INTRODUCTION TO FORTRAN 77 AND THE PERSONAL COMPUTER

INTRODUCTION TO FORTRAN 77 AND THE PERSONAL COMPUTER

Robert H. Hammond
North Carolina State University

William B. Rogers
Virginia Polytechnic Institute and State University

John B. Crittenden
Virginia Polytechnic Institute and State University

McGRAW-HILL BOOK COMPANY

New York St. Louis San Francisco Auckland Bogotá Hamburg
Johannesburg London Madrid Mexico Milan Montreal New Delhi
Panama Paris São Paulo Singapore Sydney Tokyo Toronto

This book was set in Times Roman by Interactive Composition Corporation.
The editor was Kaye Pace;
the production supervisor was Diane Renda;
the cover was designed by Rafael Hernandez.
Project supervision was done by The Total Book.
R. R. Donnelley & Sons Company was printer and binder.

INTRODUCTION TO FORTRAN 77 AND THE PERSONAL COMPUTER

1 2 3 4 5 6 7 8 9 0 DOCDOC 8 9 3 2 1 0 9 8 7

ISBN 0-07-025912-7

Library of Congress Cataloging-in-Publication Data

Hammond, Robert H.
Introduction to FORTRAN 77 and the personal computer.

Includes bibliographical references.
1. FORTRAN (Computer program language). I. Rogers, William B., II. Crittenden, John. III. Title.
QA76.73.F25H365 1987 005.26 86-21467
ISBN 0-07-025912-7

CONTENTS IN BRIEF

CONTENTS

PREFACE

Many excellent textbooks on the FORTRAN programming language, and specifically FORTRAN 77, have been written and published. Much has also been written about the operations and applications of the personal computer. However, very little has appeared in print directly relating FORTRAN and the personal computer. The availability of workable FORTRAN compiler programs designed to be used on the personal computer has created a need for a textbook which introduces a beginner to the FORTRAN language implemented on the personal computer. This textbook fills that need.

This textbook diagrams the simplified logic of computer programming and details the rudiments of programming in the 1977 version of the FORTRAN language. Appendix E provides a "how-to" procedure for compiling and executing a FORTRAN program using commercially available compiler software on the personal computer.

The hardware and software used by the authors in preparing the text descriptions and illustrative examples were, respectively: the IBM-PC with 256K of random access memory; the IBM 80 CPS Graphics Printer; the PC-Disk Operating System, version 2.1 (PC-DOS 2.1); and the Microsoft FORTRAN Compiler, version 3.1. However, allowing for minor hardware differences, the explanations should be valid for any IBM-compatible hardware with a suitable FORTRAN compiler. The material presented in the main body of the textbook (chapters 1–11) deals with the FORTRAN language and is generally independent of any specific hardware or software. The specifics of the hardware and the operating system, as well as editing, entering, compiling, and executing a FORTRAN program are described in detail in the appendixes. Pertinent appendix sections are cited, where appropriate, in the text but without digression from the FORTRAN discussion.

This textbook was written for the beginner: the beginner in FORTRAN and the beginner on the personal computer. No prior experience with either is assumed. Some explanations, rules, and cautions are repeated to the point of redundancy. Experience with beginning students has demonstrated the need for such repetition. The coverage is sufficient for a one-semester first course in FORTRAN, utilizing the disk operating system and a suitable FORTRAN compiler.

The problems cover a broad spectrum of applications but require little more than high-school-level mathematics. Most are relatively short, emphasizing one or more of the specific techniques just discussed. Beginning problems are very simple. More advanced problems are not significantly "harder"; they just require more ingenuity in the application of FORTRAN techniques. A few problems should challenge the most experienced student programmer.

Programming logic is stressed. Chapter 2 provides the details of flowcharting technique; illustrative examples throughout the text are accompanied by a flowchart. It is recommended that the logic of all but the most trivial programs be outlined in a flowchart prior to coding the FORTRAN source program.

The authors take this opportunity to thank their colleagues and former students at the North Carolina State University and the Virginia Polytechnic Institute and State University for their contribution in the form of unceasing criticism of the "work in progress." This criticism and the discussions which followed undoubtedly changed, for the better, the direction and emphasis of portions of the text and provided the seeds for useful ideas which resulted in clearer explanations.

Robert H. Hammond
William B. Rogers
John B. Crittenden

CHAPTER **1**

THE PERSONAL COMPUTER: BASIC CONCEPTS

1-1 INTRODUCTION

Computers may be broadly classified as digital or analog computers. The *digital computer* is essentially a counting device and operates with discrete numerical quantities represented by a finite sequence of digits. The *analog computer* operates by measuring the magnitudes of the quantities in an electric circuit that is set up to parallel (or be analogous to) the equation of the phenomenon being investigated. Analog-computer results are often displayed graphically on a cathode-ray tube with no discrete numerical quantities shown. The needs of modern computations have led to the increasing use of a combination of digital and analog computers, known as *hybrid computers*. Analog and hybrid computers are not in this text, which is limited to the digital computer.

The earliest digital computers were small in capacity but large in size, some occupying a full room. These early computers utilized space-consuming vacuum tubes in their circuitry. As knowledge of circuitry grew, computers decreased in size but increased in capacity. The present-day main-frame computer is capable of being addressed by a number of input devices and apparently works on a number of programs concurrently. The term "main frame" is used to differentiate this modern computer colossus from the latest development in computers—the personal computer. This is a computer, small in size, that is operated by one person at a time; hence the name *personal computer*. The application of the personal computer in the FORTRAN language to computational problems in engineering and science will be presented in this book. Figure 1-1 (see p. 2) illustrates a typical personal computer.

1-2 THE BASIC COMPONENTS OF PERSONAL COMPUTERS

All computers, whether main-frame or personal, consist of two distinctly different components. These are defined as hardware and software. *Hardware* is the physical, tangible part of the computer—the electronic circuitry, the keyboard, screen, etc.—while *software* consists of the programs which supply the computer with specific instructions for performing a given task. It is the purpose of this section to provide an elementary description of the hardware of a personal computer. This generally consists of four units: an input unit, the central processing unit (CPU), the storage units (internal and external), and the output units (printer, cathode-ray display screen, and diskette). The CPU and storage units are usually combined in a system unit (Fig. 1-2) (see p. 2).

FIGURE 1-1 An IBM Personal Computer. (*IBM.*)

FIGURE 1-2 Functional elements of the personal computer.

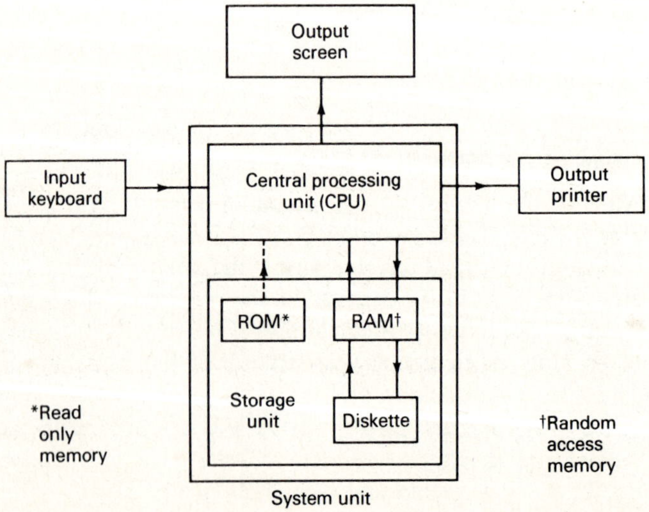

a The Input Unit

The input unit of the personal computer is the keyboard (Fig. 1-3). The center section of the keyboard is similar to the standard typewriter keyboard with the same arrangement of characters. Located to the left and right, respectively, of the typewriter section are the 10 function keys, numbered F1 through F10, and the numeric keypad. In addition, there are several other keys which perform control functions. Each of the 10 function keys can be externally programmed through the software to perform a given task. The 10 decimal digits and the algebraic signs, plus and minus, are grouped in the numeric keypad in a convenient working arrangement to facilitate numeric calculations. Depressing one key, or a combination of keys, sends a unique signal to the CPU.

b The Central Processing Unit

The central processing unit (Fig. 1-2) performs all the instructions given to the computer. It can add, subtract, or compare numbers at speeds measured in small fractions of a second. It can call for a specific instruction and execute that instruction. The CPU generally consists of three parts: the instruction counter, the instruction register, and the arithmetic unit. The *instruction counter* keeps track of which instruction to call next. The *instruction register* stores each instruction as it is called from storage and initiates the execution of that instruction. The *arithmetic unit* performs the addition, subtraction, or comparison of values as required by the instruction, temporarily holding the results in a storage unit known as the *accumulator*.

FIGURE 1-3 An IBM Personal Computer keyboard. (*IBM.*)

c The Storage Unit

The storage unit (Fig. 1-2) of a personal computer usually provides three types of storage: read-only memory (ROM), random-access memory (RAM), and diskette. The ROM is used for system instruction and is built into the permanent electronic circuitry of the computer. The contents of the ROM are used but cannot be changed by the programmer. RAM is used to hold instructions or data supplied by the programmer. Results from the arithmetic unit are also held in RAM. Diskettes provide external storage; a file (program) stored on a diskette can be retrieved for subsequent use after power to the computer has been turned off. Information stored in the RAM is temporary and is lost forever when electric power is turned off.

The RAM consists of solid-state electronic circuitry which functions as an integrated assembly of many two-state, or binary, devices. In an ON or OFF position, these binary devices may represent, respectively, YES or NO, PLUS or MINUS, ONE or ZERO, etc. A group of binary devices is referred to as a WORD,[†] each WORD having a unique retrievable address.

Distinctive features of the storage unit of a computer are destructive read-in and nondestructive readout. Each time information is stored in a given WORD, the previous contents of that WORD are erased as the new information is read in. However, the contents of that WORD can be moved (copied) to another WORD with a different address without changing the contents of the original WORD. This feature is important to remember in preparing instructions for the computer. A second characteristic of this type of storage unit, and the characteristic which gives it its name, is random access memory. "Random access" means that any WORD address is as easy to locate as any other in a given period of time. Both the CPU and the storage unit are located in the system unit (Fig. 1-2).

The amount of RAM is a measure of the capacity of the computer. Terms like 16 K, 128 K, etc., refer to the capacity of storage. This actually refers to the number of individual *storage units,* each of which can hold some amount of information. Each of these units is designed by the manufacturer to hold a number of characters of information, or bytes. The term 16 K, used above, actually means 16,384 bytes. If each storage unit required 4 bytes, then there could be 4096 units, or WORDs stored. A capacity of 256 K is the minimum recommended for FORTRAN. (K implies a multiplier of 1000.)

The storage unit is also known as the memory unit. The term "memory" is avoided in this text because it implies the human capability to remember and the ability to think. These implications are misleading. A computer does not remember, nor does it think for itself. The computer does precisely what it is instructed to do—nothing more, nothing less. The computer's sequence of operations and the results thereof depend solely upon the instructions it receives from a human programmer. A common expression among computer users is "garbage in, garbage out." This means that unless the logic of the program is correctly planned to perform the desired calculations, the output will be meaningless or misleading "garbage."

[†]In this text WORD stands for a binary word, as distinguished from the usual spoken or written (language) word.

d The Output Units

The personal computer has a cathode-ray tube (CRT) as an output device. This CRT may be either a monochrome or a color display (Fig. 1-1). As the programmer enters the program via the keyboard, every character keyed in is simultaneously displayed on the CRT. Thus, each instruction can be visually checked for correctness before the ENTER key is depressed to enter the information into the RAM. The results of the program can be displayed on the CRT. Of course these CRT displays are temporary. They disappear from the screen when the next operation is performed. If a permanent copy is desired, a printer (Fig. 1-4) is needed to print the results. The program can specify that the output is to be routed to the printer, or the programmer can, via manual instructions from the keyboard, specify that either a stored file (program) or the screen display be printed.

1-3 THE STORED-PROGRAM CONCEPT

Before any problem can be solved on the computer, a set of step-by-step instructions must be written which state precisely how to solve the problem. This set of instructions is called a *program*. Each step of the program is called a *statement*. The program must be written in a language that the computer can interpret. The computer can only interpret instructions written in a machine language, a language that is complex and cumbersome for the programmer to conveniently handle. The computer does not directly interpret a program written in a user-oriented language (such as FORTRAN) into the machine-oriented language of the computer. An intermediate program which translates FORTRAN into machine language must be used. This translator program is called a *compiler*. Most compilers

FIGURE 1-4 An IBM Matrix Printer. (*IBM.*)

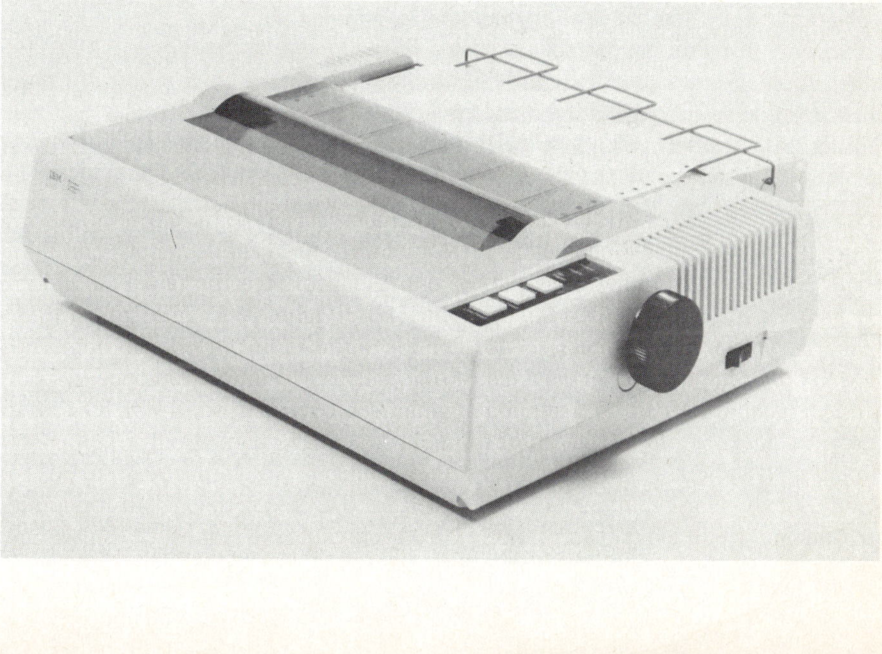

also include diagnostic routines which assist the programmer in locating errors in the FORTRAN source program.

The computer solution to a problem is a two-phase operation: compilation and execution. During the *compilation* phase, the entire set of instructions (the source program) is read, translated into machine language, and stored. Each instruction is stored in a WORD (or WORDs, as required) with a unique address. During the *execution* phase, each instruction is called sequentially from the storage unit and held temporarily in the instruction register while that instruction is executed. This two-phase operation in which the source program is first translated and stored in its entirety (compilation) and then each instruction is automatically and sequentially executed (execution) is known as the *stored-program concept*.

Consider a simple arithmetic problem such as the sum of two numbers: 32 + 18 = 5Ø. Without attempting to simulate any actual computer language but using instructions understandable to the reader and assuming computer acceptability, the following program has been written to read two numerical values, 32 and 18, and to compute and display the sum.

```
Instruction A: Read a value (from a data source) and store it
               in address 2-1.
Instruction B: Read the next value and store it in address
               2-2.
Instruction C: Copy the value in address 2-1 into the
               accumulator.
Instruction D: Add the value in address 2-2 to the value in
               the accumulator.
Instruction E: Store the value in the accumulator in address
               2-3.
Instruction F: Display (or store on a diskette) the value in
               address 2-3.
(End of instructions)
Data:          32
Data:          18
```

Figure 1-5 presents a graphical simulation of the functional units of the computer described in Sec. 1-2. The storage unit provides for 30 WORDs, whose locations are specified by a two-digit numerical address identifying the row and column, respectively. (For example, the address of the bottom right location, or WORD, is 5-6, row 5, column 6.) The XX's in the storage unit, the instruction register (IR), instruction counter (IC), and the accumulator represent miscellaneous information remaining in storage after completion of the previous program. When current information is read into storage, previously stored information will be destroyed. To start the sequence, the instructions are entered via the keyboard and action begins.

The condition of the computer after all instructions are entered and compiled is shown in Fig. 1-6. Instructions A, B, C, D, E, and F are stored sequentially in WORDs with addresses 1-1, 1-2, 1-3, 1-4, 1-5, and 1-6, respectively. The information remaining from previous calculations (XX) has been destroyed in ad-

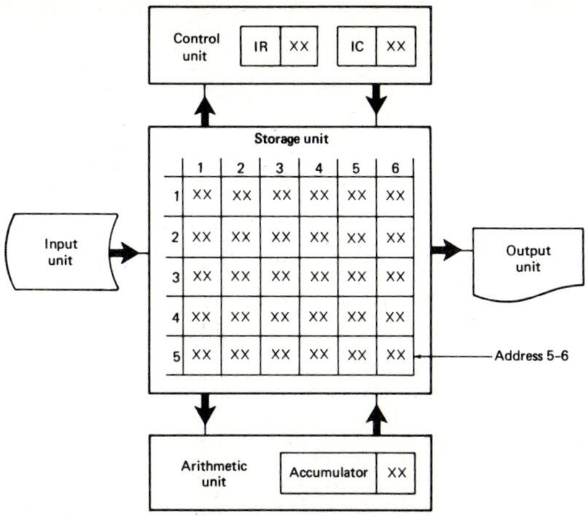

FIGURE 1-5
Simulation of computer ready for input of instructions. (IR = instruction register; IC = instruction counter.)

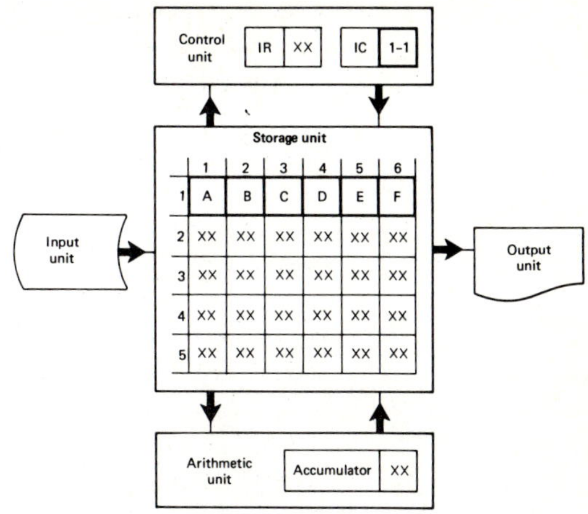

FIGURE 1-6
Simulation of computer ready for execution.

dresses 1-1 to 1-6 and replaced by the new and relevant information. Note that the instruction counter (IC) has been automatically set to the address of the first instruction (1-1). Execution of the program begins.

In Fig. 1-7 (see p. 8) the first instruction (instruction A in address 1-1) has been "copied" into the instruction register (IR), destroying the previous instruction (XX) but leaving instruction A unchanged in address 1-1. The computer then executes instruction A:

```
Read a value and store it in address 2-1.
```

The first value is entered via the keyboard, read, and the numerical value (32) is stored in address 2-1. The IC automatically increments to the next address (1-2).

Figure 1-8 (see p. 8) illustrates the execution of instruction B. The IC calls for the instruction in address 1-2 (instruction B) to be copied into the IR, destroying the previous instruction (instruction A). Note that instruction B remains unchanged in address 1-2. The computer then executes instruction B:

```
Read the next value and store it in address 2-2.
```

The next value is entered via the keyboard, read, and the numerical value (18) is stored in address 2-2. The IC automatically increments to the next address (1-3).

In Fig. 1-9 (see p. 8), the instruction in address 1-3 (instruction C) has been copied into the IR. Instruction C is executed:

```
Copy the value in address 2-1 into the accumulator.
```

The value in address 2-1 (32) is copied into the accumulator, where arithmetic op-

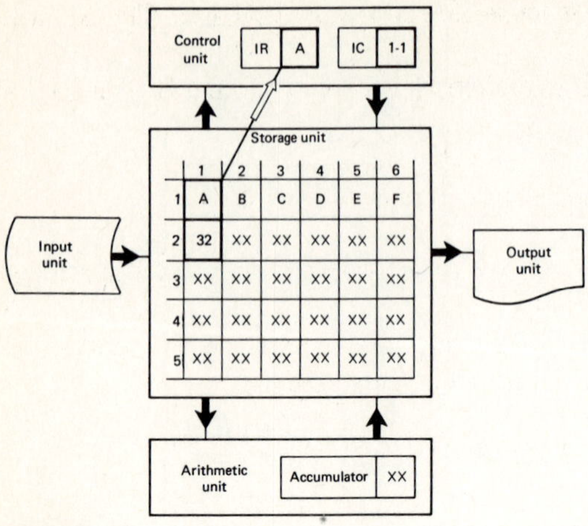

FIGURE 1-7
Simulation of computer after execution of instruction A.

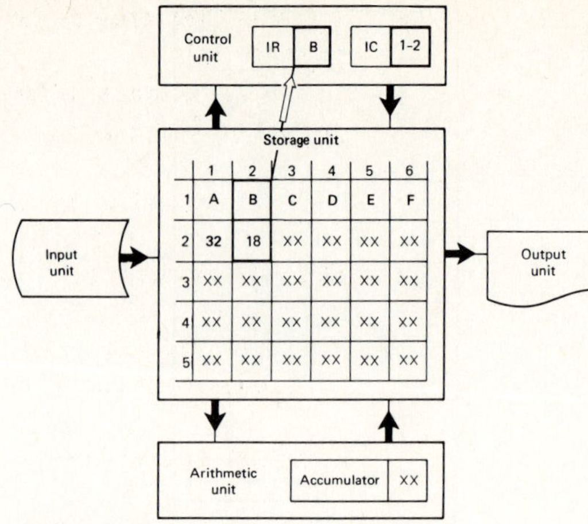

FIGURE 1-8
Simulation of computer after execution of instruction B.

erations are performed. The previous value in the accumulator has been erased. The IC now increments to 1-4.

The instruction in address 1-4 (instruction D) is copied into the IR (Fig. 1-10). Instruction D is executed:

```
Add the value in address 2-2 to the value in the accumulator.
```

The value in address 2-2 (18) is added to the value in the accumulator (32).

FIGURE 1-9
Simulation of computer after execution of instruction C.

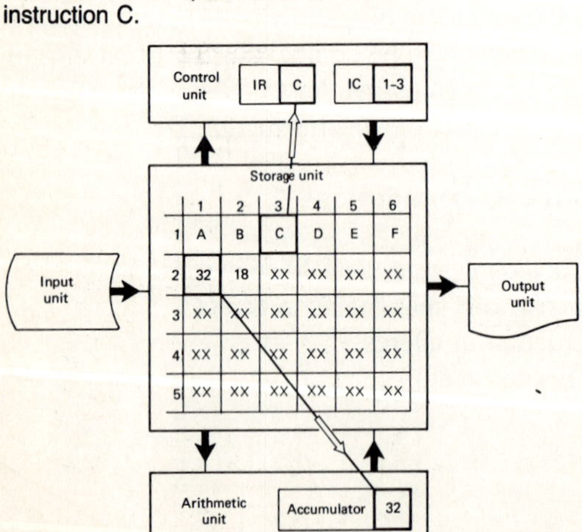

FIGURE 1-10
Simulation of computer after execution of instruction D.

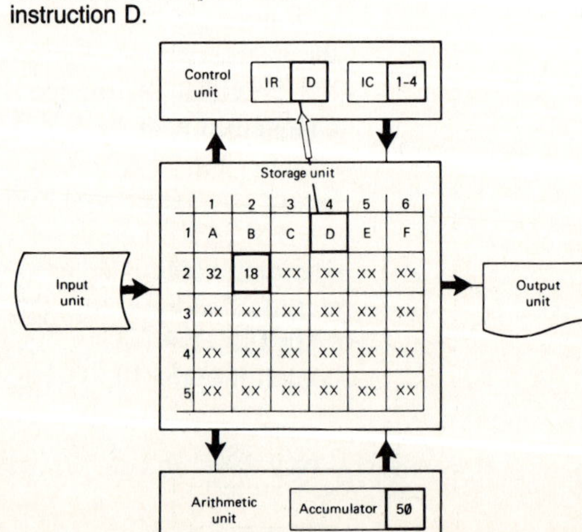

The sum (5Ø) replaces the previous value (32) in the accumulator. The IC increments to 1-5.

The instruction in address 1-5 (instruction E) is copied into the IR (Fig. 1-11). Instruction E is executed:

```
Store the value in the accumulator in address 2-3.
```

The value in the accumulator (5Ø) is copied into address 2-3. The IC increments to 1-6.

Finally, as illustrated in Fig. 1-12, the last instruction in address 1-6 (instruction F) is copied into the IR. Instruction F is executed:

```
Display the value in address 2-3.
```

The value in address 2-3 (5Ø) is transmitted to the output unit, and the result of the computation (5Ø) is displayed on the screen, printed on a sheet of paper, or stored on a diskette. Note that the zero character is overprinted with a slash (Ø). This convention is used to distinguish the digit zero (Ø) from the letter O and will be used throughout this text.

The preceding description is an oversimplified simulation of the operational sequence of a digital computer. The first computers developed could accept only one hand-fed instruction at a time, a slow process indeed. However, with the development of the stored-program concept and its related increase in speed, the use of the digital computer has rapidly grown and has been extended to many fields of application.

Succeeding chapters will discuss the preparation of computer instructions needed to solve a wide variety of numerical problems. Although no further direct

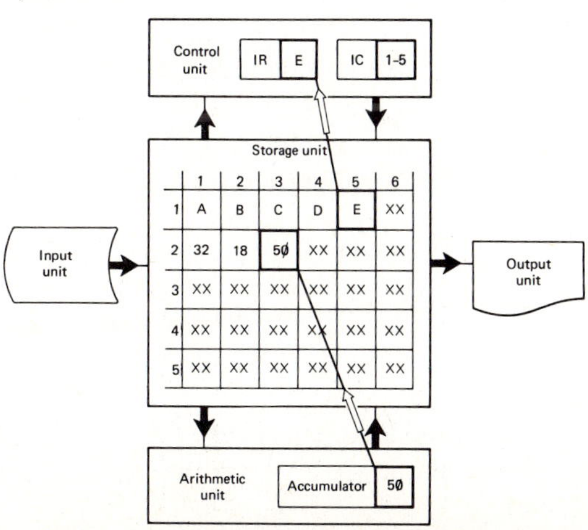

FIGURE 1-11
Simulation of computer after execution of instruction E.

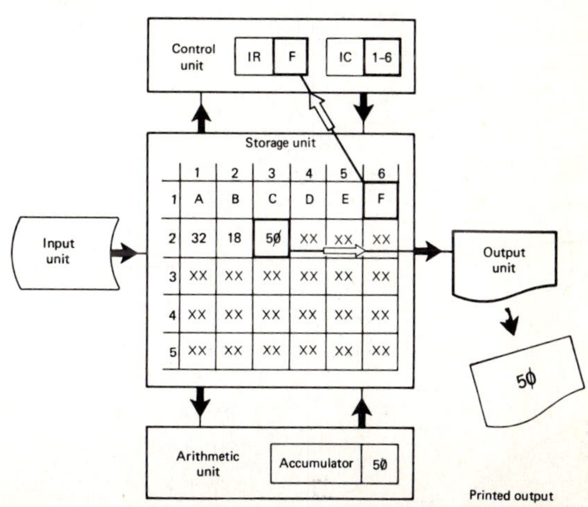

FIGURE 1-12
Simulation of computer after execution of instruction F.

reference will be made to the simplified explanation presented in this chapter, an awareness of the stored-program concept will reduce the potential for errors in logic in future computer programming.

1-4 HOW NUMBERS ARE STORED

The digital computer is basically a bistable device. Since only two states are available, representing the 10 digits of the decimal number system presents a problem. The problem is solved by using combinations of the two characters zero and one (Ø and 1) of the binary number system to represent and store all other characters.

The binary number system defines decimal numbers by expressing them in terms of the presence or absence of powers of 2. Assume that state one (of a two-state device) indicates the presence of a power of 2 and state two indicates the absence of a power of 2. Only two conditions are required. If state one signals 1 and state two signals Ø, the two-state elements of the storage unit can be employed to represent and store any number or binary-coded character.

Table 1-1 illustrates how a group of two-state storage elements (a WORD) can be used to represent decimal numbers. The digits (1 or Ø) in the first four columns represent the presence or absence of positive powers of 2, and the digits in the last three columns represent the presence or absence of negative powers of 2. The decimal number 5.ØØØ (in the sixth row from the top) is represented by Ø1Ø1.ØØØ in the binary system. The first digit Ø (state two) shows the absence of $2^3 = 8$; the second digit 1 (state one) shows the presence of $2^2 = 4$; the third digit (state two) shows the absence of $2^1 = 2$; the fourth digit (state one) shows the presence of $2^0 = 1$. The last three digits (state two) show the absence of any negative powers of 2.

For another example, the decimal number 8.875 (in the twelfth row) is represented by 1ØØØ.111 in the binary system. The first digit (state one) shows the presence of $2^3 = 8$; and the next three digits (state two) show the absence of $2^2 = 4$, $2^1 = 2$, and $2^0 = 1$. The last three digits (state one) show the presence of $2^{-1} = \frac{1}{2}$, $2^{-2} = \frac{1}{4}$, and $2^{-3} = \frac{1}{8}$. The sum of these last three (Ø.5, Ø.25, Ø.125) equals Ø.875. All seven digits in the binary number then add up to the decimal number of 8.875.

The integer portion of any decimal number (that portion to the left of the decimal point) can always be exactly represented in the binary system, but the fractional portion (that portion to the right of the decimal point) can be exactly represented in the binary system only when that fractional portion is composed of one or more negative powers of 2.

In other words, the decimal fraction Ø.125 can be exactly represented in the binary system, but the decimal fractions Ø.126 and Ø.124 can only be approximated in the binary system. The closeness of that approximation will be increased as the number of binary digits representing negative powers of 2 is increased, but the end result is still an approximation.

It is not necessary for the beginning programmer to understand the binary number system thoroughly. It is important only to know that binary digits are used to

TABLE 1-1 BINARY REPRESENTATION AND STORAGE OF DECIMAL DIGITS

Binary value								Common decimal value
Integer portion					Fractional portion			
$2^3=8$	$2^2=4$	$2^1=2$	$2^0=1$		$2^{-1}=0.5$	$2^{-2}=0.25$	$2^{-3}=0.125$	
Ø	Ø	Ø	Ø	.	Ø	Ø	Ø	Ø.ØØØ
Ø	Ø	Ø	1	.	Ø	Ø	Ø	1.ØØØ
Ø	Ø	1	Ø	.	Ø	Ø	Ø	2.ØØØ
Ø	Ø	1	1	.	Ø	Ø	Ø	3.ØØØ
Ø	1	Ø	Ø	.	Ø	Ø	Ø	4.ØØØ
Ø	1	Ø	1	.	Ø	Ø	Ø	5.ØØØ
Ø	1	1	Ø	.	Ø	Ø	Ø	6.ØØØ
Ø	1	1	1	.	Ø	Ø	Ø	7.ØØØ
1	Ø	Ø	Ø	.	Ø	Ø	Ø	8.ØØØ
1	Ø	Ø	Ø	.	1	Ø	Ø	8.5ØØ
1	Ø	Ø	Ø	.	1	1	Ø	8.75Ø
1	Ø	Ø	Ø	.	1	1	1	8.875
1	Ø	Ø	1	.	Ø	1	Ø	9.25Ø
1	Ø	Ø	1	.	Ø	1	1	9.375
1	Ø	1	Ø	.	Ø	Ø	Ø	1Ø.ØØØ

represent decimal numbers; consequently, only numbers that arc powers of 2 can be stored as exact values. All other numbers (not powers of 2) are close approximations of their exact decimal values. This fact has an important bearing on the accuracy of computer results, discussed in greater detail in Chap. 11.

1-5 THE BIG PICTURE

The preceding sections have discussed, in some detail, the components of personal digital computers, how a program can be translated and placed in the storage unit, and how the computer then executes the program. The remaining chapters will describe how the user-oriented computer language FORTRAN can be employed in preparing a computer program. But first, a brief description of the total procedure will help the student understand the "big picture" of computer usage.

The first step, as shown in Fig. 1-13 (see p. 12), is to recognize that a problem exists and the nature of the problem calls for a computer solution. Of course, one must understand the problem and the steps leading to its solution. Then the solution algorithm is prepared. An *algorithm* may be defined as a series of step-by-step instructions for solving the problem. The algorithm is usually presented in a graphical form called a *flowchart*. Flowcharts are discussed in depth in Chap. 2 and as appropriate throughout the text.

The step-by-step instructions are coded in a user-oriented language. This is the *source program,* composed on a coding form and entered via the keyboard. The instructions of the source program are translated by the compiler program into a machine-language program the computer can interpret and execute. This form of

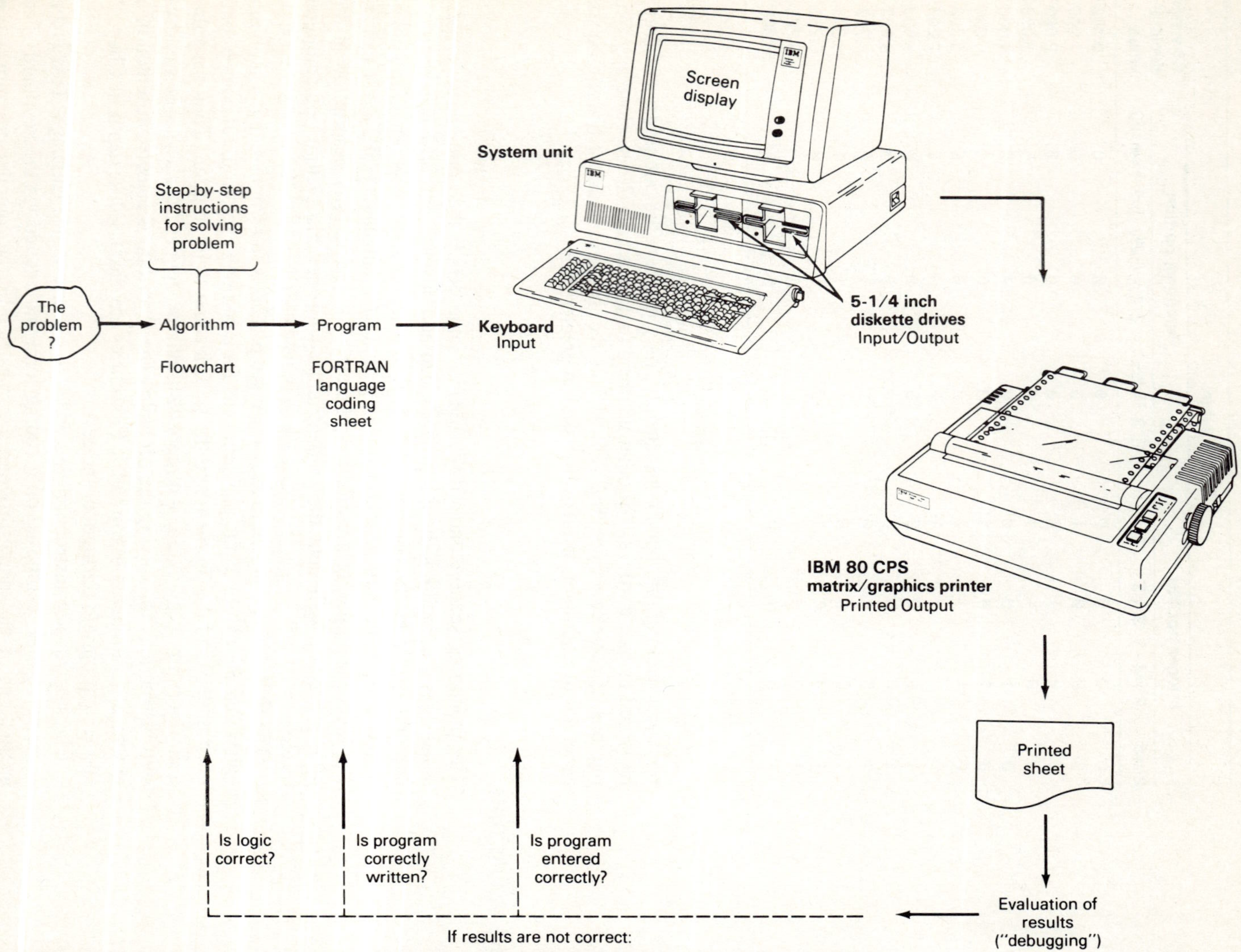

FIGURE 1-13 Diagram of a personal-computer solution from problem recognition to printed results.

the program is temporarily stored in the RAM and automatically copied to a diskette as the *execute program*.

When the translation has been completed, the instructions are sequentially executed, and the results are displayed, printed, or stored. These results must be carefully evaluated by the programmer to determine whether they are correct as planned. If errors or inaccuracies occur, the source program must be studied for errors in logic, encoding, or entering.

CHAPTER **2**

FLOWCHARTING

2-1 INTRODUCTION

Chapter 1 introduced the world of digital computer programming and outlined the most basic concepts of digital computation. This chapter will describe a planning technique applicable to any type of problem, not just those to be solved with the use of the modern digital computer. However, it should be emphasized that the various examples in this chapter illustrate how this planning technique is to be applied when programming a digital computer in the FORTRAN language.

Before using the powerful capabilities of any computer to solve a problem, it is wise to outline the steps to be followed in solving that problem. Often, the outlining procedure is done in one's head, but in learning to program the digital computer, it is advisable to place the outline on paper to ensure that no steps in the solution process are overlooked. An example indicating how it is possible to carelessly omit instructions necessary to solve a problem is illustrated in a *National Geographic* magazine article, "Behold the Computer Revolution" (Peter T. White, November 1970). The article demonstrates the difficulties in programming a robot-type girl to simply cross a street.

> Alas, how tricky it could be just to program a girl to cross a road! I had learned that from a film which, to illustrate the pitfalls of programming, shows her holding a walkie-talkie and doing only what she is told to do.
>
> Take a step forward. Have you reached the curb? NO.
> Take a step forward. Have you reached the curb? YES.
> Stop. Look to the left. Is there a vehicle within 60 yards? YES.
> Is there a vehicle within 60 yards? YES.
> Is there a vehicle within 60 yards? YES.
>
> What went wrong? The girl was stuck because the programmer forgot that vehicles can be parked. He should have asked:
>
> Is there a moving vehicle within 60 yards?
>
> The reply would have been NO and the next instruction could have been CROSS THE ROAD.

Such pitfalls are common in programming, even among experienced programmers. For this reason, most programmers, when writing long, complicated programs, first diagram the steps to be followed in solving the problem. One method commonly used in outlining the problem solution is flowcharting.

2-2 FLOWCHART SYMBOLS

A *flowchart* (or graphical representation of an algorithm) is a schematic diagram utilizing standardized symbols which, when placed in the proper sequence, outline the logical steps to solve a problem, whether it is a problem to be solved on a digital computer or by some other technique. The key to this definition is the phrase "schematic diagram." Everyone constantly plans for one event or another. We go through a planning process to ensure that we arrive at class or work on time; we plan when preparing a meal; we plan when we take a trip; etc. This planning is a type of flowcharting, but it is usually a mental exercise only. Proper flowcharting for computer programming purposes requires the transference from the brain to paper of the steps necessary to solve the problem. It sounds easy enough, but as illustrated in the excerpt from the *National Geographic,* it can be tricky. Invariably, the programmer forgets to include in the flowchart some minute detail, the omission of which may result in unforeseen problems in programming logic or execution.

The symbols commonly used in basic programming are illustrated in Fig. 2-1. These symbols conform to the standards established by the International Organization for Standardization (ISO), "Information Processing—Flowcharting Symbols" (International Standard 1028); by the American National Standards Institute (ANSI), American National Standard, Flowchart Symbols and Their Usage in Information Processing (ANSI X3.5-1970); and by the International Business Machines Corporation (IBM).

Several forms of these symbols are often used and are normally distinguished from one another through the use of words or phrases placed inside the symbol. For example, the TERMINAL, INTERRUPT symbol may be used to initiate and terminate programs. To initiate a program flowchart, the word START is placed within the symbol as shown in Fig. 2-2(*a*) (see p. 18). To indicate the end of a program flowchart, the word STOP is placed within the symbol as shown in Fig. 2-2(*b*) (see p. 18).

As illustrated in Fig. 2-3(*a*) and (*b*) (see p. 18), the PROCESS symbol may be used to indicate one or more defining operations.

The DECISION symbol, illustrated in Fig. 2-4(*a*) through (*d*) (see p. 19), indicates that any one of two or more branches may be followed after a decision is made. The decision symbol may include an arithmetic expression, as shown in Fig. 2-4(*a*) and (*b*), or logical expression, as shown in Fig. 2-4(*c*) and (*d*). The symbolism in Fig. 2-4(*a*) implies the question: "Is A positive, equal to zero, or negative?" If A is positive, the path leading to the left will be followed; if zero, the path leading downward will be followed; and if negative, the path leading to the right will be followed. In Fig. 2-4(*b*), if the value of B · C is positive or negative, the path leading to the right will be followed, while if B · C is equal to zero, the path leading downward will be used. Figure 2-4(*c*) and (*d*) imply the questions: "Is D less than F?" and "Is E equal to A · B?" respectively. In both Fig. 2-4(*c*) and (*d*), if the answer to the question is true, or yes, the logic path leading to the right will be followed, while if the answer to the question is false, or no, the logic path leading downward will be followed.

The INPUT and OUTPUT symbols, illustrated in Fig. 2-5 (see p. 19), imply that values may be supplied (input) or displayed (output) either singly or in multiple form.

TERMINAL, INTERRUPT symbol, indicating the beginning or ending of a main program or subprogram.

PROCESS symbol, indicating the assignment of a value to a variable or change in value of a variable. Also used to indicate the opening and closing of a file.

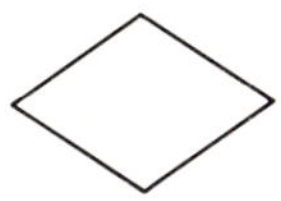

DECISION symbol, indicating a branching of the logic flow in which any one of a number of alternative paths may be followed.

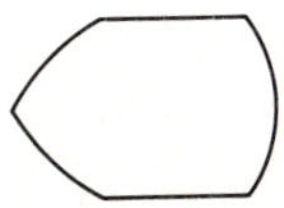

DISPLAY symbol, indicating that information is to be displayed on the cathode-ray tube monitor.

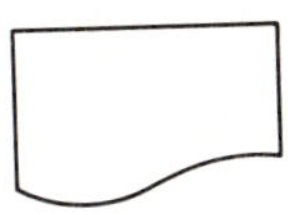

DOCUMENT symbol, indicating that information is to be printed on paper.

INPUT/OUTPUT symbol, indicating that data is to be supplied from a diskette or results are to be stored on a diskette.

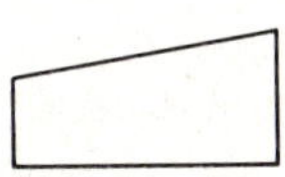

INPUT symbol, indicating that data is to be supplied during program execution from the keyboard.

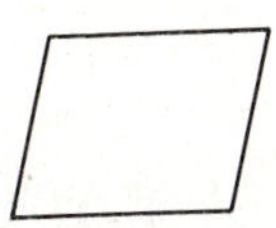

INPUT symbol, indicating that data is to be supplied during compilation of the program.

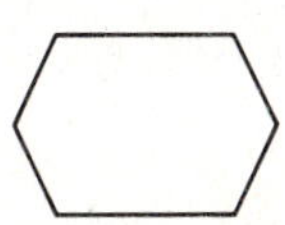

PREPARATION symbol, indicating a beginning of a looping procedure.

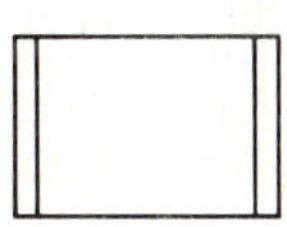

PREDEFINED PROCESS symbol, indicating the transfer of logic to a subprogram.

ONPAGE CONNECTOR symbol, indicating the transfer of logic flow from one point on a page to another point on the same page.

OFFPAGE CONNECTOR symbol, indicating the transfer of logic flow from one page to another.

FIGURE 2-1 Flowchart symbols.

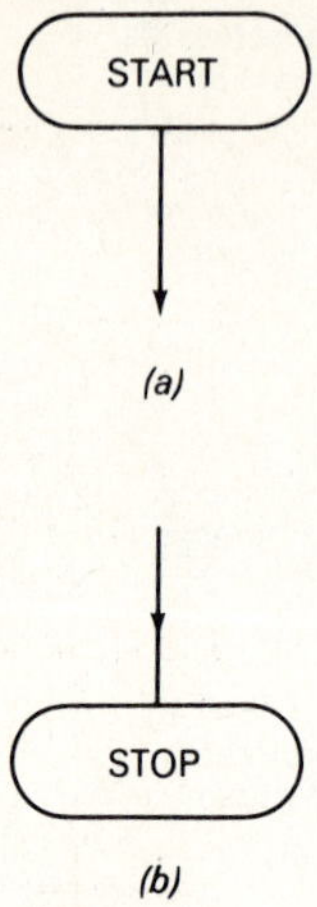

FIGURE 2-2
TERMINAL, INTERRUPT symbols.

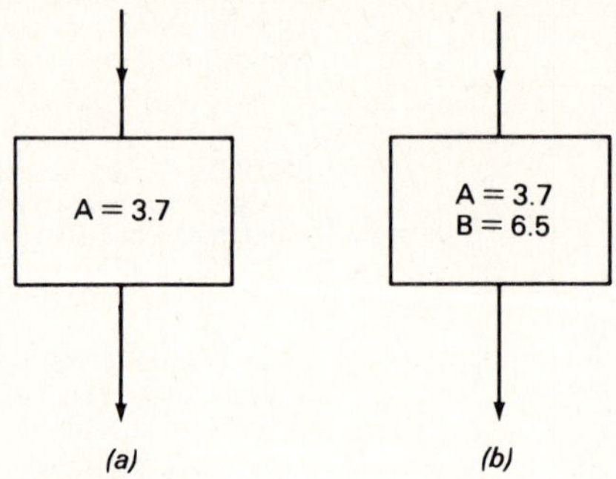

FIGURE 2-3
PROCESS symbols.

The PREDEFINED PROCESS symbol, Fig. 2-6 (see p. 20), is used to indicate transfer to a subprogram and will normally contain the NAME of the subprogram called, as will be explained in Chap. 9.

ONPAGE and OFFPAGE connectors, Fig. 2-7(*a*) and (*b*) (see p. 20), are used to continue a flowchart and are paired by numerals placed within each symbol. To fully understand the application of the various forms of flowchart symbols, several examples will be examined.

2-3 FLOWCHART DEVELOPMENT

To add two numbers, such as 6.3 and 7.8, is a simple process, but flowcharting such a problem solution requires attention to detail. First, the solution procedure must be initiated with the use of the wiener-shaped TERMINAL, INTERRUPT symbol. This symbol is always used to begin a flowchart. Next, considering that the flowchart will be used to program a digital computer, the values to be added (6.3 and 7.8) will be supplied from the keyboard. This is depicted in the INPUT symbol (the trapezoid) as shown in Fig. 2-8 (see p. 21). The ordering of the symbols is directed by flow lines, with arrowheads connecting the symbols to indicate the direction of logic flow. A PROCESS symbol depicts the addition of the values provided from the keyboard and the assignment of their sum to the variable name SUM. Either the DISPLAY symbol, the DOCUMENT symbol, or the INPUT/OUTPUT symbol is used to represent output of the result. The DISPLAY symbol indicates that the answer is to be displayed on a cathode-ray tube; the DOCUMENT symbol indicates that the answer is to be printed on paper; and the the INPUT/OUTPUT symbol indicates that the answer is to be stored on diskette. If all forms of output are required, the flowchart should include all sym-

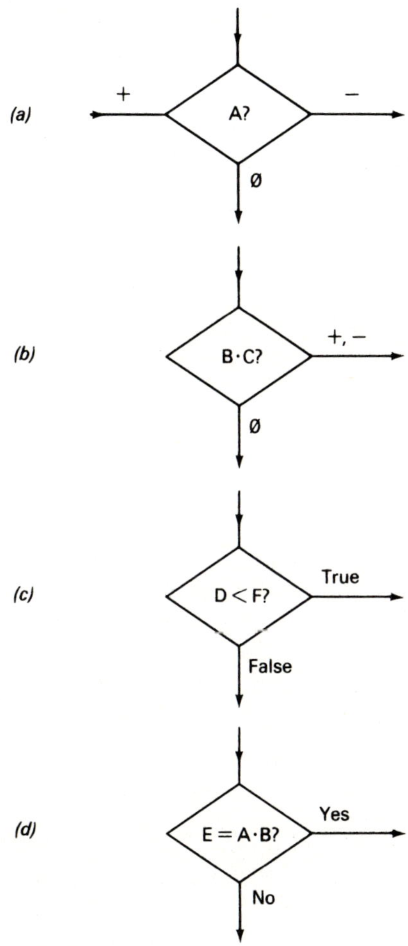

FIGURE 2-4
DECISION symbols.

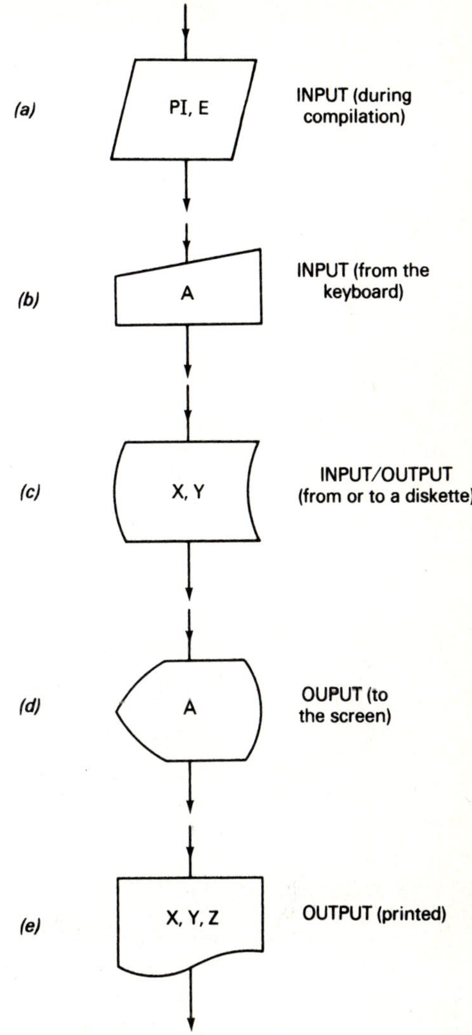

FIGURE 2-5
INPUT/OUTPUT symbols.

bols, one following the other. To indicate that the problem solution has been obtained and that no further operations are required, the TERMINAL, INTERRUPT symbol labeled STOP completes the flowchart. Once the flowchart procedure is correctly completed, the coding of the program in FORTRAN (or any other programming language) is a relatively simple task.

At first glance such a procedure may seem a waste of time. However, for problem solutions that require hundreds or even thousands of steps, this graphical procedure for laying out in detail the sequential order of the steps to be followed in

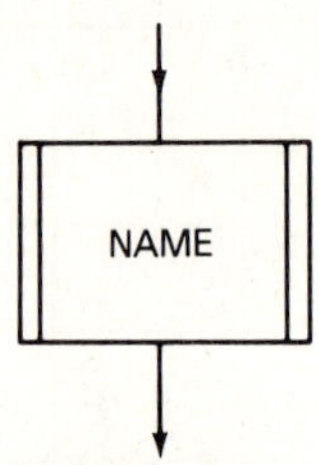

FIGURE 2-6
A PREDEFINED PROCESS symbol.

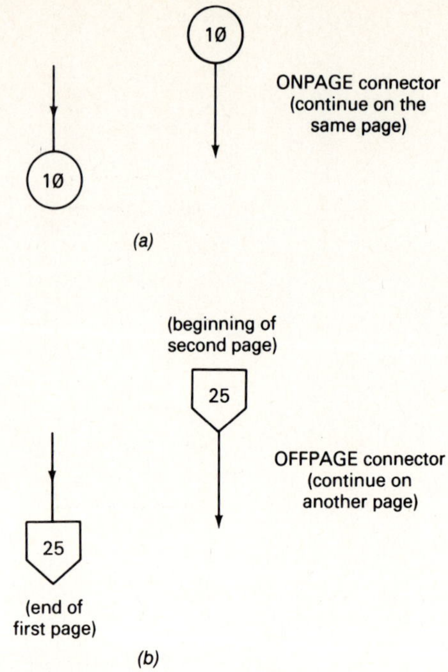

FIGURE 2-7
Connectors.

solving the problem can save countless hours of frustration. In addition, if the programmer must explain to another person precisely how the program works, the flowchart is an effective and efficient way of conveying such information. As the old saying goes, "A picture is worth a thousand words."

Another example will help. Suppose the problem is to add ten numbers supplied one at a time. In this problem there are several subtleties which must not be overlooked. There will be exactly ten numbers to add, no more and no less; only the total of the ten numbers is to be displayed, not any intermediate sums; and the numbers are being supplied one at a time, not in a group. The flowchart for this problem is shown in Fig. 2-9 and includes a DECISION symbol (a diamond).

The INPUT symbol immediately following the first PROCESS symbol, which sets the initial values of N and SUM, is used to define the value of a variable A that is to be read from keyboard input, in this case the first value of A. A counting technique utilizing the statement N = N + 1 (after first initializing N as Ø) within a PROCESS symbol is then used to increment an old value of N (to the right of the = sign) by 1 in order to produce a new value of N (to the left of the = sign). N will represent the number of values of A that have been supplied to the program. The first time this statement is executed, the initial value of N is Ø and the new value of N thus becomes Ø + 1 (or 1), the value corresponding to the number of values of A that have been entered into the program logic. The next

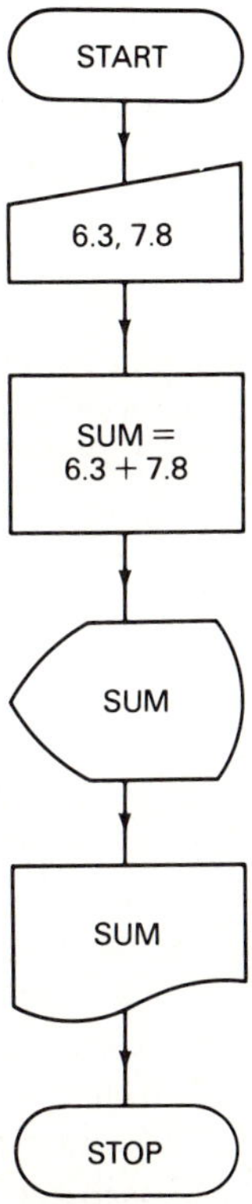

FIGURE 2-8
A simple flow-chart for adding two numbers.

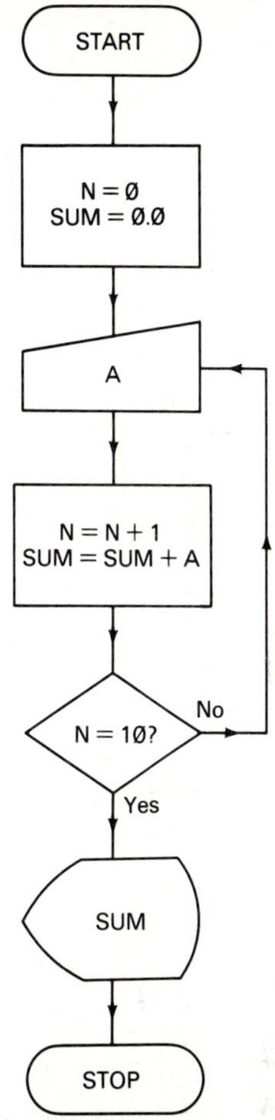

FIGURE 2-9
A flowchart loop for adding 1Ø numbers.

symbol indicates the addition of the first value of A to the old value of the variable SUM, which eventually will have the value of the sum of the ten numbers. Since the initial value of SUM was set to Ø.Ø, the new SUM will then have the value of the first A.

Next, the DECISION symbol allows a branching in the program logic. Either the logic path may return to the input symbol or it may branch to a DISPLAY symbol. The decision as to which route to follow is based on the answer to the question within the diamond. In this example the question implied is: "Is the value of the current N equal to 1Ø?" Initially, the answer to the question in the DECISION symbol is no (or false). The logic path returns to the INPUT symbol, thus repeating the sequence of steps (looping).

When the logic flow reaches the INPUT symbol a second time, the second of the ten numbers is assigned to A, automatically destroying the first value assigned to A, which is no longer needed. Next, the value of the counter variable N is incremented by 1 to a value of 2, indicating that the second of the ten numbers has been entered into the computation. A new SUM is then calculated by adding to the old SUM (the first value of A) the new A or second number. A partial summation of the ten numbers (the sum of the first two numbers) is therefore assigned to the variable SUM. A decision is made a second time. Since N will have the value of 2, the logic path returns to the INPUT symbol. A third repetition of the logical steps within the loop is performed followed by a fourth, fifth, etc. Eventually the tenth and last value will be assigned to A; the new N becomes 1Ø and the new SUM becomes the sum of the ten numbers. This time when the DECISION symbol is reached, the answer to the question within the symbol is yes, or true. The sum of the ten numbers is displayed, and the flowchart is terminated.

It is likely that a beginning programmer will overlook two specific items in trying to write the program for this problem without first drawing the flowchart: (1) omission of the counting technique and (2) the decision as to when to loop or terminate.

2-4 ADDITIONAL FLOWCHART CONVENTIONS

In addition to the use of the standardized symbols introduced, other conventions may be applied when constructing a flowchart, as illustrated in Fig. 2-10. The main logic path of the flowchart should proceed from the top of the page to the bottom or from the left of the page to the right. When this is the case, arrowheads on the flowlines connecting the flowchart symbols are not required. However, if some subordinate portion of the logic flow moves from the bottom of the page to the top or from the right of the page to the left, then arrowheads are required for clarification. Beginning flowcharters often find it useful to place arrowheads on all flowlines to avoid confusion, as is done throughout this text.

Flowlines may cross each other, but this often causes confusion. Instead, use ONPAGE connectors to eliminate the need to cross flowlines.

Comments required for explanation only may be added to the flowchart through the use of rectangles open on the right side, with commentary phrases placed within. The placement of comments is accomplished by the use of dashed lines drawn from the open rectangle to the point in the flowchart where the comment is applicable, as shown in Fig. 2-10.

2-5 CONCLUSION

The flowchart symbols used in Figs. 2-8, 2-9, and 2-10 correspond to specific statements within the FORTRAN language. Since the numerous statements in FORTRAN have yet to be introduced, these examples were necessarily simple in both mathematical operations and flowchart symbolism. In the chapters that follow, as each new FORTRAN statement is described, the corresponding flowchart

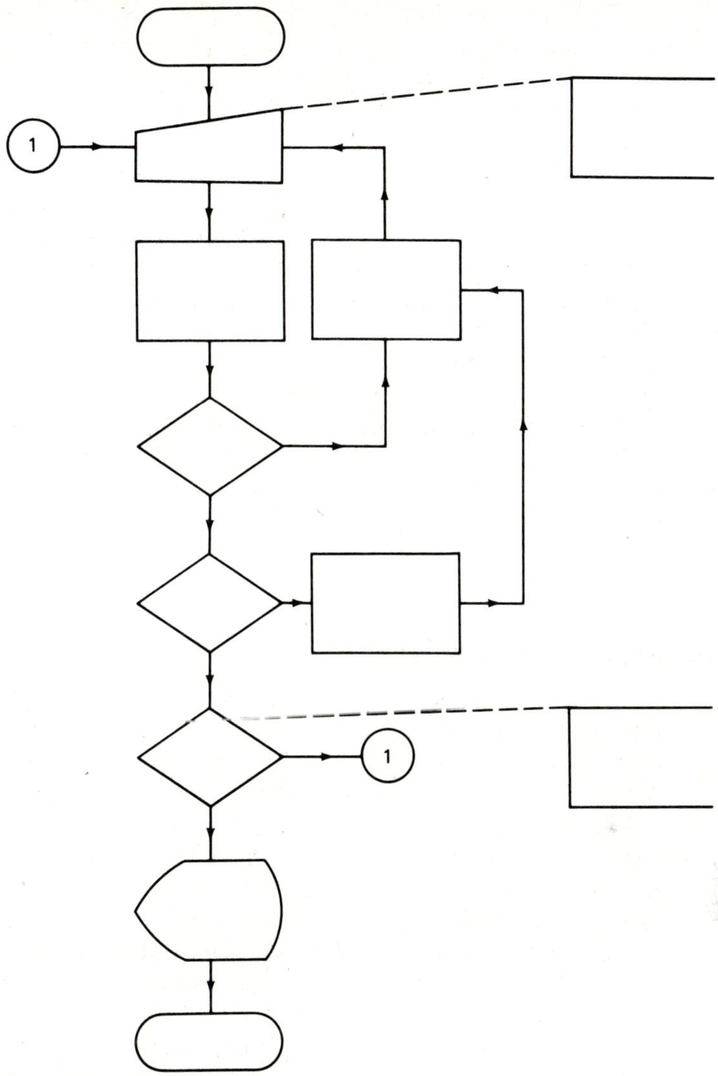

FIGURE 2-10 Additional flowchart conventions.

symbol will be identified and samples of its applications will be illustrated in increasingly complex examples.

PROBLEMS

2-1 What value of X is displayed as a result of the simple looping and incrementing flowchart indicated in Fig. 2-11 (see p. 24)?

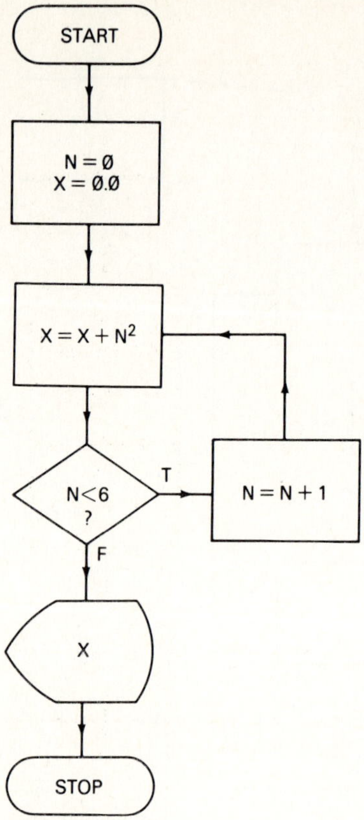

FIGURE 2-11
Problem 2-1.

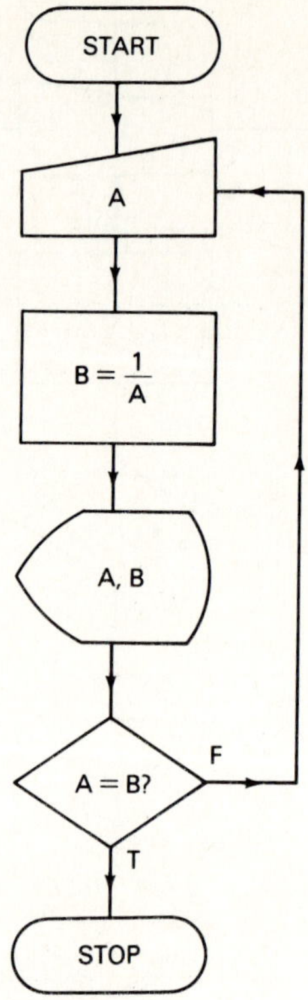

	A
DATA SET 1	5.Ø
DATA SET 2	−2.Ø
DATA SET 3	Ø.5
DATA SET 4	1Ø.Ø
DATA SET 5	1.Ø

FIGURE 2-12
Problem 2-2.

2-2 An INPUT symbol within a loop usually implies that numerous data values must be available sequentially for the algorithm to function. What values of A and B will be displayed if the logic of the flowchart of Fig. 2-12 is followed, when supplied sequentially with the values of A shown in the data table?

2-3 The flowchart of Fig. 2-13 will cause the printing of a two-dimensional array of numbers. Indicate the elements of the array in the array form in which they will be printed.

2-4 A flowchart representing the monthly compounding of interest at the rate of 1.Ø percent per month for 12 months is illustrated in Fig. 2-14. Following the logic indicated in the flowchart, determine the value to which the principal will grow during this time.

2-5 If the order of the values of X to be supplied to the flowchart of Fig. 2-15 (see p. 26) is as shown, what values of X and Y are displayed? How many of the X values are used?

2-6 For the values of A, B, and C shown in Fig. 2-16 (see p. 27), what values of X, Y,

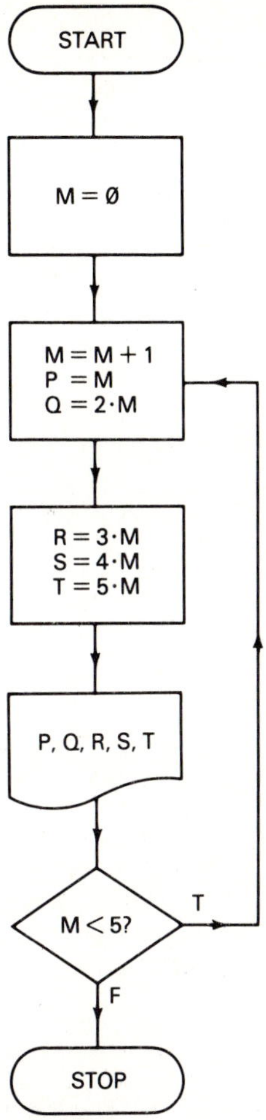

FIGURE 2-13
Problem 2-3.

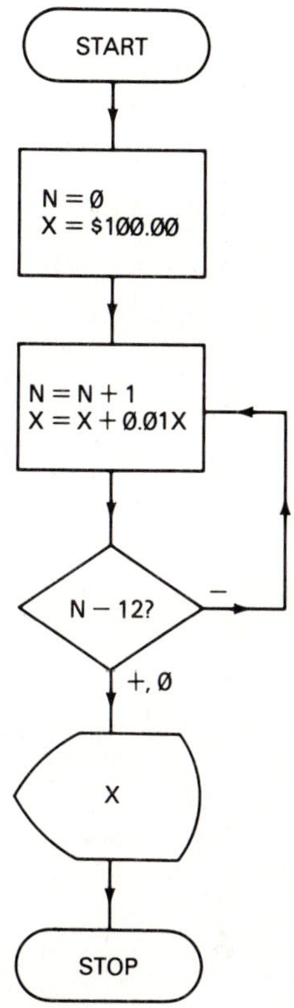

FIGURE 2-14
Problem 2-4.

and Z are printed? What alterations must be made to the flowchart so that the number of sets of data that are used to calculate Y and Z are also printed?

2-7 Looping procedures may cause many calculations to be made in order to produce only a few values. What values of I, J, and M result from the loop within a loop illustrated in Fig. 2-17 (see p. 28)?

2-8 Figure 2-18 (see p. 29) indicates the flowchart of a numerical problem with nonnumerical results. For the given sets of values of the interior angles of a triangle, what expressions are printed?

Develop a flowchart for each of Probs. 2-9 through 2-18.

2-9 Given a value for the diameter of a circle, determine the area and circumference of the circle.

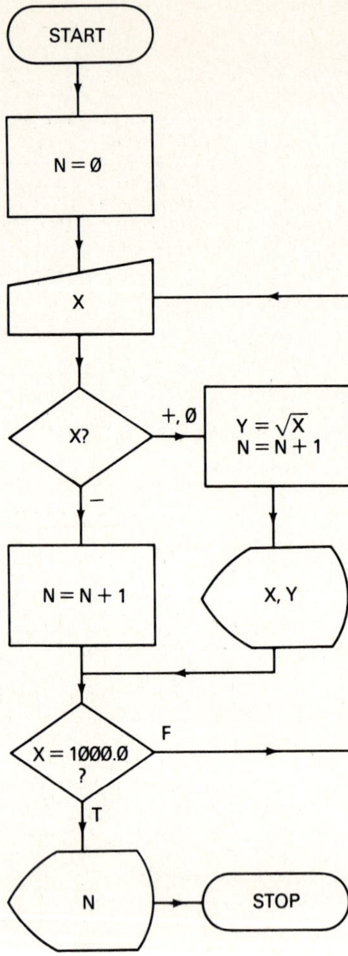

X VALUES
5.Ø
−3.7
Ø.Ø
4.Ø
1ØØØ.Ø
7.6
−3.8

FIGURE 2-15 Problem 2-5.

2-10 Add the even positive integers from 2 through 1ØØØ.

2-11 From a group of 25 positive and negative numbers, determine the sum of the positive numbers and the sum of the negative numbers.

2-12 Given 1Ø numbers one at a time, determine the smallest and the largest values from among the group.

2-13 Determine the average value and the value halfway between the largest and smallest values of 25 numbers, supplied one at a time.

2-14 For each of 1Ø numbers (named X), determine $X^2, X^3, \ldots, X^{10}$.

2-15 Given any positive integer number N, determine $N!$

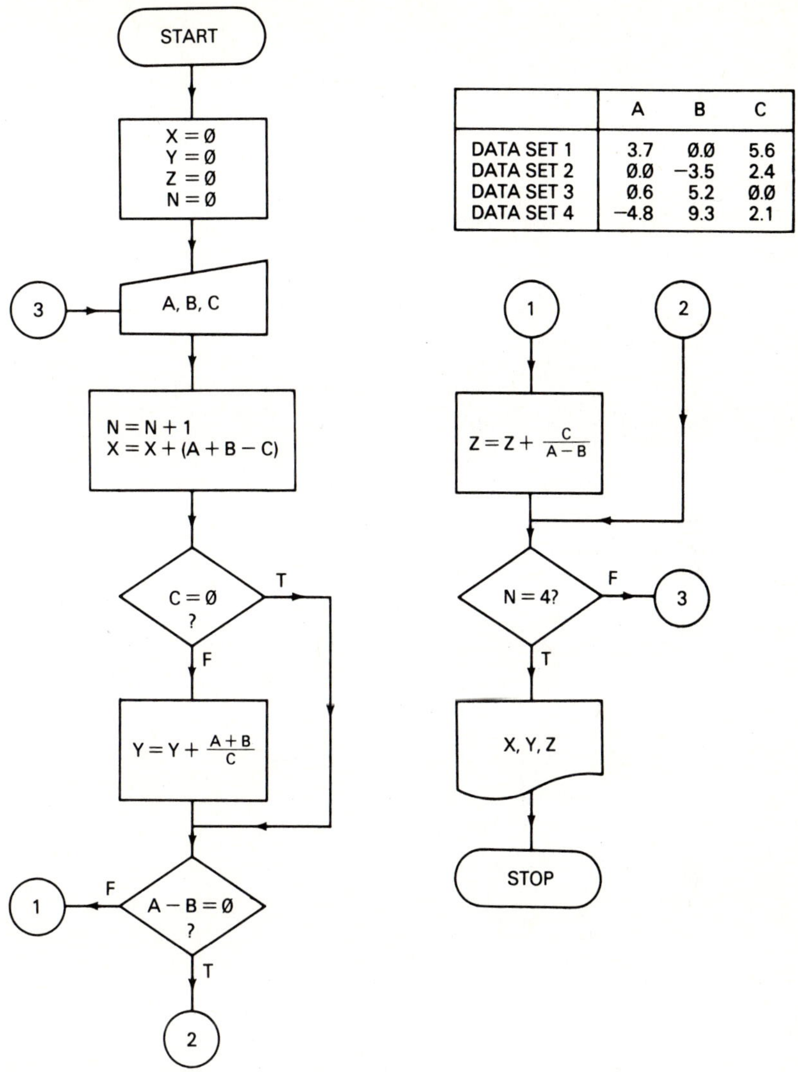

	A	B	C
DATA SET 1	3.7	Ø.Ø	5.6
DATA SET 2	Ø.Ø	−3.5	2.4
DATA SET 3	Ø.6	5.2	Ø.Ø
DATA SET 4	−4.8	9.3	2.1

FIGURE 2-16 Problem 2-6.

2-16 Given ten pairs of numbers, supplied one pair at a time, print for each pair one of the following statements, as applicable:

One number is positive; one is negative.
Both numbers are positive.
Both numbers are negative.

Assume that no zero values are supplied.

2-17 Given a group of five positive numbers, list the numbers in sequential order, beginning with the smallest and terminating with the largest.

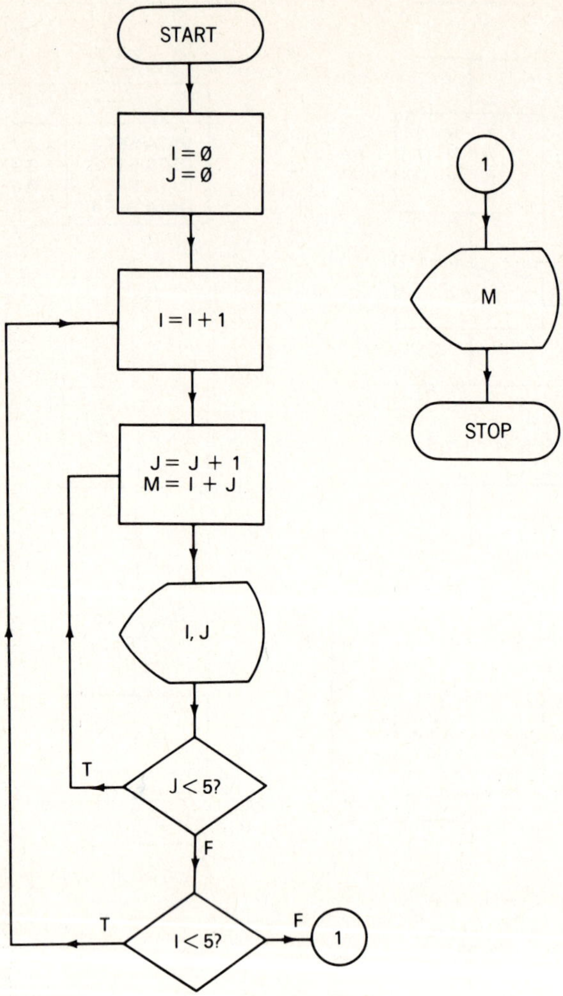

FIGURE 2-17 Problem 2-7.

2-18 Given the coordinates of five points, indicate the location of each point on a rectangular grid by using one of the following phrases:

At the origin.
On the positive *X* axis.
On the negative *X* axis.
On the positive *Y* axis.
On the negative *Y* axis.
In the first quadrant.
In the second quadrant.
In the third quadrant.
In the fourth quadrant.

	ANGLE 1	ANGLE 2	ANGLE 3
DATA SET 1	37.Ø°	37.Ø°	1Ø6.Ø°
DATA SET 2	25.Ø°	83.4°	71.6°
DATA SET 3	6Ø.Ø°	6Ø.Ø°	6Ø.Ø°
DATA SET 4	45.Ø°	9Ø.Ø°	45.Ø°
DATA SET 5	12Ø.Ø°	3Ø.Ø°	3Ø.Ø°

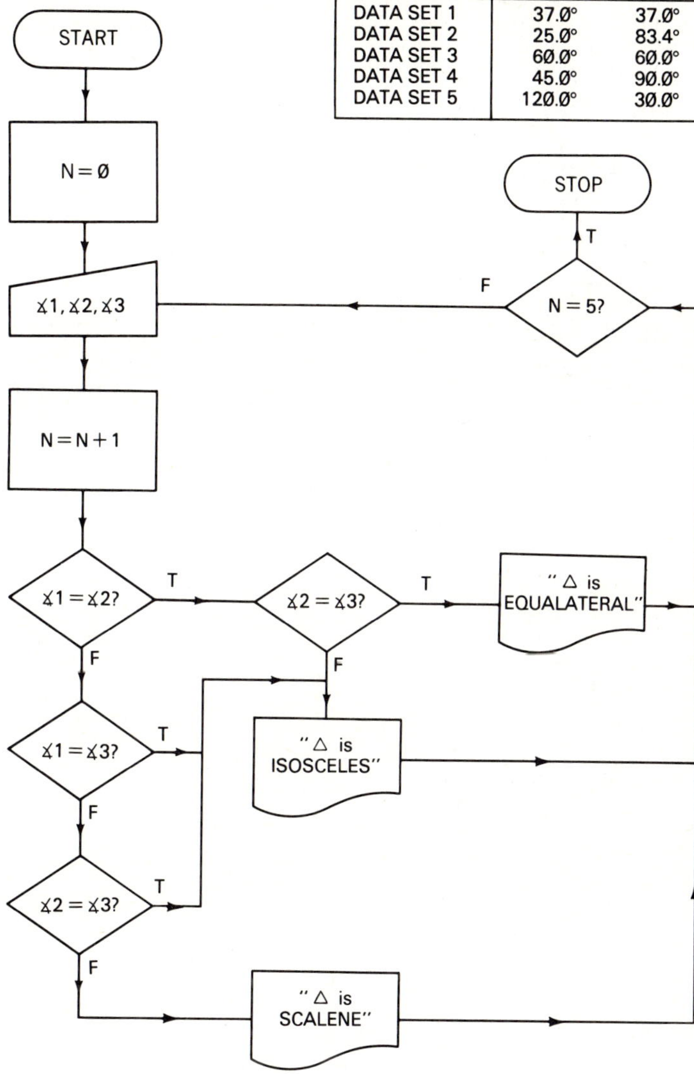

FIGURE 2-18 Problem 2-8.

CHAPTER **3**

FUNDAMENTALS OF PROGRAMMING

3-1 INTRODUCTION

Chapter 1 indicated that characters are stored in the form of binary digits in addressable locations within the storage unit of the computer. The purpose of this chapter is to describe the types of constants and variables, the evaluation of arithmetic expressions, the storage of results, the preparation of simple input/output instructions, the assembling of sequential instructions into a program, and the types of errors inherent in computer programs. The language used in this and succeeding chapters is FORTRAN 77. The name FORTRAN is derived from the words FORmula TRANslation. This version was prepared in 1977 and published in 1978.

Beginning students are often confused by the technical terminology of computer science. A complete understanding of the computer-science idiom is not a prerequisite to the intelligent preparation of a logical sequence of instructions (a program) which can be used with the computer to solve a given problem. One need only accept the premise that on an available diskette there exists a set of detailed machine-language instructions enabling the computer to execute a series of simplified user-oriented instructions prepared under the rules of FORTRAN 77. This set of machine-language instructions originates with a compiler program (Sec. 1-3 and App. E).

3-2 THE FORTRAN CHARACTER SET

The FORTRAN language uses the following alphabetic, numeric, and special characters of the English language and mathematics: the 26 characters of the English alphabet, A through Z; the 10 decimal digits, Ø through 9; and 10 special characters:

+	plus	.	period (decimal point)
−	minus	,	comma
*	asterisk (star)	'	apostrophe
/	solidus (slash)	(	left parenthesis
=	equals sign (or assignment symbol)	)	right parenthesis

While these are the most commonly used, other characters such as $, ?, #, :, and ; are also available.

These characters are combined to form words, numbers, and expressions that are used to compose FORTRAN statements. A FORTRAN *statement* may be an explicit instruction to the computer to perform a single, simple operation. For example, read a value entered from the keyboard and assign it to a given variable name; perform a mathematical operation and assign the result to a given variable name; repeat a series of operations; or print the results of a calculation. A statement may also supply information by defining an array, identifying a complex variable, or specifying an output format, as described in subsequent chapters.

A FORTRAN *program* consists of a series of these step-by-step instructions or statements organized in a logical sequence to achieve predictable results. FORTRAN statements of various types and those most frequently used will be described in detail as appropriate.

3-3 FORTRAN NUMBERS (CONSTANTS)

A mathematical value is represented by a series of numerical digits with or without a decimal point and with or without an algebraic sign. Constants (numbers) used in FORTRAN are expressed as one of two types: integer or real.

a Integer Constants

An *integer* constant is literally an integer, i.e., a whole number without a decimal point. It may be zero or any positive or negative value. In general, an integer constant should not exceed nine digits. Decimal points are *not used* in integer constants. The constant 123 is an integer, while the constant 123. is not an integer because it is written with a decimal point. Integer constants *must* be written without a decimal point so that the compiler can identify them as integers.

The maximum magnitude of an integer constant varies from computer to computer. In general, the maximum magnitude is $2^{31} - 1 = 2{,}147{,}483{,}647$, a 10-digit number. Numbers greater than this value are not permissible, hence the general rule that an integer constant should not exceed nine digits.

Integer-arithmetic operations may produce unexpected results if the rules of integer arithmetic are not understood. The compiler is programmed so that the results of arithmetic operations with integer numbers must also be integers. Consider the operation 4/5, where both 4 and 5 are integers. The true arithmetic quotient is Ø.8, a fractional value; however, the computer-evaluated quotient will be an integer. The decimal fraction is dropped and the integer Ø is the result. Ignoring this characteristic of FORTRAN integer arithmetic can cause significant errors in the final results. *Integers should be avoided in computations, except when used as exponents*. Occasionally the peculiarities of integer-arithmetic operations may be applied advantageously in certain decision-making situations. One such application is discussed in Sec. 6-14. However, in general, use of integer numbers should be limited to counting, identification, or exponentiation. Table 3-1 summarizes the rules pertaining to integer numbers.

TABLE 3-1 INTEGER NUMBERS

1. No decimal point.
2. No fractional values.
3. Used as counters, exponents, and identification numbers.
4. Results of integer arithmetic reduced to next-lower integer.
5. Remainders resulting from division are lost (truncated).

4/3	value is 1
4/5	value is Ø
17/5	value is 3

b Real Constants

Most numbers used in FORTRAN arithmetic operations are decimal numbers called *real* constants. There are two forms in which real constants can be expressed: with an exponent and without an exponent. The number 123. is a real constant without an exponent. The decimal point following the last digit identifies the number as a real constant. A zero following the decimal point (123.Ø) is not required but may be included.

A real constant can also be expressed in exponential form, i.e., a decimal number times a power of 10. For example, the real constant 123. can be expressed in the familiar mathematical notation, $1.23 \times 1Ø^2$. Coded in FORTRAN exponential form, this becomes 1.23E2, with the E2 indicating that the exponent, or power of 10, is 2. This number might also be coded 12.3E1, 123.EØ, or Ø.123E3.

As with integer constants, the maximum number of digits depends on the capacity of the computer used. In general, real constants should not exceed seven digits. For example, the constant π can be written as a seven-digit number without an exponent, 3.141593. The value may also be coded Ø.3141593E1 or 3.141593EØ. Whichever way the number is coded in the program, every real constant is stored in exponential form as a decimal number between Ø.1ØØØØØØ and Ø.9999999 times an appropriate power of 10.

A confusing concept involves the *magnitude* of a real number that can be stored versus the *precision* with which a real numerical value can be read (defined). The personal computer is capable of storing real numbers whose magnitude ranges from $+3.4Ø2823 \times 1Ø^{38}$ to $-3.4Ø2823 \times 1Ø^{38}$, inclusive. As the value approaches zero, the minimum positive and maximum negative values (other than zero) that can be stored are $\pm 1.175495 \times 1Ø^{-38}$. All values between the latter two limits are stored as zero. Seven digits is the maximum number of digits allowed (in single-precision calculations) for real numbers and defines the precision with which a real number can be specified, not the magnitude of the number that can be stored. (See Sec. 11-9 for a description of double-precision calculations.) This limit on the digit count means that numbers greater than 9999999. or less than Ø.ØØØØØØ1 must be expressed in exponential form. Table 3-2 on p. 34 summarizes the rules pertaining to real numbers.

TABLE 3-2 REAL NUMBERS

1. Used in most computations.
2. Decimal point must be included.
3. Should not be used as an exponent for integer numbers.
4. Remainders resulting from division are not lost.

4.Ø/3.Ø	value is 1.3333333
4.Ø/5.Ø	value is Ø.8ØØØØØØ
17.Ø/5.Ø	value is 3.4ØØØØØØ
Ø.5E2/Ø.2E1	value is 25.ØØØØØØØ

3-4 FORTRAN VARIABLE NAMES

A quantity whose numerical value is temporarily unknown or which may vary in numerical value is called a *variable* and is expressed by a *variable name*. A variable name is created by the programmer and may consist of from one to six letters or letters and numbers, depending on the computer system used. Most FORTRAN compilers permit six alphanumeric characters. Whatever the acceptable length, the first character of the variable name must be a letter of the alphabet. Succeeding characters must be either letters or numbers. Other characters *are not* allowed. The numerical value assigned to a variable name may be either integer or real, the type being determined by the first letter of the variable name.

a Integer-Variable Names

When the value of the variable is to be considered an integer number, the variable *must* be designated by an *integer-variable name*. The first letter of an integer-variable name must be I, J, K, L, M, or N, the *integer designators*. After the first letter, succeeding characters may be any letter or number. Examples of acceptable integer-variable names are I, J2, and NUMBER. Examples of unacceptable integer-variable names are X (not an integer designator), 2K (first character is not a letter), NUMBERS (more than six characters), and NO. (contains a character other than a letter or a digit).

b Real-Variable Names

When the value of a variable is to be considered a *real number*, the variable must be designated by a *real-variable name*. The first letter of a real-variable name may be any letter of the alphabet other than those reserved for the first letter of integer-variable names, i.e., the integer designators I, J, K, L, M, and N. The letters A through H and O through Z are the *real designators*. After the first letter, succeeding characters may be any letter or digit. Examples of acceptable real-variable names are ALPHA, BIG, YCUBED, PART2, and X. Examples of unacceptable real-variable names are 2XRAY (first character is not a letter), KAPPA (first letter is an integer designator), and XYZ?A (contains characters other than letters or digits). Table 3-3 summarizes the rules that must be followed in establishing variable names.

TABLE 3-3 RULES FOR VARIABLE NAMES

1. First character must be a letter.
2. Subsequent letters may be any combination of letters and digits (other characters cannot be used).
3. Variable names must not exceed six characters (for most computers).
4. Integer-variable names must begin with letters I through N only.
5. Real-variable names must begin with any other letter (A through H or O through Z).
6. Blank spaces may be inserted to improve readability and do not count as one of the six allowable characters.
7. The same name must not be used for more than one variable in a given program.
8. Before a variable name can be used in computation, it must be assigned a numerical value by either an assignment statement, a READ statement, or a DATA statement.
9. Terms that are part of the FORTRAN vocabulary, e.g., READ, WRITE, REAL, IF, should not be used as variable names.

	Integer-variable names			Real-variable names		
Designators	I, J, K, L, M, N			A through H, O through Z		
	NUMBER	NUM	NO	RADIUS	RAD	R
	MONTH	MO	M	AREA	AR	A
	ITEM	JOHN	J	CIRCUM	CIR	C
	NUM2	ITEM3		R1	R2	R3

c Mnemonic Names

Using a number of randomly chosen one- or two-letter variable names to represent a variety of quantities in a single program is likely to confuse the human reader. Carefully composed mnemonic variable names help in reading and understanding a long and complex program. A *mnemonic name* is a group of six (or fewer) characters that form a valid variable name suggestive of the quantity represented. The mnemonic names RADIUS, DIAM, CIRCUM, and AREA are more suggestive of the radius, diameter, circumference, and area than, say, R or RAD (which may suggest radians), D, C, and A.

The mnemonic name should be as descriptive as possible within the limitations imposed by the rules applying to FORTRAN variable names. Names that are easily misspelled or ambiguous should be avoided. Names too similar in their spelling are easily confused. For example:

```
N=K
NN=K+K
NNN=K+K+K
```

(The meaning of the above statements will be discussed in Sec. 3-7.) The multiple-N variation may be confusing and encourage mistakes. Better names for these variables are:

```
N=K
NSUM=K+K
NTOT=K+K+K
```

If two variable names must be similar, differences should occur at the beginning of the names rather than at the end. For example, XPOS and YPOS are preferable to POSX and POSY. Note that in the examples above the names could not have been SUMN or TOTN since the initial real-designator characters S and T would change the type of the variable from integer to real.

3-5 FORTRAN STATEMENTS

A FORTRAN program is composed of a sequence of step-by-step instructions called statements. There are two general categories of FORTRAN statements: executable and nonexecutable.

a Executable Statements

Executable statements instruct the computer to perform (execute) some specific action; e.g., read a value, assign a value, print a result, or stop execution. Assignment statements, transfer statements, control statements, and input/output statements are all examples of executable statements. (These statements will be described as required in this and subsequent chapters.)

b Nonexecutable Statements

Nonexecutable statements direct no specific action but provide information essential to the proper execution of some executable statement. Declaration statements, DATA statements, and FORMAT statements are examples of nonexecutable statements. (These statements will be discussed as required in this and subsequent chapters.) With the exception of the FORMAT statement, nonexecutable statements should appear in the program sequence before any executable statement. Within flowcharts, nonexecutable statements are not usually identified by a unique symbol, but may be identified by annotation. Table 3-4 shows the most common FORTRAN statements and the category of each.

Programming consists of correctly coding appropriate FORTRAN statements and assembling them in proper sequential order to achieve the desired results. If the logical sequence of operations has been carefully planned on a flowchart (the algorithm), writing and assembling the FORTRAN statements in a FORTRAN program becomes a somewhat routine operation. However, great care must be exercised to ensure that the rules of syntax (the prescribed arrangement of characters in a FORTRAN statement) are understood and obeyed. Violating these rules will cause much frustration and lost time with seemingly endless reruns of incorrect programs. Almost correct is not good enough; a single misplaced, added, omitted, or incorrect character can abort compilation and/or execution of the program.

3-6 TYPE-DECLARATION STATEMENTS

The compiler distinguishes between integer- and real-variable names by the first letter of the variable name. However, the programmer may wish to use variable

TABLE 3-4 FORTRAN STATEMENTS

Executable		Nonexecutable	
Type	**Statement**	**Type**	**Statement**
Input/output	READ WRITE	Type-declaration	INTEGER REAL DIMENSION DOUBLE PRECISION CHARACTER COMPLEX
Transfer	GOTO IF		
Looping	DO		
Control	CONTINUE CALL RETURN STOP	Specification	FORMAT EQUIVALENCE
		Definition	DATA FUNCTION SUBROUTINE COMMON END
Assignment	PI = 3.141593		

Note: The END statement can be considered either executable or nonexecutable.

names that do not begin with the appropriate letter designator. The type of a variable name can be declared, regardless of the first-letter designator, by using a *type-declaration statement*. The general forms for type-declaration statements are:

INTEGER *a*, *b*, *c*
REAL *i*, *j*, *k*

where *a, b, c* represent a list of variable names whose type is to be integer, and *i, j, k* represent a list of variable names whose type is to be real. In the case of the INTEGER statement, the number assigned to each variable named in the list is treated as an integer number regardless of the first letter of the variable name. In the case of the REAL statement, the number assigned to each variable named in the list is treated as a real number regardless of the first letter of the variable name. The variable names in the list must be separated by commas. Examples of type-declaration statements are:

INTEGER A, DELTA, LAST
REAL LOAD, MASS, B

These two statements declare that the variable names A and DELTA are to be integer throughout the program and that the variable names LOAD and MASS are to be real throughout the program. LAST could have been omitted from the INTEGER statement and B could have been omitted from the REAL statement because the first-letter designator establishes the type. But it is not incorrect to list them, and some programmers prefer to declare the type of all variable names used in a program. The type-declaration statement is a nonexecutable statement and *must appear* in the program *before* any executable statement. Other type-declaration statements, e.g., DIMENSION, DOUBLE PRECISION, CHARACTER, and COMPLEX, will be described later in applicable chapters.

3-7 FORTRAN ARITHMETIC OPERATIONS

FORTRAN provides for five basic arithmetic operations: *addition, subtraction, multiplication, division,* and *exponentiation* (raising to a power). Each operation is represented by an easily distinguishable symbol, called an *arithmetic operator:*

+	addition
−	subtraction
*	multiplication
/	division
**	exponentiation

The double asterisk (**) is considered one symbol.

a FORTRAN Expressions

A FORTRAN *expression* describes the mathematical relationship of a group of constants and/or variables. In some cases, an expression may consist of a single constant, variable, or function (Chap. 5). More often, several of these elements are combined with arithmetic operators and grouped within parentheses. X, X*Y, X**2, and (X+1.)*(Y−1.) are examples of FORTRAN arithmetic expressions (see Table 3-5 for additional examples).

Note that two or more arithmetic operators must not appear in succession. Using consecutive arithmetic operators in an arithmetic expression constitutes a syntax error. When the minus sign is used to indicate a negative number, it may be necessary to rearrange the symbols of the expression to avoid successive symbols of arithmetic operations. For example, $X/-Y$ may be rewritten with parentheses (Sec. 3-8*i*) as X/(−Y) or −X/Y without changing the meaning or value of the expression. Table 3-5 summarizes the rules pertaining to arithmetic operations and expressions.

b Hierarchy of Arithmetic Operations

Computer evaluation of a FORTRAN arithmetic expression follows a strictly ordered sequence or hierarchy of operations:

1 *Clear parentheses:* clearing from inside out, scanning from left to right.

2 *Function evaluation:* scanning from left to right (Chap. 5).

3 *Exponentiation:* scanning from left to right, exponentiating from right to left.

4 *Multiplication and/or division:* scanning and multiplying or dividing, as required, from left to right.

TABLE 3-5 ARITHMETIC OPERATIONS AND EXPRESSIONS

Operations

Operation	Math notation	FORTRAN symbol	FORTRAN expression
Addition	$A + B$	+	A+2
Subtraction	$A - B$	−	A−B
Multiplication	$A \times B$	*	A*B
Division	A/B	/	A/B
Exponentiation	A^2	**	A**2

Expressions

Math notation	FORTRAN expression
πr	3.141593*R
πr^2	3.141593*R**2
$\pi d^2/4$	3.141593*D**2/4.Ø
$(a + b)^3$	(A+B)**3
$\sqrt{a^2 + b^2}$	(A**2+B**2)**Ø.5

Expressions must be either integer or real. Mixed mode expressions should not be used.

Note: An integer exponent may be used with a real constant or a real variable base, but a real exponent should not be used with an integer constant or an integer-variable base.

Correct:	X**2	6.Ø**2
Incorrect:	N**2.Ø	6**2.Ø

No two arithmetic operators may appear in sequence. $A/-B$ must be written: A/(−B) or −A/B.

5 *Addition and/or subtraction:* scanning and adding or subtracting, as required, from left to right.

The hierarchy of arithmetic operations and proper use of parenthetical groupings must be clearly understood and carefully practiced when coding arithmetic expressions. When parentheses are used, it is important that the parentheses be matched; there *must be the same number* of right and left parentheses. Unmatched parentheses constitute a syntax error.

Consider the mathematical expression:

$$\frac{a+b}{c-d}$$

This might be erroneously coded in FORTRAN as in (*a*), or properly coded as in (*b*):

(*a*) A+B/C−D (*b*) (A+B) / (C−D)

With the following numerical values assigned to the variable names:

A=4.Ø B=3.Ø C=2.Ø D=1.Ø

the two FORTRAN expressions are evaluated, respectively, as

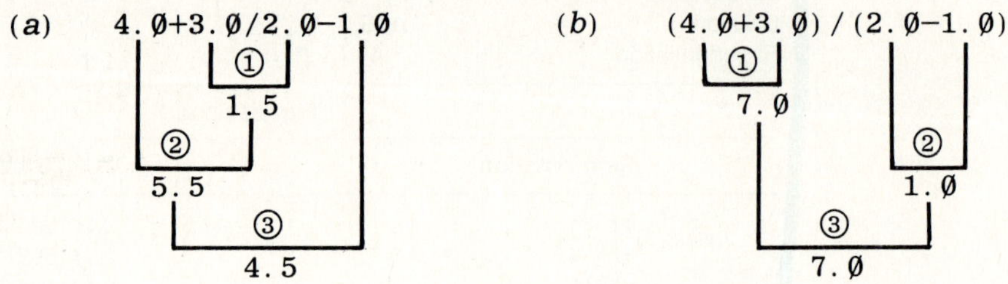

Substitution of the given numerical values in the original mathematical expression shows that the result of the sum of 4.Ø plus 3.Ø divided by the difference of 2.Ø and 1.Ø is 7.Ø, the result obtained from FORTRAN expression (*b*). The result obtained from evaluating FORTRAN expression (*a*), 4.5, is obviously incorrect. These examples illustrate situations where the hierarchy of operations dictates the use of parentheses so that the sequence of calculations will be performed correctly. Many incorrect answers are the result of incorrectly coded arithmetic expressions.

Examples 3-1 through 3-3 below illustrate the hierarchy of operations followed in evaluating an arithmetic expression. COS(C) and SIN(PI/B) are examples of (trigonometric) functions in an arithmetic expression. A knowledge of functions is not essential to understanding these examples of the hierarchy of operations. It is sufficient to know that when the evaluation occurs, a real number replaces the function. Both functions will be discussed in Chap. 5.

Example 3-1

Mathematical expression: $\dfrac{ab^3}{\cos c} + d - e$

FORTRAN expression: A*B**3/COS(C) + D − E

Assign the following numerical values to the variable names:

A=2.Ø B=3.Ø C=Ø.Ø D=4.Ø E=5.Ø

The FORTRAN expression is evaluated:

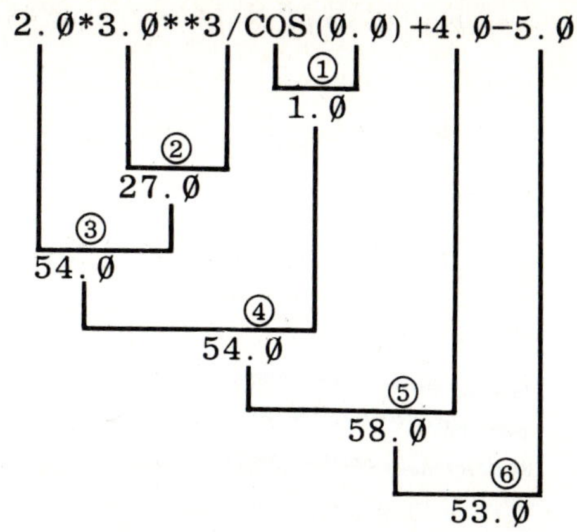

Example 3-2

Mathematical expression: $\dfrac{a + b}{(c + d)\sin^2(\pi/b)}$

FORTRAN expression: `(A+B)/((C+D)*SIN(PI/B)**2)`

Assign the following numerical values to the variable names:

A=4.Ø   B=6.Ø   C=2.Ø   D=3.Ø   PI=3.141593

The FORTRAN expression is evaluated:

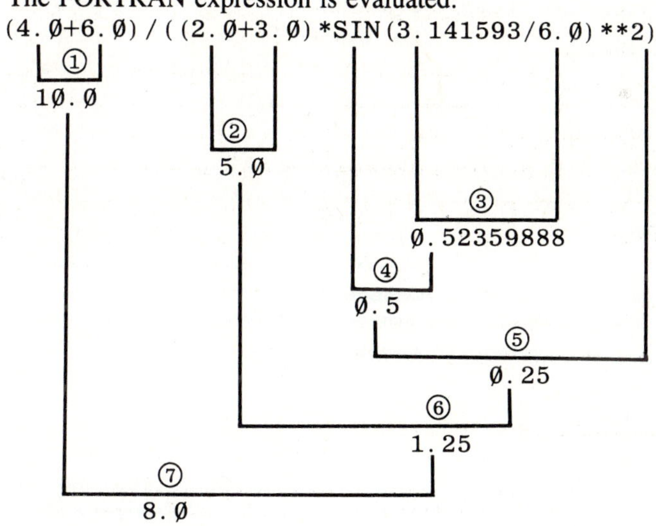

Example 3-3

Mathematical expression: (*a*) x^{2^3} (*b*) $(x^2)^3$

FORTRAN expression: (*a*) X**2**3   (*b*) (X**2)**3

Assign the following numerical value to the variable name:

X=5.Ø

The FORTRAN expressions are evaluated:

c Mixed-Mode Expressions

The term "mixed-mode" refers to expressions containing both integer and real constants and/or variables. The compiler used in this text will evaluate a mixed-mode expression and return a real value, which, depending upon the arithmetic operations performed, may or may not be the intended value. For example:

```
Operation 1: 1.5 * (1./2.) / (5./2.)   is evaluated Ø.3Ø
Operation 2: 1.5 * (1./2 ) / (5 /2.)   is evaluated Ø.3Ø
Operation 3: 1.5 * (1 /2 ) / (5 /2 )   is evaluated Ø.ØØ
Operation 4: 1.5 *  1 /2   /  5 /2     is evaluated Ø.Ø75
```

The first example contains no mixed modes, and the expression is evaluated as expected, Ø.3Ø. The second example is a mixed-mode expression. The mixed-mode divisions of 1./2 and 5/2. are both evaluated by the compiler in real arithmetic as Ø.5 and 2.5, respectively, and no problem occurs. The expression in the second example is also evaluated as Ø.3Ø. In the third example, the integer divisions of 1/2 and 5/2 are evaluated as Ø and 2, respectively, and the expression is evaluated as Ø.ØØ, an "incorrect" evaluation. The fourth example is evaluated in real arithmetic and, since all parentheses are removed, is evaluated from left to right as explained in Sec. 3-7*b*. Hence the expression in the fourth example is evaluated as Ø.Ø75, another "incorrect" evaluation. Indiscriminate mixing of real and integer constants or variables in a single arithmetic expression should be avoided.

As a general rule, all arithmetic calculations should be performed with real expressions. An exception occurs in the case of exponents. Integer exponents should be used whenever possible since integer exponentiation is more efficiently executed than real exponentiation.

3-8 THE ASSIGNMENT STATEMENT

An *assignment statement* is an executable statement that assigns the numerical value of an arithmetic expression to a named variable in a specific address. The general form for the assignment statement is:

NAME=*arithmetic expression*

where NAME represents a variable name, either integer or real; = is the *assignment symbol;* and *arithmetic expression* is any arithmetic expression to be evaluated. In a flowchart, the PROCESS symbol is used to represent the assignment statement. Flowchart examples are given in Figs. 2-3, 2-8, and 2-9.

a The Assignment Symbol

Consider the statements:

```
A=2.Ø
B=3.Ø
C=(A+B)/A
```

The first statement, A=2.Ø, assigns the real value 2.Ø to the real-variable name A and stores it in location A. The second statement, B=3.Ø, assigns the real value 3.Ø to the real-variable B and stores it in location B. The third statement, C=(A+B)/A, evaluates the expression (A+B)/A by dividing the sum of A+B, (2.Ø+3.Ø), by the value of A, (2.Ø); assigns the real result, (2.5), to the real-variable C; and stores it in location C. The programmer does not have to specify the storage locations for the variable names A, B, and C or know and remember storage locations. A unique storage location will be assigned to each variable name the first time that name is used. When that name is again used in subsequent statements, the value assigned will be available when required.

If the three statements illustrated above are coded:

```
A=2
B=3
IC=(A+B)/A
```

the real values 2. and 3. will still be assigned, respectively, to A and B since A and B are real-variable names. The assignment statement will always assign a real value to a real-variable name. The value of the real expression (A+B)/A will therefore remain the same, 2.5. However, the value assigned to the integer-variable name IC will be the integer value 2; the decimal point and fraction .5 will be truncated because an integer value will always be assigned to an integer-variable name. Note that there can be *one and only one* variable name to the left of the assignment symbol.

b Incrementing the Value of a Variable

In FORTRAN, the symbol = is not used to denote mathematical equality but is strictly an assignment symbol. It signifies that the value of the expression to the right of the = symbol is to be assigned to the variable name to the left of the symbol. Therefore, the statement N=N+1 is a valid assignment statement. This statement will recall from storage the value previously assigned to N, add 1 to that value, and store the new value N+1 in the storage location designated N, replacing the old value. This technique can be used to increment (sequentially change) the numerical value assigned to a given variable name. The statements:

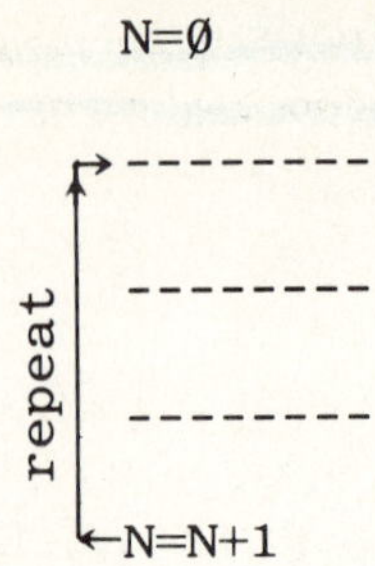

where the dashed lines represent intervening statements, are often used to record the number of repetitive operations in a computer program. The value initially assigned to N is Ø. Since the value of N is incremented by 1 each time the operation is repeated, the last value assigned to N will be the number of repetitions.

c Assigning a Constant to a Variable Name

The assignment statement can be used to assign the value of a constant to a unique variable name as described in Sec. 3-8*a*. PI=3.141593 is another good example. Here the constant 3.141593 is to be used repeatedly in subsequent calculations. This statement will store the constant in a storage location called PI; and when the constant is later needed in an expression, it can be called by using the name PI instead of repeating the longer constant. Note that the value assigned to PI in this example is a seven-digit real number, the maximum number of digits the compiler will accept for assignment to a real-variable name.

d Truncating a Real Variable or Constant

There are times when it may be desirable to truncate (drop the fractional part of) a real value or, in other words, to change from a real value to an integer value, as shown in the last part of Sec. 3-8*a*. N=Y will change the real value assigned to Y by truncating, or dropping, the decimal portion of the number and assigning the remaining integer to N. If the value assigned to Y is 6.6, the value assigned to N by the statement N=Y will be 6, an integer number. The value assigned to Y remains unchanged. The same applies if a real constant is assigned to an integer-variable name. N=2.5, for example, will result in the truncation of .5 with the integer 2 being assigned to N. Temporary truncation can also be accomplished by functions to be described in Sec. 5-4.

e Rounding (Up or Down) a Real Variable to the Nearest Integer Value

In the example used in Sec. 3-8*d*, N=Y, where the value assigned to Y is 6.6, the truncated value assigned to N is 6, which is not the nearest integer to 6.6. If the statement is changed to N=Y+Ø.5, the expression will be evaluated at 7.1, and when truncated, the integer 7 will be assigned to N. Thus, *rounding up* rather than truncation is the result. If the decimal portion of the value assigned to Y is less than Ø.5, the decimal will still be dropped and *rounding down* is the result. If the decimal portion is exactly Ø.5, the addition of Ø.5 will increase the value of the number to the next higher unit and rounding up will result. This technique is applicable only when rounding real values to the nearest integer value (Sec. 5-1Ø).

f Changing an Integer Variable or Constant to a Real Variable or Constant

There are times when it may be desirable to change an integer value to a real value. This can be done by assigning the integer variable or constant to a real-variable name. If the value assigned to the integer-variable name N is 6, the statement Y=N will assign real 6.Ø to Y by adding a decimal point to the value of N. The statement Y=6 will also add a decimal point, with a real 6.Ø being assigned to Y. There is, of course, no problem with truncation; a decimal point is simply added to the integer value. The temporary change of an integer value to a real value can also be accomplished by functions to be described in Sec. 5-4.

g Mixed-Mode Expressions

A number of examples in the preceding paragraphs in this section have included statements in which the result of an arithmetic expression evaluated in one type is to be assigned to a variable name of the other type. These are not mixed-mode expressions (as defined in Sec. 3-7*c*). The caution about mixed modes applies to the arithmetic-expression portion of the assignment statement. Table 3-6 illustrates a summation of the preceding descriptions of the assignment statement.

TABLE 3-6 ASSIGNMENT STATEMENTS

An instruction to the computer to evaluate an expression and assign its numerical value to a variable name, taking the form:

VAR=*arithmetic expression*

Examples		
	PI=3.141593	CIRCUM=PI*RAD*2.0
	AREA=PI*R**2	N=N+1

Assignment statement	Value assigned to variable
J=3*4+1	J is 13
C=3*4+1	C is 13.Ø
I=4.Ø/3.Ø	I is 1
A=4/3	A is 1.Ø
X=5.Ø*3.Ø/2.Ø	X is 7.5
L=5.Ø*3.Ø/2.Ø	L is 7
M=5*3/2	M is 7
B=5*3/2	B is 7.Ø
K=(5.Ø*3.Ø/2.Ø)+Ø.5	K is 8
N=(3.Ø/4.Ø)+Ø.5	N is 1
J=(5.Ø/4.Ø)+Ø.5	J is 1
Y=4.Ø*3.Ø**2	Y is 36.Ø
Z=(4.Ø*3.Ø)**2	Z is 144.Ø
D=(5.Ø+3.Ø)/2.Ø	D is 4.Ø
E=5.Ø+3.Ø/2.Ø	E is 6.5
F=3.Ø*(6.Ø+8.Ø/2.Ø**2)	F is 24.Ø
G=3.Ø*((6.Ø+8.Ø)/(2.Ø**))	G is 1Ø.5

h Unassigned Variable Names

All variable names used in the arithmetic-expression portion of the assignment statement must previously have been assigned a numerical value. If a variable name is not assigned a value, the compiler will automatically assign a value of zero to the variable. Attempting to use a variable name to which a numerical value has not been assigned is a potential programming error which may be difficult to locate since no error message results. Execution will continue to completion with the unassigned variable name evaluated as zero.

i Parentheses

Long and involved arithmetic expressions should include sufficient parentheses to make the mathematical relationship absolutely clear. Redundant parentheses in arithmetic expressions are well worth the effort for the beginning programmer.

3-9 THE LIST-DIRECTED READ STATEMENT, THE OPEN STATEMENT, AND THE DATA FILE

The READ statement is an executable input statement that provides a simple and direct means for supplying data values to the variable names used in a FORTRAN program. The general form for the READ statement is:

READ(*n*, *m*)*a*, *b*, *j*

where *n* represents an integer number or character designating the input unit (a data file or the keyboard)

m represents an integer number identifying another statement which specifies how the data values are structured (Sec. 6-3, the FORMAT statement), or a character denoting unstructured data

a, *b*, *j* represent variable names (referred to as a list) to which values are to be assigned

a List-Directed READ Statement

When unstructured data [data without a FORMAT statement (Secs. 6-3 and 6-8)] are to be supplied from the keyboard, the READ statement is coded:

```
READ(*, *)A, B, J
```

This is referred to as a *list-directed* READ statement. The first asterisk indicates that the data are to be manually keyed in via the keyboard. The second asterisk indicates that the data supplied will be unstructured (without a FORMAT specification). Two flowchart symbols may be used to represent the general READ statement. They are the "curved-paper" INPUT/OUTPUT symbol and the trapezoidal INPUT symbol, illustrated in Fig. 2-1.

b Numerical Data from the Keyboard

When a READ statement is included in a FORTRAN program, it must be supplied with numerical values, integer or real, ordered as required, for assignment to each variable name in the READ list. When the list-directed READ statement is coded:

```
READ(*, *)A, B, J
```

indicating input from the keyboard, a pause will occur at the execution of the READ statement. No prompt other than the blinking cursor will appear on the screen; the PC operator must respond by manually keying in the data to satisfy the READ list.

c Data from the Data File

When the values to be assigned to the variable names in the READ list are to be read from a data file stored on the diskette under a separate filename, an OPEN statement is required, preceding the READ statement, to identify and open the file from which the data are to be read. The OPEN statement is coded:

OPEN(*n*, FILE='FILENAME.DAT')

where *n* represents the unit code (an integer number chosen by the programmer, used to identify the file within the program) and FILENAME.DAT represents a unique filename and extension under which the data file is stored (Sec. 3-16 and App. C). The associated READ statement is coded:

READ(*n*, *)*a*, *b*, *j*

where *n* is the same integer number (unit code) used in the associated OPEN statement and references a specific data file from which data values are to be read

* indicates that the values in the data file are without consistent structure or that the specific structure of the data file is unknown (without FORMAT)

a, *b*, *j* again represent the list of variable names to which values so read are to be assigned.

The OPEN statement is represented in a flowchart by the PROCESS symbol, as illustrated in Figs. 3-5(*a*) and 3-6(*a*).

The OPEN and list-directed READ statements in a program require a data file, prepared by the programmer, that contains the values to be assigned to the variable names in the READ list. The data file is a separate file stored on the same diskette as the FORTRAN program under the filename and extension specified in the OPEN statement. The READ statement references the OPEN statement through the integer number (unit code) common to both statements. Execution of the READ statement "opens" the specified file and values are read from it, in the order encountered, and assigned in turn to each of the variables in the READ list. Each line of the data file is termed a *record*. Reading will cease when all variables in the READ list have been assigned a value, even though there may be more values remaining in the data file. Consider the following examples:

```
OPEN(5,FILE='FILE.DAT')
READ(5, *)A, B, J
```

FILE.DAT
1.5   2.5   9   7.5

The constants in the data file FILE.DAT are assigned in turn to the variable names in the READ list: 1.5 to A, 2.5 to B, and 9 to J. The READ list has been satisfied, i.e., all variable names in the READ list have been assigned a value, so reading from the data file ceases. The last constant in the record, 7.5, is ignored.

There may be situations when it is desired to reuse the data file. The data file can be reopened with another OPEN statement exactly like the original OPEN statement, or the REWIND statement can be used. The REWIND statement is written:

```
REWIND n
```

where REWIND repositions input control to the first record of the data file designated by the unit number *n*. For example:

```
OPEN(n, FILE='FILENAME.DAT')
READ(n, *)A, B, J

----------

----------

REWIND n
READ(n, *)X, Y, L
```

will open the data file FILENAME.DAT identified by the integer *n* and sequentially read the records therein. At a later point in the program, execution of the REWIND statement will reposition input control to the first record of the data file FILENAME.DAT. The second READ statement begins reading with the first record of FILENAME.DAT.

d Numerical Data

The values in each record of the data file must agree in number (count), order, and type with the variable names in the READ list. If the items of data supplied on a single record exceed the number of variable names in the READ list, data values will be assigned, in the order supplied, until a value has been assigned to each variable name in the READ list. Any data remaining in the record will be ignored. If the variable names in the READ list exceed the number of data values in a single record, the data values in the next record and each succeeding record will be assigned until all the variable names in the READ list have been assigned a value. Any values remaining in the last record read are ignored. The READ list is satisfied when a suitable value has been assigned to each variable name in the list. An unsatisfied READ list (not enough data values supplied) constitutes an execution error. It should be noted that if zero is included in the constant to be assigned to a variable name, the character Ø must be keyed in when preparing the data file. The list-directed READ statement will not read a blank as a zero. When an integer value is provided for a real-variable name, a decimal point will be added to the value and the program will proceed. However, if a real value is provided for an integer-variable name, an error will result. To avoid this problem, the programmer should always be sure of the one-to-one correspondence of the data values with the variable names in the READ list.

When data are to be supplied from a data file, the data file must be created separately from the program file, though filed on the same diskette. The filename of the data filc is established in an OPEN statement of the program. It is suggested that the filename given to the data file be the same as the source program in which it is referenced with the extension DAT to identify a data file (Sec. 3-9*c* and App. C).

The data is entered into the file according to the rules discussed in Sec. 3-9*e*. After the entry of data is completed, the file is stored on the same diskette as the program. Unlike the file of the FORTRAN source program, the data file is *not* compiled.

e Input of Numerical Data

Although data values supplied to the list-directed READ statement may be without consistent structure, input of data must follow a certain order and form to ensure the proper assignment of values to the variable names in the READ list. Whether the data values are entered from the keyboard or read from a data file stored on the diskette, the following rules apply:

1 Values will be assigned to the variable names in the READ list in the order supplied.

2 Values supplied to real-variable names may be either real or integer constants. The compiler will add the decimal point required to make an integer constant agree with the real-variable name. Real constants may be written with or without an exponent.

3 Values supplied to integer-variable names must be integer constants.

4 A positive algebraic sign is implied unless a negative sign is included with the value supplied.

5 When more than one variable name is in the READ list, successive values may be on separate records, or two or more values may be on the same record. The first value may begin in any column. A comma, one or more blanks, or a combination of one comma and one or more blanks must separate successive values.

3-10 LOOPING WITH THE UNCONDITIONAL GOTO STATEMENT

The READ statement is often used in a *loop*, where it can be executed repeatedly, assigning different numerical values from successive records to the variable names in the READ list with each execution. A loop can be formed by combining the READ statement with a simple transfer statement called the *unconditional* GOTO statement (Sec. 4-2). Execution of the GOTO statement temporarily interrupts the sequential execution of the program statements and transfers to another executable statement identified by an integer number called a *statement label* (Sec. 3-16). If the READ statement is given a label, say 1Ø, and the GOTO statement is GOTO 1Ø, execution of the unconditional GOTO statement will cause transfer to statement 1Ø, the READ statement, which will then be executed. If a data file is used, the first execution of the READ statement will read the data from the first record of the data file. There should be a data value for each variable name in the READ list. The second execution of the READ statement will skip the first record (which has already been read) and go to the second record of the data file. Hence the data file should have as many records as the looping will require. Sequential execution will continue with the next executable statement following the READ statement.

In the following example, five values (constants) for the variable DIA, representing the diameter of a circle, are supplied from five records of a data file and assigned in turn to the variable name DIA by the READ statement:

```
      OPEN(2,FILE='DIAM.DAT')
   1Ø READ(2,*)DIA
      AREA=3.141593*(DIA/2.Ø)**2
      WRITE(*,*)DIA,AREA
      GOTO 1Ø
```

DIAM.DAT
1.Ø
1.5
2.Ø
2.5
3.Ø

The first time the READ statement is executed, the constant in the first record, 1.Ø, is assigned to DIA. The arithmetic expression in the assignment statement is evaluated using 1.Ø as the value for DIA, and a value is assigned to AREA. Execution of the WRITE statement (to be discussed in Sec. 3-12) will display the values assigned to DIA and AREA, 1.Ø and Ø.7853983, respectively. Execution of the GOTO statement will initiate a loop back to statement 1Ø, the READ statement. The READ statement is executed for the second time, assigning the constant in the second record of the data file, 1.5, to DIA, replacing the first value, 1.Ø. Execution will continue, in sequence, from the READ statement.

A second value for AREA will be computed and assigned, replacing the first value of AREA. The second values for DIA and AREA, 1.5 and 1.767146, respectively, will be displayed. Execution of the GOTO statement again transfers the sequence back to the READ statement. The sequence through the loop continues until all data values supplied have been assigned. After the last data value has been assigned and the assignment statement and WRITE statement executed, the GOTO statement again transfers back to the READ statement. No more data values are available; the five values supplied have all been assigned. Attempting to execute the READ statement without a data value to assign constitutes an execution error (Sec. 3-21). Execution of the program terminates with an error message (End-of-file encountered) indicating no more data. The output of a similar program will be shown in Fig. 3-6. (Note the error message after the fifth line of output.) Although the desired results were obtained before the error message occurred, terminating a program by default with an error message is poor practice and should be avoided.

Transfer to another statement outside the READ loop will avoid the "End-of-file encountered" error when the READ statement is executed with no more data available. By adding an element, either the END=*n* or ERR=*m* option, to the READ statement, the end of the data file or an error in input is detected and transfer made to an appropriate statement label. Examples are:

```
READ(2,*,END=2Ø)DIA
```

or:

```
READ(2,*,ERR=3Ø)DIA
```

or both options:

```
READ(2,*,END=2Ø,ERR=3Ø)DIA
```

In the first example, transfer to statement 2Ø is made when the end of the data file is detected. In the second, transfer to statement 3Ø is made if an input error occurs, while the third example provides for both occurrences. Execution of the program will proceed from the designated statement. For example, execution can be terminated by placing the *n* label (or the *m* label) on the STOP or the END statement:

```
20 STOP
```

The program in Fig. 3-7 will illustrate this technique. See Chap. 4 for additional information on the unconditional GOTO statement and other looping and branching techniques.

3-11 TERMINATING THE PROGRAM: THE END AND STOP STATEMENTS

The stored-program concept of computer operations in which the entire FORTRAN program is first written, compiled, and then executed, one statement at a time, in sequential order is described in Sec. 1-3. Instructions must be included in the program to signal the end of compilation and to terminate execution.

a The END Statement

The last statement in a FORTRAN program must be an END statement, and an END statement can only be placed at the end of the program as the last statement. Any statement following the END statement will cause an error message during compilation and in most cases initiates several error messages (Sec. 3-21). The END statement serves two purposes: it signals completion of compilation and terminates execution. The END statement may be assigned a statement label; transfer to the END statement may be made by referencing that label in another statement.

b The STOP Statement

The STOP statement serves only one purpose, to terminate execution of the program. The STOP statement may be located anywhere in the program where termination of execution is desired, and may appear more than once in a given program; however, the STOP statement is not required. The STOP statement may be assigned a statement label. When the STOP statement is used to terminate execution, the message:

```
Stop - Program terminated.
```

is displayed on the screen. If the STOP statement is not used, the message is not displayed. The STOP and/or END statements are represented by the TERMINAL, INTERRUPT symbol in flowcharts, with the word STOP inserted within the symbol. This will be illustrated in Figs. 3-5(*a*) and 3-6(*a*).

3-12 THE LIST-DIRECTED WRITE STATEMENT AND THE OPEN STATEMENT

The WRITE statement is an executable statement used to output the results of computer computations. The *verb* "output," as used in this text, will mean to display on the CRT, to print on paper, or to store on diskette and should not be confused with the *noun* "output" meaning the results of a computer program or the *adjective* "output" as used in "output statement." The general form for the WRITE statement is:

WRITE(*n*, *m*) *a*, *b*, *j*

where *n* represents an integer number or character designating the file or output unit to which the results are to be routed

m represents an integer number identifying another statement which specifies how the output is to be structured (Sec. 6-8, the FORMAT statement), or a character denoting compiler-controlled output structure

a, *b*, *j* represent variable names whose values are to be output

a The List-Directed WRITE Statement

Numerical output in a format specified by the compiler may be obtained through the list-directed WRITE statement coded:

```
WRITE(*,*)A,B,J
```

The first asterisk indicates that the results are to be displayed on the screen. The second asterisk indicates that the output will be structured by the compiler. The programmer has no control over how the output is structured.

The first output column is reserved for a vertical-control character (Sec. 6-11) which is *always* a *blank* with list-directed output.

Integer numbers are right-justified in a 13-column field width, i.e., the number will be placed as far to the right in the field as possible, with any blanks in the field shown to the left of the number. The 13-column field includes up to 10 digits, the algebraic sign (displayed only when negative), and at least two leading blanks. (See Fig. 3-1 on p. 54.)

Real numbers with an absolute value equal to or greater than 1 and less than $1\emptyset^8$ are displayed right-justified in decimal form in an 18-column field, which includes seven digits for the decimal part of the number, the decimal point, up to seven digits for the integer part of the number, the algebraic sign (displayed only when negative), and at least two leading blanks (Fig. 3-1). Zeros are added when needed in order to display seven digits to the right of the decimal point.

Real numbers with an absolute value less than 1 and equal to or greater than $1\emptyset^8$ are displayed right-justified in exponential form, in a 15-column field, which includes a three-digit exponent, the algebraic sign of the exponent (always displayed), an E indicating exponent, six digits for the decimal part of the number, the decimal point, one digit for the integer part of the number, the algebraic sign (displayed only when negative), and at least one leading blank (Fig. 3-1). This form of the WRITE statement utilizes the DISPLAY symbol in flowcharts, as will be illustrated in Fig. 3-8.

Figure 3-1 illustrates and summarizes the use of the list-directed WRITE statement. The first two lines of numbers in the output in Fig. 3-1 identify the output

```
C234567890
      OPEN(6,FILE='PRN')
      A=567.89
      B=-1234.5
      C=54.321
      D=15.4E20
      E=25.5E-20
      F=-33.3E17
      I=-12345
      J=67890
      K=54321
      WRITE(6,*)'        1         2         3         4         5'
      WRITE(6,*)'2345678901234567890123456789012345678901234567890123345'
      WRITE(6,*)A,B,C
      WRITE(6,*)D,E,F
      WRITE(6,*)I,J,K
      WRITE(6,*)A,D,I
      WRITE(6,*)E,B,J
      WRITE(6,*)K,F,C
      STOP
      END
```

```
         1         2         3         4         5
2345678901234567890123456789012345678901234567890123345
      567.8900000       -1234.5000000          54.3210000
  1.540000E+021   2.550000E-019 -3.330000E+018
      -12345           67890           54321
      567.8900000   1.540000E+021           -12345
  2.550000E-019       -1234.5000000            67890
          54321 -3.330000E+018          54.3210000
```

FIGURE 3-1 The printing of list-directed data.

column numbers in which the results are printed. It must be realized that all compilers do not print numbers in the same structure as described in this section. If a different compiler or a revised version of the compiler described in App. E is used, a program similar to that of Fig. 3-1 should be executed to determine the list-directed output structure.

b The OPEN Statement

When the results of computations are to be printed on a sheet of paper, the output may be routed to the printer through a print file. The print file is opened with an OPEN statement, coded:

OPEN(*n*, FILE='PRN')

where *n* represents an integer number, chosen by the programmer, and PRN specifies the printer as the output unit. The associated WRITE statement is coded:

WRITE(*n*, *) *a*, *b*, *j*

where *n* is the integer number used in the associated OPEN statement

* indicates that the output will be in the structure specified by the compiler (described in Sec. 3-12*a*)

a, b, j represent the list of variables whose values are to be printed

The following example illustrates the statements required to read values from a specified data file, display those values on the screen, and then print them on a sheet of paper:

```
OPEN(5,FILE='EXMP.DAT')
READ(5,*)A,B,J
OPEN(6,FILE='PRN')
WRITE(*,*)A,B,J
WRITE(6,*)A,B,J
```

EXMP.DAT		
123.456	Ø.Ø123	123

The output will appear as follows:

```
123.456ØØØØ        1.23ØØØØEØØ2        123
```

The first WRITE statement will route output to the screen. The second WRITE statement will route the output to the printer. Whether displayed or printed, the first value, being in decimal form, will be right-justified in column 19 (column 1 is *always* a *blank*); the second value, in exponential form, will be right-justified in column 34; the third value, being integer, will be right-justified in column 47.

3-13 DATA MANIPULATION

Since most programs involve the use of large quantites of data either supplied to or generated by the computer program, further explanation and examples are presented to summarize the use of the list-directed READ and WRITE statements.

a Keyboard-Supplied Data

When data are to be supplied via the keyboard, the execution of the program halts and awaits entry of the required value(s). No prompt is supplied by the compiler; hence, it is advisable to include a prompting message in the program that will appear on the screen to inform the programmer that data are now needed. This can be accomplished as shown by the following program segment:

```
1Ø WRITE(*,*)'ENTER VALUES FOR A AND B'
   READ(*,*)A,B

   ------------

   ------------

   WRITE(*,*)A,B
   GOTO 1Ø
```

The message "ENTER VALUES FOR A AND B" will appear on the screen just prior to the execution of the READ statement. This alerts the programmer that data are required and must be entered via the keyboard. Upon keying in of the requested data, execution continues until control is transferred back to the statement labeled 1Ø, and the prompting message again appears. If the programmer does not wish to enter any further data, simultaneously depressing the Ctrl−Break keys will terminate the program and return the system prompt to the screen.

b Reading Examples

The following examples illustrate how the list-directed READ statement reads and assigns numerical values from data supplied to the variable names in the READ list.

Example 3-4

The simplest and most straightforward condition is the existence of a one-to-one correspondence between the constants supplied and the variable names in the READ list. For the program segment:

```
WRITE(*,*)'ENTER VALUES FOR J, K, and L'
READ(*,*)J,K,L
```

when the following values are entered via the keyboard:

1*b*2*b*3

1 is assigned to J, 2 is assigned to K, and 3 is assigned to L. The *b* shown in the data record is used in this text to indicate a *blank* column and is entered by depressing the space bar on the keyboard. (The data are entered and read when the ENTER key is depressed.)

Example 3-5

When more constants are supplied from the keyboard than there are variable names in the READ list, values are assigned to variable names on a one-to-one basis, beginning with the first value and continuing until the READ list is satisfied. The remaining values will be ignored, as shown below. For the program segment:

```
WRITE(*,*)'ENTER VALUES FOR J, K, AND L'
READ(*,*)J,K,L
```

when the following data are entered via the keyboard:

1*b*2*b*3*b*4*b*5*b*6

1 is assigned to J, 2 is assigned to K, 3 is assigned to L, and 4, 5, and 6 are ignored.

Example 3-6

When there are more variable names in the READ list than items of data supplied in a single data record of a data file, reading will continue in the next data record and in each succeeding data record until the READ list is satisfied. Any values remaining in the data file will be ignored. For the program segment:

```
OPEN(3,FILE='EXAM3-6.DAT')
READ(3,*)J,K,L,M,N
```

when a data file containing the following records is read:

EXAM3-6.DAT
1*b*2*b*3*b*4 5*b*6*b*7*b*8

1 is assigned to J, 2 is assigned to K, 3 is assigned to L, 4 is assigned to M, 5 is assigned to N, and 6, 7, and 8 are ignored.

Example 3-7

When more than one READ statement is included in a given program, the execution of each READ statement will assign values from the next succeeding data record beginning with the first value of that record. Remember that each READ statement must be satisfied. For the program segment:

```
OPEN(2,FILE='EXAM3-7.DAT')
READ(2,*)J,K,L
READ(2,*)M,N
READ(2,*)A,B,C
```

when a data file containing the following records is read:

EXAM3-7.DAT
1*b*2*b*3*b*4*b*5 6*b*7*b*8*b*9 1.Ø*b*2.Ø*b*3.Ø*b*4.Ø

1 is assigned to J, 2 is assigned to K, 3 is assigned to L; 4 and 5 are ignored. Then 6 is assigned to M, 7 is assigned to N; 8 and 9 are ignored. Finally, 1.Ø is assigned to A, 2.Ø is assigned to B, 3.Ø is assigned to C; 4.Ø is ignored.

Example 3-8

If provision is made for repeating a portion of the program that includes a READ statement, each execution of the READ statement will assign values from the next data record beginning with the first constant of that record. For the program segment:

```
    OPEN(4,FILE='EXAM3-8.DAT')
1Ø  READ(4,*)J,K,L
    GOTO 1Ø
```

when a data file containing the following records is read:

EXAM3-8.DAT
1*b*2*b*3 4*b*5*b*6 7*b*8*b*9

on the first execution of the READ statement, 1 is assigned to J, 2 is assigned to K, and 3 is assigned to L. On the second execution, 4 is assigned to J, 5 is assigned to K, and 6 is assigned to L. On the third execution, 7 is assigned to J, 8 is assigned to K, and 9 is assigned to L. When the fourth execution is attempted, execution terminates with an error message indicating no more data.

Example 3-9

The following example demonstrates how values are assigned when the program includes multiple READ statements with one READ statement programmed for repeated execution. Execution of a READ statement will assign the first constant of the next available data record to the first variable name in the READ list and continue until the READ list is satisfied. For the program segment:

```
    OPEN(5,FILE='EXAM3-9.DAT')
    READ(5,*)J
    READ(5,*)K,L,M,N
1Ø  READ(5,*,END=2Ø)A,B,C
    GOTO 1Ø
2Ø  STOP
```

when a data file containing the following records is read:

EXAM3-9.DAT
1*b*2*b*3 4*b*5*b*6 7*b*8*b*9 1.Ø*b*2.Ø 3.Ø*b*4.Ø 5.Ø*b*6.Ø 7.Ø*b*8.Ø

on the execution of the first READ statement, 1 is assigned to J; 2 and 3 are ignored. On the execution of the second READ statement, 4 is assigned to K, 5 is assigned to L, 6 is assigned to M, 7 is assigned to N; 8 and 9 are ignored. On the first execution of the third READ statement, 1.Ø is assigned to A, 2.Ø is assigned to B, 3.Ø is assigned to C; 4.Ø is ignored. On the second execution of the third READ statement, 5.Ø is assigned to A, 6.Ø is assigned to B, 7.Ø is assigned to C; 8.Ø is ignored. When the third execution of the third READ statement is attempted, since there are no more data, the END=2Ø option transfers to statement 2Ø and execution is terminated.

In each of the above examples, the type of the constant matched the type of the variable name to which it was assigned, i.e., integer number to integer-variable name and real number to real-variable name. If the assignment of a real number to an integer-variable name is attempted, execution of the program will be aborted and an error message displayed as previously described.

3-14 ANNOTATING NUMERICAL RESULTS

Numerical results without identification are often difficult to interpret. Referring back to the WRITE statement to relate results with the appropriate variable name can be confusing; if the program listing is not available, it is impossible. Column headings, units, or other identifying annotations along with the numerical values eliminate this problem. This can be done by using a character string in the list-directed WRITE statement. A *character string* (character constant) is formed by enclosing any string of characters between apostrophes. The following WRITE statement illustrates the character string:

```
WRITE(*,*)'DIAMETER','bAREA'
```

When more than one character string is used in a single WRITE statement, the strings are separated by commas. The WRITE statement in the example above will display on a single line the characters enclosed within each pair of leading and closing apostrophes as follows:

```
bDIAMETERbAREA
```

The *b* shown in the character string and in the output is used in this text to indicate a blank column. The first *b* in the output (always a blank) is in column 1. The second *b* is caused by a blank included in the second character string in the WRITE statement to provide a space between the two headings. (Remember that a *b* in these examples represents a *blank* and is entered by depressing the space bar on the keyboard.) The same output will result if the two character strings are combined into one string:

```
WRITE(*,*)'DIAMETERbAREA'
```

Consider the program segment:

```
PI=3.141593
DIA=4.Ø
AREA=PI*(DIA/2.Ø)**2
WRITE(*,*)DIA,AREA
```

When properly entered, compiled, and executed, this program segment will display the values assigned to DIA and AREA as real numbers in decimal form:

```
bbbbbbbbbb4.ØØØØØØØbbbbbbbb12.56637ØØ
```

Nothing is included in the output to identify these values or associate them with the quantities and units they represent. The addition of a WRITE statement with an appropriate character string to the program segment:

```
PI=3.141593
DIA=4.Ø
AREA=PI*(DIA/2.Ø)**2
WRITE(*,*)'bbbbbbbDIAMETERb(CM)bbbbbAREAb(SQCM)'
WRITE(*,*)DIA,AREA
```

will display:

```
bbbbbbbbDIAMETERb(CM)bbbbbAREAb(SQCM)
bbbbbbbbbb4.ØØØØØØØbbbbbbbb12.56637ØØ
```

Double spacing (skipping a line between each line of output) can be accomplished by including a WRITE statement to cause a blank line. For example:

```
WRITE(*,*)'bbbbbbbDIAMETERb(CM)bbbbbAREAb(SQCM)'
WRITE(*,*)
WRITE(*,*)DIA,AREA
```

will result in double spacing between the line of character output (column headings) and the line of numerical values as shown below. The *b*'s have been omitted in the display below to show the output as it would actually appear:

```
        DIAMETER (CM)        AREA (SQCM)

         4.ØØØØØØØ           12.56637ØØ
```

Planning the output with character annotation can best be accomplished by laying out the anticipated result on a sheet of grid paper. A coding form (Sec. 3-16*a*) serves this purpose very well, as illustrated in Fig. 3-2. The programmer has no control over the positioning of numerical values in the output, but by including blanks in the character strings, the characters can be spaced as desired to provide headings neatly centered in the field width above the columns of numbers. It may be advisable to first run the program without headings in order to determine whether real values will be output in decimal or exponential form.

The WRITE statement can also be used to include a string of characters on the same line with the numerical values assigned to the variable names. For example:

```
WRITE(*,*) 'DIAMETERb=',DIA,'bCM'
WRITE(*,*)
WRITE(*,*) 'AREAb=',AREA,'bSQCM'
```

will display:

```
bDIAMETERb=bbbbbbbbb4.ØØØØØØØbCM

bAREAb=bbbbbbbb12.56637ØØbSQCM
```

FIGURE 3-2 Use of a coding form to compose column headings.

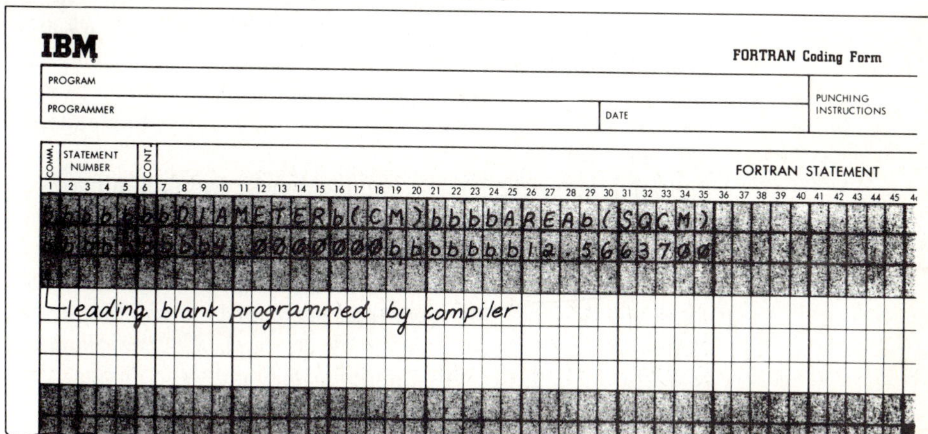

3-15 WRITING THE PROGRAM: PRELIMINARY PLANNING

Sufficient information has now been provided in this chapter to write the elementary statements of the FORTRAN language from which a simple program can be prepared. The programmer must first determine the sequential order in which the statements should be arranged and subsequently executed in order to produce the desired results. A well-prepared flowchart will expedite this process.

a Analysis of the Program

Begin the preliminary planning by carefully considering all aspects of the given problem. *Think*. Have all the parameters of the problem been defined? Is it clear what is known and what results are required? Are the mathematical models necessary for solving the problem given, or must these formulas be determined through research in appropriate reference material or by derivation? All questions relating to the solution of the problem must be resolved; all elements of the problem must be in place. *The programmer must visualize the logic of the solution and know how to solve the problem (with or without a computer) before attempting to write a computer program to solve the problem.*

b The Flowchart

The next step in preliminary planning is to develop the logic of the problem solution by constructing a flowchart that describes the sequence of operations to be followed. A flowchart (Chap. 2) is a graphical description of an algorithm, referred to in Fig. 1-13. The operations specified in the flowchart generally should be independent of any explicit programming language. The flowchart outlines only the structure and logic of the problem-solving operations. After the logic of the solution has been established and delineated by the flowchart, the actual writing of the program becomes routine and somewhat mechanical.

Usually, the flowchart is first roughly sketched. As the flowchart is developed and studied, errors in logic can be detected and corrected or more efficient sequences may become apparent. An eraser is as necessary as a pencil in the creative phase of flowcharting. After deciding on the final arrangement, the best practice calls for making a neat drawing of the flowchart by using a symbol template to outline the symbols of operation and a straightedge to draw the connecting lines.

Failure to systematically complete these two preliminaries of program preparation—conducting the analysis and constructing the flowchart—often results in programs that literally go around in circles, producing no answers at all, or programs flawlessly compiled and executed, producing neat columns of meaningless "garbage." Much time must then be spent in attempting to locate errors in logic that might have been avoided by thorough advance planning. Such results are wasteful of both the programmer's time and the computer time required for running the program—time which costs money!

In the beginning, the programmer may be pleased with any sequence of operations that results in usable answers. However, the ultimate goal in program preparation is to find the best and most efficient sequence possible. Reducing the number of statements in the program, writing instructions specifying simpler and/or shorter computer routines, and eliminating unnecessary statements or repetitions all result in more efficient programs, which save computer time and cost. Preparing efficient programs requires both knowledge and experience, but the best place to begin is with the flowchart.

3-16 WRITING THE PROGRAM: PROGRAM ORGANIZATION

Writing the program is now a simple matter of composing the FORTRAN statements needed to instruct the computer to perform the operations specified in the flowchart and organizing these statements in the proper sequence to achieve the desired results.

a The Coding Form

The beginning programmer is well advised to code the program statements on a printed form called a *coding form* before entering it into the computer. A commercially available coding form with 8Ø columns designed for the FORTRAN language is illustrated in Fig. 3-3. Coding FORTRAN statements is an exacting exercise. Correct identification of each element of the statement by the compiler depends upon that element being in its proper column. Use of a printed form reduces the potential for mistakes by constantly reminding the programmer of the proper column in which the various elements of the statement must be placed.

FORTRAN statements must be placed in columns 7 through 72. If the statement requires more than the 66 columns available between columns 7 and 72, inclusive, the statement can be continued on successive lines of the coding form, beginning each line in column 7. Each continued line must be identified as a *continuation* by a character (any character other than Ø) in column 6 of the coding

FIGURE 3-3 A coding form. (*IBM.*)

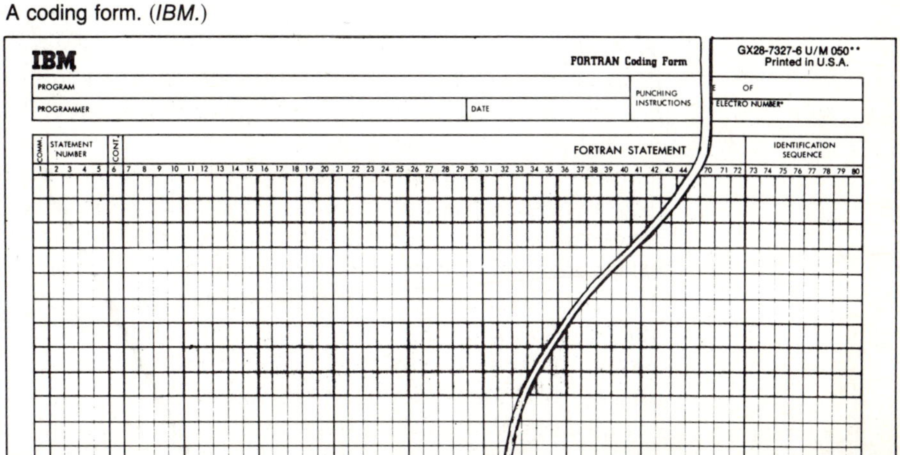

form. It is suggested that the dollar sign ($) be used since it is rarely used for anything else and is not likely to be confused with a character of the statement.

b Statement Labels

Columns 1 through 5 of the coding form are reserved for statement labels. A *statement label* is used to identify a statement to which reference is made by another statement. There is no need to label every statement in the program. A statement should be labeled *only* when specific identification of that statement is required because it will be referred to in another statement. With a single exception, nonexecutable statements [e.g., DATA (Sec. 10-4), INTEGER and REAL (Sec. 3-6), and DIMENSION (Sec. 8-3)] should not be labeled, since they are never referred to in another statement. The single exception is the FORMAT statement (Sec. 6-3) which *must always* be given a statement label since it is referenced in a READ or WRITE statement (Secs. 6-2 and 6-7). Statement labels may be from 1 to 5 digits in length and are placed in columns 1 through 5. It is recommended that the statement labels be right-justified in column 5, i.e., enter a one-digit label in column 5; a two-digit label in columns 4 and 5, etc. It is further recommended that statement labels be limited to four significant digits, reserving column 1 of the coding form for the comment designator C or * (Sec. 3-19). Although statement labels need not be in numerical, consecutive, or any other consistent order, it is suggested that the beginning programmer form the habit of labeling statements consecutively, 1Ø, 2Ø, 3Ø, etc., from top down. There is some advantage for the reader in consecutive labeling, and labeling by tens permits insertion of intermediate statement labels without disturbing the numerical consecutive order.

3-17 STORING THE PROGRAM

When using a personal computer, each FORTRAN statement is keyed in, in turn, and displayed on the screen. This is accomplished with a line or screen editor (App. D) or a suitable word processor. At this time each statement can be checked and corrected, if necessary, before entering the statement. When the program is completed, it can be entered into storage on a diskette (App. B).

Each program and each set of data records is stored in a block of storage referred to as a *file*. Each file must be assigned a unique filename (App. C) by the programmer. A *filename* consists of up to eight characters. No *blank* characters are allowed. Each filename may have an extension of up to three characters. The extension is separated from the filename by a period. The characters in the filename are the choice of the programmer; the characters in the extension are more restricted. If the filename is the name of a FORTRAN program, the extension should be FOR, i.e., FILENAME.FOR. When a file and its filename are created for data, the filename extension used in this text is DAT, i.e., FILENAME.DAT.

3-18 COMPILING AND RUNNING THE PROGRAM

After the completed program is stored on a diskette under its filename, the next step is to compile the program. This is accomplished as described in App. E. This action creates a new file, the EXEcute file, identified with the same filename but with a different extension, i.e., FILENAME.EXE. The program is actually run from the EXEcute file.

3-19 DOCUMENTING THE PROGRAM

When reviewing an old program or studying a program prepared by someone else, it may not be immediately obvious what a statement or series of statements was intended to accomplish or why a particular technique was used. Explanatory remarks or other identifying statements, which are not part of the sequential instructions constituting the program, may be included and output with the program listing. These statements are called *comments*. A comment is identified by a C or * in column 1 of the comment line. All 79 remaining columns may be used for the characters of the comment. A comment may be continued on more than one line, but a C or * must be entered in column 1 for every line of comment. The letter C or * is output along with the characters that follow. Comments are not compiled and are not included in the EXEcute program; therefore, changes, additions, and deletions can be made in the comments in the source program without affecting the EXEcute program or necessitating recompiling the program. If desired, comments may be written with lowercase characters to improve readability and to distinguish comments from FORTRAN instructions.

A documented program should contain information necessary to explain the purpose and procedures of the program to any person who may be interested in what the program accomplishes. Through the use of comment statements, the following information could be given:

NAME: Filename under which the program is stored
PROGRAMMER: Author(s)
DATE: Date program written
VERSION: Version number and date (if revised)
PURPOSE: Description of problem
INPUT: Input description and formats
OUTPUT: Output description and formats
PARAMETER: Parameter names, meanings, and functions (if used)
STRATEGY: Description of how this program attacks the problem
SUBPROGRAM: Listing and description of subprograms used
LIMITATION and RESTRICTION: Description of any limitations and/or restrictions inherent in the program
ERROR CHECK: Description of how possible errors are handled
VARIABLE: List of variable names used and what they represent

Obviously not all these items of information are required in every program. For instance, if the program is not a revision of a previous program, there is no need for a VERSION comment. Likewise, if there are no parameters, limitations, or error checks, there will be no need for these comments. On the other hand, a VARIABLE comment is always helpful.

Additional comments can be used throughout the program to explain what each section of the program is accomplishing. English is usually easier to understand than the program code. Such documentation should explain *what* is being done by the ensuing FORTRAN statements rather than *how*. Avoid comments that describe the obvious. For example:

```
C SET Y TO ZERO
      Y=Ø.Ø
```

is an unnecessary comment.

Some programmers prefer to indent comments within a program to indicate the level of the program to which the comments apply. For example, one comment might apply to a number of statements. If a comment pertaining only to the next few statements is also desired, that comment could be indented beyond the starting position of the first comment. Some programmers also prefer to emphasize the comments within the body of the program with asterisks. Such documentation is illustrated in Fig. 3-4. Note the additional indentation used for the comments pertaining to each type of solid.

3-20 WRITING THE PROGRAM: ILLUSTRATIVE EXAMPLES

It will be helpful for the beginning programmer to study simple examples of complete programs that illustrate and review the material described in this chapter. Although the explanations may appear redundant, the elements of these simple programs are the same elements used in preparing the most complex programs and they must be clearly understood before further progress can be made.

Each of the following example programs computes and prints the circumference and area of a circle from a given diameter. The mathematical models are the relationships of the constant 3.141593 (π) and the diameter of a circle to its circumference and area, where the circumference = 3.141593 × diameter, and area = 3.141593 × (diameter/2)^2. To compute the circumference and the area, values for the diameter and the constant π must be supplied to the mathematical models.

Example 3-10

Study the flowchart (the algorithm) and note the operational steps involved in Fig. 3-5(a) (see p. 68). Begin with the TERMINAL, INTERRUPT symbol. A PROCESS symbol is used to indicate the opening of the print file. The value of the constant π is established and a value assigned to the diameter. PROCESS symbols are also used here. Values for the circumference and area can then be computed using appropriate mathematical models. These steps are also represented by PROCESS symbols. Known numerical values can now be output; the output operation is represented by a symbol suggesting a CRT or a sheet of

```
C234567890
C   NAME: VOLUME CALCULATOR
C   PROGRAMMER: R. H. HAMMOND
C   DATE: 10 MAY 1985
C   PURPOSE: TO CALCULATE THE VOLUMES OF SEVERAL SOLIDS
C   INPUT: TWO REAL VALUES FROM THE KEYBOARD. VALUES
C          REPRESENT DIMENSIONS OF POSSIBLE SOLIDS
C   OUTPUT:  THE DIMENSIONS AND THE POSSIBLE VOLUMES
C   RESTRICTIONS: DATA IS ASSUMED TO BE PROPERLY ENTERED
C   STRATEGY: READ THE DIMENSIONS, THEN COMPUTE THE POSSIBLE
C             VOLUMES AND PRINT THE RESULTS
C   VARIABLES USED:
C       HEIGHT       FIRST VALUE IN DATA
C       RADIUS       SECOND VALUE IN DATA
C       PI           3.141593
C       CUBE         VOLUME TO BE CALCULATED
C       SPHERE       DITTO
C       CYLIND       DITTO
C       CONE         DITTO
C
C   ** INITIALIZE THE CONSTANT
      PI=3.141593
      OPEN(3,FILE='FIG3-4.DAT')
      OPEN(6,FILE='PRN')
C   ** READ THE VALUES, PRINT THEM
      READ(3,*)HEIGHT,RADIUS
      WRITE(6,*)'HEIGHT =',HEIGHT,'   RADIUS =',RADIUS
      WRITE(6,*)
C   ** CALCULATE AND PRINT EACH VOLUME. SKIP A LINE
C      BETWEEN EACH CALCULATION
      CUBE=HEIGHT**3
      WRITE(6,*)'CUBIC VOLUME =',CUBE
      WRITE(6,*)
C         *** ASSUME A SPHERE WHOSE RADIUS IS "RADIUS"
      SPHERE=(4.0/3.0)*PI*RADIUS**3
      WRITE(6,*)'SPHERICAL VOLUME =',SPHERE
      WRITE(6,*)
C         *** ASSUME A CYLINDER WHOSE BASE RADIUS IS "RADIUS"
C             AND ALTITUDE IS "HEIGHT"
      CYLIND=HEIGHT*PI*RADIUS**2
      WRITE(6,*)'CYLINDRICAL VOLUME =',CYLIND
      WRITE(6,*)
C         *** ASSUME A CONE WHOSE BASE RADIUS IS "RADIUS"
C             AND ALTITUDE IS "HEIGHT"
      CONE=(1.0/3.0)*PI*HEIGHT*RADIUS**2
      WRITE(6,*)'CONICAL VOLUME =',CONE
      WRITE(6,*)
C         *** INDICATE END OF PROGRAM
      WRITE(6,*)'***ALL DONE***'
      STOP
      END
```

```
1.2345 6.789
```

```
HEIGHT =           1.2345000  RADIUS =          6.7890000

CUBIC VOLUME =          1.8813660

SPHERICAL VOLUME =       1310.7080000

CYLINDRICAL VOLUME =        178.7527000

CONICAL VOLUME =         59.5842400

***ALL DONE***
```

FIGURE 3-4 A documented program.

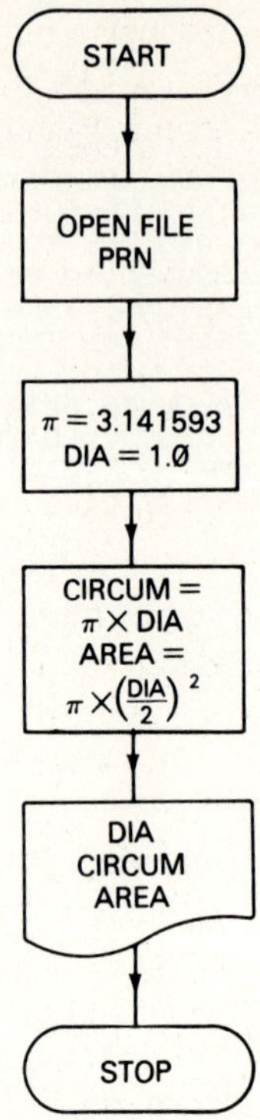


```
OPEN(6, FILE='PRN')

PI=3.141593
DIA=1.0

CIRCUM=PI*DIA
AREA=PI*(DIA/2.0)**2

WRITE(6, *) DIA, CIRCUM, AREA

STOP
END
```

(a)

```
C234567890
      OPEN(6,FILE='PRN')
      PI=3.141593
      DIA=1.0
      CIRCUM=PI*DIA
      AREA=PI*(DIA/2.0)**2
      WRITE(6,*)DIA,CIRCUM,AREA
      STOP
      END
```

```
     1.0000000          3.1415930   7.853982E-001
```

(b)

FIGURE 3-5 The circle problem, Example 3-10.

paper torn from the printer. Provision is made to terminate the program; this is represented by the TERMINAL, INTERRUPT symbol.

Each of the operations described and represented in the flowchart as a language-independent operation symbol must now be encoded in the characters and syntax of FORTRAN. A FORTRAN statement is written which, when properly compiled (translated into machine language), will instruct the computer to perform the required operation. Note the first line of the program shown in Fig. 3-5(*b*). This is a comment statement designed to show the column numbers necessary to place the FORTRAN statements in their proper column. These statements are now listed in the order indicated by the flowchart. A seven-digit (the maximum acceptable) numerical value, 3.141593, is assigned to the variable name PI by an assignment statement. A numerical value for the diameter is assigned in like manner to the variable name DIA. The appropriate mathematical models are written as arithmetic expressions and included in assignment statements, where their values are assigned to the variable names CIRCUM and AREA. The list-directed WRITE statement is used to print the values previously assigned to the variable names DIA, CIRCUM, and AREA. Execution is terminated by the STOP statement. The END statement, the last statement, signals the end of compilation. The completed program is now stored on a diskette under an appropriate filename and then compiled. The computer is then instructed to print the program listing and to execute the program. The printed output of the solution shows the values of DIA and CIRCUM printed as real numbers in decimal form, but AREA is printed as a real number in exponential form because its value is less than 1.

If a program contains identifiable errors, appropriate error messages will be displayed on the screen as an aid in program evaluation and correction (Sec. 3-21 and App. E). In most cases, compilation and/or execution of programs containing errors will be aborted before any numerical results are obtained.

It should be obvious that preparing a computer program to compute the circumference and area of a single circle is a little like hammering thumbtacks with a pile driver or hunting flies with a shotgun. There are certainly more efficient ways to accomplish the same results. Even the very short program of this example requires too much time and effort for one-time usage.

Example 3-11

The utility of the previous program can be greatly increased by using a list-directed READ statement to read values for the diameter from a data file. This will permit assigning successive values for the diameter to a variable, as in Fig. 3-6(*a*) (see p. 70). Each time the READ statement is executed, a new value is assigned to the diameter. No provision is made for exiting the loop in this example. The program is terminated by default (and an error message is displayed) when there are no more data values to read.

Three statements have been added to the basic program illustrated in Fig. 3-5—the OPEN, the list-directed READ, and the unconditional GOTO—and one statement deleted. The assignment statement, assigning a single value (a constant) to the variable DIA, has been replaced by the READ statement, which permits a succession of values to be assigned to DIA. Note the label 1Ø given to the READ statement. Execution of the unconditional transfer statement GOTO 1Ø returns the sequence of operations to statement 1Ø, the READ statement. Numerical values are assigned to the variable name DIA in succession from the data file, which is shown in the box following the END statement

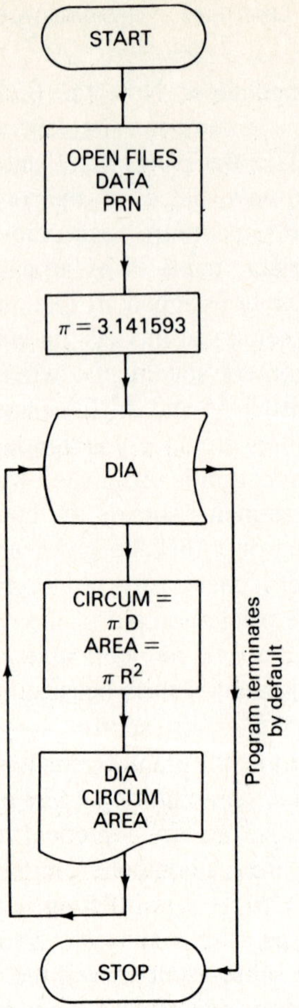


```
      OPEN(3, FILE='FIG3-6.DAT')
      OPEN(5, FILE='PRN')

      PI=3.141593

   10 READ(3, *) DIA

      CIRCUM=PI*DIA
      AREA=PI*(DIA/2.0)**2

      WRITE(5, *) DIA, CIRCUM, AREA

      GOTO 10

      STOP
      END
```

(a)

```
C234567890
      OPEN(5,FILE='PRN')
      OPEN(2,FILE='FIG3-6.DAT')
      PI=3.141593
   10 READ(2,*)DIA
      CIRCUM=PI*DIA
      AREA=PI*(DIA/2.0)**2
      WRITE(5,*)DIA,CIRCUM,AREA
      GOTO 10
      STOP
      END
```

```
1.0
1.5
2.0
2.5
3.0
```

```
           1.0000000          3.1415930  7.853982E-001
           1.5000000          4.7123890      1.7671460
           2.0000000          6.2831860      3.1415930
           2.5000000          7.8539820      4.9087390
           3.0000000          9.4247790      7.0685840
? Error: Operation error in file FIG3-6.DAT
  Error Code 1298, Status  0003
PC = 0002: 0006; SS = 0F2E, FP = 0878, SP = 1470
```

(b)

FIGURE 3-6 The circle problem, Example 3-11.

of the program. (This practice will be used in all illustrations in this text that use a stored data file.) When no more data values remain in the data file, the program is terminated with an error message indicating no more data. The STOP statement is included; however, in this program the STOP statement is never executed and could have been omitted.

By referring back to the WRITE statement in the program listing, it is possible to determine that the first column of numerical values in the output represents diameter; the second column, circumference; and the third column, area. Headings above each column identifying the numerical values and the units they represent are preferred. Although it is hardly necessary in this simple program, some comment is usually desirable to explain just what the program is intended to accomplish.

Example 3-12

Figure 3-7 (see p. 72) shows the previous program, revised, with some documentation and annotation added. A counting routine has also been included (Sec. 3-8*b*), which is used to number consecutively and record each iteration of the program.

Some of the documentation described in Sec. 3-19 has been omitted in Fig. 3-7 and will be omitted in all other illustrative programs. Since these programs are usually simple, illustrating a particular technique or routine described in the text, there is no real reason for a complete documentation.

The comments included with the program listing in Fig. 3-7 illustrate how the clarity of the procedure can be improved by the use of comments. The programmer is enjoined to document each program so that there will be no doubt in the mind of any reader as to what variables are used in the program and what is intended by the FORTRAN statements.

In Fig. 3-7 a list-directed WRITE statement with two character strings is used to locate headings above each column of numerical output. The WRITE statement specifying the character headings is placed outside the loop, since the headings are to appear only once at the top of each column. The WRITE statement is continued on a second line and illustrates how a statement too long for a single line (66 characters) can be continued on successive lines. Note that the character output has been divided into two strings separated by a comma. If the entire WRITE statement had been short enough to be completed on a single line, or if every column through column 72 in the first line had been used, all the characters could have been included in a single string between one set of apostrophes. The next WRITE statement provides the blank line (double-spacing) between the headings and the first line of numerical values in the output. Each heading is centered over the columns of numbers, taking into consideration their location within the 13- (for integer) or 18- (for decimal) output-column field. Note that the heading for the AREA column was centered for decimal-form numbers, even though it was known that the first area value would be in exponential form. This emphasizes the practicality of running the program prior to adding annotation to determine how the list-directed output will be structured.

```
C234567890
C   PROGRAM COMPUTES CIRCUMFERENCE AND AREA OF A
C   CIRCLE FROM THE DIAMETER PROVIDED AS DATA.

C   OPEN FILES FOR DATA AND PRINTER.

      OPEN(3,FILE='FIG3-7.DAT')
      OPEN(5,FILE='PRN')

C   PRINT COLUMN HEADINGS. DOUBLE SPACE BETWEEN
C   COLUMN HEADINGS AND NUMERICAL VALUES.

      WRITE(5,*)'           NO.          DIAMETER (CM)',
     $'       CIRCUM (CM)          AREA (SQCM)'
      WRITE(5,*)

C   DEFINE PI AND INITIATE THE COUNTER.

      PI=3.141593
      N=0

C   READ A DATA VALUE AND ASSIGN TO DIA.
C   TERMINATE PROGRAM WHEN ALL DATA READ.

   10 READ(3,*,END=20)DIA

C   COMPUTE CIRCUMFERENCE AND AREA. ASSIGN TO
C   RESPECTIVE VARIABLES.

      CIRCUM=PI*DIA
      AREA=PI*(DIA/2.0)**2
      N=N+1

C   PRINT VALUES OF N, DIA, CIRCUM, AND AREA.

      WRITE(5,*)N,DIA,CIRCUM,AREA

C   TRANSFER TO STATEMENT NUMBER 10.

      GOTO 10

C   END OF PROGRAM. TERMINATE.

   20 STOP
      END
```

```
1.0
1.5
2.0
2.5
3.0
```

```
           NO.          DIAMETER (CM)       CIRCUM (CM)          AREA (SQCM)

             1              1.0000000         3.1415930    7.853982E-001
             2              1.5000000         4.7123890        1.7671460
             3              2.0000000         6.2831860        3.1415930
             4              2.5000000         7.8539820        4.9087390
             5              3.0000000         9.4247790        7.0685840
```

FIGURE 3-7 The circle problem, Example 3-12.

Note the use of the END=*n* option in the READ statement. This prevents termination of the program with an error message when the data in the data file FIG3-7.DAT have all been read.

The column of integer numbers headed by NO. is generated from the counting routine N=N+1 with an initial value of Ø assigned to N and successive printings of each value assigned to N. The number of program iterations is recorded, and each line of output is consecutively numbered.

3-21 PROGRAM EVALUATION—ERRORS

Few programmers consistently achieve first-run success with significant programs. Many programs that run without obvious errors either do not run to completion or do not yield the intended results. In such cases the problem is to find out what went wrong, or to locate the "bug" in the program. In the jargon of the computer world, this search for and correction of errors is called *debugging*.

Every computer capable of accepting programs in FORTRAN can do so only because there is available a set of instructions that translates the statements of the source program written by the programmer into a machine language acceptable to the computer. This set of instructions, the compiler program (Sec. 1-3), not only interprets the program statements but also includes routines which detect and identify many common and predictable mistakes. Mistakes, *errors* in computer terminology, are identified and located with the help of *error messages,* which are automatically displayed when errors are detected by the compiler during the compilation or execution of the program.

Large main-frame computers with vast storage space can accommodate compilers containing very detailed and specific error messages. Compilers designed for use on the personal computer must be stored on limited diskette space, and the error messages displayed on the screen are terse, numbered phrases referencing the compiler user's guide. In many instances, the user's guide reveals no more helpful information than simply repeating the same phrase displayed on the screen. But, however enigmatic the message may be, it is sufficient to establish that an error exists, which must be located and corrected before compilation and/or execution can continue (App. E-6).

Errors in computer programs are of three types: *compilation, execution,* and *logic errors*. Compilation errors are detected during compilation and are usually the result of mistakes made while keying in the program. An incorrectly spelled FORTRAN term; an incorrect, omitted, or added character; a missing statement label; unmatched parentheses; and a statement beginning in column 6 (instead of 7) are examples of compilation errors. Most of these errors in FORTRAN *syntax* are caused by carelessness and can be avoided by carefully checking each statement and the entire program listing before entering the program on the diskette. A single syntax error will often cause several error messages to be displayed. Compilation errors are the easiest to locate and correct since they are identified by error messages indicating the line number in which they (probably) occur and suggesting the cause of the error. Compilation errors should be corrected from the beginning of the program to the end. Execution will not begin until all compilation errors have been eliminated.

Execution errors are detected during execution and may be referred to as *run-time errors*. Execution errors are caused by instructions that are mathematically undefined or violate the rules of FORTRAN. Examples of execution errors include:

Attempts to divide by zero
Taking the square root or logarithm of a negative number (Secs. 5-2, 5-7)
Calculating the arcsine of a number greater than one (Sec. 5-8)
Using an improper type in the argument of an intrinsic function (Chap. 5)
Outputting an integer value with a real edit descriptor (Chap. 6)
Improperly entering a data file
Using an array (Sec. 8-1) that exceeds the space reserved for it

The specific cause of execution errors in a long program or loop may be difficult to locate. Sometimes such errors can be isolated by inserting temporary output (WRITE) statements into the program at selected intervals, particularly in loops. Studying this output may disclose, for example, that the value assigned to a variable in a loop is zero or negative at some point, thereby creating a mathematically undefined condition.

A logic error is an error in the composition and organization of the source program. Occasionally a logic error is revealed by compilation and execution error messages, but the compiler cannot be depended upon to detect logic errors. Logic errors can be located and corrected only by carefully studying the algorithm (flowchart), the source program listing, and the results which have been output (if any). Locating and correcting logic errors in long and complex programs may be exceedingly difficult and tedious. Long programs should be tested in short segments with simple data values that produce known results. A common logic error that plagues the beginning (and sometimes the experienced) programmer is the *endless loop*. An endless loop will continue forever if it is not terminated by the programmer. An endless loop can be avoided by including statements that will count the number of passes through the loop and transfer out of the loop after a specified number of repetitions. A thorough knowledge of all the ramifications of the problem, its solution, and the nature and magnitude of the probable results is prerequisite to the successful debugging of logic errors.

Just because a program runs without apparent error and neatly displays the results is no reason to unthinkingly accept the output as correct. Faulty logic may have yielded incorrect values (garbage). In any program, at least some of the results, including critical values, should be calculated by hand in order to ensure that the output is correct. Test the program for boundary values. For example, if an interest-rate program is designed to accept principal amounts between $100 and $1 million, inclusive, for interest rates between 5 and 20 percent, inclusive, be sure to test the program for combinations of both the minimum and maximum values, i.e., $100 at both 5 and 20 percent, and $1 million at both 5 and 20 percent, as well as at selected intervals between the limiting values. Do not hesitate to take paper and calculator in hand and work through the program, step by step, statement by statement, loop after loop, with simple data until the error is located and corrected.

It is tempting (and ego-salving) to believe that the computer made an error. Most programmers have been guilty of that notion at one time or another. It is possible, but unlikely, for one or more of the hundreds of thousands of components and complex circuits that make up the computer hardware to fail, causing an error. A faulty diskette may create a problem. It is also possible for a bug to be lurking somewhere in the compiler program. However, computer hardware, high-quality diskettes, and compiler programs are generally very reliable. Practically all errors are programmer errors: grammatical (syntactical) errors, improper statement errors, errors in knowledge of how the computer operations are performed, etc. Most errors are caused by just plain carelessness! Errors can be eliminated by analysis of the problem, preparing a complete algorithm (flowchart), exercising great care in writing and encoding the source program, and evaluating and comparing the results computed from critical-condition test data, with known answers.

Table E-1 in App. E-6 lists a number of typical programming errors gleaned from countless student problems. These mistakes should be studied carefully. With this foreknowledge, repetition of many of these mistakes may be avoided.

PROBLEMS

3-1 What are the results of the following arithmetic operations?

(a) 8/2 **(b)** 6/1Ø **(c)** (6 + 8)/5
(d) 4*5/3/2 **(e)** (4*5)/(3/2) **(f)** (4*(5/3))/2

3-2 Express the following numbers in exponential form.

(a) 1Ø.3 **(b)** 2345.7 **(c)** 378.66
(d) Ø.453 **(e)** Ø.ØØØ56 **(f)** Ø.ØØ678

3-3 Are the following acceptable integer-variable names? If not, why not?

(a) JACK **(b)** NEG5X **(c)** PREFER
(d) I*JACK **(e)** OPTION2 **(f)** INTEGRAL
(g) ITEM-1 **(h)** NUM(1) **(i)** LOCK 12

3-4 Are the following acceptable real-variable names? If not, why not?

(a) ACTION **(b)** BETA/2 **(c)** OPTION2
(d) LITTLE **(e)** XRAY **(f)** HEIGHT
(g) RADIANS **(h)** RAD 123 **(i)** RAD(1)

3-5 Write the following algebraic expressions as FORTRAN arithmetic expressions:

(a) $\dfrac{a^2 + b^2}{c}$ **(b)** $a^2b - \dfrac{b^2 c}{d}$ **(c)** $3(x^2 y - y^2)$

(d) $4x^{a+b}$ **(e)** $\dfrac{a^2 y^b}{c} + e$ **(f)** $(ab + ac)/d^4$

(g) $a/b + \dfrac{b - c}{d}\left(\dfrac{e^5}{f}\right)$ **(h)** $(x^2 + y^2)^3 - 5ab + 2a/3b$

3-6 Write the following algebraic equations as FORTRAN assignment statements:

(a) $R = \dfrac{Pb^3}{L^2}(3a + b)$ **(b)** $X = 2\pi fy - fc/2$

(c) $S = vt + at^2/2$ **(d)** $F = Wv^2/g$

3-7 Show the step-by-step order in which the following FORTRAN assignment statements would be evaluated:

(a) S=VØ*T+A*T**2/2.Ø **(b)** A=(VT−VØ)/T
(c) C=(A+C)*(A−2.Ø*B) **(d)** A=P*(1.Ø+XI/XM)**(XN+XM)

3-8 Write the following FORTRAN assignment statements as algebraic equations. (Note the effect of the use of parentheses.)

(a) A=X**2+2.Ø*X*Y+Y**2/A+B
(b) A=X**2+2.Ø*X*Y+Y**2/(A+B)
(c) A=(X**2+2.Ø*X*Y+Y**2)/A+B
(d) A=(X**2+2.Ø*X*Y+Y**2)/(A+B)

3-9 Analyze the flowchart and data supplied in Fig. 3-8 and list the displayed results.

3-10 Analyze the flowchart and data supplied in Fig. 3-9 (see p. 78) and list the displayed results.

In Probs. 3-11 through 3-25, write a FORTRAN source program to perform the specified operations.

3-11 Write and run a FORTRAN program to compute the total surface area and volume of a rectangular box whose width is 5.5, depth is 7.25, and height is 3.75. Prepare a flowchart and use appropriate column headings.

3-12 Write a FORTRAN program to compute the surface area and volume of a sphere whose diameter is 7.75. Include appropriate column headings.

3-13 Write a FORTRAN program to compute the initial velocity and present displacement of a body moving with uniform acceleration at 33 ft/s^2, when the time is 2.5 s and the velocity is 1ØØ ft/s. Print the *given* values on one line; print the *calculated* values on a second line. Include appropriate column headings and annotation.

3-14 Read the values for the diameter and altitude of a right circular cylinder given below. Compute the area of the base and the volume in liters (L); 1 L = 1ØØØ cm^3. Include appropriate column headings.

Diameter, cm	Altitude, cm
37.4	45.5
2Ø.3	12.8
12.7	51.3
45.1	39.9

3-15 Write a program to compute the area of the ring between two concentric circles whose radii are 173.Ø and 55.5. Values for both radii are on the same data line. Then repeat for a least four other pairs of radii of your choice. Print the values of the radii and the area. Include appropriate column headings.

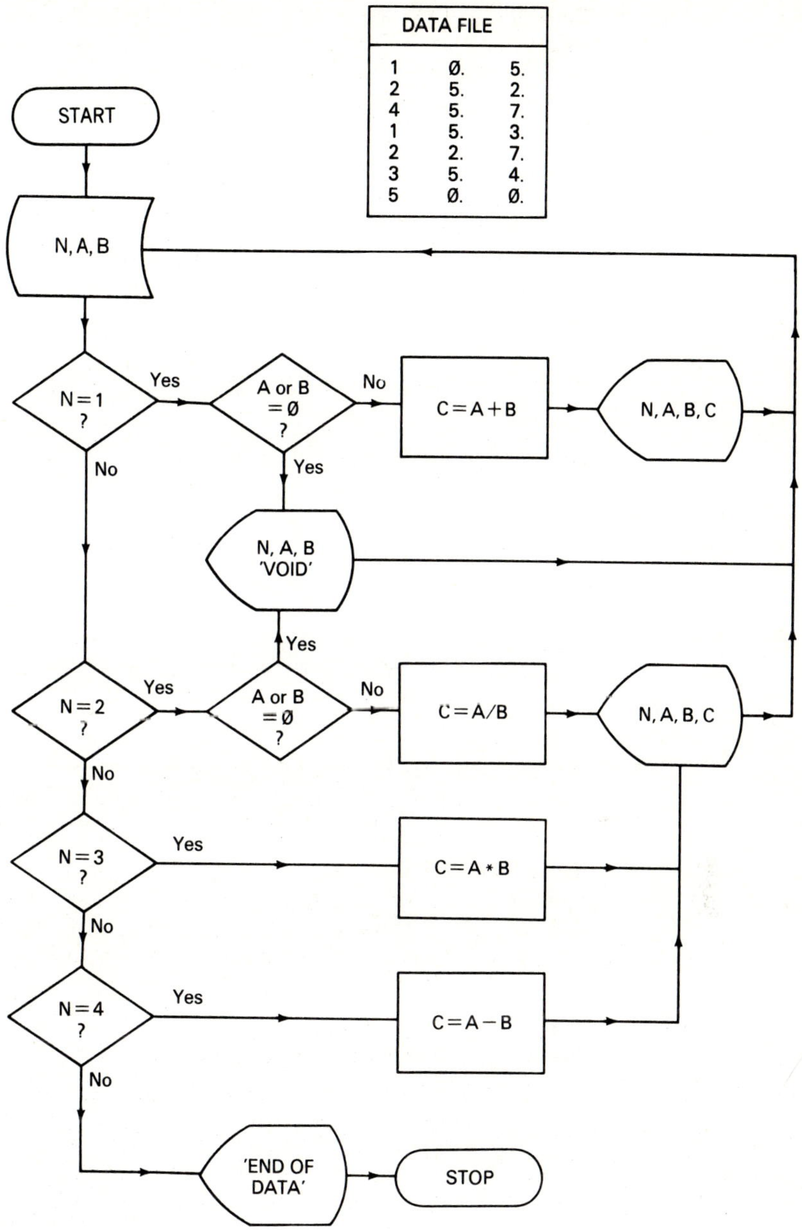

FIGURE 3-8 Problem 3-9.

3-16 The area of a trapezoid is:

$$A = \frac{h}{2}(b + c)$$

where A = area
h = altitude
b, c = lengths of the two parallel sides

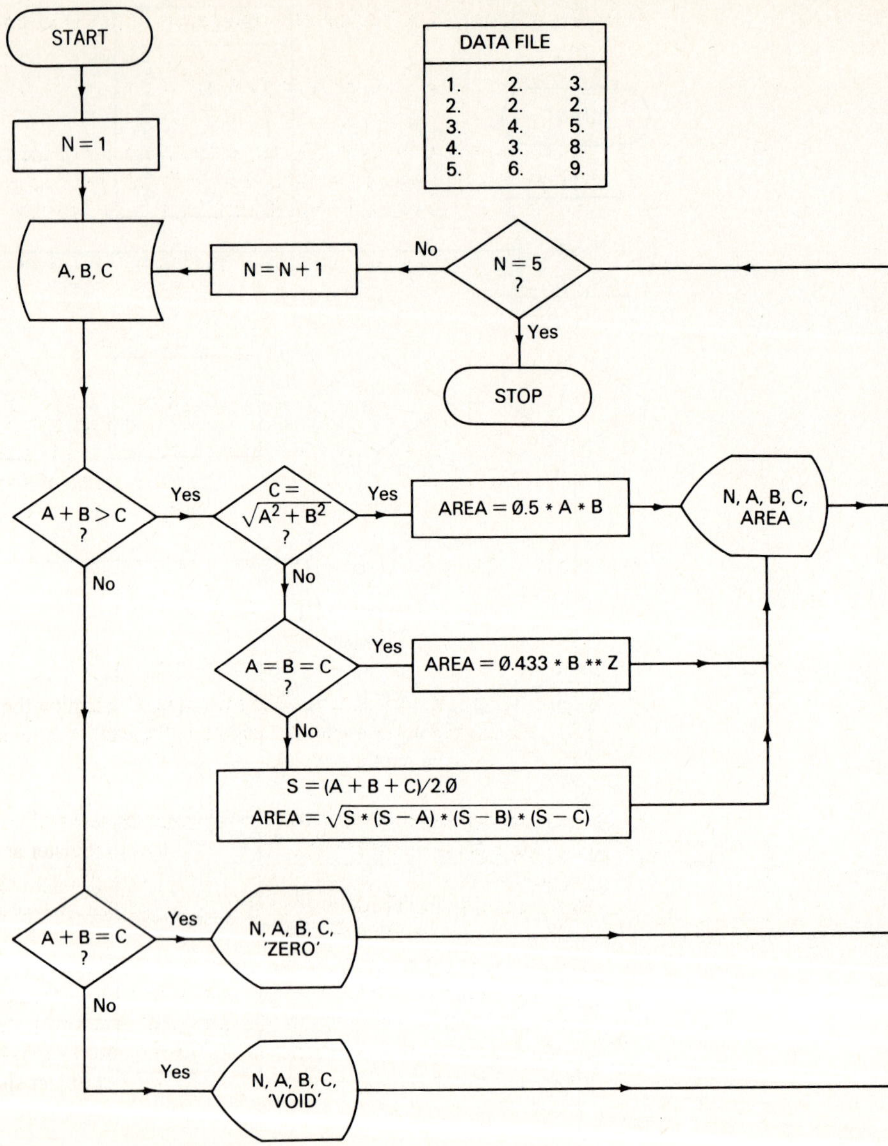

FIGURE 3-9 Problem 3-10.

Determine the area of a trapezoid whose altitude is 8.375 and whose parallel sides are 4.75 and 1Ø.25. Repeat for at least four other sets of data. Print the values of the parallel sides, altitude, and area. Include appropriate column headings.

3-17 The coefficient of linear expansion is the change in unit length of a body for each unit change in temperature. Determine the coefficient of expansion for a steel rod that measures 25Ø.ØØ cm at 6Ø°C and 25Ø.Ø6 cm at 12Ø°C.

3-18 The volume of the frustum of a right circular cone is given by:

$$V = \frac{h}{3}(A_1 + A_2 + \sqrt{A_1A_2})$$

where h is the altitude and A_1 and A_2 are the areas of the two bases. Determine the volume when the diameter of one base is 7Ø cm, the diameter of the other base is 24 cm, and the altitude is 5Ø cm. Repeat for at least four sets of data.

3-19 Figure 3-10 shows a triangle *ABC*. The cosine of the angle *A* can be computed using the formula:

$$\cos A = \frac{b^2 + c^2 - a^2}{2bc}$$

The value of side a is 24.62, side b is 16.39, and side c is 33.ØØ. Compute the value of the cosine for each of the three angles *A*, *B*, and *C* and print on separate lines, skipping a line between each value. *Note:* The cosine of angle *C* should be negative. What does this signify? Repeat for at least four other triangles.

3-20 The moment of inertia of a rectangle about its diagonal is:

$$I = \frac{b^3h^3}{6(b^2 + h^2)}$$

where b and h are the sides of the rectangle. Determine the moment of inertia for a 3 in × 6 in rectangle about its diagonal. Repeat for at least four other rectangles. Print the result in sentence form.

3-21 Write a program that will read in the number of half-dollars, quarters, dimes, nickels, and pennies that are in the drawer of the cash register at the end of the day. Print the initial data and identify, then compute and print the total dollar value of the coins. Provide the initial data and check the computer calculations.

3-22 A standard problem in a beginning physics course concerns energy calculations for an object vibrating at the end of a spring in simple harmonic motion. The energy terms used are: kinetic energy (the energy of motion), potential energy (stored energy), and total energy (the sum of the kinetic and potential energy). Without going into detail about theory, the formulas used for the object shown in Fig. 3-11 are:

FIGURE 3-10
Problem 3-19.

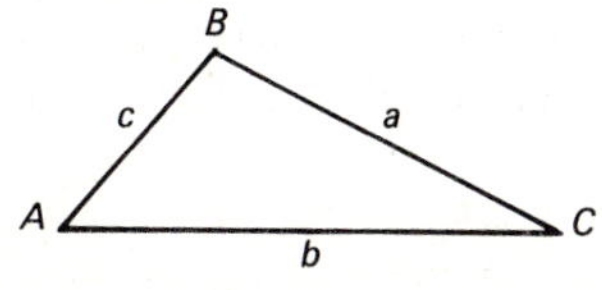

FIGURE 3-11
Problem 3-22.

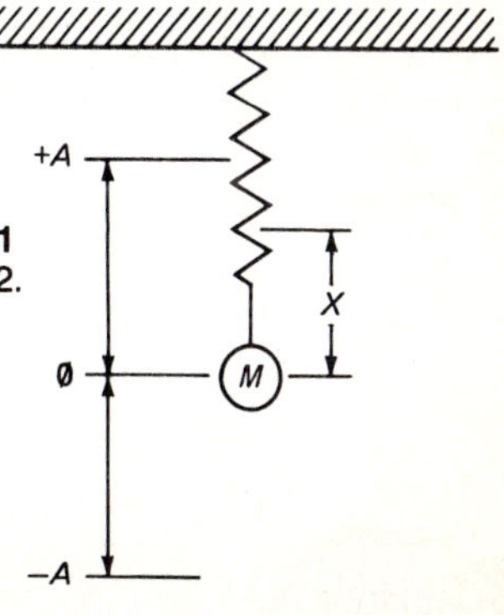

$$K = \frac{4\pi^2 M}{T^2} \qquad \text{TE} = \frac{KA^2}{2} \qquad \text{PE} = \frac{KX^2}{2} \qquad \text{KE} = \text{TE} - \text{PE}$$

where K is the spring constant
TE = the total energy
PE = the potential energy
KE = the kinetic energy
A = the amplitude of motion
X = the displacement being considered
M = the mass of the object
T = the time of the period (one cycle of motion)

Write a program to determine the spring constant, expressed in kilograms per second squared (kg/s^2), and the three related energies when the displacement is Ø.2 meter (m) for an object whose mass is Ø.ØØ6 kg. The period is Ø.5 s, and the amplitude is Ø.4 m. The energy, expressed in these units, is in joules (J). Print the results with appropriate annotation.

3-23 A pair of simultaneous equations of the form:

$$A \cdot X + B \cdot Y = C$$
$$AA \cdot X + BB \cdot Y = CC$$

where A, AA, B, BB, C, and CC are constants, can be solved for X and Y by the equations:

$$X = \frac{BB \cdot C - B \cdot CC}{A \cdot BB - AA \cdot B} \qquad Y = \frac{A \cdot CC - AA \cdot C}{A \cdot BB - AA \cdot B}$$

when $A \cdot BB - AA \cdot B$ is not equal to zero. Write a program that will read values for the constants A, B, and C for the first equation from one data record, and the values for constants AA, BB, and CC for the second equation from the next data record. Solve for the values of X and Y. Use the following constants: A = 1Ø.ØØ, B = 7.5Ø, C = 23.22, AA = 7.66, BB = 33.33, and CC = 9.75.

3-24 Write a program to read in a variable representing the area of a plane figure. Then determine the side of the square, the radius of the circle, and the side of the equilateral triangle that have that area. Print the area and the three results under appropriate headings. The formulas for the area of a square and circle are known. The area of an equilateral triangle can be proved to be $A = \sqrt{3}\,(S^2/4)$, where S is the length of the side of the triangle. For the value of $\sqrt{3}$ use 1.732Ø51. Solve for the required values for the areas 12.34567, 23.45678, 34.56789, 45.67891, and 56.78912.

3-25 A student in a computer programming class is asked to determine, to the nearest Ø.Ø1 m, the distance between floors of the building in which the class is held. The student looks around the classroom and sees a personal computer, chalk, stopwatch, and erasers. Remembering that a falling body obeys the formula $S = GT^2/2$ and that G = 9.8Ø665 m/s^2, the student grabs an eraser and drops it from a windowsill, timing its eight-story fall to the ground at 2.55 s. The height of the windowsill is 1.Ø m above the floor. Working with the computer, the student announces the answer. What program might have been written, and what is the distance between floors in meters and feet?

CHAPTER **4**

LOOPING AND BRANCHING

4-1 INTRODUCTION

Chapter 3 described how to prepare assignment statements that perform arithmetic operations and assign results to a variable name. It also showed how to read data and print answers and briefly introduced looping with the unconditional GOTO statement. To exploit the full power of the computer it is necessary to know how to repeat a given sequence of operations, to make decisions based on simple comparisons, and to branch to a specified statement in the program as the result of a simple decision. Iteration, or repetition of calculations, is called *looping* and is accomplished through various transfer and control statements.

A *transfer statement* is an executable statement that transfers or branches to another statement designated by a unique statement label. A transfer statement may be either unconditional or conditional. An *unconditional* transfer statement *always* branches to a single designated statement, while a *conditional* transfer statement *may* branch to one of several different designated statements, depending upon conditions of the data. Typical transfer statements are the GOTO and IF statements, which will be discussed in this chapter.

A *control statement* may repeat a given set of statements a specified number of times. The DO statement, described in Chap. 7, is such a control statement.

4-2 THE UNCONDITIONAL GOTO STATEMENT

The *unconditional* GOTO statement is the unconditional transfer statement, first discussed in Sec. 3-10, that always transfers to a designated executable statement. The general form for the unconditional GOTO statement is:

GOTO *n*

where *n* is an integer number identifying the statement label of the executable statement to which the transfer is to be made. Transfer is always to the statement labeled *n*. An example of the unconditional GOTO statement is:

```
GOTO 1Ø
```

Every time this statement is executed, a transfer is made to statement 1Ø.

In a flowchart there is no special symbol to represent the unconditional GOTO statement. As illustrated by the program segment and accompanying flowchart in

Fig. 4-1, this statement is represented by a line connecting two conventional symbols or by lines drawn to similarly labeled on page connectors.

4-3 THE COMPUTED GOTO STATEMENT

The *computed* GOTO statement is a conditional transfer statement that transfers to one of several executable statements, depending on the value of an integer numerical indicator. The general form for the computed GOTO statement is:

GOTO $(n_1, n_2, n_3, \ldots n_i)$, *intexp*

where n_1, n_2, n_3, . . . , n_i are the first, second, third, etc., statement labels in a list of statement labels and *intexp* is an integer-variable or integer-arithmetic expression (the numerical indicator) whose value determines to which of these labeled statements (first, second, third, etc.) transfer is to be made. The comma following the rightmost parenthesis is optional and may be omitted. If the value of the numerical indicator *intexp* is less than one (zero or a negative integer) or greater than the number of statement labels in the list, the computed GOTO statement is ignored and execution continues with the next executable statement following the computed GOTO statement. An example of the computed GOTO statement is:

FIGURE 4-1 Using the unconditional GOTO statement.

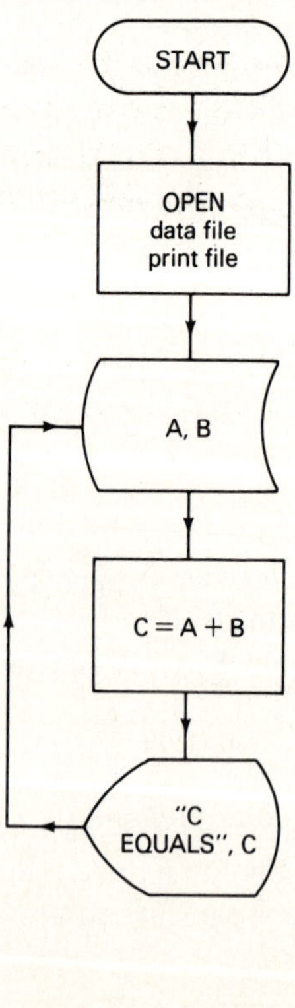


```
C234567890
      OPEN(5,FILE='FIG4-1.DAT')
      OPEN(6,FILE='PRN')
   10 READ(5,*)A,B
      C=A+B
      WRITE(6,*)'   C EQUALS',C
      GOTO 10
      STOP
      END
```

```
1.0 3.0
-4.5 7.8
0.0 3.4
2.6 -4.5
```

```
 C EQUALS               4.0000000
 C EQUALS               3.3000000
 C EQUALS               3.4000000
 C EQUALS              -1.9000000
```

```
GOTO (1Ø,25,5Ø,35),K-J
```

Transfer is made to statement 1Ø if K−J = 1; to statement 25 if K−J = 2; to statement 5Ø if K−J = 3; and to statement 35 if K−J = 4. Since there are four statement labels, the value K−J must equal 1 through 4, inclusive, if the computed GOTO statement is to be executed, and values for K and J must have been assigned earlier in the program.

The flowchart symbol for the computed GOTO statement is the diamond illustrated in Fig. 4-2. In this diagram, one line indicates the flow of logic into the decision step, and any number of lines may be used to indicate the logic paths to which branching may occur.

An example of a program segment using a computed GOTO statement is illustrated in Fig. 4-3 (see p. 84). When the larger of any two integer numbers between 1 and 1Ø, inclusive, is divided by the smaller, one of five different remainders is possible: Ø, 1, 2, 3, or 4. In this example, the value of the calculated remainder (REM) is used as the numerical indicator in a computed GOTO statement. Transfer is to the statement labeled 2Ø when REM = 1, to the statement labeled 5Ø when REM = 2, to the statement labeled 4Ø when REM = 3, and to the statement labeled 8Ø when REM = 4. When REM = Ø, the GOTO statement is ignored and execution continues sequentially with the first executable statement following the GOTO statement. Note that the variable REM has been declared an integer by the INTEGER declaration statement.

4-4 THE ARITHMETIC IF STATEMENT

The *arithmetic* IF statement is a conditional transfer statement that evaluates a given variable or arithmetic expression and transfers (branches) to one of three designated statements, depending on whether the given variable or arithmetic expression is negative, zero, or positive. The general form for the arithmetic IF statement is:

FIGURE 4-2 Flowchart symbol and FORTRAN code for a computed GOTO statement.

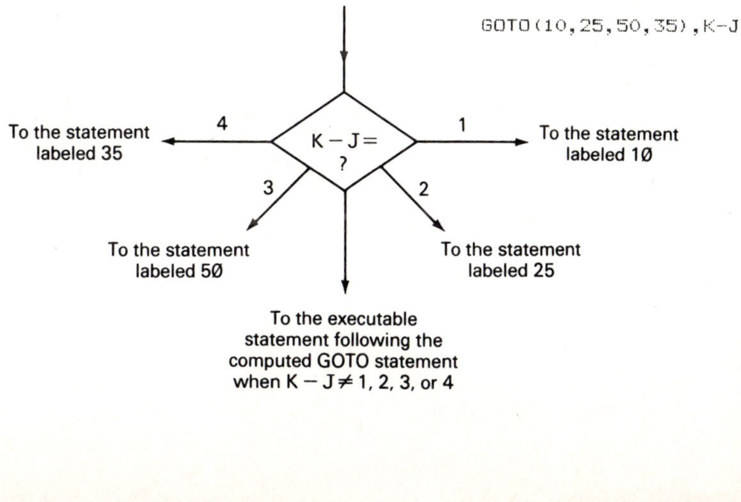

```
      INTEGER REM
      .....
      .....
      WRITE(*,*)'ENTER TWO POSITIVE',
     $' NUMBERS FROM 1 TO 10, LARGE',
     $ST FIRST.'
      READ(*,*)N,M
      REM=N-N/M*M
      GOTO(20,50,40,80)REM
      WRITE(*,*)'THE REMAINDER OF',N,
     $' DIVIDED BY',M,' IS ZERO.'
      GOTO 100
   20 WRITE(*,*)'THE REMAINDER OF',N,
     $' DIVIDED BY',M,' IS ONE.'
      GOTO 100
   50 WRITE(*,*)'THE REMAINDER OF',N,
     $' DIVIDED BY',M,' IS TWO.'
      GOTO 100
   40 WRITE(*,*)'THE REMAINDER OF',N,
     $' DIVIDED BY',M,' IS THREE.'
      GOTO 100
   80 WRITE(*,*)'THE REMAINDER OF',N,
     $' DIVIDED BY',M,' IS FOUR.'
  100 ....
      ....
```

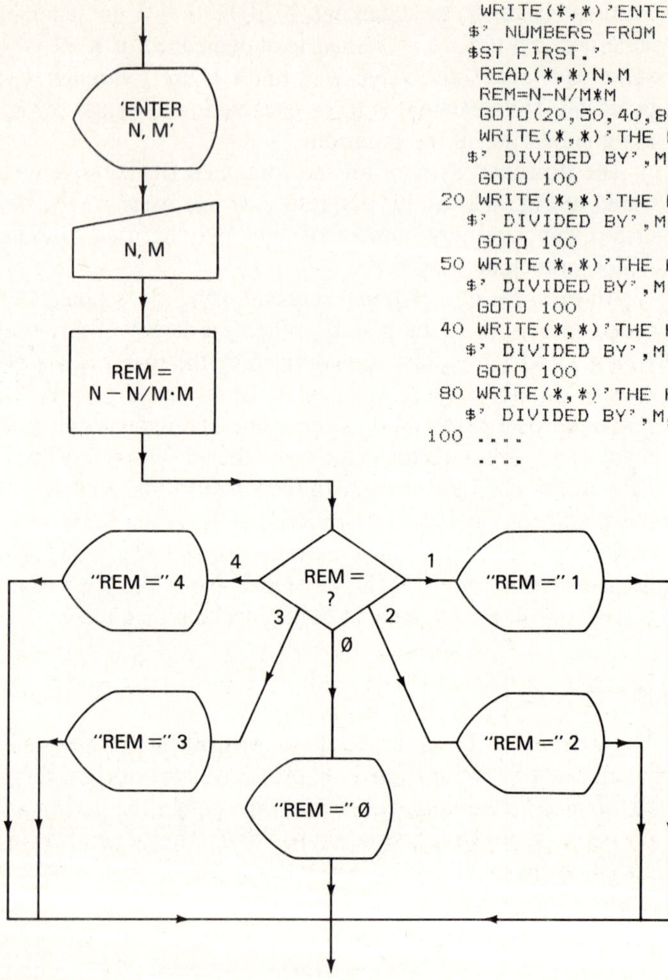

FIGURE 4-3 Using the computed GOTO statement.

IF (*exp*) n_1, n_2, n_3

where *exp* is any variable or arithmetic expression and n_1, n_2, and n_3 are integer numbers representing three statement labels. *exp* can be either a single variable name or an arithmetic expression; the type can be either integer or real. If *exp* is *negative,* the transfer is to statement n_1; if *exp* is *zero*, to statement n_2; and if *exp* is *positive*, to statement n_3.

The following examples illustrate the arithmetic IF statement:

IF (A–B) 1Ø, 2Ø, 3Ø

If A is less than B, the algebraic sign of the expression is negative and the transfer is to statement 1Ø. If A and B are exactly equal, the value of the expression is zero and the transfer is to statement 2Ø. If A is greater than B, the algebraic sign of the expression is positive and the transfer is to statement 3Ø. As discussed in Sec. 1-4, many real numbers cannot be stored as exact values. If the value stored in A is not exactly the same as the value stored in B, A−B will never be exactly zero. In the example:

```
IF (N−J) 1Ø, 2Ø, 3Ø
```

the same transfers are indicated, but the value of the arithmetic expression will be an integer instead of a real number. There is no problem in this case with the value of the expression being exactly zero when N is equal to J. When possible, comparisons that must transfer when the value of the arithmetic expression is zero should be made with integers.

Three statement labels must be listed, but they need not be different labels. However, there should be at least two different statement labels in the list. For example:

```
IF (N) 2Ø, 1Ø, 1Ø
```

will transfer to statement 2Ø when N is less than zero and to statement 1Ø when N is equal to or greater than zero. Other examples of the arithmetic IF statement are included in Sec. 4-6, and further examples can be found in selected illustrative problems in succeeding chapters.

The flowchart symbol for the arithmetic IF statement is a diamond, just as for the computed GOTO statement. However, for the arithmetic IF statement, there are at most three paths that the problem logic may follow, as illustrated in Fig. 4-4. Note that the paths are distinguished from one another by the use of +, Ø, and − symbols placed next to the various paths corresponding to the sign of the arithmetic expression within the statement. If only two paths are required, the flowchart symbol may appear in any of the forms shown in Fig. 4-5 (see p. 86).

FIGURE 4-4 Flowchart symbol and FORTRAN code for an arithmetic IF statement.

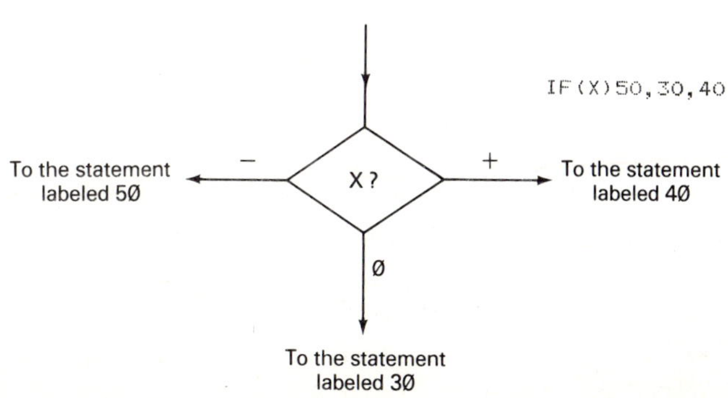

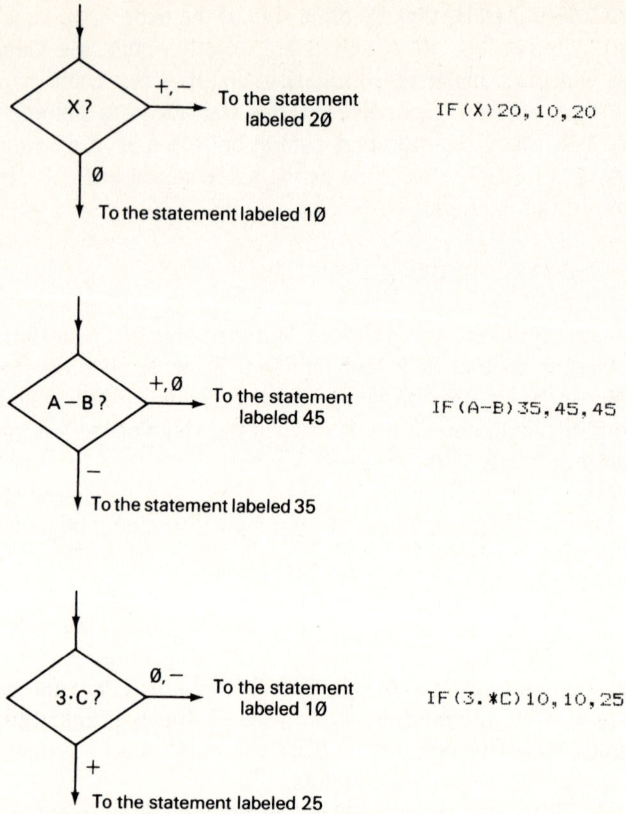

FIGURE 4-5 Flowchart symbols and FORTRAN codes for variations of arithmetic IF statements.

4-5 THE LOGICAL IF STATEMENT (LOGICAL DECISIONS)

Another, and perhaps more useful, conditional transfer statement is the *logical* IF statement. This statement employs *logical expressions* using *relational operators* and makes decisions based on the relationship between the values of two or more variables or arithmetic expressions. Some programming experience is necessary to appreciate fully the power of the logical IF statement.

a Logical Expressions and Relational Operators

A *logical expression* is one that asks a question about two or more variables or arithmetic expressions. Is A less than B? Is C greater than D? Is E equal to F? The six basic *relational operators* in Table 4-1 are used to ask such relational questions. The periods are necessary parts of the operator. These relational operators are used to develop logical expressions as illustrated in Table 4-2. In the last two expressions the parentheses are advisable to show clearly that the comparison called for by the relational operator applies to the value of the expression within the parentheses.

TABLE 4-1 RELATIONAL OPERATORS

Operator	Symbol	Meaning
.LT.	$<$	Less than
.LE.	$\leq$	Less than or equal to
.EQ.	$=$	Equal to
.GE.	$\geq$	Greater than or equal to
.GT.	$>$	Greater than
.NE.	$\neq$	Not equal to

All logical expressions are either true or false. In the expression A.LT.B, if A is less than B, the expression is true; but if A is equal to or greater than B, the expression is false. As in the arithmetic expression, the logical expression should not be of mixed type. All variables and constants in a logical expression should be either real or integer.

Two other operators, .AND. and .OR., called *logical operators,* greatly extend the flexibility of a logical expression. The .AND. operator is used as follows:

```
A.LT.B.AND.C.GT.D
```

This expression asks: Is A less than B *and* is C greater than D? The .AND. requires that *both* conditions be satisfied for the expression to be true. The .OR. operator is used as follows:

```
E.GE.F.OR.G.LE.(H-X)
```

This expression asks: Is E greater than or equal to F *or* is G less than or equal to the value of H minus X? The .OR. means that when *either* condition is true, the expression is true.

An example of an INCORRECT logical expression is:

```
D.AND.E.LT.F
```

The reason this form is not acceptable is that the logical operators .AND. and .OR. relate logical expressions, not individual variable names.

TABLE 4-2 LOGICAL EXPRESSIONS

Logical expression	Meaning
A.LT.B	Is A less than B?
C.EQ.(D/E)	Is C equal to the quotient of D divided by E?
X.GT.(R+S)	Is X greater than the sum of R plus S?

Note: The use of parentheses as illustrated above is optional in these examples but may be used for clarity.

b The Logical IF Statement

The general form for the logical IF statement is:

```
IF (logical expression) executable statement
```

The *executable statement* must not be another logical IF statement; DO statement (Chap. 7); IF THEN, ELSEIF, ELSE, or ENDIF statement (Sec. 4-7); or END statement (Chap. 3). Execution of the logical IF statement occurs in the following order:

1 The logical expression is evaluated as being either true or false.
2 If the expression is *true,* the executable statement is executed. If the executable statement is an arithmetic IF statement or either type of GOTO statement, the transfer is made as indicated. If the statement is an assignment statement (or any other allowable statement), that statement is executed and the program continues with the first executable statement following the logical IF statement.
3 If the expression is *false,* execution continues with the first executable statement following the logical IF statement.

Note that whether the logical expression is true *or* false, the statement immediately following the logical IF statement is *always* executed unless the executable statement of the logical IF is a transfer statement (an arithmetic IF or either type of GOTO statement).

Example 4-1

Consider a situation where the value assigned to Y is determined by the value of N and the value assigned to Z is Y^2. When N is less than or equal to 2, Y equals X. When N is greater than 2, Y equals 2X. In either case, Z must be assigned a value equal to Y^2. With values previously assigned to N and X, the program segment of Fig. 4-6 will establish the given conditions. Notice that the diamond symbol in the flowchart segment is also used for the logical IF statement, but only two paths are needed for branching. One path is identified with a Yes or True, indicating the logic path when the logical expression is true, while the other is identified with a No or False, indicating the logic path when the logical expression is false.

In Example 4-1, when N is less than or equal to 2, the logical expression in the first IF statement is true, and the statement Y=X will be executed. Since N is less than or equal to 2, the logical expression in the second IF statement (N.GT.2) must be false. The statement Y=2.*X will be ignored, and the next statement in sequence (Z=Y**2) will be executed. The value assigned to Z will be the square of the value assigned to Y in the first IF statement. When N is greater than 2 (the logical expression in the first IF statement is false), the statement Y=X will be ignored and the next statement in sequence, the second IF statement, will be executed. The logical expression in the second IF statement (N.GT.2) is true, so the

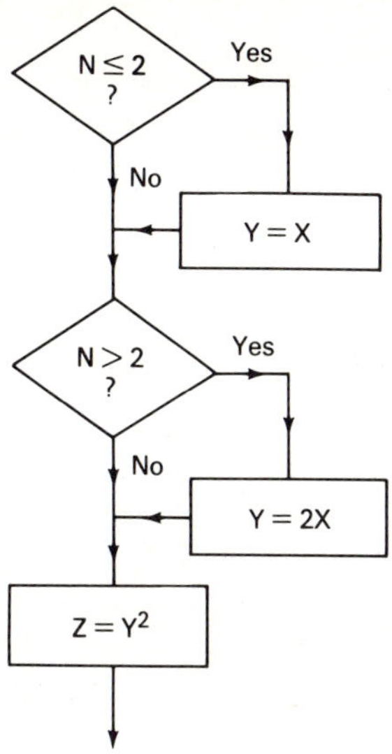


```
....
....
IF(N.LE.2)Y=X
IF(N.GT.2)Y=2.*X
Z=Y**2
....
....
```

FIGURE 4-6 The correct use of a logical IF statement—Example 4-1.

statement Y=2.*X will be executed. The next statement in the sequence, Z=Y**2, is executed. The value assigned to Z will be the square of the value assigned to Y in the second IF statement.

Are two IF statements really necessary in Example 4-1? Perhaps the same result could have been accomplished using the program segment of Fig. 4-7 (see p. 90). When N is less than or equal to 2 (the logical expression in the IF statement is true), the statement Y=X will be executed. Then the next statement in sequence, Y=2.*X, is executed, and a new value is assigned to Y. When N is greater than 2 (the logical expression in the IF statement is false), the statement Y=X will be ignored and the next statement in sequence, Y=2.*X, will be executed. No matter what the value of N, Y will always have the same value when it is used in the last statement Z=Y**2, and the value assigned to Z will always be the same. This sequence of statements does *not* satisfy the given conditions. Therefore, two logical IF statements are necessary.

Figure 4-8 (see p. 91) demonstrates how two other techniques might have been used to achieve the same result. Figure 4-8(*a*) uses a logical IF statement and Fig. 4-8(*b*) uses an arithmetic IF statement to make the basic decision: Is N less than or equal to 2? The unconditional GOTO statement transfers around the unwanted assignment statement in each case. Both these techniques require more statements and represent less efficient programming than the first example, illustrated in Fig. 4-6.

When the logical IF statement is used for branching or looping with the GOTO statement as its "statement," execution time can be reduced if the logical IF statement is written so that the most probable condition of the logical expression is false—*dropping through* rather than branching occurs.

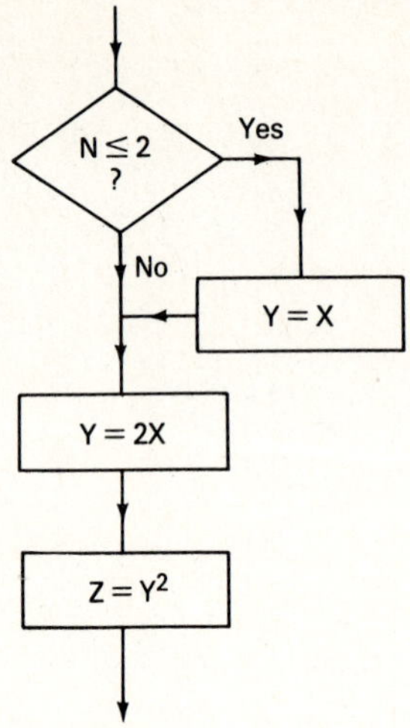


```
....
....
IF(N.LE.2)Y=X
Y=2.*X
Z=Y**2
....
....
```

FIGURE 4-7 The incorrect use of the logical IF statement—Example 4-1.

For example, the integer value assigned to N—incremented from 1 through a maximum value 1Ø in increments of 1—is used to effect a branch or loop when the value assigned to N becomes greater than 8. Eight values must be assigned to N and compared before N is greater than 8. The logical IF statement can effect this result in either of two ways:

(*a*)

```
     N=Ø
1Ø   N=N+1
     ---------
     ---------
     IF (N. GT. 8) GOTO 3Ø
2Ø   ---------
     ---------
3Ø   ---------
     ---------
     IF (N. EQ. 1Ø) STOP
     GOTO 1Ø
```

(*b*)

```
     N=Ø
1Ø   N=N+1
     ---------
     ---------
     IF (N. LE. 8) GOTO 2Ø
     GOTO 3Ø
2Ø   ---------
     ---------
3Ø   ---------
     ---------
     IF (N. EQ. 1Ø) STOP
     GOTO 1Ø
```

Most of the integer values of N between 1 and 1Ø will be less than 8; the value of the logical expression in program segment (*a*) will be false most of the time, and a dropping through to the statement labeled 2Ø will occur. The transfer statement GOTO 3Ø will be executed only twice, when the value assigned to N is 9 or 1Ø. In (*b*) the logical expression will be true most of the time; the transfer statement GOTO 2Ø will be executed 8 times. When the value assigned to N is 9 or 1Ø, the logical statement is false and the dropping through occurs; another transfer statement is required to branch to the statement labeled 3Ø. The logical IF statement as

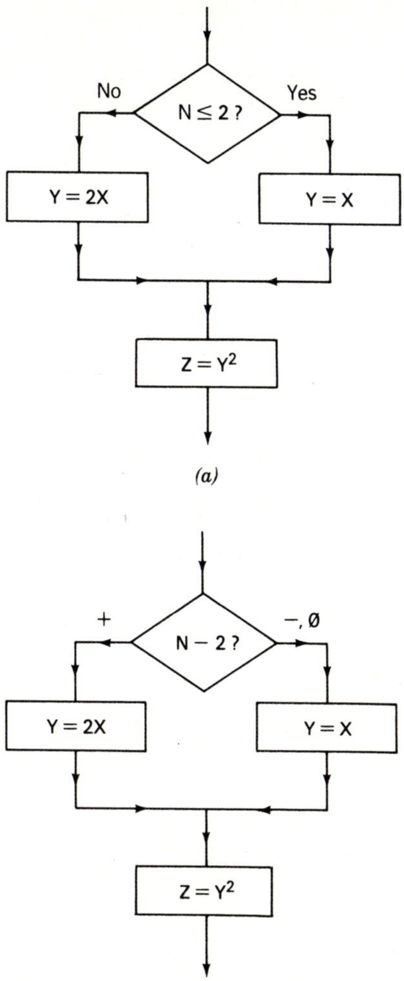


```
      ....
      ....
      IF(N.LE.2)GOTO 10
      Y=2.*X
      GOTO 20
   10 Y=X
   20 Z=Y**2
      ....
      ....
```

```
      ....
      ....
      IF(N-2)10,10,20
   10 Y=X
      GOTO 30
   20 Y=2.*X
   30 Z=Y**2
      ....
      ....
```

FIGURE 4-8 Different decision techniques—Example 4-1.

written in (*a*) uses computer time more efficiently and therefore is the preferred method.

With the introduction of logical expressions, an extension to the hierarchy of operations (Sec. 3-7*b*) is required. Within a logical expression, such as:

```
A+B.GT.C/D**3
```

the arithmetic expressions to either side of the relational operator are evaluated first. Then the relational comparison between the two values is made.

For an expression involving the .AND. or .OR. operator, such as:

```
A+B.GT.C.AND.D.LT.F/6.7
```

the arithmetic expressions are first evaluated, from the leftmost to the rightmost. Next the comparison in each relational expression is made, from the left to the right. Then the comparison with the .AND. (or .OR.) logical operator is made.

If a logical expression includes both .AND. and .OR. logical operators, arithmetic expressions are first evaluated, from the leftmost to the rightmost. Next the comparison in each relational expression is made, from the left to the right. Then the .AND. comparison is made followed by the .OR. comparison. Thus the expression:

```
A.GT.B.OR.C.LT.D.AND.D.EQ.7.6
```

will have the same logical value as the expression:

```
A.GT.B.OR.(C.LT.D.AND.D.EQ.7.6)
```

If more than one .AND. or .OR operator is included, all the .AND. comparisons are made, from left to right, then all the .OR. comparisons are made, from left to right. Thus the expression:

```
A.GT.B.AND.B.EQ.7.5.OR.D.NE.E.AND.C.GT.F.OR.A.NE.G
```

will have the same logical value as the expression:

```
((A.GT.B.AND.B.EQ.7.5).OR.(D.NE.E.AND.C.GT.F)).OR.A.NE.G
```

A summary of the hierachy of relational and logical operations may be listed in five levels:

1 Parentheses cleared
2 Arithmetic-expression evaluation (Sec. 3-7*b*)
3 Comparison with relational operators, from left to right
4 Comparison with the logical operator .AND., from left to right
5 Comparison with the logical operator .OR., from left to right

An IF statement (either arithmetic or logical) in a program indicates an important decision. Therefore, an explanatory comment statement will be useful.

4-6 LOOPING TECHNIQUES COMPARED

The examples in this section will illustrate how identical results can be obtained using, in turn, the computed GOTO statement, the arithmetic IF statement, and the logical IF statement combined with unconditional GOTO statements.

Example 4-2

The sequential execution of a program is to be interrupted and a given sequence of operations repeated a specified number of times with different values assigned to one or more variables. Sequential execution of the program continues after the specified number of repetitions has been completed. The variable name DELTA is assigned an initial value of 1.Ø. After the given sequence of operations has been executed once, the value assigned to DELTA is changed to Ø.1, and the sequence is repeated. The value assigned to DELTA is again changed, to Ø.Ø1, and the sequence of operations is executed for the third time. After the given sequence of operations has been executed 3 times with 3 different values assigned to DELTA, the program continues in sequential order.

a Looping with the Computed GOTO Statement

Figure 4-9 (see p. 94) shows the program segment for this sequence. An integer counter, N, is initially assigned a value of Ø, and DELTA is assigned its first value, 1.Ø. The given sequence of operations is executed the first time. The value of N is incremented by 1 using N=N+1. The computed GOTO statement is executed with N assigned a value of 1; transfer is made to the first labeled statement in the list, statement 4Ø. Execution of statement 4Ø assigns a new value, Ø.1, to DELTA. Execution of GOTO 2Ø transfers to statement 2Ø, and the given sequence is repeated from statement 2Ø with the new value, Ø.1, assigned to DELTA. The value of N is incremented by 1, again using N=N+1. The computed GOTO statement is executed with N assigned a value of 2; transfer is made to the second labeled statement in the list, statement 5Ø. Execution of statement 5Ø assigns a new value, Ø.Ø1, to DELTA; the GOTO 2Ø statement transfers to statement 2Ø, and the given sequence is again repeated with the new value, Ø.Ø1, assigned to DELTA. The value of N is, as before, incremented by 1 using N=N+1. The computed GOTO is executed with N assigned a value of 3; transfer is made to the third labeled statement in the list, statement 6Ø, and the program sequence continues.

b Looping with the Arithmetic IF Statement

Figure 4-10 (see p. 94) shows the program segment for this method. An integer counter, N, is initially assigned a value of Ø, and DELTA is assigned its first value, 1.Ø. The given sequence of operations is executed the first time. The value of N is incremented by 1 using N=N+1. The arithmetic IF statement is executed with N = 1, and since arithmetic expression N − 2 is negative, transfer is to statement 4Ø. Execution of statement 4Ø assigns a new value, Ø.1, to DELTA. Execution of GOTO 2Ø transfers to statement 2Ø, and the given sequence is repeated from statement 2Ø with the new value, Ø.1, assigned to DELTA. The value of N is again incremented by 1 using N=N+1. The arithmetic IF statement is executed with N = 2, and since arithmetic expression N − 2 is zero, transfer is to statement 5Ø. Execution of statement 5Ø assigns a new value, Ø.Ø1, to DELTA; the GOTO 2Ø statement transfers to statement 2Ø, and the given sequence is again repeated with the new value, Ø.Ø1, assigned to DELTA. The value of N is incremented for a third time by 1. The arithmetic IF statement is

```
       ....
       ....
       N=0
       DELTA=1.0
 20    ....
       ....
       N=N+1
       GOTO (40,50,60),N
 40    DELTA=0.1
       GOTO 20
 50    DELTA=0.01
       GOTO 20
 60    ....
       ....
```

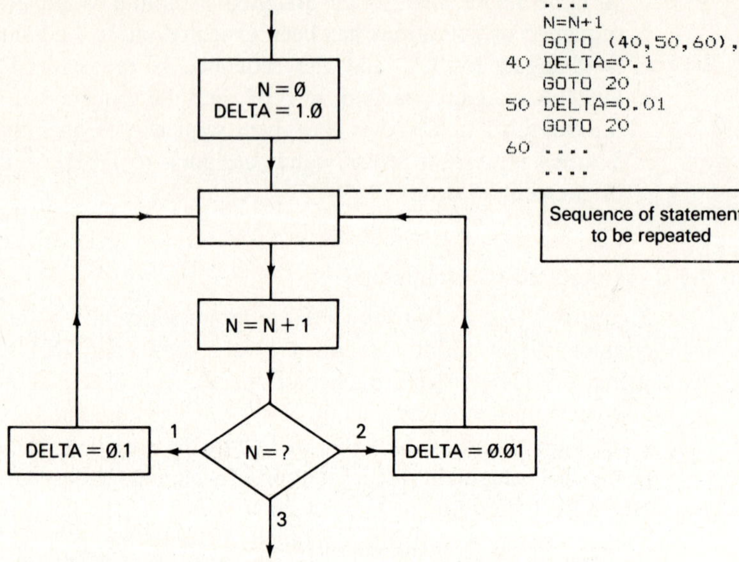

FIGURE 4-9 Looping with the computed GOTO—Example 4-2.

FIGURE 4-10 Looping with an arithmetic IF—Example 4-2.

```
       ....
       ....
       N=0
       DELTA=1.0
 20    ....
       ....
       N=N+1
       IF(N-2)40,50,60
 40    DELTA=0.1
       GOTO 20
 50    DELTA=0.01
       GOTO 20
 60    ....
       ....
```

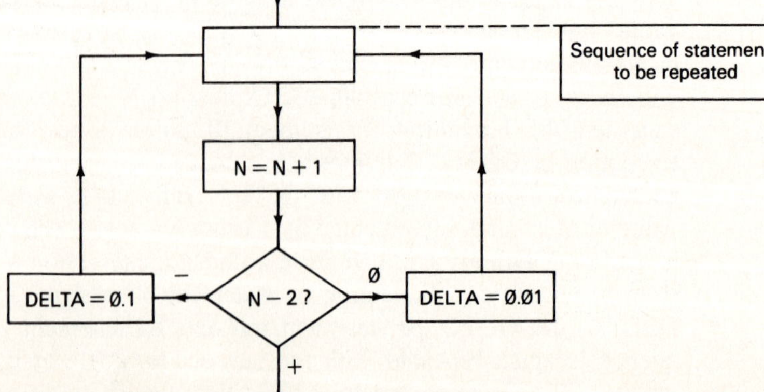

executed with N = 3; the arithmetic expression N − 2 is positive, so transfer is to statement 6Ø, and the program sequence continues. Since only three transfers are possible with the arithmetic IF statement, this technique cannot be used if more than three executions of the given sequence of operations is required.

c Looping with the Logical IF Statement

Figure 4-11 shows the program segment for this method. When the first IF statement is executed, DELTA has a value of 1.Ø (the logical expression is true) and the transfer statement GOTO 4Ø is executed. The statement labeled 4Ø assigns a new value, Ø.1, to DELTA. The next statement in sequence, GOTO 2Ø, is executed, and the given sequence is repeated from statement 2Ø with the new value, Ø.1, assigned to DELTA. When the first IF statement is executed for the second time, the logical expression is false. The transfer statement GOTO 4Ø therefore will be ignored. Then the second IF statement is executed. Since the logical expression in the second IF statement is true (DELTA is greater than Ø.Ø5), the transfer statement GOTO 5Ø is executed. Statement 5Ø assigns a new value, Ø.Ø1, to DELTA. The next statement in sequence, GOTO 2Ø, is executed, and the given sequence is again repeated from statement 2Ø with the new value, Ø.Ø1, assigned to DELTA. This time the logical expressions in both IF statements are false; both transfer statements GOTO 4Ø and GOTO 5Ø will be ignored, and the next statement in sequence following the second IF statement, GOTO 6Ø, will be executed. Execution of the program will continue from statement 6Ø.

```
      ....
      ....
      DELTA=1.0
20    ....
      ....
      IF(DELTA.GT.0.5)GOTO 40
      IF(DELTA.GT.0.05)GOTO 50
      GOTO 60
40    DELTA=0.1
      GOTO 20
50    DELTA=0.01
      GOTO 20
60    ....
      ....
```

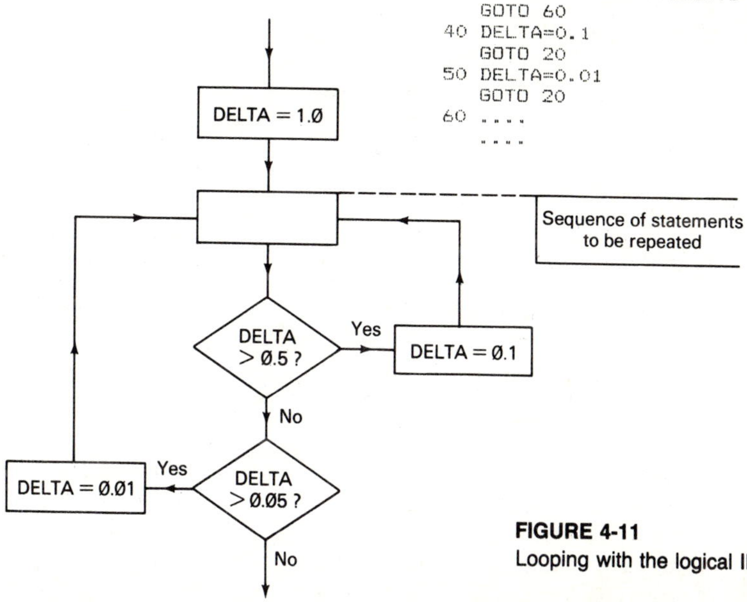

FIGURE 4-11
Looping with the logical IF—Example 4-2.

In each of these solutions, eight statements are required to assign three values to DELTA and effect the three repetitive executions of the given sequence of operations. In this case, one procedure has little, if any, significant advantage over another, but if more than three executions of the given sequence are required, the arithmetic IF statement cannot be used. The logical IF solution requires writing a logical IF statement for every repetition of the sequence. The single computed GOTO statement must be modified by adding additional statement labels to the list corresponding to the statement labels given to the assignment statements changing the value assigned to DELTA. In short, for simple programs it makes little difference which looping or branching procedure is used. In longer, more complex programs, some thought should be given to selecting the most efficient looping or branching technique.

4-7 BLOCK IF STRUCTURES

The somewhat limited looping procedures illustrated in previous sections of this chapter may be enhanced through the use of BLOCK IF structures. These structures consist of two or more blocks, or sets of statements, ordered in such a manner that more complex branching procedures may be executed. This branching, although having characteristics similar to those initiated by the logical IF statement (Sec. 4-5), allows the programmer much greater flexibility.

a The BLOCK IF Structure (IF THEN, ELSE, and ENDIF Statements)

The BLOCK IF structure allows the programmer to control logic flow while minimizing the number of transfer steps. The general form for this structure is illustrated in Fig. 4-12(*a*).

In this structure, the logical expression in the IF THEN statement is identical to the form(s) used in the logical IF statement. Statement set 1 and statement set 2 normally consist of one or more statements to be executed. If the logical expression is true, control is transferred to the first statement in statement set 1 and the statements between the IF THEN statement and the ELSE statements are executed. When the execution of the statements within statement set 1 is completed, control is transferred to the statement immediately following the ENDIF statement. The statements in statement set 2 are ignored. If, however, the logical expression is false, the statements in statement set 1 are ignored and control is transferred to the first statement of statement set 2. When completion of the execution of the statements within statement set 2 is accomplished, control is transferred to the statement immediately following the ENDIF statement.

The flexibility of the BLOCK IF structure may be illustrated with the calculation of the square root of the difference between two numbers. As in Fig. 4-12(*b*), the programmer must consider the possibility of both real and imaginary answers. After assigning values to the variables A and B, the value of A − B is compared to zero. If the difference is positive, the statements between the IF-THEN and

```
IF(logical expression) THEN
   .  }
   .  }   statement set 1
   .  }
ELSE
   .  }
   .  }   statement set 2
   .  }
ENDIF
```

(a)

```
C234567890
      OPEN(5,FILE='FIG4-12.DAT')
      OPEN(6,FILE='PRN')
      N=0
   10 READ(5,*)A,B
      N=N+1
      IF(A-B.GE.0.0)THEN
      ROOT=(A-B)**0.5
      WRITE(6,*)'  THE REAL ROOT'
     $' OF A-B IS',ROOT
      ELSE
      ROOT=(B-A)**0.5
      WRITE(6,*)'  THE IMAGINARY SQUARE',
     $' ROOT OF A-B IS',ROOT,'j'
      ENDIF
      IF(N.NE.5)GOTO 10
      STOP
      END
```

```
7.0 3.0
4.5 -3.2
5.6 5.6
-3.2 7.8
0.0 0.0
```

```
THE REAL ROOT OF A-B IS           2.0000000
THE REAL ROOT OF A-B IS           2.7748870
THE REAL ROOT OF A-B IS            .0000000
THE IMAGINARY SQUARE ROOT OF A-B IS              3.3166250j
THE REAL ROOT OF A-B IS            .0000000
```

(b)

FIGURE 4-12 Basic BLOCK IF structure.

ELSE statements are executed, causing the real value of ROOT to be displayed. Control is then transferred to the first executable statement following the ENDIF statement. If the difference is negative, only those statements between the ELSE and ENDIF statements are executed, causing the imaginary value of ROOT to be displayed. The "j" following the imaginary answer is used to represent the square root of -1, implying that the answer is imaginary. Control is then transferred to the first executable statement following the ENDIF statement.

b The BLOCK IF Structure without the ELSE Statement

If no statements are to be executed when the logical expression of the IF THEN statement is false, the general form for the BLOCK IF structure is as shown in Fig. 4-13(*a*) (see p. 98). In this case, if the logical expression is true, statement set 3 is executed, followed by a transfer of control to the first executable statement following the ENDIF statement. If the logical expression is false, control is transferred immediately to the first executable statement following the ENDIF statement. The statements in statement set 3 are ignored. Figure 4-13(*b*) illustrates the use of this form of the BLOCK IF structure in a short program.

c Nested BLOCK IF Structures

BLOCK IF structures may be placed within any statement set of another BLOCK IF structure, a procedure known as *nesting*. A general form for a nest of two BLOCK IF structures is illustrated in Fig. 4-14(*a*).

In this general form, execution begins with the first IF THEN statement, the initial statement of the outer BLOCK IF structure. If the logical expression of this statement is true, statement set 4 is executed, followed by a transfer of control to the first executable statement following the last ENDIF statement. If the logical expression is false, statement set 4 is ignored and control is transferred to the statement immediately following the first ELSE statement (belonging to the outer BLOCK IF structure), which, in this general form, is the IF THEN statement of the inner BLOCK IF structure. Execution of the inner BLOCK IF structure occurs in the normal manner, and control is eventually transferred to the first statement of statement set 7. When completion of the execution of the statements in statement set 7 is accomplished, control is transferred to the first executable statement

FIGURE 4-13 BLOCK IF structure without an ELSE statement.

```
IF(logical expression) THEN
  .  }
  .  }   statement set 3
  .  }
ENDIF
```

(a)

```
C234567890
      OPEN(5,FILE='FIG4-13.DAT')
      OPEN(6,FILE='PRN')
      N=0
   10 READ(5,*)A
      N=N+1
      IF(A.GE.0.0)THEN
      ROOT=SQRT(A)
      WRITE(6,*)'   THE SQUARE ROOT OF',
     $' A IS',ROOT
      ENDIF
      IF(N.NE.3)GO TO 10
      END
```

```
4.5
-3.0
0.0
```

```
 THE SQUARE ROOT OF A IS          2.1213200
 THE SQUARE ROOT OF A IS           .0000000
```

(b)

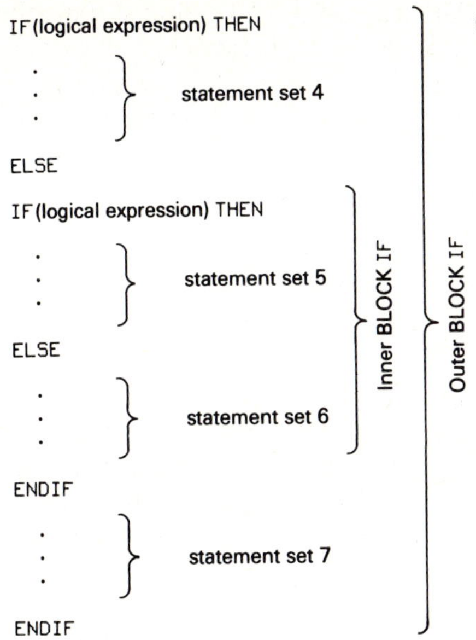


```
C234567890
      OPEN(5,FILE='FIG4-14.DAT')
      OPEN(6,FILE='PRN')
      N=0
   10 READ(5,*)A,B
      N=N+1
      IF(A.EQ.0.0)THEN
      WRITE(6,*)'SINCE A=0.0, THE ',
     $'QUOTIENT OF B DIVIDED BY A IS',
     $' UNDEFINED.'
      ELSE
      IF(B.LT.A)THEN
      WRITE(6,*)'THE QUOTIENT OF B ',
     $'DIVIDED BY A IS LESS THAN 1.0.'
      ELSE
      IF(A-B)30,40,50
   30 WRITE(6,*)'THE VALUE OF B DIVID',
     $'ED BY A IS GREATER THAN 1.0.'
      ENDIF
      GO TO 50
   40 WRITE(6,*)'THE QUOTIENT OF B ',
     $'DIVIDED BY A IS 1.0.'
      ENDIF
   50 IF(N.NE.4)GOTO 10
      STOP
      END
```

(a)

```
3.0,3.0
2.0,7.0
5.0,3.0
0.0,3.0
```

```
THE QUOTIENT OF B DIVIDED BY A IS 1.0.
THE VALUE OF B DIVIDED BY A IS GREATER THAN 1.0.
THE QUOTIENT OF B DIVIDED BY A IS LESS THAN 1.0.
SINCE A=0.0, THE QUOTIENT OF B DIVIDED BY A IS UNDEFINED.
```

(b)

FIGURE 4-14 Nesting of BLOCK IF structures.

following the last ENDIF statement. Figure 4-14(*b*) illustrates the use of this form of BLOCK IF structure in a short program.

More complex nesting may occur, involving not only the normal BLOCK IF structures, but also the BLOCK IF structure without the ELSE statement. Any inner BLOCK IF structure must lie completely between the IF THEN and ELSE statements or completely between the ELSE and ENDIF statements of the outer BLOCK IF structure, except as noted in the section that follows.

d The ELSEIF Statement

Additional versatility may be obtained by using the ELSE statement of an outer BLOCK IF structure to initiate an inner BLOCK IF structure. The general form of such a statement, called the ELSEIF statement, is:

ELSEIF *(logical expression)* THEN

Figure 4-15(*a*) illustrates a general form for a nesting of BLOCK IF structures. Notice that the ELSEIF statement allows two BLOCK IF structures to terminate on the same ENDIF statement. In this general form, if the logical expression of the outer BLOCK IF structure is true, statement set 8 is executed, followed by a transfer of control to the first executable statement following the ENDIF statement. If the logical expression of the outer BLOCK IF structure is false, statement set 8 is ignored and control is transferred to the ELSEIF statement, the first

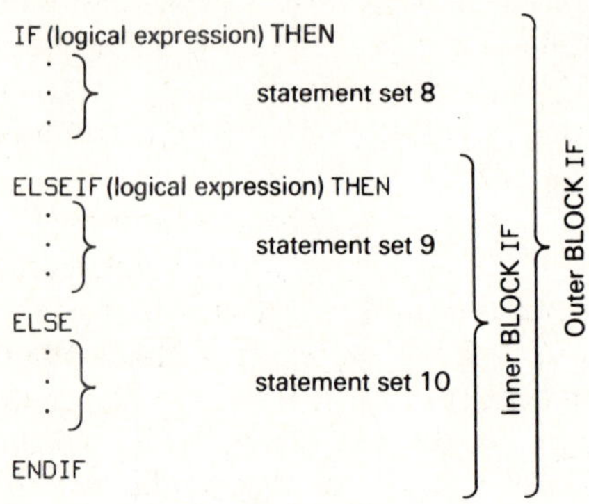

(a)

```
C234567890
      OPEN(5,FILE='FIG4-15.DAT')
      OPEN(6,FILE='PRN')
      N=0
   10 READ(5,*)A
      N=N+1
      IF(A.LT.5.0.AND.A.GT.0.0)THEN
      WRITE(6,*)A,' IS LESS THAN ',
     $'5.0 BUT GREATER THAN 0.0.'
      ELSEIF (A.LT.10.0)THEN
      WRITE(6,*)A,' IS LESS THAN ',
     $'10.0 BUT GREATER THAN OR ',
     $'EQUAL TO 5.0.'
      ELSE
      WRITE(6,*)A,' IS GREATER THAN',
     $' OR EQUAL TO 10.0.'
      ENDIF
      IF(N.NE.5)GOTO 10
      END
```

```
3.5
6.9
12.4
5.0
10.0
```

```
 3.5000000 IS LESS THAN 5.0 BUT GREATER THAN 0.0.
 6.9000000 IS LESS THAN 10.0 BUT GREATER THAN OR EQUAL TO 5.0.
12.4000000 IS GREATER THAN OR EQUAL TO 10.0.
 5.0000000 IS LESS THAN 10.0 BUT GREATER THAN OR EQUAL TO 5.0.
10.0000000 IS GREATER THAN OR EQUAL TO 10.0.
```

(b)

FIGURE 4-15 Nesting BLOCK IF structures using the ELSEIF statement.

statement of the inner BLOCK IF structure. The inner BLOCK IF structure is executed in the normal manner, using the outer ENDIF statement to terminate its execution. Control is then transferred to the first executable statement following the ENDIF statement. A short program using the ELSEIF statement is presented in Fig. 4-15*(b)*.

Flowcharting BLOCK IF structures involves the use of the same diamond symbol used for the arithmetic and logical IF statements; a flowchart illustrating this and the corresponding FORTRAN code are shown in Fig. 4-16 (see p. 102). Note that there is no flowchart symbol for the ELSE or ENDIF statements. The IF THEN and ELSEIF statements are represented by the diamond.

4-8 BRANCHING FROM THE READ STATEMENT AT THE END OF A DATA FILE

The example program (the circle problem), introduced in Sec. 3-20 and shown in Fig. 3-5 to illustrate repetitive execution of the READ statement by looping with the unconditional GOTO statement, terminated by default with an error message when no more data were supplied (the last record had been read). This is often undesirable and can be eliminated by including a decision-making routine that will identify the last record and branch to another part of the program when that record has been read. In this example, the unconditional GOTO statement transfers to the READ statement even though there are no more data to be read. The attempted execution of the READ statement without data causes the default and displays the ERROR message. An addition to the READ statement (the END and ERR options), which allows the program to avoid this error, was introduced in Sec. 3-1. Other techniques can also be used. A conditional transfer, employing either the arithmetic IF statement or the logical IF statement, can be written which will transfer to the READ statement until the last record has been read and the last item(s) of data processed; then, instead of looping back to the READ statement, a branch (transfer to another statement) will be made. If program termination is desired, transfer (branch) can be to a STOP or END statement.

a Branching after the Last Data Value, When the Number of Records Is Known

If the number of records in the data file is known, a counting routine can be used to tally the number of repetitions through the loop, as was done in Fig. 3-7. A decision can then be made based on comparing the known number of records with the repetition count. In the example of Fig. 4-17 (see p. 103), there are five records. A counting technique using the statements N=Ø and N=N+1 tallies the number of repetitions of the loop. Transfer is to the READ statement until the loop has been completed 5 times, implying N = 5, with five different data values read from five consecutive records. When N is equal to or greater than 5, a transfer (branch) is made to the STOP statement. Either the arithmetic IF (Fig. 4-17) or the logical IF (Fig. 4-18, p. 104) can be used to accomplish the branch.

```
....
....
IF(A.LT.B) THEN
A=A+B
B=A-B
ELSEIF(A.EQ.B) THEN
C=A**2
D=B**2
ELSE
E=(A+B)**2
ENDIF
....
....
```

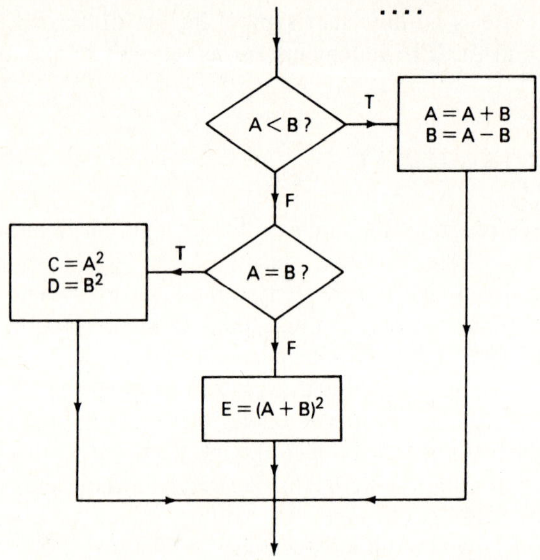

FIGURE 4-16 Flowchart and FORTRAN code of a BLOCK IF structure.

b Branching after the Last Data Value, When the Number of Records Is Not Known

If the number of records in the data file is not known, an additional, final "signal" record can be added, following the last record containing the actual data. This signal record should consist of numbers compatible with the form of the actual data but use values that will never occur in the actual data set. The data values in the example of Fig. 4-19 (see p. 105) represent the diameter of a circle and are all positive values. The final record can therefore include a negative number. When the algebraic sign of DIA is negative, a transfer out of the loop (branch) is made to the STOP statement.

Another way to accomplish the same result is to add a variable LVAL to the READ list. Two values are supplied in each record, the second value in all but the last record being zero. As long as the value assigned to LVAL is zero, the loop will continue. In the last record a value greater than zero is supplied for LVAL. When LVAL is greater than zero, transfer is to the STOP statement. This method is shown in Fig. 4-20 (see p. 106).

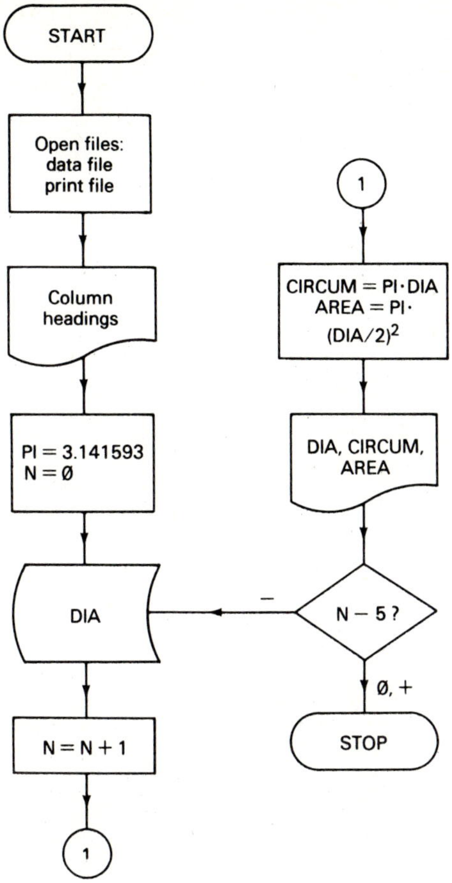


```
C234567890
      OPEN(3,FILE='FIG4-17.DAT')
      OPEN(5,FILE='PRN')
      WRITE(5,*)'            DIAMETER (CM)',
     $'   CIRCUMFERENCE (CM)    AREA (SQCM)'
      WRITE(5,*)
      PI=3.141593
      N=0
   10 READ(3,*)DIA
      N=N+1
      CIRCUM=PI*DIA
      AREA=PI*(DIA/2.0)**2
      WRITE(5,*)DIA,CIRCUM,AREA
      IF(N-5)10,20,20
   20 STOP
      END
```

```
1.0
1.5
2.0
2.5
3.0
```

```
DIAMETER (CM)      CIRCUMFERENCE (CM)    AREA (SQCM)

   1.0000000             3.1415930   7.853982E-001
   1.5000000             4.7123890       1.7671460
   2.0000000             6.2831860       3.1415930
   2.5000000             7.8539820       4.9087390
   3.0000000             9.4247790       7.0685840
```

(a) *(b)*

FIGURE 4-17 The circle problem with a known number of data—branching with the arithmetic IF.

A different problem is used to illustrate a variation in the use of a counter. Suppose an unknown number of values are to be read and when all values have been read the average of these values is to be computed. This requires the use of a counter to determine the number of values read and the use of a summing variable, SUM, to compute the cumulative total of the values. When all values have been read, the average can be determined by dividing the cumulative total by the number of values (AVE=SUM/N). Figure 4-21 (see p. 107) shows the flowchart and the program. A second value, Ø, to be assigned to LVAL was included in each data record. A value greater than zero assigned to LVAL indicates the last data value.

Note that in the program an integer variable N is used as a counter. Then when the average is determined, the integer variable N is assigned to a real variable (DIVIS) to avoid mixed-mode arithmetic. Also note that the counter is initialized

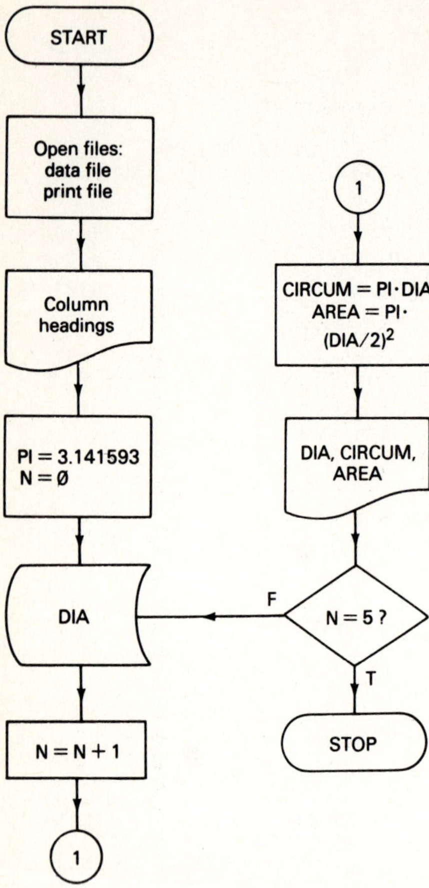


```
C234567890
      OPEN(2,FILE='FIG4-17.DAT')
      OPEN(5,FILE='PRN')
      WRITE(5,*)'          DIAMETER (CM)',
     $'   CIRCUMFERENCE (CM)   AREA (SQCM)'
      WRITE(5,*)
      PI=3.141593
      N=0
   10 READ(2,*)DIA
      N=N+1
      CIRCUM=PI*DIA
      AREA=PI*(DIA/2.0)**2
      WRITE(5,*)DIA,CIRCUM,AREA
      IF(N.EQ.5)GOTO 20
      GOTO 10
   20 STOP
      END
```

```
1.0
1.5
2.0
2.5
3.0
```

```
DIAMETER (CM)     CIRCUMFERENCE (CM)    AREA (SQCM)

   1.0000000            3.1415930  7.853982E-001
   1.5000000            4.7123890      1.7671460
   2.0000000            6.2831860      3.1415930
   2.5000000            7.8539820      4.9087390
   3.0000000            9.4247790      7.0685840
```

(a) (b)

FIGURE 4-18 The circle problem with a known number of data—branching with the logical IF.

with a value of 1. This is done because the incrementation of the counter follows the transfer statement used to identify the last value.

4-9 CONCLUSION

Preparing an error-free computer program is a time-consuming effort on the part of a programmer or a team of programmers. Processing the program requires sophisticated and expensive electronic equipment. Writing a computer program to perform one simple calculation once, such as calculating the circumference and area of a circle from its diameter, obviously wastes time, money, and personnel; some other method of calculation should be employed. However, if that same calculation is to be made not once, not 5 times, not 50 times, but perhaps 50,000

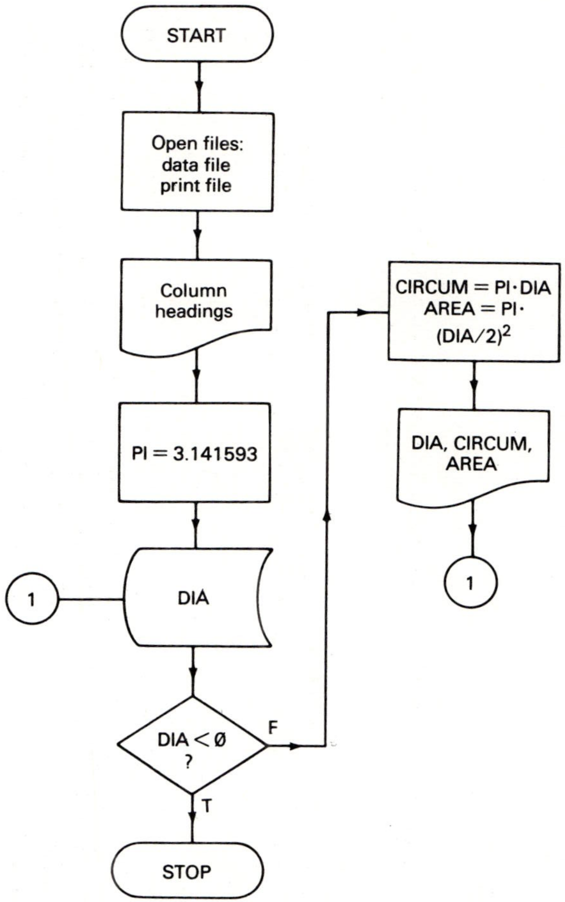

(a)

```
C234567890
      OPEN(2,FILE='FIG4-19.DAT')
      OPEN(5,FILE='PRN')
      WRITE(5,*)'         DIAMETER (CM)',
     $'   CIRCUMFERENCE (CM)    AREA (SQCM)'
      WRITE(5,*)
      PI=3.141593
   10 READ(2,*)DIA
      IF(DIA.LT.0.0)GOTO 20
      CIRCUM=PI*DIA
      AREA=PI*(DIA/2.0)**2
      WRITE(5,*)DIA,CIRCUM,AREA
      GOTO 10
   20 STOP
      END
```

```
1.0
1.5
2.0
2.5
3.0
-3.5
```

```
DIAMETER (CM)    CIRCUMFERENCE (CM)    AREA (SQCM)

   1.0000000          3.1415930   7.853982E-001
   1.5000000          4.7123890       1.7671460
   2.0000000          6.2831860       3.1415930
   2.5000000          7.8539820       4.9087390
   3.0000000          9.4247790       7.0685840
```

(b)

FIGURE 4-19 The circle problem with an unknown number of data—branching with meaningless data.

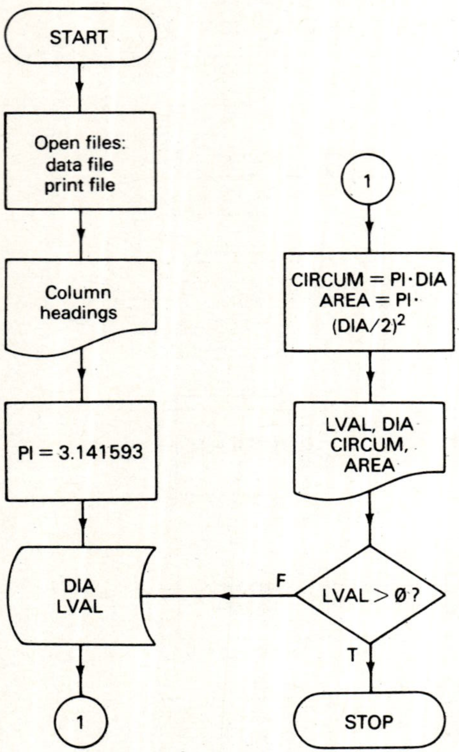

(a)

```
C234567890
      OPEN(3,FILE='FIG4-20.DAT')
      OPEN(6,FILE='PRN')
      WRITE(6,*)'                LVAL
     $'DIAMETER  (CM)    CIRCUMFERENCE  (CM)',
     $'    AREA  (SQCM)'
      WRITE(6,*)
      PI=3.141594
   10 READ(3,*)DIA,LVAL
      CIRCUM=PI*DIA
      AREA=PI*(DIA/2.0)**2
      WRITE(6,*)LVAL,DIA,CIRCUM,AREA
      IF(LVAL.GT.0)GOTO 20
      GOTO 10
   20 STOP
      END
```

```
1.0 0
1.5 0
2.0 0
2.5 0
3.0 1
```

LVAL	DIAMETER (CM)	CIRCUMFERENCE (CM)	AREA (SQCM)
0	1.0000000	3.1415940	7.853985E-001
0	1.5000000	4.7123910	1.7671470
0	2.0000000	6.2831880	3.1415940
0	2.5000000	7.8539850	4.9087410
1	3.0000000	9.4247820	7.0685860

(b)

FIGURE 4-20 The circle problem with an unknown number of data—branching with "last-record" variable.

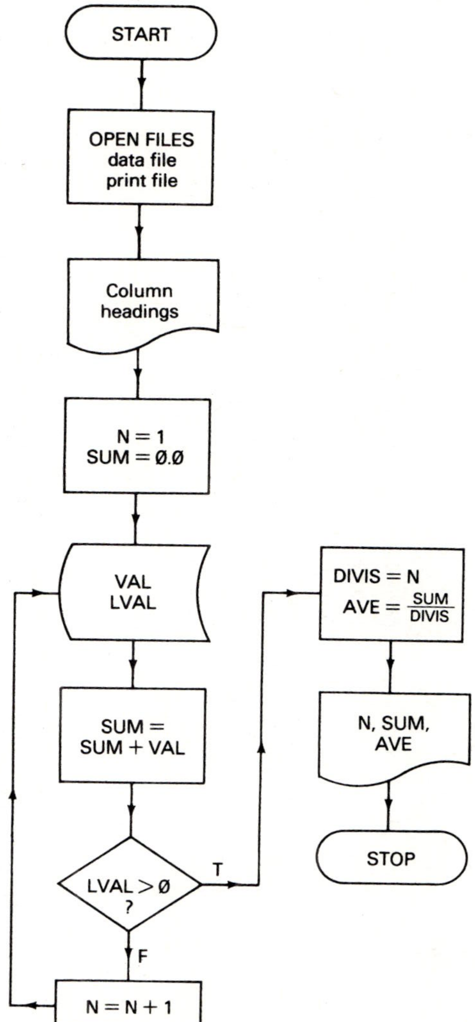

(a)

```
C234567890
      OPEN(4,FILE='FIG4-21.DAT')
      OPEN(7,FILE='PRN')
      WRITE(7,*)'          NO. DATA',
     $'         SUM',
     $'                AVERAGE'
      WRITE(7,*)
      N=1
      SUM=0.0
   10 READ(4,*)VAL,LVAL
      SUM=SUM+VAL
      IF(LVAL.GT.0)GOTO 20
      N=N+1
      GOTO 10
   20 DIVIS=N
      AVE=SUM/DIVIS
      WRITE(7,*)N,SUM,AVE
      STOP
      END
```

```
1.2 0
2.3 0
3.4 0
4.5 0
5.6 0
6.7 0
7.8 0
8.9 0
9.0 1
```

```
NO. DATA          SUM                  AVERAGE

       9       49.4000000            5.4888890
```

(b)

FIGURE 4-21 The averaging problem with an unknown number of data records.

times without human intervention in a time frame of seconds rather than hours or days and the calculations are to be correct (without possibility of human error) 100 percent of the time, a computer program and the facilities required to process it are justified. A savings bank's use of a computer to maintain and update records of its accounts is a good example. The data entered and the calculations involved are simple—adding dollar deposits, subtracting dollar withdrawals, computing and adding dollar interest, and subtracting dollar service charges—but the calculations must be made hundreds of thousands of times without error and the results must be reported on demand and/or stored in a retrievable form for further calculations. The only human intervention required is the entry of dollar data identified as a deposit or withdrawal and minor modification as interest rates and other parameters change.

The full power of the computer is realized only when it is properly programmed to repeat a series of calculations (looping) a specified number of times, to make decisions based on predictable numerical values, and to transfer to another part of the program (branching) based on these decisions. The simple looping and branching statements explained in this chapter provide the computer with the ability to decide, loop, and branch.

PROBLEMS

4-1 Expand Prob. 3-11 to handle any number of rectangular boxes. End the program when there are no more data values. Prepare your own data.

4-2 Expand Prob. 3-12 to handle any number of spheres. End on a last-value indicator. Prepare your own data.

4-3 Write a program to sum the values of the odd integers between 1 and 1ØØ.

4-4 Write a program to determine whether any integer value is odd or even by using the logical IF statement. The program must be able to handle the case when the value of the integer is zero. Use at least three integer values to test the program (Ø, an even value other than 2, and an odd value other than 1). Print the answer as a sentence.

4-5 The torque (T) in pound-inches (lb·in) transmitted through a shaft delivering a given horsepower (hp) at a given rotational rate in revolutions per minute (rpm) can be calculated by:

$$T = \frac{\text{hp} \times 63{,}ØØØ}{\text{rpm}}$$

The required shaft diameter (D) in inches can be determined from:

$$D = \sqrt[3]{\frac{16T}{\pi S}}$$

where S is the allowable stress in pounds per square inch (lb/in^2). Write a program that will read in the horsepower, revolutions per minute, and allowable shear stress for any number of shafts and then determine the required shaft diameter. Print all data. Prepare suitable data to test the program. Use an allowable shear stress of 8000 lb/in^2.

4-6 Using the information from Prob. 4-5, determine the required shaft diameters for transmitting from 5 to 45 hp (in increments of 10) at 2000 rpm.

4-7 Write a program to read any three values representing three lengths and determine whether they can form a triangle; if they can, determine whether the triangle is a right triangle. Appropriate messages should then be printed, together with the values of each of the three sides. The program should be able to handle any number of triangles. Test the program with appropriate data.

4-8 Using the list-directed READ statement, read values (in feet) for the diameter and altitude of a right circular tank (cylinder) whose bases are horizontal. Compute the volume of the tank in cubic feet and liters. Print all values. The program should handle any number of data. Provide for terminating the program when data from the last record has been processed. Use the following data:

D, ft	*H*, ft
1.00	2.00
2.30	2.35
5.55	4.50
4.75	6.75

4-9 A storage tank originally contains 800 gal of a solution made by mixing 150 lb of a dry hormone concentrate with water. Assume that in these proportions the concentrate can be mixed with water without significantly changing the volume. Every day 1.5 gal of the hormone-treated solution is removed from the tank and added to the drinking water provided for cattle. After the solution is removed each day, 1.5 gal of fresh, untreated water is added to the tank. No more hormone concentrate need be added to the solution in the tank until the amount of concentrate falls to 100 lb or below. Then enough concentrate must be added to bring the total weight back to 150 lb. Determine the time in days, counting the original day, until concentrate must be added, and the amount that must be added.

4-10 Write and run a program that will read four real numbers A, B, C, D and an integer number J from records of a data file. Then the program is to perform one of the following calculations, depending upon the value of J:

If J = 1:	X=A+B+C+D
If J = 2:	X=(A+B+C+D)/4.0
If J = 3:	X=(A+B)/(C+D)
If J = 4:	X=A/B+C/D
If J = 5:	X=A/B−C/D

All initial data and the value of X are to be printed with appropriate notations. Provide an escape in the program if J is greater than 5. The program is to be terminated when the last record is read. Use as test data:

A	B	C	D	J
1.Ø	2.Ø	3.Ø	4.Ø	1
5.6	2.Ø	1Ø.4	4.Ø	4
−1Ø.5	3.5	25.2	6.3	5
27.8	38.33	45.75	−41.Ø2	2
33.68	21.46	13.21	14.36	3

4-11 Write a program that will read three values from each record of a data file. The first two values (X and Y) are real values; the third value is an integer value used to indicate the last data record. If X−Y is greater than zero, determine the value of Z=X/Y; if X−Y is zero, determine the value of Z=X*Y; if X−Y is less than zero, determine the value of Z=Y/X. Print the values of X, Y, and Z. The values of X and Y should vary between Ø and 1ØØ.Ø. Prepare a data file and test the program.

4-12 A given county in a mountainous state contains 156 mi^2 and is capable of supporting three people per square mile. At present the population is 8Ø people, but the population is increasing at the rate of 1Ø percent annually. In how many years will the population first be in excess? Each calculation of the new population should be rounded to the nearest integer.

4-13 The owner of a cattle ranch in Texas has an opportunity to purchase an adjacent ranch. There will not be another chance to purchase additional land for 15 years. The present ranch is capable of supporting 13,ØØØ cattle; at present there are only 45ØØ cattle, but the herd is increasing at an annual rate of 12 percent. Should the owner purchase the additional land now or wait? All calculations of herd size should be rounded to the nearest integer.

4-14 Many engineering problems require the value of e, defined as:

$$e = 1 + \frac{1}{1!} + \frac{1}{2!} + \frac{1}{3!} + \frac{1}{4!} + \cdots + \frac{1}{n!}$$

Write a program to determine the value of e correct to six decimal places (the first six decimal places of two successive solutions are the same). Note that a plan must be devised to compute the values of factorials. Build into the program a method of counting the number of factorial terms necessary to achieve the desired precision. Print the value of e and the number of terms required.

4-15 Given the formulas below, write a program to compute and print, in tabular form, the resulting data for N's from 1 to 15. Provide appropriate column headings and double-space the output.

$$\sum_{J=1}^{N} J = N\frac{N+1}{2} \qquad \sum_{J=1}^{N} J^2 = N(N+1)\frac{2N+1}{6} \qquad \sum_{J=1}^{N} J^3 = N^2\frac{(N+1)^2}{4}$$

4-16 Many computer problems require the sorting of numerical data, usually from the smallest value to the largest. One method is to start by comparing the first and second values. If the second value is smaller than the first, switch the two values. (Think when you do this.) Next, compare the second and third values, and again switch if the third is the smaller. This is continued until the largest value is in the last position. This process is repeated until the second largest value is in the second to last position, and so on, until all the values are arranged in ascending order. This process is termed a "bubble sort."

Write and run a bubble sort that will read and print 15 integer values arranged in any order. After the sort, the values should be arranged in ascending order. A BLOCK IF structure will simplify the programming. It should be realized that the program can be revised to handle any number of values and can also be revised to arrange the values in descending order. The program can further be revised as a subprogram. Refer to Secs. 8-2*a* and 8-9*a* before attempting this problem.

4-17 A company is offering a gidget where shipping costs and price per unit vary with the size of the order. If the order size is less than 1ØØ, the shipping charge is $25 and the unit price is $1Ø. If the order size is between 1ØØ and 299, the shipping charge is $20 and the unit price is $8. If the order size is 3ØØ or greater, the shipping charge is $15 and the unit price is $6. Write a program that will compute (given the order size) the cost of the order. Use the BLOCK IF structure in programming your solution. Use order quantities of 8Ø, 2ØØ, and 4ØØ.

CHAPTER **5**

COMMON MATHEMATICAL FUNCTIONS

5-1 INTRODUCTION

Many mathematical procedures are used repeatedly in a variety of programming applications. To rewrite the program segment—often a complex and lengthy sequence of operations required to extract the square root, evaluate a logarithm, or calculate the sine of an angle—each time the procedure is used is wasteful of the programmer's time and leads to unnecessary mistakes. The most common mathematical procedures can be evaluated by using preprogrammed packages available as system-supplied or *intrinsic functions*. Evaluation of such a function will call a prestored subprogram, the execution of which performs the calculation indicated by the function name and returns a single numerical value to the expression where the function was used. The value resulting from a function calculation can also be assigned to a variable name and used in subsequent calculations.

The number of intrinsic functions available depends upon the choice of compiler. This chapter will describe the intrinsic functions that are most likely to be needed by the beginning programmer and that are usually available on the personal computer compiler.

The general form for all the functions is:

FUNCT(*argument*)

where FUNCT is a unique name identifying the function, and *argument* is a constant, variable, or arithmetic expression. The FORTRAN term used to identify a function (FUNCT) must not be used as a variable name in a statement where the function name is also used and, to avoid confusion, should not be used as a variable name at all. The argument of each function must meet the individual specifications of each function, as explained in the following sections. *Note:* All angles, whether used as arguments or calculated as a result of an operation, are in radian measure.

5-2 SQUARE-ROOT FUNCTION

The square root of a number can be calculated by simply raising the number to the one-half power, for example, 25.Ø**Ø.5; however, the exponential calculation does not always yield the most nearly exact root. It is generally better to use the *square-root function*. The general form for the square-root function is:

```
SQRT (a)
```

where *a*, the argument of the function, represents a real constant, real variable, or real arithmetic expression whose value is equal to or greater than zero. Some examples of the square-root function are:

```
A=SQRT (9.Ø)
B=SQRT (16.Ø)
C=SQRT (A**2+B**2)
```

where the value assigned to A is 3.Ø, to B is 4.Ø, and to C is 5.Ø.

Remember that the argument of the square-root function *must* be real and positive (or zero). An attempt to evaluate the SQRT function with a negative real argument or an integer argument will abort execution of the program with an error message at the statement in which the erroneous argument occurs. However, if the negative real argument is first written as the argument of the absolute value function (Sec. 5-3), the negative sign will be ignored and the square root of the absolute value of the argument will be calculated. The root will be positive. It is also possible to change an integer argument to type real, temporarily, by writing it as an argument of a type-conversion function (Sec. 5-4). The root will be a real number.

5-3 ABSOLUTE-VALUE FUNCTIONS

The *absolute-value function* does just what the name implies. The value of the function is the absolute value of the argument. The absolute-value function has two common forms, a generic form:

```
ABS (a)
```

and an integer form:

```
IABS (k)
```

where *a*, the argument of the generic form, represents a real or integer constant, real or integer variable, or real or integer arithmetic expression, and *k*, the argument of the integer form, represents an integer constant, integer variable, or integer arithmetic expression. The use of the generic function ABS will return either a real value if the argument is real or an integer value if the argument is integer.

If A = −25.Ø, the following is an example of how an absolute function might be used:

```
B=SQRT (ABS (A) )
```

Note the use of nested functions in this example, a practice that is often advantageous. In the above example, the negative sign of A is disregarded and only the absolute value of A (25.Ø) is used as the argument of the SQRT function. The value assigned to B is 5.Ø. A second example is:

```
NUM=IABS(6-1Ø)
```

The value assigned to NUM is 4, the absolute value of the argument. The generic ABS function could also have been used in this case.

5-4 TYPE-CONVERSION FUNCTIONS

The type of a constant, variable, or arithmetic expression can be changed temporarily by the appropriate *type-conversion function*. For example, a number may be converted from integer to real, from real to integer, from real to complex, from single precision to double precision, etc., through the use of the appropriate type-conversion function. This function has many general forms. Two common forms that change a type-real argument to type integer are the generic form, which accepts all types of arguments (either real or integer):

INT(*a*)

and the real-argument form

IFIX(*a*)

where *a,* the argument of the function, represents a real constant, real variable, or real arithmetic expression whose value is to be changed to type integer. Evaluation of either function truncates the decimal fraction and drops the decimal point, leaving an integer number for use in further calculations or assignment to a variable name. Two other forms of the type-conversion function that change integer arguments to type real are the generic form which accepts all types of arguments (either integer or real):

REAL(***k***)

and the real-argument form

FLOAT(***k***)

where *k,* the argument of the function, represents an integer constant, integer variable, or integer arithmetic expression whose value is to be changed to type real. Evaluation of this function adds a decimal point, creating a real number for use in further calculations or assignment to a variable name.

In either form, the type change is effective only for that specific evaluation in the type-conversion function. If the argument, without the function, is used elsewhere following its use in the type-conversion function, the default or declared type designation prevails.

Consider the following program segments used to extract the square root of an integer number:

(*a*)
```
N=25
AN=N
NRT=SQRT(AN)
```

(*b*)
```
N=25
NRT=SQRT(FLOAT(N))
```

In (*a*) the value assigned to N, the integer 25, is assigned to a real-variable name AN. The real variable AN, whose value is now 25.Ø, is used as the argument of the SQRT function which is evaluated at 5.Ø. The integer number 5 is assigned to NRT. In (*b*) the mode of integer N is changed to type real with the FLOAT function. This provides the SQRT function with a real argument. The result in both cases is the same; the SQRT function is evaluated as 5.Ø, and the integer number 5 is assigned to NRT. Note the nested functions in example (*b*), where the FLOAT function is the argument of the SQRT function. The FLOAT function could be replaced by the REAL function, with the same result.

If the value of N is both integer and negative, either of the following can be used to extract the square root:

(*a*)
```
N=-25
NRT=SQRT(FLOAT(IABS(N)))
```

(*b*)
```
N=-25
NRT=SQRT(ABS(FLOAT(N)))
```

Note the use of IABS in (*a*); the argument of the absolute function is integer. In (*b*) the argument of the absolute function is real (the type has been changed by the FLOAT function), so the real form of the absolute function, ABS, must be used.

The average of the sum of N real values is calculated by dividing the sum by N, or AVE=SUM/N. A counting routine utilizing integer variables in the statements N=Ø and N=N+1 might be used to tally the number of values included in the sum. To avoid mixed-mode division (dividing by integer N), either of the following procedures can be used:

(*a*)
```
AN=N
AVE=SUM/AN
```

(*b*)
```
AVE=SUM/FLOAT(N)
```

The real value (the average) assigned to AVE is the same in either case, but procedure (*b*), using the type-conversion function, is shorter by one statement. Note that the sequence shown in (*a*) was used in Fig. 4-16. Again, the REAL function could be used instead of the FLOAT function.

The IFIX function is used in a similar manner. The variable A in the following example represents a real value, the integer part of which is to be subtracted from an integer variable N:

```
I=A
J=N-I
```

The first statement truncates the real value assigned to A and assigns the remaining integer number to I; the second statement subtracts the integer value assigned to I from the integer value N and assigns the difference to J. The use of the IFIX function, however, requires only one statement, such as:

```
J=N-IFIX(A)
```

The IFIX function could be replaced by the INT function, with the same result. Two other functions, the CMPLX and DBLE functions, are also classified as type-conversion functions. These and related functions are explained in Secs. 5-12 and 5-13.

5-5 EXPONENTIAL FUNCTION

In scientific calculations Euler's[†] number *e*, a constant equal to 2.718281..., appears repeatedly. Exponentiating *e* (raising *e* to a power) is so common that a function called the *exponential function* has been written to perform this calculation. The general form for the exponential function is:

```
EXP(a)
```

where *a*, the argument of the function, is a real constant, real variable, or real arithmetic expression. Evaluating the exponential function is the same as raising *e* to the *a* power or 2.718282^a.

Compare the following examples:

```
(a)  E=2.718282        (b) EX=EXP(Ø.25)
     EX=E**Ø.25
```

In both these examples the same value, $1.284Ø25 = 2.718282^{0.25}$, is assigned to EX. In (*b*) the use of the exponential function EXP avoids the requirement to define the value of the constant *e*, uses one less statement to accomplish the same result, and also eliminates the possibility of programmer error in assigning the value of the constant *e*.

5-6 LOGARITHMIC FUNCTIONS

Two logarithm systems are in general use, the *common* (base 1Ø) *system* and the *natural* (base *e*) *system* (*e* = 2.718281...). Four logarithmic functions are available to calculate the logarithms of real numbers. The generic form for the common or base 1Ø logarithm function is:

```
LOG1Ø(a)
```

but the form:

```
ALOG1Ø(a)
```

[†]After Leonard Euler (1707–1783), the Swiss mathematician who introduced this constant.

may also be used. The argument of both functions, *a*, is a real constant, real variable, or real arithmetic expression.

The generic form for the natural or base *e* logarithmic function is:

```
LOG(a)
```

but the form:

```
ALOG(a)
```

may also be used. The argument of both functions, *a*, is a real constant, real variable, or real arithmetic expression. LOG1Ø(*a*) and ALOG1Ø(*a*) are equivalent to the mathematical expression log *a* and evaluate the common logarithm of *a*. LOG(*a*) and ALOG(*a*) are equivalent to ln *a* and evaluate the natural logarithm of *a*.

Note the following examples:

```
(a) A=LOG1Ø(2.Ø)
```

The value assigned to A is Ø.3Ø1Ø3ØØ, the common logarithm of 2.

```
(b) B=LOG(2.Ø)
```

The value assigned to B is Ø.6931471, the natural logarithm of 2.

```
(c) CUBRT=EXP(LOG(125.Ø)/3.Ø)
```

The value assigned to CUBRT is 5.Ø, the cube root of 125.Ø. In each of the above examples, the ALOG or ALOG1Ø function could have been used, instead of LOG and LOG1Ø, respectively.

In example (*c*), the natural logarithm of 125.Ø was divided by 3.Ø, then used as a power of *e*, which takes the antilogarithm and assigns the resulting value to the name CUBRT. This is equivalent to evaluating the mathematical expression, $(2.718282)^{\ln 125.0/3.0}$. The intrinsic functions do not include a cube root function, but the FORTRAN expression illustrated above can be used effectively to find the cube root of a given real constant, variable, or arithmetic expression. Any other root can also be determined by appropriately changing the divisor in the expression.

5-7 TRIGONOMETRIC FUNCTIONS

The *sine, cosine,* or *tangent* of an angle can be evaluated using the appropriate *trigonometric function*. The general forms for the trigonometric functions are:

```
SIN(a)      COS(a)      TAN(a)
```

where SIN, COS, and TAN are the respective trigonometric functions sine,

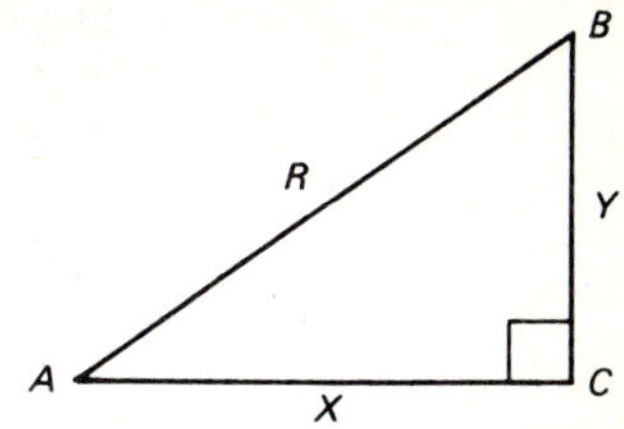

$$\sin A = \frac{Y}{R}, \quad \cos A = \frac{X}{R}, \quad \tan A = \frac{Y}{X}$$

$$A = \arcsin\frac{Y}{R} = \arccos\frac{X}{R} = \arctan\frac{Y}{X}$$

$$\sin B = \frac{X}{R}, \quad \cos B = \frac{Y}{R}, \quad \tan B = \frac{X}{Y}$$

$$B = \arcsin\frac{X}{R} = \arccos\frac{Y}{R} = \arctan\frac{X}{Y}$$

$$C = 90^\circ = \frac{\pi}{2}\ \text{radians}$$

$$A + B + C = 180^\circ = \pi\ \text{radians}$$

FIGURE 5-1 Right-triangle relationships.

cosine, and tangent, as shown in Fig. 5-1, and *a,* the argument of the function, represents a real constant, real variable, or real arithmetic expression. The argument of a trigonometric function, *a,* represents the magnitude of an angle and must be expressed in radians. Most instruments used for measuring plane angles are calibrated in degrees and fractions of a degree. Numerical values representing degree units must be converted to radians in an appropriate assignment statement before being used as the argument of a trigonometric function, or the conversion to radians must be made in an arithmetic expression as part of the argument.

Consider the following examples of the use of the trigonometric functions in sequential statements with a given angle A of 3Ø°:

```
ADEG=3Ø.Ø
ARAD=ADEG*3.141593/18Ø.Ø
SINA=SIN(ARAD)
```

Here an angular value of 3Ø° is assigned to ADEG. The degree value 3Ø° is converted to radians and Ø.5235988 is assigned to ARAD. Then the SIN function is evaluated, and Ø.5ØØØØØØ is assigned to SINA. The last two statements can be combined as:

```
SINA=SIN(ADEG*3.141593/18Ø.Ø)
```

Here conversion from degrees to radians is part of the argument of the function, and again Ø.5ØØØØØØ is assigned to SINA.

The trigonometric relationships (*identities*) in Table 5-1 are expressed mathematically and as a FORTRAN assignment statement. Assuming the value of *a* to

TABLE 5-1 TRIGONOMETRIC RELATIONS

Example mathematical expression	FORTRAN assignment statement
(a) $\sin a = \cos(9\emptyset° - a)$	SINA=COS(1.570796-ARAD)
(b) $\sin 2a = \sin 2a$	SIN2A=SIN(2.0*ARAD)
$= 2 \sin a \cos a$	SIN2A=2.0*SIN(ARAD)*COS(ARAD)
(c) $\sin^2 a = (\sin a)^2$	SINSQA=SIN(ARAD)**2
$= \frac{1}{2}(1 - \cos 2a)$	SINSQA=0.5*(1.0-COS(2.0*ARAD))
(d) $\tan a = \dfrac{\sin a}{\cos a}$	TANA=SIN(ARAD)/COS(ARAD)

FIGURE 5-2 Mathematical quadrants and the functions of angles in them.

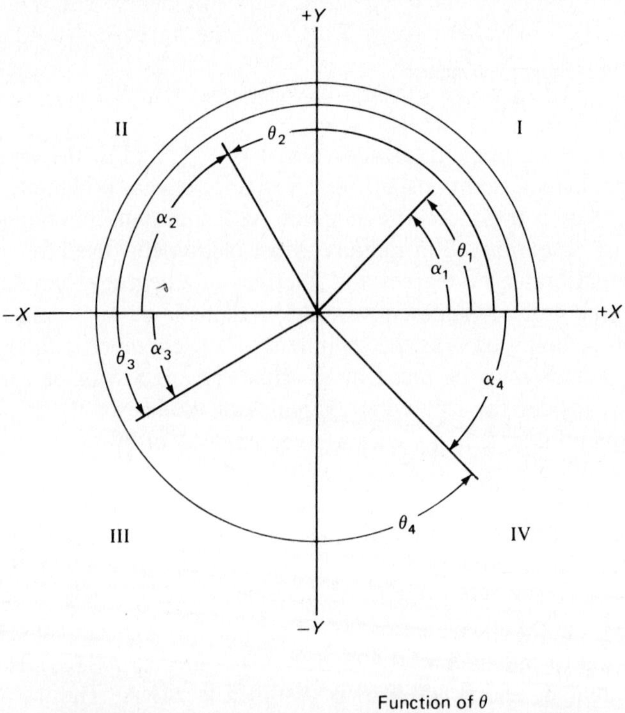

Quadrant	θ	$\sin\theta$	$\cos\theta$	$\tan\theta$
		Function of θ		
I	$\theta_1 = \alpha_1$	$\sin\alpha_1$	$\cos\alpha_1$	$\tan\alpha_1$
II	$\theta_2 = 18\emptyset - \alpha_2$	$\sin\alpha_2$	$-\cos\alpha_2$	$-\tan\alpha_2$
III	$\theta_3 = 18\emptyset + \alpha_3$	$-\sin\alpha_3$	$-\cos\alpha_3$	$\tan\alpha_3$
IV	$\theta_4 = 36\emptyset - \alpha_4$	$-\sin\alpha_4$	$\cos\alpha_4$	$-\tan\alpha_4$

be 3Ø° in example (*a*), Ø.5ØØØØØØ is assigned to SINA. Note that 9Ø° = 1.57Ø796 radians and must be so expressed in the argument of the function. Example (*b*) can be written two ways. Either way, the sine of twice the given angle, Ø.866Ø254, is assigned to SIN2A. In example (*c*) the sine of the given angle is squared and Ø.25ØØØØØ is assigned to SINSQA. In example (*d*) the sine of 3Ø°, Ø.5ØØØØØØ, is divided by the cosine of 3Ø°, Ø.866Ø254, and the quotient Ø.57735Ø3—the tangent of 3Ø°—is assigned to TANA.

Note that the variable names ADEG, ARAD, SINA, SIN2A, SINSQA, and TANA used in the examples in Table 5-1 are suggestive of the values assigned to them. However, they are not function names and should not be so construed. The only function names used are SIN and COS.

Often angles greater than 9Ø° must be used. Mathematicians divide two-dimensional space (the X-Y plane) into four quadrants, numbered counterclockwise, as shown in Fig. 5-2. All positive angles are then measured counterclockwise from the positive X axis as shown. The angle used to determine the value and algebraic sign of the sine, cosine, and tangent of any positive angle is shown in the table in Fig. 5-2. Note that in each quadrant the acute angle is used to determine the value of the function. Figure 5-3 shows how the algebraic signs of the functions of the acute angles in Fig. 5-2 are established. It should be observed that the sign of R is positive in each quadrant since $R = X^2 + Y^2$.

FIGURE 5-3 Proof of the signs of the sine, cosine, and tangent in each quadrant.

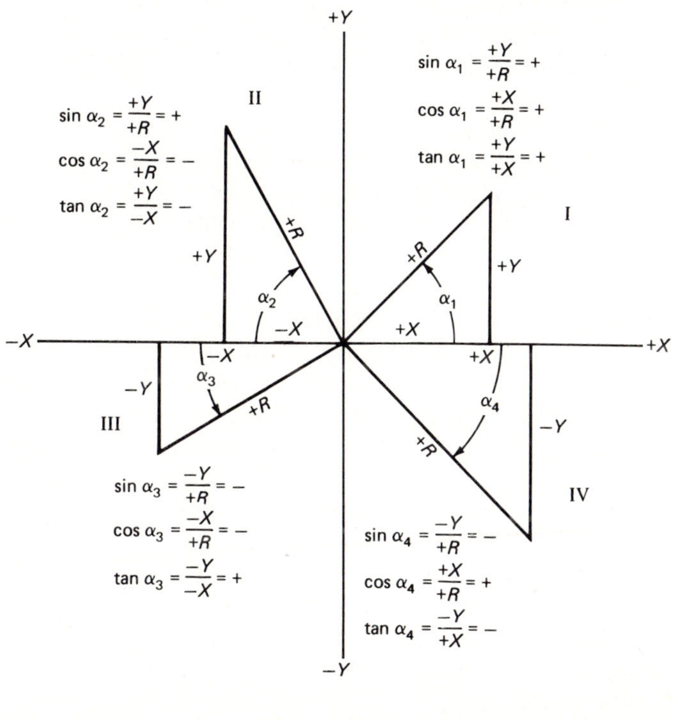

Figure 5-4 is a listing of a program calculating the values of the SIN, COS, and TAN functions in each of the four quadrants. The sine, cosine, and tangent of 15Ø, 21Ø, and 33Ø° have the same absolute numerical values as does 3Ø°, the first-quadrant angle. The algebraic signs of the functions are appropriate to the quadrant of each angle. The slight variances in the function values of the four angles are due to differences in how different values are stored, but when the function values are rounded to five-place precision, the result is the same value as found in standard trigonometric tables.

5-8 INVERSE TRIGONOMETRIC FUNCTIONS

Determining the inverse function (arcsine, arccosine, or arctangent), i.e., calculating the magnitude of the angle when the sine, cosine, or tangent of the angle is known, is a common trigonometric operation. The general forms for the functions for evaluating the *inverse trigonometric functions* are:

```
ASIN(s)      ACOS(cs)      ATAN(t)
```

where ASIN, ACOS, and ATAN identify the inverse trigonometric functions shown in Fig. 5-1 and the arguments *s*, *cs*, and *t* represent, respectively, the numerical value of the sine, cosine, and tangent of a given angle. The resulting value of these intrinsic functions is in each case returned in radians; for example:

```
(a)   ARAD=ASIN(Y/R)    or    ADEG=ASIN(Y/R)*18Ø.Ø/3.141593
(b)   ARAD=ACOS(X/R)    or    ADEG=ACOS(X/R)*18Ø.Ø/3.141593
(c)   ARAD=ATAN(Y/X)    or    ADEG=ATAN(Y/X)*18Ø.Ø/3.141593
```

where X, Y, and R are defined in Fig. 5-1. The values assigned to ARAD are in radians. The values assigned to ADEG have been converted to degrees.

When the values of the angles determined by the ASIN, ACOS, and ATAN functions are greater than 9Ø°, the results can be bewildering unless the decision processes employed by the compiler for evaluating these functions are understood. Figure 5-5 demonstrates the effect of these decisions. Figures 5-2 and 5-3 show that the sine of angles in the first and second quadrants is positive. There is no provision in the function for identifying the quadrant by algebraic sign. Since both sines are positive, the compiler is programmed to select the first-quadrant (acute) value of the angle when the value of sine is positive. The sixth line in Fig. 5-5 sets the value of S1 at + Ø.5ØØØØ, which could be the sine of either 3Ø° or 15Ø°. The ASIN(S1)—converted and rounded to the nearest degree, and printed by the WRITE statement on the sixteenth line—shows the value of the angle to be 3Ø°, as discussed above. (The angle is rounded to an integer value for simplicity in this and the succeeding discussion.) If the second-quadrant angle (15Ø°) is desired, additional programming following the ASIN function is required.

Figures 5-2 and 5-3 show that the sine of angles in both the third and fourth quadrants is negative. In this case, the compiler is programmed to select the fourth-quadrant (acute) value of the angle α_4. The eighth line in Fig. 5-5 sets the

```
C234567890
      OPEN(5,FILE='PRN')
      WRITE(5,*)'        ALL ANGLES ARE IN DEGREES'
      N=1
C   ANGLE IN FIRST QUADRANT
      A=30.0
      ANGLE=A
   10 ARAD=ANGLE*3.141593/180.0
      B=SIN(ARAD)
      C=COS(ARAD)
      D=TAN(ARAD)
      WRITE(5,*)
      WRITE(5,*)'      THIS ANGLE IS IN QUADRANT',N
      WRITE(5,*)'          ANGLE      SINE',
     $'           COSINE          TANGENT'
      I=ANGLE+0.5
      WRITE(5,*)I,B,C,D
      WRITE(5,*)
      GOTO(20,30,40,50)N
C   CHANGE ANGLE TO SECOND QUADRANT
   20 ANGLE=180.0-A
      N=N+1
      GOTO 10
C   CHANGE ANGLE TO THIRD QUADRANT
   30 ANGLE=180.0+A
      N=N+1
      GOTO 10
C   CHANGE ANGLE TO FOURTH QUADRANT
   40 ANGLE=360.0-A
      N=N+1
      GOTO 10
   50 STOP
      END
```

```
  ALL ANGLES ARE IN DEGREES

 THIS ANGLE IS IN QUADRANT              1
     ANGLE      SINE           COSINE          TANGENT
       30  5.000001E-001  8.660254E-001  5.773504E-001

 THIS ANGLE IS IN QUADRANT              2
     ANGLE      SINE           COSINE          TANGENT
      150  4.999998E-001 -8.660255E-001 -5.773500E-001

 THIS ANGLE IS IN QUADRANT              3
     ANGLE      SINE           COSINE          TANGENT
      210 -5.000004E-001 -8.660251E-001  5.773509E-001

 THIS ANGLE IS IN QUADRANT              4
     ANGLE      SINE           COSINE          TANGENT
      330 -4.999993E-001  8.660258E-001 -5.773492E-001
```

FIGURE 5-4 Values of the functions of angles from Ø to 36Ø°.

value of S2 as $-$ Ø.5ØØØØ. The value of the angle printed by the statement on the sixteenth line shows the value $-3Ø°$. Note that $36Ø° - \alpha$ and $-\alpha$ are the same angle. If the third-quadrant angle (21Ø°) is desired, additional programming following the ASIN function is required.

```
C234567890
      OPEN(6,FILE='PRN')
      WRITE(6,*)'ALL ANGLE VALUES TO NEAREST DEGREE'
      WRITE(6,*)
C  THIS ANGLE SHOULD BE 30 DEGREES
      S1=0.5000000
C  THIS ANGLE SHOULD BE -30 (330) DEGREES
      S2=-0.5000000
      WRITE(6,*)'       ANGLES FROM ASIN FUNCTION'
      WRITE(6,*)'         POSITIVE      NEGATIVE'
      WRITE(6,*)'           SINE          SINE'
      A=ASIN(S1)*180.0/3.141593
      B=ASIN(S2)*180.0/3.141593
      I=A+0.5
      J=B-0.5
      WRITE(6,*)I,J
      WRITE(6,*)
C  THIS ANGLE SHOULD BE 30 DEGREES
      C1=0.86603
C  THIS ANGLE SHOULD BE 150 DEGREES
      C2=-0.86603
      WRITE(6,*)'       ANGLES FROM ACOS FUNCTION'
      WRITE(6,*)'         POSITIVE      NEGATIVE'
      WRITE(6,*)'          COSINE        COSINE'
      C=ACOS(C1)*180.0/3.141593
      D=ACOS(C2)*180.0/3.141593
      K=C+0.5
      L=D+0.5
      WRITE(6,*)K,L
      WRITE(6,*)
C  THIS ANGLE SHOULD BE 30 DEGREES
      T1=0.57735
C  THIS ANGLE SHOULD BE -30 (330) DEGREES
      T2=-0.57735
      WRITE(6,*)'       ANGLES FROM ATAN FUNCTION'
      WRITE(6,*)'         POSITIVE      NEGATIVE'
      WRITE(6,*)'          TANGENT       TANGENT'
      E=ATAN(T1)*180.0/3.141593
      F=ATAN(T2)*180.0/3.141593
      M=E+0.5
      N=F-0.5
      WRITE(6,*)M,N
      STOP
      END
```

```
 ALL ANGLE VALUES TO NEAREST DEGREE

        ANGLES FROM ASIN FUNCTION
          POSITIVE      NEGATIVE
            SINE          SINE
             30           -30

        ANGLES FROM ACOS FUNCTION
          POSITIVE      NEGATIVE
           COSINE        COSINE
             30           150

        ANGLES FROM ATAN FUNCTION
          POSITIVE      NEGATIVE
           TANGENT       TANGENT
             30           -30
```

FIGURE 5-5 Values of angles determined by ASIN, ACOS, and ATAN functions.

Figures 5-2 and 5-3 also show that angles in the first and fourth quadrants have positive cosines, and angles in the second and third quadrants have negative cosines. The ACOS function returns the value of the first-quadrant angle when the cosine is negative. Figure 5-5 assigns positive and negative values, respectively, to C1 and C2. When the corresponding angles are determined by the ACOS functions and displayed, the values are 3Ø° and 15Ø°, respectively. If the fourth-quadrant angle (33Ø° when the cosine is positive) or third-quadrant angle (21Ø° when the cosine is negative) is desired, additional programming following the ACOS function is required.

In addition, Figs. 5-2 and 5-3 show that angles in the first and third quadrants have positive tangents, and angles in the second and fourth quadrants have negative tangents. The ATAN function returns the value of the first-quadrant angle if the tangent is positive, and the fourth-quadrant angle if the tangent is negative. Figure 5-5 assigns positive and negative values to T1 and T2. When the corresponding angles are determined by the ATAN functions and printed, the values are 3Ø° and −3Ø°, respectively, as shown. If the third-quadrant angle (21Ø° when the tangent is positive) or fourth-quadrant angle (33Ø° when the tangent is negative) is desired, additional programming following the ATAN function is required.

In summary, the range of angular values for the ASIN and ATAN functions is $\pm\pi/2$ rad (± 9Ø°). The range of angular values for the ACOS function is from Ø to π radians (Ø to 18Ø°). Note that in no case is the third-quadrant angle selected. The compiler does not relate the inverse trigonometric function to the quadrant because there is only one radian value associated with a given signed argument for each of the inverse trigonometric functions. The programmer must be aware of the angle values returned by these three functions when the algebraic sign is either positive or negative.

If the sides (*X* and *Y* values) of the angle (Fig. 5-1) are known, another function can be used to determine the size of an angle. In general form the function is:

```
ATAN2(opp, adj)
```

where *opp* represents the signed value of the side opposite the angle (*Y* side) and *adj* represents the signed value of the side adjacent to the angle (*X* side), as in Fig. 5-1 for the value of acute angle *BAC*. Because there are two signed arguments, this function can determine the proper quadrant of the angle. The result is expressed in radians between Ø and $\pm\ \pi$ radians. The angle can be expressed in degrees between Ø and 36Ø° by converting the resulting radian value to degrees and adding 36Ø° to all negative values (angles in the third or fourth quadrants) as follows:

```
ANGLE=ATAN2(Y,X)*18Ø.Ø/3.141593
IF(ANGLE.LT.Ø.Ø)ANGLE=36Ø.Ø+ANGLE
```

The effect of these two statements is shown in Fig. 5-6, where values for angles in all four quadrants are computed and expressed in degrees between Ø and 36Ø°.

```
C   THESE ARE THE SIDE VALUES FOR 60 DEGREES
C   WHERE A IS THE Y SIDE AND B IS THE X SIDE
C234567890
      OPEN(7,FILE='PRN')
      A=1.000000
      B=0.57735
      N=1
   10 ANGLE=ATAN2(A,B)*180.0/3.141593
      IF(ANGLE.LT.0.0)ANGLE=360.0+ANGLE
      I=ANGLE+0.5
      WRITE(7,*)'THIS ANGLE IS IN QUADRANT',N
      WRITE(7,*)'AND THE ANGLE =',I,' DEGREES'
      WRITE(7,*)
      GO TO(20,30,40,50)N
C   CONVERTS TO SECOND QUADRANT (180-60)
   20 B=-B
      N=2
      GO TO 10
C   CONVERTS TO THIRD QUADRANT (180+60)
   30 A=-A
      N=3
      GO TO 10
C   CONVERTS TO FOURTH QUADRANT (360-60)
   40 B=-B
      N=4
      GO TO 10
   50 STOP
      END
```

```
THIS ANGLE IS IN QUADRANT                 1
AND THE ANGLE =             60 DEGREES

THIS ANGLE IS IN QUADRANT                 2
AND THE ANGLE =            120 DEGREES

THIS ANGLE IS IN QUADRANT                 3
AND THE ANGLE =            240 DEGREES

THIS ANGLE IS IN QUADRANT                 4
AND THE ANGLE =            300 DEGREES
```

FIGURE 5-6 Values of angles determined by the ATAN2 function.

Surveying and mapping problems in civil engineering usually employ a coordinate reference system with a north–south meridian corresponding to the *Y-Y* axis and an east–west parallel corresponding to the *X-X* axis (Fig. 5-7). Angular measurements, called azimuths, are customarily measured clockwise starting from north (the *Y-Y* axis) from Ø to 36Ø°, as illustrated in Fig. 5-7. Note that the functions of azimuth angles as shown in Fig. 5-7 are identical to the functions of angles as shown in Fig. 5-2. Therefore, azimuth angles can be determined by the ATAN2 function by considering the argument *opp* to be the *X* side and the argument *adj* to be the *Y* side, as shown in Fig. 5-8. Compare the results of Fig. 5-8 with those of Fig. 5-6 and note the results of interchanging the values of the arguments *opp* and *adj*.

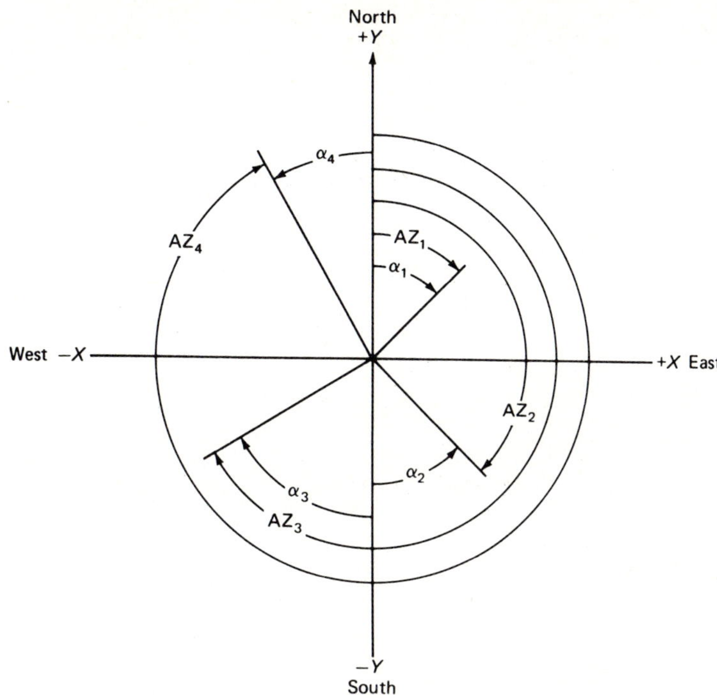

Function of azimuth

Azimuth	sin	cos	tan
$AZ_1 = \alpha_1$	$\sin \alpha_1$	$\cos \alpha_1$	$\tan \alpha_1$
$AZ_2 = 18\emptyset - \alpha_2$	$\sin \alpha_2$	$-\cos \alpha_2$	$-\tan \alpha_2$
$AZ_3 = 18\emptyset + \alpha_3$	$-\sin \alpha_3$	$-\cos \alpha_3$	$\tan \alpha_3$
$AZ_4 = 36\emptyset - \alpha_4$	$-\sin \alpha_4$	$\cos \alpha_4$	$-\tan \alpha_4$

FIGURE 5-7 Azimuth angles and their functions.

5-9 MAXIMUM-MINIMUM FUNCTIONS

A variety of intrinsic functions are available for determining the maximum or minimum value within a sequence of values. For instance, a single function can determine the largest or smallest value in a sequence such as 4.6, −5.6, 12.Ø, −7.8, etc. For all of these functions, which may handle either positive or negative numbers, the range from minimum to maximum values extends from minus infinity to plus infinity, respectively, as will be illustrated.

The generic form for determining the maximum value from among two or more values is:

MAX (*x*, *y*, *z*, . . .)

```
C   THESE ARE THE SIDE VALUES FOR AN AZIMUTH OF
C   30 DEGREES, WHERE A IS THE X SIDE AND B IS
C   THE Y SIDE
C234567890
      OPEN(8,FILE='PRN')
      A=0.57735
      B=1.00000
      N=1
   10 ANGLE=ATAN2(A,B)*180.0/3.141593
      IF(ANGLE.LT.0.0)ANGLE=360.0+ANGLE
      WRITE(8,*)'THE AZIMUTH =',ANGLE,' DEGREES'
      WRITE(8,*)
      GO TO(20,30,40,50)N
   20 B=-B
      N=2
      GO TO 10
   30 A=-A
      N=3
      GO TO 10
   40 B=-B
      N=4
      GO TO 10
   50 STOP
      END
```

```
THE AZIMUTH =          29.9999900 DEGREES

THE AZIMUTH =         150.0000000 DEGREES

THE AZIMUTH =         210.0000000 DEGREES

THE AZIMUTH =         330.0000000 DEGREES
```

FIGURE 5-8 Values of azimuth angles determined by the ATAN2 function.

x, y, z, etc., may be either all real or all integer constants, variables, arithmetic expressions, or any combination of these, as long as types are not mixed. This function returns a real maximum value if the arguments are real and an integer maximum value if the arguments are integer. In addition, there are four general forms for determining the maximum value from among two or more values:

MAXØ (*i*, *j*, *k*, . . .)

which determines the maximum value from among a group of integers and returns an integer value,

MAX1 (*a*, *b*, *c*, . . .)

which determines the maximum value from among a group of real values and returns an integer value (the truncated value of the real-mode maximum),

AMAXØ (*i*, *j*, *k*, . . .)

which determines the maximum value from among a group of integer values and returns a real value (the integer maximum value with a decimal point added), and:

AMAX1 (*a*, *b*, *c*, . . .)

which determines the maximum value from among a group of real values and returns a real value. The arguments of these functions may consist of constants, variables, arithmetic expressions, or any combination of these forms. Care must be taken to ensure that all arguments of the MAXØ and AMAXØ functions are integer and that all arguments of the MAX1 and AMAX1 functions are real. Some examples of the use of the maximum functions are:

```
I=MAXØ(23,-34,16)
J=MAXØ(-15,-67,-3,-45)
K=MAX1(3.4,-5.6,27.3)
A=AMAXØ(-15,-23,-5)
B=AMAX1(-3.Ø,17.8)
C=AMAX1(-34.6,-67.2,-Ø.74E+Ø3,-4.6)
```

where the value assigned to I is 23, to J is −3, to K is 27, to A is −5., to B is 17.8, and to C is −4.6. Two more complicated examples are:

```
K=MAXØ(I,J,INT(A),I-J,67,IABS(J-I),IFIX(B))
```

and:

```
C=AMAX1(-4.Ø,A-3.2,ABS(FLOAT(J-I))**2)
```

where values must be assigned to the variables I, J, A, and B before these two statements can be executed.

The generic form for determining the minimum value from among two or more values is:

MIN(*x*, *y*, *z*, . . .)

x, *y*, *z*, etc., may be either all real or all integer constants, variables, arithmetic expressions, or any combination of these, as long as types are not mixed. This function returns a real minimum value if the arguments are real or an integer minimum value if the arguments are integer. In addition, there are four general forms for determining the minimum value from among two or more values:

MINØ(*i*, *j*, *k*, . . .)

which determines the minimum value from among a group of integers and returns an integer value,

MIN1(*a*, *b*, *c*, . . .)

which determines the minimum value from among a group of real values and returns an integer value (the truncated value of the real minimum),

AMINØ (*i*, *j*, *k*, . . .)

which determines the minimum value from among a group of integer values and returns a real value (the integer minimum value with a decimal point added), and:

AMIN1 (*a*, *b*, *c*, . . .)

which determines the minimum value from among a group of real values and returns a real value. The arguments may consist of constants, variables, arithmetic expressions, or combinations of these forms, just as for the functions used to calculate the maximum value from among a group of values. Care must be taken to ensure that all arguments of the MINØ and AMINØ functions are integer and that all arguments of the MIN1 and AMIN1 functions are real. Some examples of the use of the minimum functions are:

```
II=MINØ(23,-34,16)
JJ=MINØ(-15,-67,-3,-45)
KK=MIN1(3.4,-5.6,27.3)
AA=AMINØ(-15,-23,-5)
BB=AMIN1(-3.Ø,17.8)
CC=AMIN1(-34.6,-67.2,-Ø.74E+Ø3,-4.6)
```

where the value assigned to II is −34, to JJ is −67, to KK is −5, to AA is −23., to BB is −3. and to CC is −74Ø.

5-10 TRUNCATION AND ROUNDING FUNCTIONS

The *truncation function* does exactly what its name implies. The value of the argument is truncated (the decimal point and the decimal fraction are dropped, leaving a type-integer number). This function has the generic form:

AINT (*a*)

where *a* is a real constant, real variable, or real arithmetic expression. This function truncates *a* to an integer value but returns the answer as type real. Some examples of truncation function usage are:

```
A=AINT(15.6)
```

and:

```
B=AINT(-4.8+1.6)
```

where the values assigned to A and B are, respectively, 15.Ø and −3.Ø.

Two generic functions are available for *rounding* values. They are:

ANINT (*a*)

and:

```
NINT(a)
```

where *a* is a real constant, real variable, or real arithmetic expression. Both round a real value to the nearest whole number, but ANINT returns a real value while NINT returns an integer value. Some examples of the use of these rounding functions are:

```
D=ANINT(-3.5)
E=ANINT(9.7)
J=NINT(4.5-2.1)
```

The values assigned to D, E, and J are −3.Ø, 1Ø.Ø, and 2, respectively.

5-11 REMAINDERING (OR MODULO) FUNCTIONS

It is often necessary to determine the remainder when one number, N, is divided by another, M. This mathematical operation is referred to as N *modulo* M. The generic form for determining the remainder of either real or integer arguments is:

```
MOD(i,j)
```

When used with integer arguments, this is equivalent to the arithmetic expression:

```
I-INT(I/J)*J
```

When used with real-mode arguments, the MOD function performs the same function as:

```
AMOD(a, b)
```

which is equivalent to the arithmetic expression:

```
A-AINT(A/B)*B
```

and applicable only when the arguments are real numbers. In both cases, the arguments may be constants, variables, arithmetic expressions, or combinations of these forms. The programmer must exercise caution to ensure that the correct argument type is used. Several examples of modulo-function usage are:

```
I=MOD(63,6)
J=MOD(-18,4)
K=MOD(7**2,5-2)
A=AMOD(2.4,1.3)
B=AMOD(2.4,-1.3)
C=AMOD(3.6*SQRT(3.Ø**3),-6.7+2.3)
```

where the values assigned to I, J, K, A, B, and C are respectively, 3, −2, 1, 1.1, 1.1, 1.1Ø615Ø. Since the beginning programmer may see little use for such a function, an example may help. Consider a case where it must be determined whether a series of numbers in a data file are evenly divisible by 7. The program segment to determine this might appear as:

```
1Ø READ(*,*)M
   K=MOD(M,7)
   IF(K.EQ.Ø) WRITE(*,*) 'THE NUMBER',M,'IS EVENLY
  $DIVISIBLE BY 7.'
   GOTO 1Ø
```

This type of operation may be useful when writing a program to find all prime numbers (numbers evenly divisible only by 1 and itself) between 1 and a certain upper limit.

5-12 FUNCTIONS FOR USE IN COMPLEX ARITHMETIC

Although the use of complex variables is not discussed until Chap. 10, several functions used in complex arithmetic are described below.

a The Complex Function

The *complex function* converts an ordered pair of real numbers to a complex number, which consists of both real and imaginary parts. A general form for this function is:

CMPLX(*x*, *y*)

where *x* and *y* may be constants, variables, arithmetic expressions, or any combination of the these forms. The type of *x* and *y* may be real, integer, single- or double-precision (Sec. 3-3 and Chap. 11), but both arguments must be of the same type. In this general form the value of the argument *x* becomes the real part of the complex number and the value of *y* becomes the imaginary part.

Another general form for this function is:

CMPLX(*x*)

where, as for the first general form, *x* may be a constant, a variable, or an arithmetic expression of real, integer, or single- or double-precision type. In this case, the value of *x* becomes the real part of the complex number and the imaginary part is Ø. For both forms, the resulting complex number is type real.

Examples of the complex function are:

CMPLX(1.2,3.4)	which implies 1.2+3.4*j*
CMPLX(3,4)	which implies 3.Ø+4.Ø*j*

```
CMPLX(1.2+5.6,7.5-13.1)     which implies 6.8-5.6j
CMPLX(3.6)                  which implies 3.6+Ø.Øj
CMPLX(4)                    which implies 4.Ø+Ø.Øj
```

b The Real Part of a Complex-Number Function

In complex arithmetic, it is often desirable to separate the real part of a complex number from the imaginary part. An intrinsic function is available to assign the real part of a complex number to a separate variable. The general form for this function (also explained in Sec. 5-4, but for a different use) is:

```
REAL(z)
```

where z is a complex variable having both real and imaginary parts. This function returns a number x, corresponding to the real part of $z = x + yj$. An example program segment, in Sec. 5-12*c* will indicate its use.

c The Imaginary Part of a Complex-Number Function

An intrinsic function is also available to separate the imaginary part from the real part of a complex number. This function reduces the imaginary part of a complex number to a simple real number. The general form for this function is:

```
AIMAG(z)
```

where z is a complex variable. This function returns a number y, corresponding to the coefficient of j of the complex number $x + yj$. The program segment below illustrates the use of these functions.

```
A=3.5
B=7.8
C=CMPLX(A,B)
D=REAL(C)
E=AIMAG(C)
```

The value assigned to C is the complex number $3.5 + 7.8j$, the value assigned to D is 3.5, and the value assigned to E is +7.8.

d The Complex-Conjugate Function

This function develops the complex conjugate of its argument by changing the sign of the imaginary part. The general form for the function is:

```
CONJG(z)
```

where z is a complex number. If the following values are assumed:

```
A=3.5
B=7.8
C=CMPLX(A,B)
F=CONJG(C)
```

The value assigned to C is the complex number $3.5 + 7.8j$. The complex conjugate, $3.5 - 7.8j$, will be assigned to F. No attempt should be made to use the functions applicable in complex arithmetic until Sec. 10-10 has been studied.

5-13 DOUBLE-PRECISION FUNCTIONS

As will be discussed in Chap. 11, an improvement in arithmetic accuracy may be possible through the use of more significant digits for each value used in arithmetic calculations. This programming technique requires the use of double-precision constants, variables, and functions having approximately double the number of significant digits as compared to single-precision constants. Most of the functions mentioned in this chapter have a corresponding function which must be used in double-precision calculations. Table 5-2 lists those functions explained in this chapter that are applicable for single-precision calculations. Table 11-1 lists the corresponding double-precision functions.

One other type-conversion function applicable to double-precision calculations only is the double-precision function, having the general form:

DBLE (*x*)

where *x* may be a real or integer constant, a real or integer variable, or a real or integer arithmetic expression. The purpose of this function is to convert the storage of the argument value from one WORD to two WORDs. More on this topic and the DBLE function will be given in Chap. 11, Computer Accuracy, which should be studied before attempting to use the functions associated with double-precision calculations.

PROBLEMS

5-1 Compute the square and cube roots of N. Start with $N = 2$ and end when $\sqrt{N} = 2\sqrt[3]{N}$. Increment N in steps of 2. Print the values of N and its two roots. Note that the two roots of N must be real values and therefore may not be exact.

5-2 Write a program that will read various values of X and compute and print the square root, common logarithm, and the exponential of X. Examine the library functions required and determine whether any limits must be placed on the values of X to avoid computational errors. Include appropriate headings. Test values for X that are less than 1, between 1 and 9, and between 1Ø and 99.

5-3 Prepare a flowchart and write a program to compute the diameter in feet of right circular cylinders with an altitude of 3.5Ø ft whose volume varies from 5Ø through 5ØØ gal in 5Ø-gal increments. Use an IF statement. Print appropriate column

TABLE 5-2 INTRINSIC FUNCTIONS PRESENTED IN CHAPTER 5

Definition	Single-precision function	Definition	Single-precision function
Square root	SQRT(*a*)	Maximum	MAX(*a,b,c,...*)
Absolute value	ABS(*a*)		MAX(*i,j,k,...*)
	ABS(*k*)		MAXØ(*i,j,k,...*)
	IABS(*k*)		MAX1(*a,b,c,...*)
Type conversion:			AMAXØ(*i,j,k,...*)
Change to integer	INT(*a*)		AMAX1(*a,b,c,...*)
	INT(*k*)	Minimum	MIN(*a,b,c,...*)
	IFIX(*a*)		MIN(*i,j,k,...*)
Change to real	REAL(*k*)		MINØ(*i,j,k,...*)
	REAL(*a*)		MIN1(*a,b,c,...*)
	FLOAT(*k*)		AMINØ(*i,j,k,...*)
Exponential	EXP(*a*)		AMIN1(*a,b,c,...*)
Logarithm:		Truncation	AINT(*a*)
Common	LOG1Ø(*a*)	Rounding:	
	ALOG1Ø(*a*)	To real	ANINT(*a*)
Natural	LOG(*a*)	To integer	NINT(*a*)
	ALOG(*a*)	Remainder	MOD(*a,b*)
Trigonometric:			MOD(*i,j*)
Sine	SIN(*a*)		AMOD(*a,b*)
Cosine	COS(*a*)	Complex:	
Tangent	TAN(*a*)	Convert to	CMPLX(*x,y*)
Arccosine	ASIN(*s*)		CMPLX(*x*)
Arctangent	ACOS(*cs*)	Isolate real part	REAL(*z*)
Arctangent	ATAN(*t*)	Isolate imaginary part	AIMAG(*z*)
	ATAN2(*y, x*)	Conjugate	CONJG(*z*)
		Double Precision, convert to	DBLE(*x*)

headings for the two columns, showing the volume (1 ft^3 = 7.481 gal) and the diameter. The output should also show the altitude.

5-4 The time of oscillation T in seconds of a pendulum whose length L is in inches can be determined from the formula:

$$T = \pi\sqrt{\frac{L}{g}}$$

where g is the gravitational acceleration in inches per second squared. Determine the time of oscillation for pendulums whose lengths vary from 4Ø to 1ØØ in, in increments of 1Ø in. Let g = 386.088 in/s^2. Include appropriate headings.

5-5 The maximum height in feet of a projectile fired at some angle above the horizontal is given by:

$$H = \frac{V^2 \sin^2 \alpha}{2g}$$

where V = initial velocity, ft/s
α = angle, rad
g = acceleration of gravity, ft/s^2

Read in the initial velocity and the angle (in degrees) and compute the maximum height. The program should be capable of handling any number of data. Select your own values. Include appropriate column headings.

5-6 Calculate and print a table showing the sine, cosine, and tangent of angles from Ø to 9Ø° in increments of 5°. Knowing the tangent of 9Ø° is infinity, program to avoid the computer error thus caused. Also note the results when printing with the list-directed WRITE statement. Include appropriate column headings.

5-7 Prepare a flowchart and write a program that will read values for rectangular coordinates X and Y, compute values for the corresponding polar coordinates R and A (in degrees), and print all four values under appropriate column headings. The program should handle any number of records and terminate after the last record. Use as test values:

X	Y
3.ØØ	4.ØØ
4.ØØ	3.ØØ
5.ØØ	8.66
14.14	14.14

5-8 Prepare a flowchart and write a program that will read values for polar coordinates R and A°, compute values for the corresponding rectangular coordinates X and Y, and print all four values under appropriate headings. The program should be able to handle any number of data and terminate after the data from the last record have been evaluated. Use as test data:

R	A°
5.ØØ	53.12
5.ØØ	36.88
1Ø.ØØ	3Ø.ØØ
2Ø.ØØ	45.ØØ
1Ø.ØØ	6Ø.ØØ

5-9 Prepare a flowchart and write a program that combines the requirements of Probs. 5-7 and 5-8. Two values will be read from each data record, a decision is then made as to whether they represent rectangular or polar coordinates, and then the appropriate coordinate conversion is made. How is the program to decide as to the form of the coordinate? Combine the data from Probs. 5-7 and 5-8.

5-10 The radius of a circle inscribed in a triangle is given by:

$$R = \frac{[S(S - a)(S - b)\ (S - c)]^{1/2}}{S}$$

where $S = \frac{1}{2}(a + b + c)$ and a, b, and c are the lengths of the sides of a triangle. Compute the radius of the inscribed circle after first testing to see whether the three sides do, in fact, form a triangle. Test the program with three sets of data, one of which does not form a triangle.

5-11 Revise Prob. 3-19 to compute the size of the three interior angles in degrees. Make sure the program can handle the angles formed by any three sides that may occur. Test the program with data for at least three triangles. Ensure that the selected sides do form a triangle. Remember that the cosine of 9Ø° is zero. Write the program to avoid division by zero. Is the sum of the three interior angles of each triangle equal to 18Ø°?

5-12 The value of e^x can be approximated by iteration of the formula:

$$e^x = 1 + \sum_{i=1}^{n} \frac{x^i}{i!}$$

Write the program so that the iteration will continue until the value of iteration n differs by less than Ø.ØØØØ5 from the value of iteration $n - 1$. Show the number of iterations required for each X and the value of e^x after iteration n. Select your own data.

5-13 The sine of X (expressed in radians) can be determined by using the infinite series:

$$\sin X = X - \frac{X^3}{3!} + \frac{X^5}{5!} - \frac{X^7}{7!} + \frac{X^9}{9!} - \cdots$$

Determine the sine of various values of X by summing the series until the last term is smaller than $1Ø^{-5}$. Terminate the program after the last data record has been read. Note the alternating signs of the terms. The program must provide for these signs.

5-14 The magnitude and direction of the resultant vector R of two vectors V_1 and V_2 can be computed:

$$R = \sqrt{V_1^2 + V_2^2 + 2V_1V_2 \cos \alpha}$$

$$\tan \theta = \frac{V_2 \sin \alpha}{V_1 + V_2 \cos \alpha}$$

where V_1, V_2 = magnitudes of two vectors
α = angle between V_1 and V_2
θ = angle between V_1 and R

(See Fig. 5-9.) Write a program that will read values of α, V_1, and V_2 and compute the corresponding values of R and θ for any number of pairs of vectors. The angles are to be expressed in degrees. All results should be given appropriate column headings. Terminate the program as desired.

5-15 Given the lengths of the four sides of a quadrilateral and the acute angle (from Ø to 9Ø° inclusive) included between two adjacent sides, first determine whether a quadrilateral can be formed; if it can, calculate the area of the quadrilateral. The program should be capable of handling any number of sets of data. Prepare your own data to test the program. (*Hint*: Think of the quadrilateral as two triangles.)

5-16 A braced separator, whose cross section is shown in Fig. 5-10, is to be designed. Specifications require that the height of wall *AC* be 2ØØ mm and the height of wall *BD* be 12Ø mm. A conduit (right circular cylinder) containing electrical wires is to run through the separator beneath the cross braces *AD* and *BC* as shown. The diameter of the conduit is to be as close as possible to 5Ø mm. The width *AB* is to be determined such that the conduit will just fit (tangent to *AB*, *BC*, and *AD*). Since this will require many repetitive solutions, a computer solution is indicated. Write and run such a program. Determine the width to the nearest millimeter and the corresponding diameter of the conduit. Print the width, diameter, and the required lengths of the cross braces. Refer to Prob. 5-10 for some necessary formulas.

5-17 The common mathematical method of determining the square root of a number is taught to all grade school students. It is a rather simple but tedious process. Two problems exist with this method: (1) it is difficult to program and (2) it is impossible to obtain the square root accurately to the same number of decimal places as are in the original value.

Another method of determining the square root is to estimate an approximate root, test it, and then arrive at a closer approximation using the formula:

$$R_{i+1} = \frac{R_i^2 + A}{2R_i}$$

where R_i is the first approximation of the square root of A and R_{i+1} is the next approximation. This process can be repeated until the desired precision (number of decimal places) is attained. The precision is established by comparing the square of the calculated root with the original value after each repetition.

Since this repetition (iteration) can be accomplished rapidly on a computer, write a program to determine the value of the square root of π (3.141593) that is precise to six decimal places (the square of the root is the same value as π through six decimal places). Print the value of π and its square root together with the number of iterations necessary. Provide a method of halting the program if the desired precision is not attained after 1ØØ iterations. Remember that the value of the calculated square root may be either a little larger or smaller than its true value.

FIGURE 5-9
Problem 5-14.

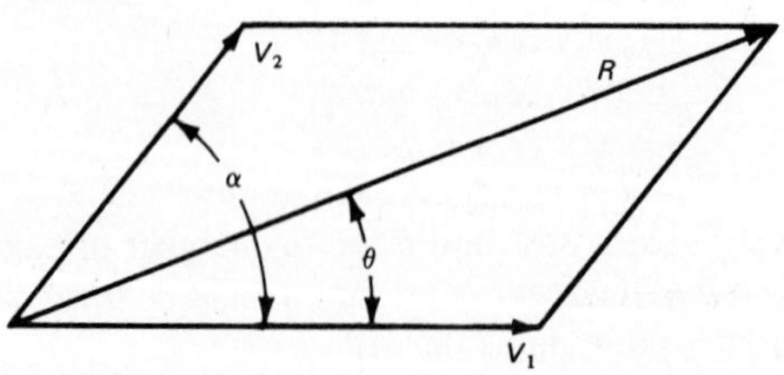

FIGURE 5-10
Problem 5-16.

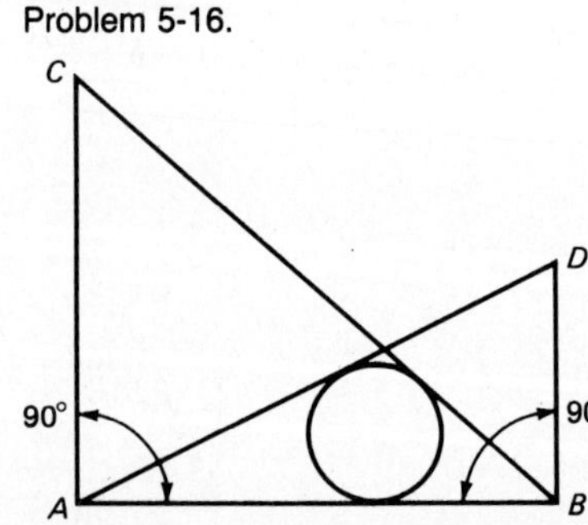

5-18 Another method of arriving at the square root of a number is to approach the square root by using successively smaller increments. If the number X, whose square root R is to be determined, is between Ø and 1Ø, assume an initial value of the root of R=Ø and increment that root by XINC=1.Ø until R is greater than X. Then reduce the root by the increment then being used and change the increment to 1/1Ø of XINC. Repeat this sequence until XINC is less than the desired precision. Write a program using this method to determine the square root of e (2.718282) to a precision of six decimal places (the square of R will be the value as e through six decimal places). Then print the value of e and its square root. Also count and print the number of iterations required. Build into the program a provision to halt the calculations if the desired precision is not attained after 1ØØ iterations.

5-19 If it is assumed that the effect of air friction and the curvature of the earth are negligible (the earth's surface is a horizontal plane), points on the curve of the trajectory of a projectile (Fig. 5-11) can be calculated using the formulas:

$$X = V_{\emptyset}T \cos \alpha \qquad \text{and} \qquad Y = V_{\emptyset}T \sin \alpha - \frac{GT^2}{2.\emptyset}$$

where V = initial velocity
T = time of flight
α = initial angle
G = effect of gravity

Write a program that will calculate and print the X and Y values of the trajectory at time intervals of 1 s until the projectile is less than 1 s from the endpoint. At that time have the program compute and print the X and Y values of the last point above the horizontal with a time accuracy of Ø.Ø1 s. The program should be able to handle any number of trajectories. Test the program with G = 32.174 ft/s^2, $V_{\emptyset}$ = 1ØØØ.Ø ft/s, and an initial angle of 3Ø°. Then rerun the program for $V_{\emptyset}$ = 8ØØ.Ø ft/s and an initial angle of 6Ø°.

5-20 A Coast Guard cutter is at sea in a dense fog with the visibility estimated at 3ØØ ft. Its radar locates a ship suspected of smuggling 1Ø nautical miles (nmi) due east of their position. The suspect is proceeding due north at 1Ø knots (1 kn = 1 nmi/h; 1 nmi = 6Ø76.1Ø3 ft); the cutter is capable of a top speed of 18 kn. The cutter's navigator has studied vector geometry and instantly recognizes that the fastest intercept course is to head at top speed on a course of NαE, where α = arccos(1Ø/18). The cutter accordingly sets out on this course. Assume the coordinates of the cutter

FIGURE 5-11 Problem 5-19.

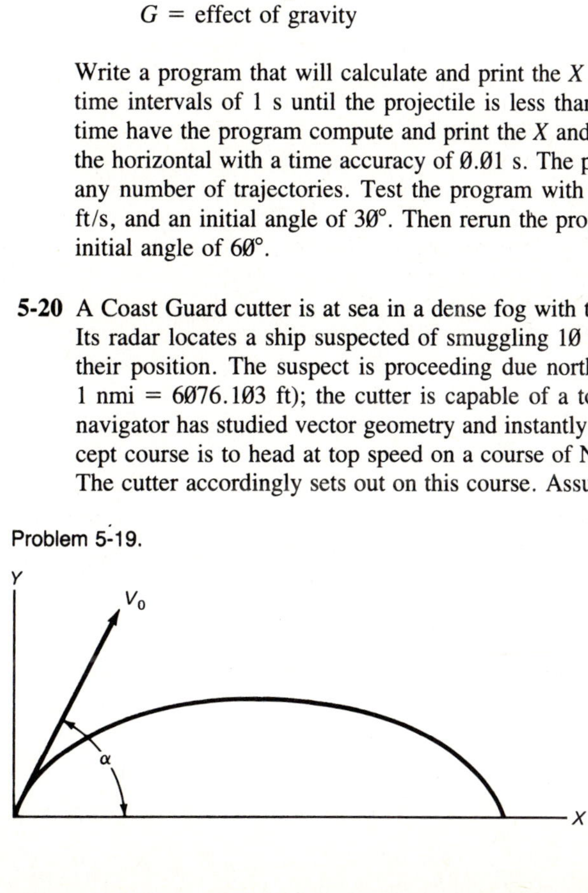

to be (Ø, Ø) and those of the suspect to be (1Ø, Ø), where the coordinates are in nautical miles. Starting with a time interval of 5 min, compute the coordinates of each vessel until calculations show that the vessels will be in sight of each other. Then by successive reductions of the time interval, calculate and print the distance in feet and the time to the nearest Ø.Ø1 min when the suspect will first be visible to the cutter. If the intercept is not made within 1 h, provide a means of ending the program. Assume the dense fog prevents the suspect from spotting the cutter and changing its course.

CHAPTER 6

CONTROLLING INPUT/OUTPUT

6-1 INTRODUCTION

The input/output instructions introduced in Chap. 3 were the list-directed READ/WRITE statements. These provided a quick and simple procedure for the input and output of numerical data, but there were drawbacks. The list-directed READ statement provides a convenient means for inputting numerical data from the keyboard; however, a more structured form of input may be needed when reading from a data file. The list-directed WRITE statement allows the programmer no choice in the output format. Using the list-directed WRITE statement to annotate numerical results is clumsy and inefficient. There are other input/output procedures that place the input/output formats under the control of the programmer. Through the use of READ/WRITE statements that refer to nonexecutable FORMAT statements, a variety of data arrangements are possible, and the programmer can plan and control exactly how and where on the screen or printed page the results will be displayed. In this text, such statements are termed: *format-directed* READ/WRITE *statements*.

6-2 THE FORMAT-DIRECTED READ STATEMENT

The executable *format-directed* READ statement, used with a nonexecutable FORMAT statement, has the same general form and flowchart symbol as the input statement introduced in Chap. 3. This general form is:

READ (*n*, *m*) *a*, *b*, *k*

where *n* represents an integer constant or character designating the input unit
m represents an integer constant (the statement label) referencing another statement (the FORMAT statement) that specifies how the values are to be read
a, *b*, *k* represent the variable names to which the values so read are to be assigned.

An example of the format-directed READ statement is:

```
    READ (*, 1ØØ) RADIUS
1ØØ FORMAT (F5.2)
```

This means that one real value is to be supplied from the keyboard (denoted by the *) and assigned to the real-variable name RADIUS. The data must be arranged by the keyboard operator to a specification contained in an associated FORMAT statement labeled 1ØØ. The value to be assigned to RADIUS must be entered via the keyboard in real-decimal form with two-decimal-place precision, with the last digit right-justified in the fifth column of a five-column field.

Another example is:

```
    OPEN(3,FILE='FILE.DAT')
    READ(3,15Ø)ALPHA,BETA,LAST
15Ø FORMAT(2F4.1,I4)
```

FILE.DAT
*b*1.5*b*2.5*bbb*3

Here three values are to be read from a data file called FILE.DAT, according to the specifications in the FORMAT statement labeled 15Ø. The first two values in the data file will be assigned, respectively, to the real-variable names ALPHA and BETA. The third value in the data file will be assigned to the integer-variable name LAST. Statement label 15Ø refers to the FORMAT statement which specifies how the values in the data file are to be arranged. The first two values in the record should be real-decimal form to one-decimal-place precision, right-justified in columns 4 and 8, respectively, in two consecutive 4-column fields. The third value should be integer, right-justified in column 12, the next consecutive 4-column field. As discussed in Chap. 3, the programmer should provide a prompting message to appear on the screen whenever values are to be input from the keyboard. Figure 6-1 illustrates the elements of the READ statement.

6-3 THE FORMAT STATEMENT WITH THE FORMAT-DIRECTED READ STATEMENT

The FORMAT statement is a nonexecutable statement that specifies how the data must be structured. It is also used with the format-directed WRITE statement to specify the structure of the output. The general form for the FORMAT statement is:

nnn FORMAT(*n*X, *r*F*w*.*d*, *r*E*w*.*d*, *r*I*w*)

where *nnn* represents a statement label of from one to five digits and the elements enclosed in parentheses (called *edit descriptors*) represent the format specification. The edit descriptors in the specification direct the precise number, arrangement, type, and form of the data values to be read—either from the keyboard or from a data file—and assigned to the variable names of the associated READ statement. The edit descriptors F, E, I, and X are described in the following paragraphs. Other edit descriptors and control characters and their applications will be explained as they are needed in association with other statements. The FORMAT statement is not represented in a flowchart.

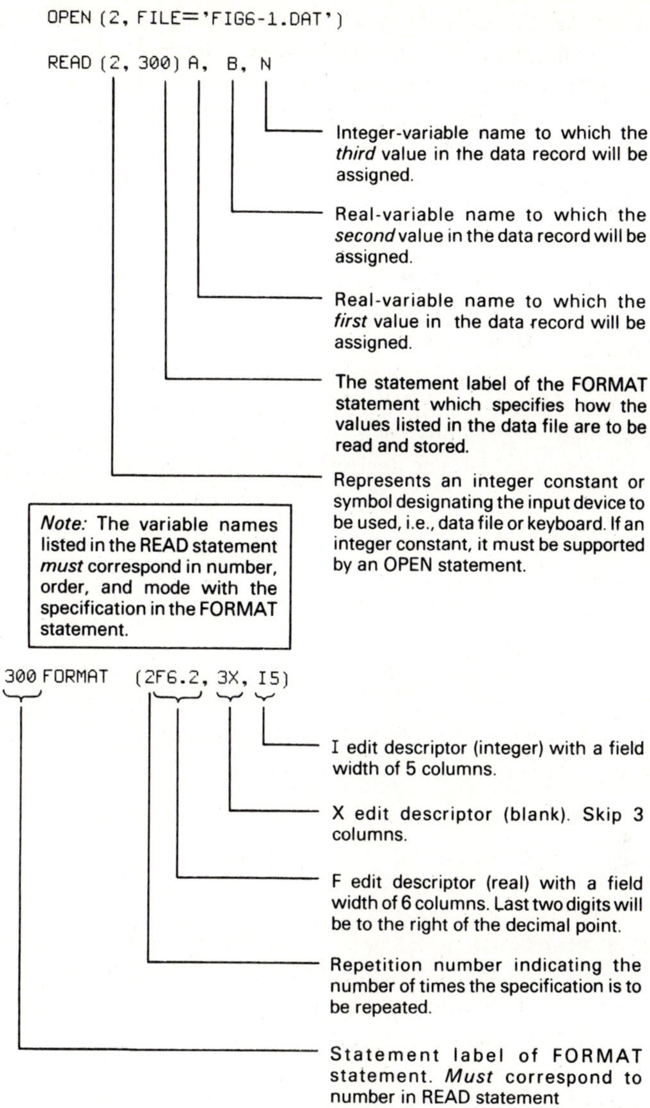

FIGURE 6-1 Elements of the format-directed READ and FORMAT statements.

a The F Edit Descriptor

The F edit descriptor is used for specifying a real-decimal-form constant to be supplied from a data file (or from the keyboard) and assigned to the appropriate real-variable name listed in the associated READ statement. The general form for the F edit descriptor is:

*r*F*w*. *d*

where *r* represents an integer repetition number indicating how many times the descriptor is to be used (omitted when 1)
F indicates a type-real, decimal form (without an exponent)
w establishes the field width (number of columns from which value is to be read)
d specifies the number of digits following the decimal point (number of decimal places)

The decimal point between *w* and *d* is an essential part of the edit descriptor.

An F1Ø.3 edit descriptor used with an input statement, for example, means that the corresponding constant in the record must be real-decimal form (without an exponent) and the corresponding variable name in the READ list must be real. The value will be read from 1Ø columns of the record. The number 1Ø specifies the number of columns (field width) covered by the descriptor. There are three decimal places (.3). The decimal point need not be included in the value supplied since the edit descriptor in the FORMAT specification (F1Ø.3) will place the decimal point so that the last 3 digits in the 1Ø-column field are to the right of the decimal point. However, it is advisable for the beginner to include the decimal point in the value supplied. If the decimal point in the value supplied does not match the decimal point specified by the edit descriptor, the decimal point in the value will override the format-specified location of the decimal point. A decimal point occupies a column and must be included in the field width, thus reducing by one the number of digits that can be placed in a given field. If the value is positive, a positive algebraic sign is implied. If the value is negative, the negative sign (−) must be explicit and the column occupied by the sign must be included in the field width of the edit descriptor. In the following example:

```
      OPEN(3,FILE='FILE.DAT')
      READ(3,15Ø)ALPHA,BETA
15Ø   FORMAT(F4.1,F4.1)
```

FILE.DAT
*b*1.5*b*2.5

there are two variable names in the READ list, ALPHA and BETA, and two edit descriptors in the FORMAT specification, F4.1 and F4.1. The data file must be structured with two data values per record, ordered in accordance with the specification of the FORMAT statement to be assigned, in turn, to the two variable names in the READ list. The values in the record should be arranged as shown, in two consecutive four-column fields, with each constant right-justified in the fourth column of its four-column field (columns 4 and 8, respectively). When the READ statement is executed, 1.5 is assigned to ALPHA and 2.5 to BETA. Of prime importance is the compatibility between the edit descriptor in the FORMAT specification, the constant in the record, and the variable name in the READ list. Any inconsistency among these three elements will cause an error when execution of the READ statement is attempted.

Note that edit descriptors in the FORMAT specification are separated by commas, and, since each edit descriptor is used once, the repetition number, an implied 1, is omitted. The two edit descriptors are identical and could be written once with a repetition number of 2, making the specification (2F4.1).

b The E Edit Descriptor

When a real value that is either very small or very large is to be read from a data file, it is often advantageous (and sometimes necessary) to use the E edit descriptor in the FORMAT specification. The E edit descriptor specifies the exponential form for a real value (Sec. 3-3*b*). The general form for the E edit descriptor is:

*r*E*w*.*d*

where *r* represents an integer repetition number indicating how many times the edit descriptor is to be used (omitted when 1)
- E indicates a type-real exponential form
- *w* establishes the field width (number of columns from which value is to be read)
- *d* specifies the number of decimal places

The decimal point between the *w* and *d* is an essential part of the edit descriptor. The field width *w* must include columns for the E; the decimal point; a one-, two-, or three-digit exponent; and, if the number or the exponent is negative, the column(s) for the negative algebraic signs. Thus a value of *w* that is seven larger than the value of *d* would provide an E edit descriptor (E14.7) that can be used to read any properly expressed exponential value. However, when the size of the value supplied is known (the usual case), the E edit descriptor can be written specifically for the manner in which that value is expressed. For example, if the keyboard-supplied value, which begins in column 1, is:

```
.3141593E1
```

the value can be read by the statements:

```
    READ(*,25Ø)PI
25Ø FORMAT(E1Ø.7)
```

The value read using the READ/FORMAT statements and assigned to π will be stored as Ø.3141593EØ1. It is the exponential form of the value of π, 3.141593. Note that the leading zero need not be included.

It is good programming practice and important for the beginning programmer to express the values in a record in a form consistent with the corresponding specifications in the READ statement and to include the decimal point in real constants. (However, the compiler may permit a real constant expressed in decimal form without an exponent to be read with an E edit descriptor without an error.) When the decimal point is included in the data value, there is no problem with the value assigned to the variable name. If the decimal point is omitted from the data value, placement of the decimal point is controlled by the E edit descriptor. Omitting the decimal point from the data value specified with an E edit descriptor may result in an unexpected, and probably incorrect, value being assigned to the variable name.

c The I Edit Descriptor

The I edit descriptor is used for specifying an integer constant to be supplied from a data file or from the keyboard and assigned to the appropriate integer-variable name listed in the associated READ statement. The general form for the I edit descriptor is:

*r*I*w*

where *r* represents an integer-repetition number indicating how many times the edit descriptor is to be used (omitted when 1)
I indicates a type-integer form
w establishes the field width (number of columns from which the value is to be read)

An example of the use of I edit descriptors is:

```
    READ(*,2ØØ)J,K
2ØØ FORMAT(I4,I6)
```

where the value for J is supplied in the first four columns (right-justified in column 4) and the value for K is supplied in the next six columns (right-justified in column 1Ø). Note the correspondence in type: two integer I edit descriptors in the FORMAT specification and two integer-variable names in the READ list. The values supplied via the keyboard must be integers. Also note that since each I edit descriptor is used only once, the repetition number, an implied 1, is omitted.

A *blank* within a field defined by an edit descriptor is interpreted as a zero. It is therefore important that integer constants in a record be right-justified within their fields. For example, if the integer value 3, specified to be read with an I4 descriptor, is placed in the first column of the four-column field followed by three *blanks* (3*bbb*), the value assigned to the variable name will be 3ØØØ, the *blanks* in the second, third, and fourth columns being interpreted as zeros. If the digit 3 of the integer constant 3 is placed in the last (rightmost) column of the field (*bbb*3), ØØØ3 will be assigned, the leading zeros having no effect on the value.

As with real values, the algebraic sign of the integer values must be considered; if the sign is negative, the minus sign must be included as part of the data value. The algebraic sign occupies a column and must be included in the field width defined by the edit descriptor. Figure 6-2 provides additional examples of the READ and FORMAT statements and how they relate to the data file.

d The X Edit Descriptor

The X edit descriptor in the FORMAT specification means that a column is skipped when reading a record. The general form for the X edit descriptor is:

*r*X

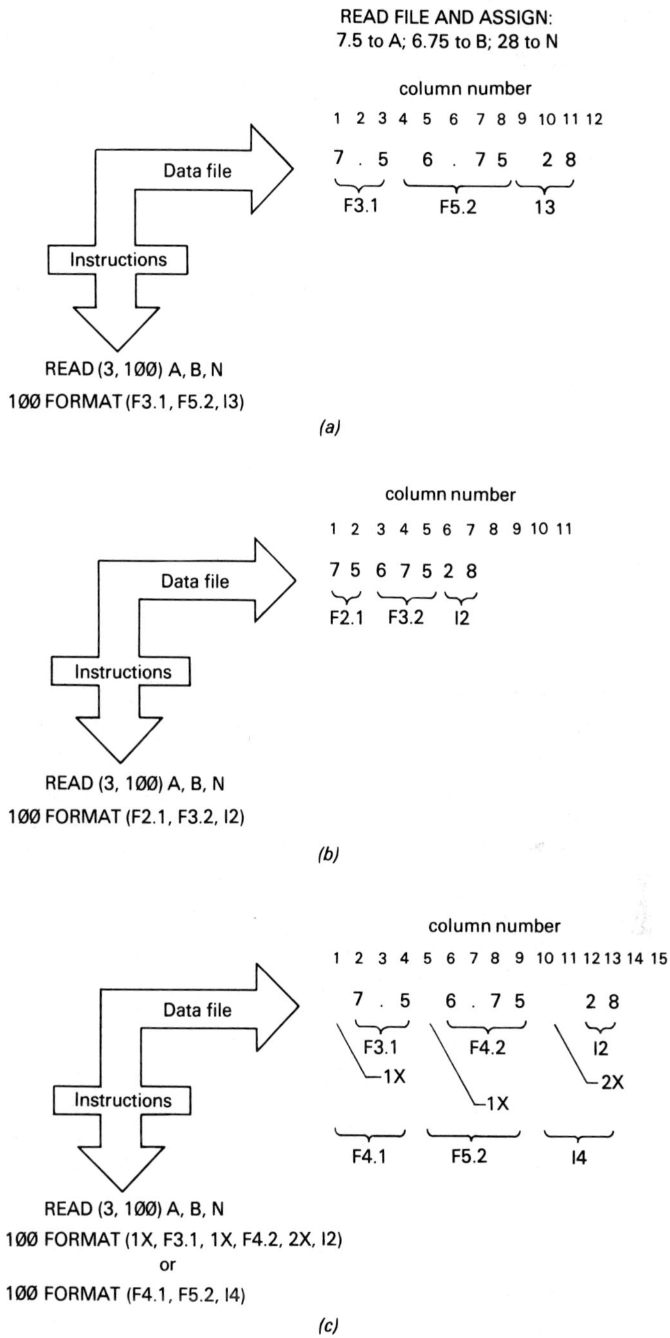

FIGURE 6-2 Variations of the format-directed READ and FORMAT statements.

where *r* represents a *mandatory* integer-repetition number, indicating how many times the edit descriptor is to be used
X indicates that a data column is to be skipped

If only one column is to be skipped, the repetition number 1 *must* be placed before the X. A repetition number is *always* used with the X edit descriptor.

If the READ and associated FORMAT statements are:

```
    READ (*, 2ØØ) NUM, CASH
2ØØ FORMAT(2X, I4, 1X, F5.2)
```

and the string of digits entered via the keyboard is:

```
123456789Ø123456789Ø123456789Ø
```

execution of the READ statement will skip the first two columns (2X); the digits from the next four columns, 3456 (I4), are assigned to NUM; the next column is skipped (1X); and the digits from the next five columns, 89Ø12 (F5.2), with a decimal point setting off the last two digits, 89Ø.12, are assigned to CASH. The remaining digits in the record are ignored. Figure 6-2 illustrates additional applications of the X edit descriptor.

It was assumed in the above explanation that the field width defined by the edit descriptor in the FORMAT specification and the field actually occupied by the constant in the record are the same. If the defined and actual field widths differ, the value assigned as a result of the READ statement will not be the value intended. Extreme care must be exercised to ensure that the field width defined by the edit descriptor and the field actually occupied by the value in the record are the same.

6-4 ARRANGING A DATA FILE

Structuring the data file so that values are arranged according to the edit descriptors in the FORMAT specification can be a tedious and error-ridden task since column numbers are not built into the editing software. The task of ensuring proper column alignment of the characters of the data values can be simplified if the programmer provides an initial record of "column headings" in the data file that is simply a line of consecutive digits, such as

```
123456789Ø123456789Ø12345
```

These digits identify the first 25 columns of input. The formatted data now can be placed with each digit or character of the data value in the correct column. This record of column headings can be deleted before storing in a diskette file, or a "dummy" list-directed READ statement can be placed in the source program immediately following the OPEN statement, which will read the record (the column headings), thus eliminating that record from further consideration by subsequent READ statements.

6-5 SATISFYING THE READ LIST

The variable names listed in the READ statement, the edit descriptors F, E, and I in the associated FORMAT statement, and the values listed in the defined fields of each record of the data file normally should be the same in number, order, and type. This means that if the first variable name in the READ list is designated real, the first edit descriptor in the FORMAT specification should be an F (or E if the data is in exponential form) and the first value in the record should be real. If the second variable name in the READ list is designated integer, the second edit descriptor in the FORMAT specification must be I, and the second value in the record must be integer, and so on. When the READ list is satisfied by this one-to-one correspondence of the variable names in the READ list, the FORMAT specification, and the values in the record, a *balanced termination* of the READ statement occurs. The compiler then indexes the reading control to the first column of the next record.

When the number of variable names listed in the READ statement differs from the number of edit descriptors in the specification of the associated FORMAT statement, an *unbalanced termination* of the READ statement will occur. This can lead to unexpected results if the rules governing unbalanced terminations are not understood. This discussion is deferred until Sec. 6-13, where illustrative programs are provided to demonstrate the results of unbalanced termination of the READ statement.

6-6 CONTROL OF INPUT: TERMINATING A RECORD WITH THE SLASH EDIT DESCRIPTOR

It may at times be convenient to read data from several consecutive records of a data file using a single, format-directed READ statement. This can be accomplished using the slash (/) edit descriptor. (The slash is the same character described in Sec. 3-7 and used as an arithmetic operator to indicate division.) Slashes placed in the specification of the associated FORMAT statement permit the programmer to terminate reading before the end of the record. In a FORMAT statement associated with a READ statement, the slash instructs the compiler, at that point, to stop reading the record presently being read and to index control to the first column of the next record (begin a new record). The data on the next record is read starting in column 1, from left to right, as the next edit descriptor following the slash directs. For example:

```
    OPEN(3,FILE='FILE.DAT')
    READ(3,*)
    READ(3,1ØØ)A,B,N,K
1ØØ FORMAT(2F6.1,/,I4,/,I1Ø)
```

FILE.DAT
12345678901234567 *bb*12.3*bb*45.6*bb*345 789Ø123 *bbbbb*12345678

The first READ statement is a "dummy" list-directed READ statement included for the sole purpose of eliminating the first record, the line of column headings used to properly align the actual records that follow. Execution of the second READ statement will begin by reading from column 1 of the second record according to the edit descriptors in the specification of the 1ØØ FORMAT statement. The 2F6.1 edit descriptor directs the assignment of the two values from the second record, 12.3 and 45.6, to the real-variable names A and B, respectively. The first slash indexes the reading cycle to column 1 of the next record. The I4 directs the assignment of 789Ø to the integer-variable name N. The second slash again indexes to column 1 of the next record, where the I1Ø directs assignment of 12345 to the integer-variable name K. Any characters beyond the twelfth, fourth, and tenth columns, respectively, of the three effective records will be ignored.

Use of the slash for reading control is further demonstrated by the program in Fig. 6-3. A data file of eight records is supplied to the program, each record containing one integer value (digits Ø1 through Ø8) in columns 1 and 2 of the respective record. The READ statement instructs the compiler to read values from the records according to the edit descriptors in the specification of the 1ØØ FORMAT statement and assign these values, in turn, to the four integer-variable names J, K, L, and M.

Examine the 1ØØ FORMAT statement in the program of Fig. 6-3. The value to be assigned to J will be read from columns 1 and 2 (I2) of the first record. The integer value Ø1 is assigned to J. The single slash indexes the compiler to column 1 of the next record, and the following edit descriptor (I2) provides for reading from columns 1 and 2 the value to be assigned to K. The integer Ø2 will be assigned to K. The next two slashes instruct the compiler to advance to the third record (Ø3) and then immediately advance to the fourth record (Ø4). The third record is skipped entirely. The integer Ø4 will be assigned to L. The next three slashes instruct the compiler to advance to the fifth record (Ø5), advance to the sixth record (Ø6), and advance to the seventh record (Ø7); read the value from columns 1 and 2, and assign Ø7 to M. The fifth and sixth records are skipped en-

FIGURE 6-3 Effects of slashes in the input format.

```
C234567890
      OPEN(5,FILE='FIG6-3.DAT')
      OPEN(8,FILE='PRN')
      READ(5,100)J,K,L,M
  100 FORMAT(I2,/,I2,//,I2,///,I2)
      WRITE(8,200)J,K,L,M
  200 FORMAT(1X,4I5)
      STOP
      END
```

```
01
02
03
04
05
06
07
08
```

```
    1    2    4    7
```

tirely. The READ statement is satisfied with the reading and assignment of four values to the four variables in the READ list. The last record (Ø8) is ignored. Note the results when the program of Fig. 6-3 is executed.

6-7 THE FORMAT-DIRECTED WRITE STATEMENT

The format-directed WRITE statement is an executable output statement that directs the compiler to display the results. The flowchart symbols for this statement are the symbols introduced in Chap. 2 to OUTPUT to diskette, to DISPLAY or to DOCUMENT. The general form for the format-directed WRITE statement is:

WRITE(*n*, *m*) *a*, *b*, *k*

where *n* represents an integer number or character designating a file or output unit to which the results are to be routed

m represents an integer constant (the statement label) referencing another statement (the FORMAT statement) which specifies how the output is to be structured

a, b, k represent a list of variable names whose values are to be displayed

An example of the format-directed WRITE statement with its associated FORMAT statement is:

```
      WRITE(*,2ØØ)RADIUS,CIRCUM,AREA
2ØØ   FORMAT(1X,F1Ø.3,5X,F1Ø.3,5X,F1Ø.3)
```

The asterisk (*) in the WRITE statement routes the output to the screen. Remember that if printed output is desired, the format-directed WRITE statement must be supported with a statement opening a print file (Sec. 3-12*b*), such as:

```
OPEN(8,FILE='PRN')
WRITE(8,2ØØ)RADIUS,CIRCUM,AREA
```

Note that PRN is the filename reserved for a print file. Figure 6-4 on p. 152 outlines the elements of the format-directed WRITE statement.

6-8 THE FORMAT STATEMENT WITH THE FORMAT-DIRECTED WRITE STATEMENT

Although use of the FORMAT statement with the WRITE statement is quite similar to its use with the READ statement, several important differences must be considered. The algebraic sign of a positive value is not displayed; the algebraic sign of a negative value is displayed. Therefore, unless all output values are known to be positive, the output field width defined by the edit descriptor must include an output column for the algebraic sign. The first output column of every line of output is reserved for a vertical-control character (Sec. 6-11). *Nothing* is

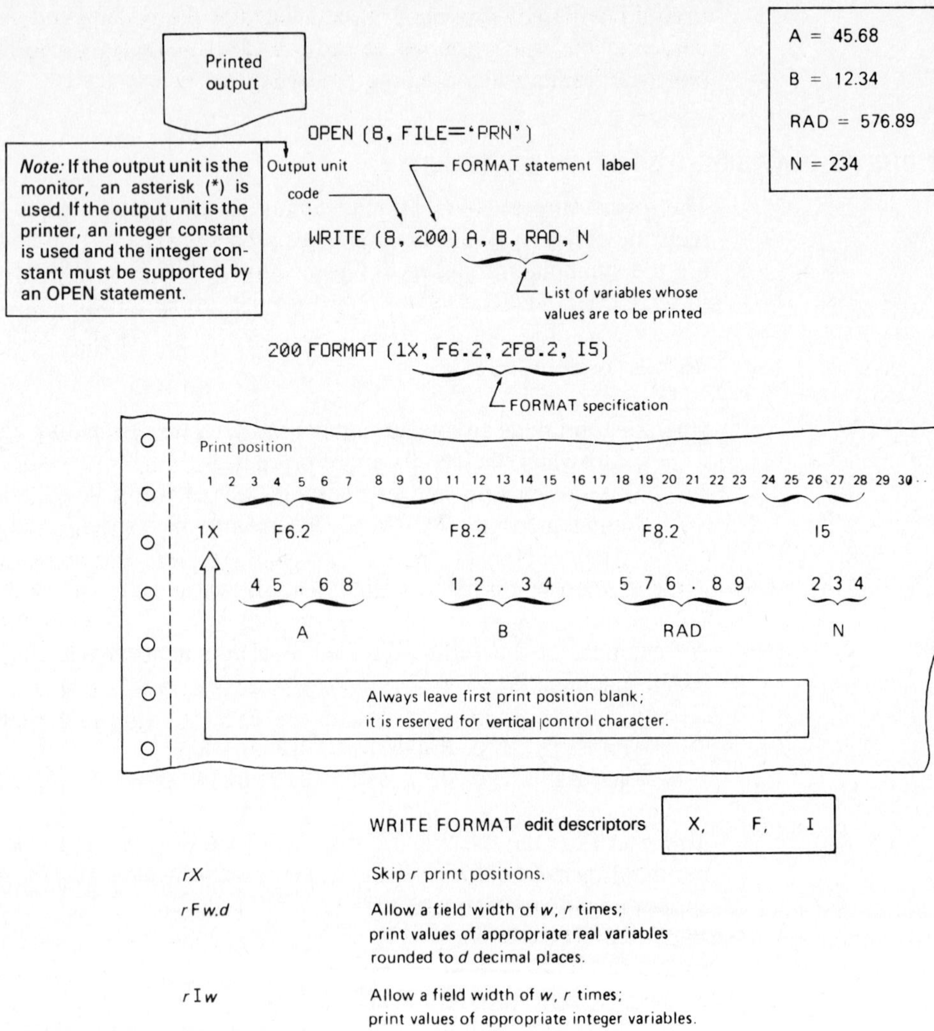

FIGURE 6-4 Elements of the format-directed WRITE and FORMAT statements.

ever displayed or printed in output column 1. The 1X, as the first edit descriptor in the FORMAT specification, provides the blank in the first output column which advances output one line for single spacing. The edit descriptors F, E, I, and X are used as follows in the specification of the FORMAT statement associated with the WRITE statement for controlling output.

a The F Edit Descriptor

The F edit descriptor is used for the output of real numbers in decimal form (without an exponent). A seven-digit number is the largest real number that can be displayed or printed. (See Sec. 11-4 for double-precision techniques, which can be used for processing numbers with more than seven digits.) The general form for the F edit descriptor, when used for output, is:

```
rFw.d
```

where *r* represents an integer-repetition number indicating how many times the descriptor is to be used (omitted when 1)
F indicates a type-real decimal form (without an exponent)
w establishes the field width (number of output columns)
d specifies the number of digits following the decimal point (number of decimal places)

The decimal point between *w* and *d* is an essential part of the edit descriptor.

Since a real value includes a decimal point, the output column occupied by the decimal point must be included in the field width. The field width must also include an output column for the algebraic sign (−) of a negative value. The algebraic sign of a positive value is not displayed and may be ignored provided the variable to be displayed will never be a negative value. A Ø must be included in the F edit descriptor (F5.Ø) to indicate that there are no digits following the decimal point in the value displayed when this is the desired format.

The minimum field width *w* must exceed the number of decimal places *d* by the number of characters (including the algebraic sign) to the left of the decimal point plus 1 (for the decimal point). For example:

```
      A=-123.4567
      WRITE(*,1ØØ)A
1ØØ   FORMAT(1X,F9.4)
```

A minimum field width *w* of nine output columns is required to display the value assigned to A. With four decimal places ($d = 4$) and four characters to the left of the decimal point (−123), $w = 4 + 4 + 1 = 9$. This provides for an output column for each of the seven digits of the number plus a column each for the negative sign and the decimal point. An F8.4 edit descriptor will provide sufficient columns for the same number with positive algebraic signs, since the positive algebraic sign is not displayed.

It is good practice for all field descriptors to specify a field width greater by 2 than the minimum required, in order to provide blanks that separate successive values. If the F edit descriptor does not provide for a field width with sufficient output columns to accommodate the number of characters in the value (including the decimal point and algebraic sign of a negative value), a row of asterisks—equal in number to the specified field width—will be displayed instead of the value intended. For example:

```
      PI=3.141593
      WRITE(*,1ØØ)PI
1ØØ   FORMAT(1X,F7.6)
```

displays a blank followed by a row of seven asterisks:

```
b*******
```

Since the field width $w = 7$ is only one larger than the number of decimal digits specified ($d = 6$), there is a column for the decimal point but no column for the digit to the left of the decimal point. Therefore, the specified value cannot be displayed and the row of seven asterisks results. A minimum field width of eight output columns is required.

The F edit descriptor provides for rounding the last digit displayed; up when the next digit is 5 or greater, and down when it is less than 5. For example:

```
      PI=3.141593
      WRITE(*,2ØØ)PI
2ØØ   FORMAT(1X,F6.4)
```

will display:

```
b3.1416
```

Real values displayed with the F edit descriptor are right-justified in the field. That is, the rightmost digit of the number is located in the rightmost output column of the field. For example:

```
      PI=3.141593
      WRITE(*,3ØØ)PI
3ØØ   FORMAT(1X,F1Ø.5)
```

will display:

```
bbbb3.14159
```

with the 9 in output column 11. Counting from right to left, the five digits to the right of the decimal point (the value is rounded to five decimal places) account for columns 11 through 7. The decimal point is in column 6, and the 3 is in column 5. Columns 4, 3, and 2 are blank, and the 1X ensures that column 1 will be blank.

Figure 6-5 gives other examples of the F edit descriptor, with three different field widths. Although the value of X is defined in the program with nine digits, the value of X in the line of output contains only the first seven of the original digits. The last two digits, in excess of the seven maximum, were used in rounding the seventh digit. They were then replaced by zeros to comply with the four-decimal-place requirement of the F12.4 edit descriptor in the specification of the 1ØØ FORMAT statement. Note that the first line of output has three leading *blanks,* the result of the 1X,F12.4 edit descriptors. The second line of output has only one leading *blank,* the result of the 1X edit descriptor; however the F1Ø.4

```
C234567890
      OPEN(6,FILE='PRN')
      X=12345.6789
      WRITE(6,100)X
  100 FORMAT(1X,F12.4)
      WRITE(6,200)X
  200 FORMAT(1X,F10.4)
      WRITE(6,300)X
  300 FORMAT(1X,F8.4)
      STOP
      END
```

```
  12345.6800
 12345.6800
********
```

FIGURE 6-5 Printing with F edit descriptors with narrowing fields.

edit descriptor in the specification of the 200 FORMAT statement provides exactly the number of output columns required by the value. The third line of output is only a row of eight asterisks (after the blank in the first column) because the F8.4 edit descriptor in the specification of the 300 FORMAT statement does not provide sufficient columns to contain all the characters of the value.

b The E Edit Descriptor

When the magnitude of the value is uncertain, it may be advantageous to specify the numerical output with an E edit descriptor. The E edit descriptor is used for the output of real values in exponential form. The general form for the E edit descriptor is:

*r*E*w*. *d*

where *r* represents an integer-repetition number indicating how many times the descriptor is to be used (omitted when 1)
E indicates a real exponential form
w establishes the field width (number of output columns)
d specifies the number of decimal places

The decimal point between the *w* and *d* is an essential part of the edit descriptor.

The E edit descriptor is applicable to real values, and the output is in exponential form (Sec. 3-3*b*). Up to seven digits can be specified. Another six columns are needed in the exponential form as follows: the algebraic sign of the value (displayed only if negative), a decimal point, the character E, the algebraic sign of the exponent (displayed whether positive or negative), and a two-digit exponent. The minimum field width specified by an E edit descriptor must be the number of digits of the value, plus 6. For a seven-digit number, the minimum field width is E13.7—a 13-output-column field with seven digits following the decimal point. For example:

```
    X=1234.567
    Y=-Ø.Ø12345678
    Z=.1234567E-Ø2
    WRITE(*,1ØØ)X
    WRITE(*,1ØØ)Y
    WRITE(*,1ØØ)Z
1ØØ FORMAT(1X,E13.7)
```

will display:

```
bb.1234567E+Ø4
b-.1234568E-Ø1
bb.1234567E-Ø2
```

Note that three different WRITE statements reference the same FORMAT statement. A single FORMAT statement may be referenced by several WRITE and/or READ statements.

Figure 6-6 illustrates how the E edit descriptor prints a single value using five different field widths.

c The I Edit Descriptor

The I edit descriptor is used for displaying integer numbers. The general form for the I edit descriptor is:

*r*I*w*

where *r* represents an integer-repetition number indicating how many times the

FIGURE 6-6 Printing with E edit descriptors with narrowing fields.

```
C234567890
      OPEN(6,FILE='PRN')
      X=-0.123456789E-10
      WRITE(6,100)X
  100 FORMAT(1X,E22.9)
      WRITE(6,200)X
  200 FORMAT(1X,E17.7)
      WRITE(6,300)X
  300 FORMAT(1X,E15.7)
      WRITE(6,400)X
  400 FORMAT(1X,E13.7)
      WRITE(6,500)X
  500 FORMAT(1X,E11.7)
      STOP
      END
```

```
           -.123456800E-10
        -.1234568E-10
      -.1234568E-10
    -.1234568E-10
***********
```

descriptor is to be used (omitted when 1)
I indicates a type-integer form
w establishes the field width (number of output columns)

No decimal points are involved, but, as with real values, a column must be provided in the field width of the I edit descriptor for the algebraic sign (−) of a negative value. Integer numbers are right-justified in the specified field. For example:

```
      MI=528Ø
      WRITE(*,4ØØ)MI
4ØØ   FORMAT(1X,I5)
```

will display:

```
bb528Ø
```

with the zero in the rightmost column of the five-column field. The 1X provides the blank in column 1, and the display of four digits in a five-column output field accounts for the second blank in column 2.

d The X Edit Descriptor

The X edit descriptor, already encountered in the examples of this section, is used to skip a column in a line of output. The general form for the X edit descriptor is:

```
rX
```

where *r* represents a *mandatory* integer-repetition number, indicating how many times the descriptor is to be used, and X indicates that an output column is to be skipped. If only one column is to be skipped, the repetition number is 1. A repetition number must *always* be used with the X edit descriptor. For example:

```
      A=1.25
      B=2.5Ø
      N=7755
      WRITE(*,1ØØ)A,B,N
1ØØ   FORMAT(1X,F4.2,1X,F4.2,2X,I4)
```

will display:

```
b1.25b2.5Øbb7755
```

the X edit descriptors included in the FORMAT specification provide the *blanks* in columns 1, 6, 11, and 12. Expanding the field width of the F, E, and I descriptors to incorporate the columns skipped by the X descriptors will also accomplish the same result. The 1ØØ FORMAT statement of the above example could also be written as 1ØØ FORMAT(2F5.2,I6).

Note that in each of the above examples, the line of output occupies 16 columns including *blanks*. The specification in the FORMAT statement, however composed, must specify a total output field width equal to the number of characters, including *blanks,* to be displayed. The field width specified by the first edit descriptor must include a *blank* in output column 1. Such an expansion of the field width for the first value may result in unexpected problems unless the programmer is positive that the number of characters in the first value will never exceed the specified field width minus 1. The total field width specified in both the FORMAT statements illustrated above is 16 and corresponds to the 16 columns occupied by the line of output.

e The Use of Commas in the FORMAT Statement

When more than one edit descriptor is used in a FORMAT specification, the descriptors should be separated by a comma. It is not necessary to separate consecutive slashes (//) with commas or to separate a slash and another edit descriptor with a comma, but comma separation of slashes is not incorrect and will cause no problem.

f Placement of FORMAT Statements

In the illustrative programs shown in this text, the FORMAT statements referred to in a READ or WRITE statement are placed immediately following the associated READ or WRITE statement. This way the reader can more easily relate the FORMAT statement with the associated input/output statement. However, it is common practice to group all FORMAT statements together, at the beginning or end of the program.

In any case, the statement labels of FORMAT statements should, to aid in visual location, be significantly different from the labels given to executable statements of the program. If the labels of the executable statements are 1Ø, 2Ø, 3Ø, etc., labels such as 1ØØ, 2ØØ, 3ØØ, etc., or 1ØØØ, 2ØØØ, 3ØØØ, should be used to identify FORMAT statements.

6-9 ANNOTATING THE OUTPUT

The recommended method for annotating numerical results in the output with alphabetic character information is *apostrophe editing* with the apostrophe edit descriptor. The apostrophe edit descriptor is used to specify the output of alphabetic, numeric, or other character constants. Apostrophe editing is simply a matter of enclosing the list of characters between two apostrophes ('). For example:

```
      WRITE(*,1ØØ)
1ØØ  FORMAT(3X,'DIA.bCIRCUMFERENCEbAREA')
```

will display:

```
bbbDIA.bCIRCUMFERENCEbAREA
```

Another example of apostrophe editing is:

```
    X=3.75
    Y=25.5Ø
    WRITE(*,2ØØ)X,Y
2ØØ FORMAT(1X,'WHENbX=',F6.2,'bTHENbY=',F6.2)
```

The above statements will display:

```
bWHENbX=bb3.75bTHENbY=b25.5Ø
```

The displayed line of output is in sentence form with the numerical values assigned to X and Y displayed as specified by the F edit descriptor following each character constant specified by the apostrophe edit descriptor.

Note that all characters, including *blanks,* between the leading and closing apostrophes are literally displayed in the output as they appear in the FORMAT specification. The apostrophes are *not* displayed. Note also that the leading apostrophe does *not* provide an automatic *blank* in output column 1 as it does in the list-directed WRITE statement (Sec. 3-12).

6-10 THE REPETITION NUMBER

The general form for the F, E, I, and X edit descriptors includes a repetition number, *r*F, *r*E, *r*I, and *r*X, where *r* represents an integer constant indicating the number of times that the descriptor is to be used. A repetition number of 1 is implied when no repetition number is included with the F, E, and I descriptors. An explicit repetition number is mandatory and must be included with the X descriptor, even if the descriptor is to be used only once, in which case the repetition number is 1.

A repetition number can also be used with parentheses to repeat a group of edit descriptors a given number of times. For example, the FORMAT specification in:

```
    WRITE(*,1ØØ)A,B,I,R,S,J,X,Y,K
1ØØ FORMAT(1X,F6.2,F6.2,I4,F6.2,F6.2,I4,F6.2,F6.2,I4)
```

can be rewritten with appropriate parentheses and repetition numbers as:

```
1ØØ FORMAT(1X,3(2F6.2,I4))
```

and have the same effect. The 3 preceding the inner left parenthesis is a repetition number. Grouping a repetitive sequence of edit descriptors with parentheses and repeating with a repetition number has obvious advantages when knowledgeably applied (Sec. 6-13*b*).

A repetition number can also be used with parentheses to repeat an apostrophe edit descriptor a given number of times. When associated with a suitable WRITE statement, each of the FORMAT statements:

```
200 FORMAT(1X, '***************')
```

or

```
300 FORMAT(1X,15('*'))
```

will display:

```
b***************
```

The 1X descriptor in each FORMAT specification provides the blank control character in output column 1; the apostrophe edit descriptors will cause a row of 15 asterisks to be displayed. The 300 FORMAT statement makes use of a repetition number to repeat the asterisk 15 times. This technique is particularly advantageous when the same character must be repeated to display a long line of dashes, asterisks, etc. This is immediately apparent if, instead of 15 asterisks as in the example above, the output must be a row of 75 asterisks. Figure 6-7 shows how the technique can be applied.

6-11 VERTICAL CONTROL OF OUTPUT

When used in a FORMAT statement associated with a WRITE statement, the *r*X edit descriptor described in Sec. 6-8*d* causes any desired number of output columns to be skipped (horizontal output control). Thus the horizontal composition of the output can be controlled. Instructions can also be written that control the vertical composition of the output by advancing the paper through the printer or spacing the lines one or two lines apart, single- or double-spaced. Furthermore, the paper can be advanced through the printer by whole-page increments, beginning a line of output at the top of a new page. It is also possible to hold the paper so that characters from more than one WRITE statement are printed on the same line. Controlling the advance of the paper through the printer, or advancing lines of output, will be referred to as *vertical control* (also termed *carriage control*).

When the WRITE list has been satisfied according to the specification in the associated FORMAT statement, the output control indexes back to column 1 of the same output line. This is true whether the output is being printed on the printer, displayed on the screen, or stored on a diskette. The output control then waits for the next WRITE statement. The FORMAT statement referenced by the next WRITE statement must include an instruction to advance control to the next line of output. Specific characters are employed for controlling the vertical spac-

```
C234567890
      OPEN(6,FILE='PRN')
      WRITE(6,100)
  100 FORMAT(5X,28('*'))
      WRITE(6,150)
  150 FORMAT(5X,'*',26X,'*')
      WRITE(6,200)
  200 FORMAT(5X,'* COMPUTING CENTER WILL BE *')
      WRITE(6,300)
  300 FORMAT(5X,'* CLOSED ON  CHRISTMAS DAY *')
      WRITE(6,400)
  400 FORMAT(5X,'* CLOSE - 1200 24 DECEMBER *')
      WRITE(6,500)
  500 FORMAT(5X,'* OPEN -  0800 26 DECEMBER *')
      WRITE(6,600)
  600 FORMAT(5X,'*',26X,'*')
      WRITE(6,650)
  650 FORMAT(5X,28('*'))
      STOP
      END
```

```
****************************
*                          *
* COMPUTING CENTER WILL BE *
* CLOSED ON  CHRISTMAS DAY *
* CLOSE - 1200 24 DECEMBER *
* OPEN -  0800 26 DECEMBER *
*                          *
****************************
```

FIGURE 6-7 Use of repetition number for boxing in a message.

ing of output. The FORMAT statements in the previous examples have all specified a *blank* in output column 1, generally by using 1X as the first edit descriptor. This is required because the first output character (the character specified for output column 1) is programmed by the compiler to be a vertical-control character. A *blank* is a vertical-control character that provides for single-spacing (advancing one line) of the output. There are four vertical-control characters, each with a unique effect:

blank	advances one line before output begins
Ø	advances two lines before output begins
1	advances paper through printer to the first line of the next page, provided the printing head is set at line 1 of the first page of continuous forms when the printer is activated (printer only—does not apply to screen display or diskette storage)
+	prevents paper advance to next line (Example 6-4)

The vertical-control character is never actually displayed or printed. (Nothing ever appears in output column 1.)

The first three vertical-control characters from the list above (*blank*, Ø, and 1) are used to structure the output. The fourth vertical-control character (+) should be used only for special effects such as overprinting.

Example 6-1

The FORMAT specification includes a *blank* in output column 1, producing single-spaced output:

```
100 FORMAT(1X,F8.2,    etc,     )
```

or the field width of the first F, E, or I edit descriptor can be expanded to include a *blank* in output column 1:

```
200 FORMAT(F9.2,    etc,     )
```

or the apostrophe edit descriptor can be used:

```
300 FORMAT('b',F8.2,    etc,     )
```

All of the above create the same results on the screen display, the printed output, or diskette storage.

Example 6-2

The apostrophe edit descriptor can be used to specify a Ø vertical-control character in output column 1 to produce double-spaced output:

```
400 FORMAT('Ø',F8.2,    etc,     )
```

This results in double-spacing on either the screen display, the printed output, or diskette storage.

Example 6-3

The apostrophe edit descriptor can be used to specify 1 as the vertical-control character to advance the paper to the first line of the next page:

```
500 FORMAT('1',F8.2,    etc,     )
```

The use of vertical-control character 1 for output on the display screen or diskette storage results in single-spacing by default.

Example 6-4

The apostrophe edit descriptor can be used to prevent line advance:

```
600 FORMAT('+',F8.2,    etc,     )
```

One application of the + vertical-control character, underlining a line of printed output, is illustrated by:

```
     OPEN(6,FILE='PRN')
     WRITE(6,1ØØ)
1ØØ  FORMAT(1X,'NOTE UNDERLINING IN PRINTED OUTPUT')
     WRITE(6,2ØØ)
2ØØ  FORMAT('+',34('_'))
```

Execution of the first WRITE statement will print the line specified by the apostrophe edit descriptor in the 1ØØ FORMAT statement:

```
bNOTE UNDERLINING IN PRINTED OUTPUT
```

Upon encountering the closing (right) parenthesis of the 1ØØ FORMAT statement, the printer will index to output column 1 on that line. When executing the second WRITE statement as instructed by the 2ØØ FORMAT statement, the vertical-control character, specified in output column 1 as character constant "+" will hold the paper on the line just printed. The underline character, as specified by the apostrophe edit descriptor, will be overprinted in the 34 columns occupied by the character constants printed by the first WRITE statement, resulting in:

```
bNOTE UNDERLINING IN PRINTED OUTPUT
 __________________________________
```

Note that this overprinting technique can only be used with the printer. If this is attempted with the screen display or diskette storage, the characters specified by the first FORMAT statement will be replaced by the characters specified by the second FORMAT statement when the second WRITE statement is executed.

If either by ignorance or accident the programmer specifies a value that places a vertical-control character in output column 1, it will perform its intended function unnoticed until its effects appear in the output. The Ø and 1 are the vertical-control characters most likely to turn up inadvertently in output column 1. No distinction is made between Ø or 1 as vertical-control characters versus Ø or 1 as digits in a numerical value or as characters in a character string.

Consider the program of Fig. 6-8 (see p. 164). As each succeeding value assigned to N (2, 4, 6, and 8) is printed according to the I2 edit descriptor, a blank is specified in column 1 and the lines of print are single-spaced. When the value of N reaches 1Ø, the program attempts to place a vertical-control character, 1, in output column 1, resulting in a paper advance to the top of a new page. The 1 in column 1 is suppressed; a zero is printed in output column 2. Succeeding values of N with a 1 as the first digit (12, 14) will each have their second digit printed in output column 2 at the top of a new page. Therefore, the last three numbers printed do not represent the true value of the variable.

6-12 THE SLASH EDIT DESCRIPTOR IN THE WRITE/FORMAT SPECIFICATION

The slash (/) edit descriptor, used in the READ/FORMAT specification for control of input from a data file (Sec. 6-6), can also be used in the WRITE/FORMAT

```
C234567890
      OPEN(6,FILE='PRN')
      N=0
   10 N=N+2
      WRITE(6,100)N
  100 FORMAT(I2)
      IF(N.LE.14)GO TO 10
      STOP
      END
```

```
                     Top of First Page
--------------------------------------
2
4
6
8
                    Top of Second Page
--------------------------------------
0
                     Top of Third Page
--------------------------------------
2
                    Top of Fourth Page
--------------------------------------
4
↑
└── output column 2
    (First digit (1) is lost)
```

FIGURE 6-8 Accidental use of vertical-control characters.

specification to index to output column 1. The slash is classified as an edit descriptor and should not be considered a vertical-control character per se, even though the effect on the output may be similar to that of a vertical-control character. Unlike the vertical-control characters discussed in Sec. 6-11, the slash does not occupy an output column and is not restricted to column-1 usage. When used as part of a FORMAT specification, the slash is never displayed. The slashes may be placed at the beginning of the specification, between two other edit descriptors, or at the end of the specification in the FORMAT statement. The slashes may be the only edit descriptors in the FORMAT specification. Slashes may be used singly, or two or more may be used successively in any of these locations. Slashes have the same effect on all forms of output.

a The Slash at the Beginning of the Specification

Slashes at the beginning of the specification in a FORMAT statement referenced by a WRITE statement advance the line of output one line for each slash. For example:

```
    WRITE(*,1ØØ)
1ØØ FORMAT(1X,'THISbISbLINEbONE')
    WRITE(*,2ØØ)
2ØØ FORMAT(//,1X,'THISbISbLINEbFOUR')
```

will display:

```
bTHISbISbLINEbONE
line 2 is blank
line 3 is blank
bTHISbISbLINEbFOUR
```

Execution of the first WRITE statement will display THIS IS LINE ONE according to the specification of the 1ØØ FORMAT statement. When the closing (right) parenthesis of the 1ØØ FORMAT statement is encountered, control is returned to output column 1 of the line just displayed. When the second WRITE statement is executed according to the specifications of the 2ØØ FORMAT statement, the first slash will cause an advance to line 2; the second slash will advance to line 3. The control remains at output column 1 for both operations. The 1X, a *blank* vertical-control character, will cause an advance to line 4, and THIS IS LINE FOUR will be displayed, beginning in output column 2 of the fourth line. When slashes are used at the beginning of the specification, the first descriptor following the slashes must include a vertical-control character.

b The Slash at the End of the Specification

Slashes at the end of the specification in a FORMAT statement referenced by a WRITE statement index to output column 1 and advance one line for each slash. For example:

```
    WRITE(*,1ØØ)
1ØØ FORMAT(1X,'THISbISbLINEbONE',//)
    WRITE(*,2ØØ)
2ØØ FORMAT(1X,'THISbISbLINEbFOUR')
```

will display:

```
bTHISbISbLINEbONE
line 2 is blank
line 3 is blank
bTHISbISbLINEbFOUR
```

Execution of the first WRITE statement will display THIS IS LINE ONE according to the specifications of the 1ØØ FORMAT statement. The first slash will index to column 1 and advance to line 2; the second slash will advance to line 3, the control remaining at column 1. Execution of the second WRITE statement according to the specifications of the 2ØØ FORMAT statement will advance to line 4 (the 1X specifies a *blank* vertical-control character in column 1), and THIS IS LINE FOUR will be displayed beginning in column 2 of the fourth line. Note that the output of the second example is identical to the output of the example in Sec. 6-12*a*. In that example the specification for displaying line 4 contained, at the beginning of the specification, two slashes which skipped lines 2 and 3 before line 4 was displayed. In this example the specification for displaying line 1 contains two slashes at the end of the specification, which skipped lines 2 and 3 after displaying line 1. The net effect on the output is the same.

c The Slash between Edit Descriptors

A single slash between two edit descriptors in the specification of a FORMAT statement referenced by a WRITE statement indexes to output column 1 of the line just displayed. Two slashes index to column 1 and advance one line. Three slashes index to column 1 and advance two lines. N slashes between two edit descriptors index to column 1 and advance N−1 lines. When slashes are used between edit descriptors, the first descriptor following the slash(es) must include a vertical-control character. The following examples illustrate the effect of slashes between edit descriptors:

Example 6-5

```
      WRITE(*,1ØØ)
1ØØ   FORMAT(1X,'LINEb1',/,1X,'LINEb2',//,1X,
     *'LINEb4',///,1X,'LINEb7')
```

will display:

```
bLINEb1
bLINEb2
line 3 is blank
bLINEb4
line 5 is blank
line 6 is blank
bLINEb7
```

Example 6-6

```
      OPEN(6,FILE='PRN')
      WRITE(6,2ØØ)
2ØØ   FORMAT(1X,'UNDERLINING',/,'+',11('_'))
```

will print:

b<u>UNDERLINING</u>

This example does not apply to the screen display. Note also that in the examples in this text, slashes are separated from other edit descriptors by a comma. This was done for clarity; the comma is not necessary.

d The Slash as the Only Edit Descriptor in the Specification

When the specification of the FORMAT statement referenced by a WRITE statement contains only slashes, the number of lines advanced will be one line more than the number of slashes. One slash advances two lines; two slashes advance three lines; three slashes advance four lines; etc. N slashes advance N+1 lines. For example:

```
    WRITE(*,1ØØ)
1ØØ FORMAT(1X,'THISbISbLINEbONE')
    WRITE(*,2ØØ)
2ØØ FORMAT(//)
    WRITE(*,3ØØ)
3ØØ FORMAT(1X,'THISbISbLINEbFIVE,)
```

will display:

```
bTHISbISbLINEbONE
line 2 is blank
line 3 is blank
line 4 is blank
bTHISbISbLINEbFIVE
```

Execution of the first WRITE statement according to the specification of the 1ØØ FORMAT statement will display THIS IS LINE ONE as the first line of output. Execution of the second WRITE statement, which references the 2ØØ FORMAT statement with a specification containing only two slashes, will advance three lines, leaving lines 2, 3, and 4 blank. Execution of the third WRITE statement according to the specification of the 3ØØ FORMAT statement will advance one line (the 1X specifies a *blank* vertical-control character in output column 1) and displays THIS IS LINE FIVE, beginning in output column 2 on the fifth line.

6-13 SATISFYING THE INPUT/OUTPUT LIST

Just as the variable names listed in the READ statement should agree in number, order, and type with the edit descriptors in the specification of the associated FORMAT statement, so the variable names listed in the WRITE statement should agree in number, order, and type with the edit descriptors in the associated FORMAT statement (Sec. 6-5). In most cases the beginning programmer should strictly comply with this requirement, but there are exceptions. To cope with this situation and get predictable results, the programmer needs to be aware of how execution of the READ and WRITE statements is terminated.

When the number and type of the variable names in a READ or WRITE statement are the same as the number and type of the edit descriptors in the specification of the associated FORMAT statement, the values assigned to all the variable names in the READ/WRITE list are read or displayed in a one-to-one correspondence with the edit descriptors in the specification of the associated FORMAT statement, and a *balanced termination* occurs. When the number of variable names in a READ or WRITE statement is less or more than the number of edit descriptors in the specification of the associated FORMAT statement, an *unbalanced termination* of the READ or WRITE statement will occur. In the case of fewer variable names than edit descriptors, the unused edit descriptors in the FORMAT specification are ignored when the READ/WRITE statement is terminated. In the case of more variable names than edit descriptors, the edit descriptors in the FORMAT specification must be repeated one or more times before all the variable names in the READ/WRITE statement are read or displayed. In either case, the READ/WRITE list is "satisfied" when a value has been assigned or displayed for each variable name in the READ/WRITE list. If the READ/WRITE list cannot be satisfied by the edit descriptors in the specification of the associated FORMAT statement, execution will be aborted with an error message.

Although several special considerations may affect the unbalanced termination of input/output statements, there are only two simple rules of immediate interest to the beginning programmer. They cover the two cases where (1) there are more edit descriptors in the FORMAT specification than variable names in the associated READ/WRITE list, and (2) there are more variable names in the READ/WRITE list than edit descriptors in the associated FORMAT specification.

> Rule 1: If there are more edit descriptors in the specification than variable names listed in the associated READ or WRITE statement, the extra descriptors are ignored.

The READ/WRITE list is satisfied when a value has been assigned to each variable name in the READ list, or a value displayed for each variable name in the WRITE list. When the READ/WRITE list has been satisfied, execution of the READ or WRITE statement is terminated. Input control is reset to read the next record, or the output control is indexed to output column 1 of the line just displayed. Program control then passes to the next sequential executable statement.

Example 6-7

Rule 1 can be illustrated as follows:

```
      OPEN(5,FILE='FILE.DAT')
      READ(5,1ØØ)I,J,K
1ØØ   FORMAT(3I3,I5,F6.2)
      WRITE(*,1ØØ)I,J,K
```

FILE.DAT
*b*11*b*12*b*13

This program segment will display:

```
b11b12b13
```

Both the READ and WRITE statements, with the same three integer-variable names I, J, and K, in each list, reference the 1ØØ FORMAT statement with five edit descriptors in the specification. Both the READ and WRITE lists are satisfied by the three I3 descriptors. The additional descriptors (I5,F6.2) are simply ignored.

Rule 2: If there are more variable names in the READ or WRITE list than edit descriptors in the associated FORMAT specification, the specification is repeated until the READ or WRITE list is satisfied.

a FORMAT Specifications without Interior Parentheses

When the closing (right) parenthesis of the FORMAT statement is encountered and the READ/WRITE list has not been satisfied, input control is reset to read the next record or output control is indexed to column 1. Repetition of the edit descriptors begins with the first edit descriptor following the opening (left) parenthesis. Continuing execution of the READ statement assigns the first value from the next record to the next variable name in the READ list. Continuing execution of the WRITE statement displays the value assigned to the next variable name beginning on a new line of output (Sec. 6-11). The edit descriptors in the FORMAT specification are repeated as many times as necessary until the READ or WRITE list is satisfied.

Example 6-8

This application of Rule 2 can be illustrated as follows:

```
      OPEN(1,FILE='FILE.DAT')
      READ(1,2ØØ)L,M,N
2ØØ   FORMAT(1X,I2)
      WRITE(*,2ØØ)L,M,N
```

FILE.DAT
b11b12b13 b21b22b23 b31b32b33

This program segment will display:

```
b11
b21
b31
```

Both the READ and WRITE statements, with the same three integer-variable names L, M, and N, in each list, reference the 200 FORMAT statement, which provides only one integer edit descriptor, I2. To satisfy the three integer-variable names in the READ and WRITE lists, the edit descriptor must be repeated three times. Each time the closing (right) parenthesis of the FORMAT statement is encountered during execution of the READ statement, the read sequence is reset and the value assigned to the next variable name is read from the *next* record according to the edit descriptor in the specification (repeated). Three records are needed, but only the first value in each record is read and assigned: 11 to L, 21 to M, and 31 to N. Each time the closing (right) parenthesis is encountered during execution of the WRITE statement, control is returned to output column 1, vertical-control character 1X causes a one-line advancement, and the value assigned to the next variable name is displayed according to the I2 descriptor in the specification (repeated). If the first edit descriptor following the opening (left) parenthesis prescribes, as it should, a vertical-control character for output column 1, the output line will be controlled accordingly and the value displayed. The values assigned to L, M, and N are displayed on three successive lines, right-justified in output column 3. The 1X edit descriptor provides a blank in output column 1 which causes a one-line advancement before displaying the first character.

b FORMAT Specifications with Interior Parentheses

When a FORMAT specification contains interior parentheses, Rule 2 is applied somewhat differently, as illustrated in Fig. 6-9. Here three sets of integer-variable names, A, B, C, D, E, F; I, J, K, L, M, N; and R, S, T, U, V (note the INTEGER type-declaration statements) are assigned the values 11, 12, 13, 14, 15, 16; 21, 22, 23, 24, 25, 26; and 31, 32, 33, 34, 34, 35, respectively. These values are assigned to the variable names by reading a data file of three records. All the variable names are included in a single WRITE list and the values printed according to the edit descriptors in the specification of the 200 FORMAT statement. Note there are seventeen variable names in the WRITE list and, considering the repetition numbers, only six I edit descriptors in the FORMAT specification. This means that Rule 2 applies; the specification must be repeated until the WRITE list is satisfied. To help relate each variable to the descriptor applied in printing the variables, character constants (the letters A, B, or C) have been included to identify each value.

The first time the FORMAT specification is used, the entire list of edit descriptors is applied, in order, and the values assigned to the first six variable names (11, 12, 13, 14, 15, 16) are printed on the first line of output along with the identifying letter of the adjacent I descriptor. When the closing (right) parenthesis of the specification is encountered, the printer control is returned to output column 1 and, since the WRITE list is not satisfied, the specification is repeated. However, repetition of the specification begins with the edit descriptor following the opening (left) parenthesis of the *rightmost set of interior parentheses* (including the repetition number, if any, applying to that set of parentheses). If the first edit de-

```
C234567890
      INTEGER A,B,C,D,E,F
      INTEGER R,S,T,U,V
      OPEN(3,FILE='FIG6-9.DAT')
      OPEN(6,FILE='PRN')
      READ(3,100)A,B,C,D,E,F
  100 FORMAT(6I3)
      READ(3,100)I,J,K,L,M,N
      READ(3,100)R,S,T,U,V
      WRITE(6,200)A,B,C,D,E,F,I,J,K,L,M,N,R,S,T,U,V
  200 FORMAT(1X,3(2X,'A',I2),2(6X,'B',I2),10X,'C',I2)
      STOP
      END
```

```
11 12 13 14 15 16
21 22 23 24 25 26
31 32 33 34 35
```

```
  A11  A12  A13      B14       B15        C16
      B21      B22        C23
      B24      B25        C26
      B31      B32        C33
      B34      B35        C
```

FIGURE 6-9 Effect of interior parentheses in FORMAT statements.

scriptor in that set of parentheses is a *blank*, the paper will advance one line. Execution continues to the closing (right) parenthesis of the specifications, or until the WRITE list is satisfied, at which time execution of the WRITE statement terminates. Each time the closing (right) parenthesis of the specification is encountered with the WRITE list unsatisfied, printer control is returned to output column 1 and the specification is repeated from the opening (left) parenthesis (including the repetition number, if any) of the rightmost set of interior parentheses. Note that the set of edit descriptors identified as 3(2X,'A',I2) is not repeated.

Repetition of the edit descriptor list in this example includes only 2(6X,'B',I2),10X,'C',I2). This portion of the descriptor list is repeated 4 times before the remaining 11 variables in the WRITE list are printed and the WRITE list satisfied. In the last repetition observe that the character constant C is printed but no value is printed for the accompanying I2 edit descriptor because the WRITE list has been previously satisfied and the edit descriptor therefore ignored. If the WRITE list contains a mix of integer, real, character, or other variable names and the programmer is unaware of or overlooks the repetition pattern of the edit descriptor list, the variable names are likely to be "out of step" with the specification after the first time through, and execution of the WRITE statement may terminate at that point with an error message.

6-14 SKIPPING LINES AT INTERVALS IN THE OUTPUT

A long table of data can be made more readable if a skipped line (double spacing) is programmed at regular intervals in the table. This can be accomplished by taking advantage of the fact that the result of the division of two integers (the integer quotient) is always an integer; any fractional parts are truncated. Thus, when N is used as a counter, the result of the expression:

```
N/3*3-N
```

is zero only when N is a multiple of 3. For example when N = 1, the value of the expression is −1; when N = 2, the value is −2; when N = 3, the value is Ø; when N = 4, the value is −1; when N = 5, the value is −2; when N = 6, the value is Ø; etc. Double spacing at regular intervals in a table of data can be programmed by using N as a counter of single-spaced output, equating the value of the constant to the desired number of single-spaced lines between a double-spaced interval. The value of the expression can be compared with zero, and double spacing programmed whenever that value equals zero. An example of this routine is:

```
IF(N/3*3-N.EQ.Ø) WRITE(*,*)
```

Each time the arithmetic expression is zero the logical expression is true and a blank line will occur. When the arithmetic expression is not zero, the WRITE statement will be ignored and execution will proceed with the next sequential executable statement. This routine is shown in Figs. 7-15 and 8-14. The same concept can be used to display results at any regular interval in a long sequence of iterative calculations.

6-15 ADDITIONAL EDIT DESCRIPTORS

The F, E, I, X, apostrophe, and slash edit descriptors have been discussed in this chapter. Some FORTRAN compilers provide additional edit descriptors. The Hollerith (H), positional (T), scale-factor (P), optional-plus (S), general (G), character (A), and blank-interpretation (BN and BZ) edit descriptors will be presented in Chap. 10. The double-precision edit descriptor (D) will be presented in Chap. 11.

6-16 EXAMPLE PROBLEMS

Example 6-9

Now that methods for controlling input/output and annotating the output with character constants have been discussed, the circle problem presented in Secs. 3-19 and 4-8 can be rewritten to apply these concepts. Figure 6-10 shows the flowchart used, which is essentially the same as the flowchart of Fig. 4-20(*a*). Figure 6-11 on p. 174 shows the program. The format-directed READ/WRITE statements are used. The WRITE statement prints the results in the form of a sentence.

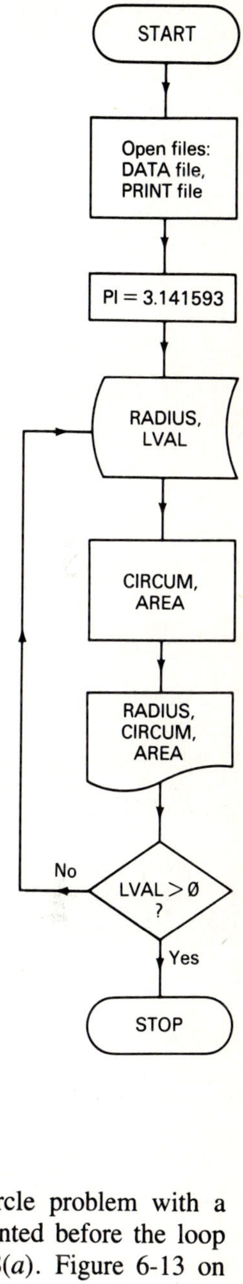

FIGURE 6-10 Flowchart of circle problem.

Example 6-10

Figure 6-12 on p. 175 shows the flowchart of the circle problem with a counter variable. Note that the column headings are printed before the loop starts. Figure 6-12 is essentially the same as Fig. 4-18(*a*). Figure 6-13 on p. 176 shows the program and the results.

Example 6-11

Surveying instruments (transit and theodolite) used for measuring angles are

```
C234567890
C   OPEN FILES FOR DATA AND PRINTER
      OPEN(3,FILE='FIG6-11.DAT')
      OPEN(6,FILE='PRN')
C   PUT IN THE VALUE OF PI
      PI=3.141593
C   READ VALUES FOR RAD AND LAST VALUE INDICATOR
   10 READ(3,100)RAD,LVAL
  100 FORMAT(F10.3,I5)
C   COMPUTE THE CIRCUMFERENCE AND AREA
      CIRCUM=PI*RAD*2.0
      AREA=PI*RAD**2
C   PRINT OUT THE RESULTS
      WRITE(6,200)RAD,CIRCUM,AREA
  200 FORMAT(1X,'WHEN THE RADIUS =',F10.3,', THE CIRCUMFERENCE IS THEN
     $',F10.3,/,1X,'AND THE AREA IS',F10.3,/)
C IF THE LAST VALUE, TERMINATE
      IF(LVAL.GT.0)STOP
      GOTO 10
      END
```

```
10.000    0
20.000    0
32.400    0
40.750    0
75.823    1
```

```
WHEN THE RADIUS =    10.000, THE CIRCUMFERENCE IS THEN     62.832
AND THE AREA IS   314.159

WHEN THE RADIUS =    20.000, THE CIRCUMFERENCE IS THEN    125.664
AND THE AREA IS  1256.637

WHEN THE RADIUS =    32.400, THE CIRCUMFERENCE IS THEN    203.575
AND THE AREA IS  3297.919

WHEN THE RADIUS =    40.750, THE CIRCUMFERENCE IS THEN    256.040
AND THE AREA IS  5216.812

WHEN THE RADIUS =    75.823, THE CIRCUMFERENCE IS THEN    476.410
AND THE AREA IS 18061.420
```

FIGURE 6-11 Program for circle problem.

calibrated in degrees, minutes, and seconds. Computer computations involving angular measurement require that the angle be expressed in radians. Write a program that will read from a data file the value of an angle in degrees, minutes, and seconds and calculate and print the value of that angle in decimal degrees and radians. Figure 6-14 on p. 177 illustrates the flowchart for this problem. This program uses the END=*n* option (Sec. 3-10) in the READ statement. The attempt to execute the READ statement after the last record has been read will cause a transfer to the STOP statement. Figure 6-15 on p. 178 shows the program for this problem and generally summarizes by application the statements and programming techniques discussed thus far.

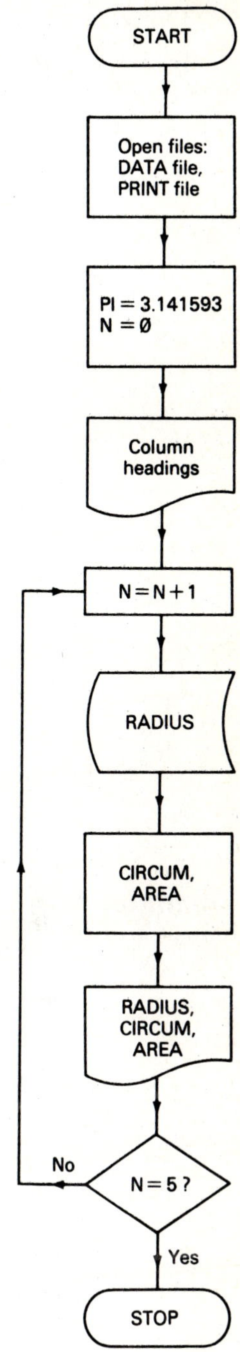

FIGURE 6-12 Flowchart of circle problem with a counter loop.

```
C234567890
      OPEN(3,FILE='FIG6-13.DAT')
      OPEN(6,FILE='PRN')
      PI=3.141593
      N=0
      WRITE(6,*)'          COUNT          RADIUS',
     $'          CIRCUMFERENCE          AREA'
   10 N=N+1
      READ(3,*) RAD
      CIRCUM=PI*RAD*2.0
      AREA=PI*RAD**2
      WRITE(6,*)N,RAD,CIRCUM,AREA
      IF(N.EQ.6)STOP
      GOTO 10
      END
```

```
10.0
25.0
32.4
40.75
75.823
100.0
```

```
COUNT        RADIUS          CIRCUMFERENCE         AREA
  1        10.0000000          62.8318600        314.1593000
  2        25.0000000         157.0797000       1963.4960000
  3        32.4000000         203.5752000       3297.9190000
  4        40.7500000         256.0398000       5216.8120000
  5        75.8230000         476.4100000      18061.4200000
  6       100.0000000         628.3186000      31415.9300000
```

FIGURE 6-13 Program for circle problem with a counter loop.

PROBLEMS

6-1 A file identified by the statement: OPEN(3,FILE = 'PROB1.DAT') contains the following data (starting in column 1):

124.56843.72*b*54.38*bb*7.85932

What values will be assigned to each of the given variables as the result of the following pairs of statements?

```
(a)     READ (3, 3ØØ) A, B
    3ØØ FORMAT (2F6.2)
(b)     READ (3, 4ØØ) A, B, C
    4ØØ FORMAT (3F6.2)
(c)     READ (3, 5ØØ) A, B, C
    5ØØ FORMAT (2F5.2, 6X, F6.2)
(d)     READ (3, 6ØØ) A, B, C, D, LVAL
    6ØØ FORMAT (4F7.3, I1)
(e)     READ (3, 7ØØ) A, B, I
    7ØØ FORMAT (12X, 2F6.2, 1X, I2)
```

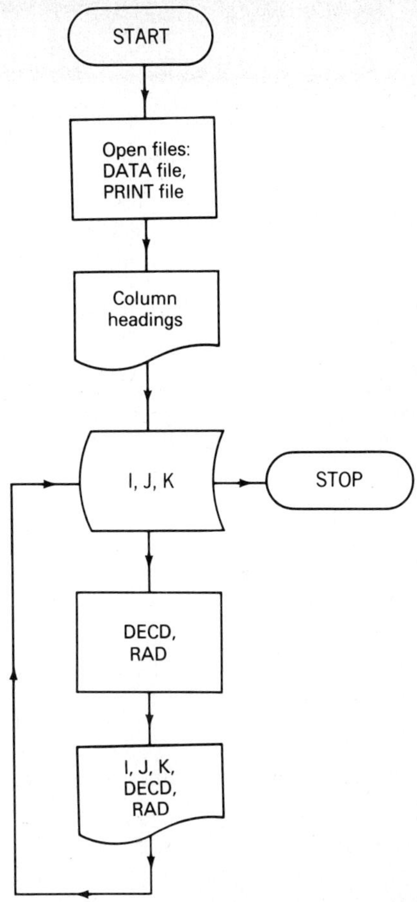

FIGURE 6-14 Flowchart for degree-conversion problem.

6-2 The following values are assigned to the given variable names.

```
X=Ø.1234567E3       I=158
Y=Ø.4682EØ          J=3Ø3
A=Ø.876543E-1       K=5
```

With the statement OPEN(6,FILE = 'PRN'), what will be printed as the result of the following pairs of statements?

```
(a)         WRITE(6,1ØØ)X,Y
        1ØØ FORMAT(2F1Ø.3)
(b)         WRITE(6,2ØØ)X,J
        2ØØ FORMAT(1X,F8.4,I3)
(c)         WRITE(6,3ØØ)X,Y,A,K
        3ØØ FORMAT(1X,3F1Ø.5,I6) .
```

```
C234567890
C   THIS IS A PROGRAM TO READ ANY ANGLE IN DEGREES, MINUTES, AND
C   SECONDS AND THEN TO CHANGE THE ANGLE TO A DECIMAL VALUE,
C   AND THEN CHANGE THE ANGLE TO RADIANS.

C   OPEN FILES AND PRINT HEADINGS.
      OPEN(2,FILE='FIG6-15.DAT')
      OPEN(8,FILE='PRN')
      WRITE(8,100)
  100 FORMAT(2X,'DEG MIN SEC     DECDEG        RADIANS')
C READ IN VALUES OF DEGREES, MINUTES, AND SECONDS AS INTEGERS.
C   TERMINATE PROGRAM WHEN ALL DATA IS READ.
   10 READ(2,200,END=20)I,J,K
  200 FORMAT(3I5)
C   CONVERT ANGLE TO DECIMAL AND TO RADIANS.
      DECD=FLOAT(I)+FLOAT(J)/60.0+FLOAT(K)/3600.0
      RAD=DECD*3.141593/180.0
C   PRINT ANGLE AND RESULTS.
      WRITE(8,300)I,J,K,DECD,RAD
  300 FORMAT(1X,3I4,F11.5,E14.6,/)
C   READ THE NEXT DATA CARD.
      GO TO 10
   20 STOP
      END
```

```
360    0    0
229   57   38
111    3    7
 45    0    0
 26   18   11
  0    0    1
```

```
DEG MIN SEC     DECDEG        RADIANS
360   0   0  360.00000    .628319E+01

229  57  38  229.96060    .401357E+01

111   3   7  111.05190    .193822E+01

 45   0   0   45.00000    .785398E+00

 26  18  11   26.30305    .459075E+00

  0   0   1     .00028    .484814E-05
```

FIGURE 6-15 Program for degree-conversion problem.

```
(d)         WRITE(6,4ØØ)X
        4ØØ FORMAT(F8.4)
(e)         WRITE(6,5ØØ)X,A,I
        5ØØ FORMATI(1X,F1Ø.5,/,F1Ø.5,I4)
```

6-3 Study the program shown in Fig. 6-16 and determine the numerical values that will be printed. The data in data file PROB6-3.DAT are: Ø1234567890Ø, starting in column 1.

6-4 Study the program shown in Fig. 6-17 and determine the numerical values that will be printed. The data in data file PROB6-4.DAT are: 2468101214161820, starting in column 1.

```
C  PROB 6-3
C234567890
      OPEN(6,FILE='PRN')
      OPEN(3,FILE='PROB6-3.DAT')
      READ(3,100)A,B,N
  100 FORMAT(2X,F2.1,F2.0,3X,I2)
      C=N
      D=C/B
      WRITE(6,*)'   PROB 6-3'
      WRITE(6,*)'THE PRINTED VALUES ARE:'
      WRITE(6,200)A,B,C,D,N
  200 FORMAT(4F5.1,I5)
      STOP
      END
```

FIGURE 6-16
Problem 6-3.

```
C  PROB 6-4
C234567890
      OPEN(3,FILE='PROB6-4.DAT')
      OPEN(6,FILE='PRN')
      READ(3,100)N,A,B
  100 FORMAT(I2,8X,F2.0,F4.2)
      C=N
      D=C/A
      WRITE(6,200)A,B,C,D,N
  200 FORMAT(4F5.1,I3)
      STOP
      END
```

FIGURE 6-17
Problem 6-4.

6-5 This problem demonstrates various methods for the format-directed reading and printing of numerical values. Write a program that will read from the first seven columns of a record the digits 4561785, and assign Ø.456 to X and 1.785 to Y. On successive lines of output, print:

Values of X and Y with edit descriptors of (2F1Ø.3)
Value of X with edit descriptors of ('*b*X = ',F5.3)
Values of X and Y with edit descriptors of (2X,2F4.3)
Values of X and Y with edit descriptors of (2F5.3)
Value of Y with an edit descriptor of (F5.3)

Explain the results printed with the last three lines.

6-6 This problem demonstrates the power of the FORMAT statement to selectively read values from a record. Create a record of the digits: 123456789Ø, starting in column 1. Write a program that will read this record and assign the integer value 2 to the variable name N, the real value 3.4 to the variable name A, and the real value 6.7 to the variable name B. Compute the square root of $A^N + B^N$, and assign that value to the variable name C. Under appropriate column headings print the values of N, A, B, and C.

6-7 Given a file of records each containing a single integer value, which may vary from 1 through 999, read the value from each record and determine whether the value is an odd or even integer. Count the total number of values read and the number of odd and even values. Separately sum and average the odd values and the even values. Appropriately annotate and print on the first line of output the number of even values and the number of odd values. On the second line print the sums of the even and odd values. On the third line print the average of the even and odd values. On the fourth line print the total number of values read. Make up your own data file using values that can be easily checked.

6-8 The American Institute of Steel Construction gives the following formulas for the allowable stress for secondary columns:

$$S = 17{,}ØØØ - Ø.485\left(\frac{\ell}{r}\right)^2 \quad \text{where } \frac{\ell}{r} \le 12Ø$$

and $$S = \frac{18{,}000}{1 + \ell^2/18{,}000r^2} \qquad \text{where } 120 \le \frac{\ell}{r} < 200$$

where S = unit stress, lb/in^2
ℓ = length of column, in
r = radius of gyration, in

The value of ℓ/r is known as the slenderness ratio. Write a program that will read in the values of ℓ and r, select the appropriate formula, and calculate the allowable unit stress. If the value of the slenderness ratio is 200 or greater, an appropriate message should be printed. Terminate the program with a last-value indicator. Select data to test all parts of the program.

6-9 A computer can test a variety of hypotheses about a collection of data. Read the integer numbers I, J, and K from a record and test the following hypotheses:

K is the product of I and J.
K is the sum of I and J.
K is a common factor of I and J; i.e., it can be divided into both I and J a whole number of times.

Prepare a suitable data file and write the program.

6-10 Values for ten sets of numbers, each set having three values, are to be prepared for a data file. The values should be arranged in order of descending magnitude. Test the records in the data file for proper arrangement. If they are properly arranged, compute the sum of the three values and print the values and their sum. If they are not properly arranged, print the three values and an appropriate message.

6-11 The ellipse in Fig. 6-18 with the semiaxes *OA* and *OB* has the mathematical relationships:

$$\text{AREA} = \pi\,(OA)\,(OB)$$

$$\text{CIRCUM} = 2\,\pi\sqrt{\frac{(OA)^2 + (OB)^2}{2}}$$

$$\text{OR} = \sqrt{\frac{(OA)^2(OB)^2}{(OA)^2(\sin^2\theta) + (OB)^2(\cos^2\theta)}}$$

Assume that the dimensions of seven ellipses are as follows:

OA, cm	*OB*, cm	$\theta°$
3.	1.	0
3.	1.	15.
3.	5.	30.
4.	4.	45.
5.	3.	60.
1.	3.	75.
1.	3.	90.

Read the given data and compute the values for the AREA, CIRCUM, and OR. Print out the given data, the value of the angle in radians, and the results of the computations. Include column headings.

6-12 Figure 6-15 illustrates a program to read values for angles in degrees, minutes, and seconds and convert them to decimal degrees and radians. Other conversions that might be required are to convert to mils and grads. Use the data in Fig. 6-15. Print values of the angles in degrees, minutes, and seconds. Compute the conversions to mils and grads to a comparable degree of precision. (*Note:* 36Ø° ØØ′ ØØ″ = 64ØØ mils = 4ØØ grads.)

6-13 Write a program that will read a value for an angle in radians, and convert it to degrees, minutes, and seconds. Print the results as integer values with seconds, precise to the nearest second. Use as test data the following angles in radians: 6.283185, 4.Ø13567, 1.938221, Ø.7853982, Ø.459075Ø, and Ø.ØØØØØØ48.

6-14 The values for the volume and surface area of a spherical segment can be determined from the relationships:

$$V = \pi H^2\left(\frac{L^2 + 4H^2}{8H} - \frac{H}{3}\right) \qquad A = \frac{\pi}{2}(2H^2 + L^2)$$

where H and L are as shown in Fig. 6-19. Use the data:

H	L
3.5Ø	1Ø.5Ø
3.5Ø	15.ØØ
2.25	8.5Ø
3.ØØ	9.75

Write a program that will read the data for H and L. For each set of values compute and print the values of the volume and surface area. Print the given and computed values under appropriate headings. Terminate the program by using the END=*n* option. Submit a flowchart.

6-15 Write a program that will read any number of temperature values in degrees Celsius.

FIGURE 6-18
Problem 6-11.

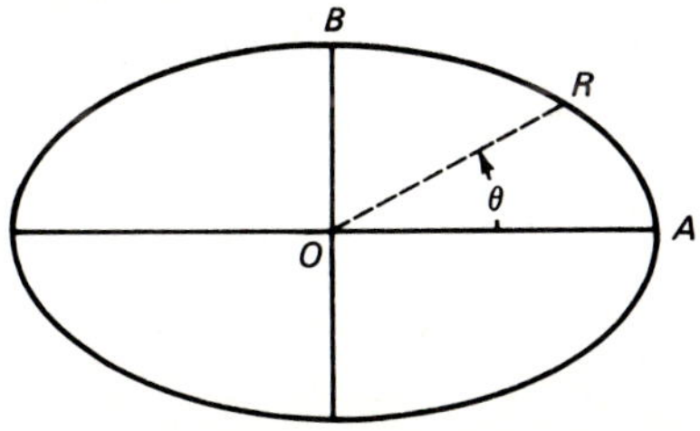

FIGURE 6-19
Problem 6-14.

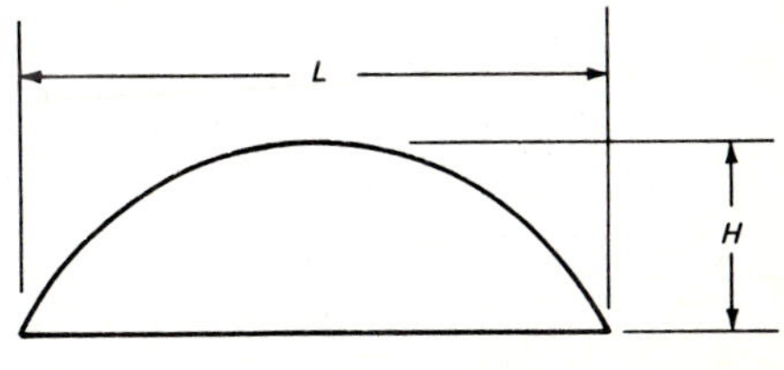

Compute the corresponding temperatures in degrees Fahrenheit and Rankine. Terminate the program with a last-value indicator. Prepare your own data. Print column headings. Submit a flowchart.

6-16 The distributers of natural gas plan to computerize their bill preparation. Rates are:

Consumption, cu ft	Cost per 1ØØ cu ft
First 3ØØØ	$5.ØØ (Minimum flat charge)
Second 3ØØØ	Ø.15
Next 2Ø,ØØØ	Ø.13
Next 15Ø,ØØØ	Ø.1Ø
All remaining	Ø.Ø55

Each record of the data file contains the customer's identification (social security number) and the number of cubic feet of gas consumed. Write a program that will determine the charges for any quantity of gas consumed. Output should show the social security number, the consumption, and the dollar charge. Prepare data as desired.

6-17 In a simple beam *AB* with a single concentrated load *F* at any point *P* (Fig. 6-20), the reactions at the ends are:

$$R_A = \frac{Fb}{\ell} \qquad R_B = \frac{Fa}{\ell}$$

From the left end of the beam to the load, the shear force is the value of R_A. From the load to the right end of the beam, the shear force is R_B. The units of the reactions and shear are pounds. The bending moment (BM) and deflection (DE) at any distance X are determined by the following equations when $X \leq a$:

$$(\mathrm{BM})_X = \frac{FbX}{\ell} \qquad (\mathrm{DE})_X = -\frac{FbX(\ell^2 - b^2 - X^2)}{6EI\ell}$$

FIGURE 6-20 Problem 6-17.

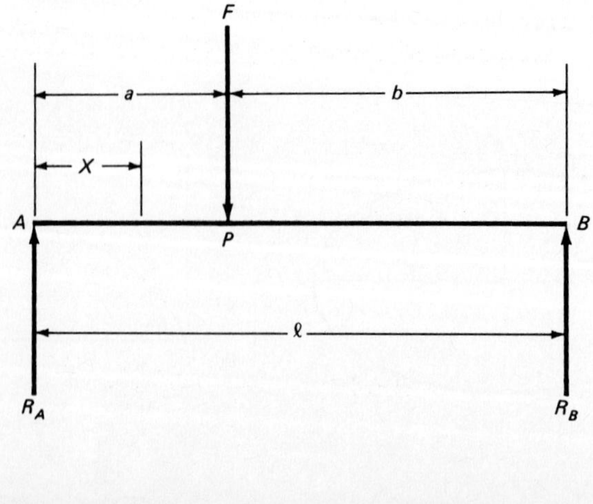

and when $X > a$:

$$(BM)_X = \frac{Fa(\ell - X)}{\ell} \qquad (DE)_X = -Fa(\ell - X)\,\frac{\ell^2 - a^2 - (\ell - X)^2}{6EI\ell}$$

where $(BM)_X$ = bending moment at X, lb·in
$(DE)_X$ = deflection at X, in
E = modulus of elasticity, lb/in^2
I = moment of inertia, in^4

ℓ, a, and b are as in Fig. 6-20. The maximum bending moment is:

$$(BM)_{max} = \frac{Fab}{\ell}$$

and the maximum deflection when $a > b$ is as follows:

$$X = \sqrt{\frac{a(\ell + b)}{3}}$$

measured from A, and

$$(DE)_{max} = -\frac{FbX^3}{3EI\ell}$$

If $a < b$:

$$X = \sqrt{\frac{b(\ell + a)}{3}}$$

measured from B and

$$(DE)_{max} = -\frac{FaX^3}{3EI\ell}$$

where X is the location of the maximum deflection $(DE)_{max}$. Write a program to calculate the reactions, shear force, bending moment, and deflections at 6-in intervals across a simple beam whose span is 24Ø in, with a concentrated load of 1Ø,ØØØ lb located 185 in from the left end. Assume I = 1222.7 in and E = 3Ø × 1Ø^6 lb/in^2.

6-18 In a cantilever beam with a uniformly distributed load (Fig. 6-21, p. 184) the following equations apply:

$$(VS)_X = -WX$$

$$(BM)_X = -\frac{WX^2}{2}$$

$$(DE)_X = -\frac{W(X^4 - 4\ell^3X + 3\ell^4)}{24EI}$$

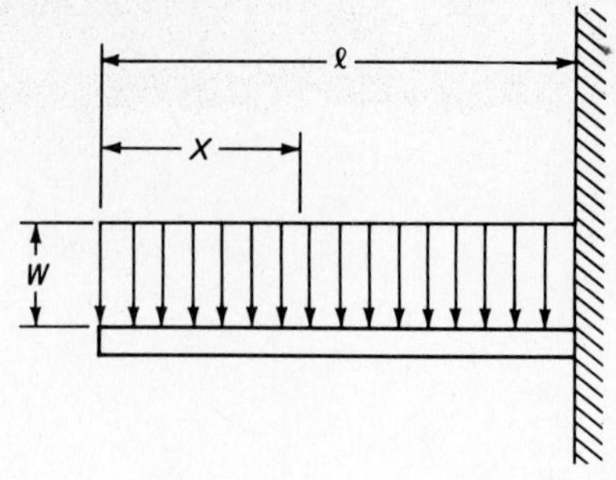

FIGURE 6-21 Problem 6-18.

where $(\mathrm{VS})_X$ = vertical shear at point X, lb
$(\mathrm{BM})_X$ = bending moment at point X, lb·in
$(\mathrm{DE})_X$ = deflection at point X, in
I = moment of inertia, in^4
E = modulus of elasticity, $\mathrm{lb/in}^2$
ℓ = length, in

The uniform load is W lb/in, and the distance from the free end is X in. Write a program that will read the initial data; then calculate and print, in appropriately annotated tabular form, the results of the given equations for uniform intervals along the beam. Select your own interval, but it must be one that divides evenly into the length. The length of the beam is 18Ø in; the uniform load is 25 lb/in; the modulus of elasticity is $3Ø \times 1Ø^6$ lb/in^2; and the moment of inertia is 625 in^4.

6-19 Each record of a given data file contains the X, Y, and Z coordinates of points A, B, and C. Note that these coordinates define the position of each point in three-dimensional space. Coordinate values are positive and range from Ø.Ø to 9.9. As each record is read, assign it a sequence number (1, 2, 3, etc.). Then compute the length of each of the three sides (AB, AC, and BC), the area of the triangle ABC formed by the three sides, and the value in decimal degrees of the interior angles A, B, and C of the triangles. Under appropriate column headings, print the sequence number and the results of all calculations. Print all values to the nearest tenth. Repeat the loop, ending after the last record is read. The following formulas will be useful:

$$\text{Length of side } AB = \sqrt{(X_B - X_A)^2 + (Y_B - Y_A)^2 + (Z_B - Z_A)^2}$$

$$\text{Semiperimeter } S = \frac{AB + BC + CA}{2}$$

$$\text{Area} = \sqrt{S(S - AB)\,(S - BC)\,(S - CA)}$$

$$\sin A = \frac{2(\text{area})}{(AB)\,(CA)} \qquad \cos A = \sqrt{1 - \sin^2 A} \qquad \tan A = \frac{\sin A}{\cos A}$$

Use the following data:

A			*B*			*C*		
X	*Y*	*Z*	*X*	*Y*	*Z*	*X*	*Y*	*Z*
8.2	2.5	7.3	9.7	8.4	3.3	3.2	6.6	9.8
5.2	4.5	8.Ø	6.5	4.5	1.Ø	1.3	4.5	4.5
2.Ø	3.Ø	9.Ø	8.Ø	3.Ø	4.Ø	2.Ø	9.Ø	4.Ø
8.1	9.3	8.5	6.7	2.4	1.5	2.7	5.3	2.4
5.Ø	4.Ø	8.Ø	6.Ø	4.Ø	1.Ø	1.Ø	4.Ø	4.Ø

6-20 Transits and theodolites are used in most surveying work. An instrument operator looking through the telescope sees three horizontal cross hairs. The center horizontal cross hair is used when measuring the vertical angle VA in degrees and minutes to some point on a Philadelphia rod, which is graduated in feet to the nearest Ø.Ø1 ft (Fig. 6-22). The height of this point above the ground is called the rod reading (RR). At the same time the instrument operator can determine the distance subtended on the rod between the upper and lower horizontal cross hairs (the stadia hairs). This distance is called the stadia intercept SI. These cross hairs are precisely located in the telescope to subtend 1.ØØ ft on a vertical rod at a horizontal distance of 1ØØ.ØØ ft. The stadia intercept thus gives the distance from the focal point of the telescope to the rod. The distance *C* is the distance from the focal point to the center of the telescope, which is also the axis of its rotation and is constant for a given telescope. The value of *C* may vary from Ø.75 to 1.25 ft. The height of the center of the telescope above ground (HI) can be determined in a number of ways, usually by holding the Philadelphia rod beside the transit before starting out to radial points. When these values are known, the vertical distance VD between the center of the transit and the point on the rod at which the rod reading was made can be calculated.

FIGURE 6-22 Problem 6-20.

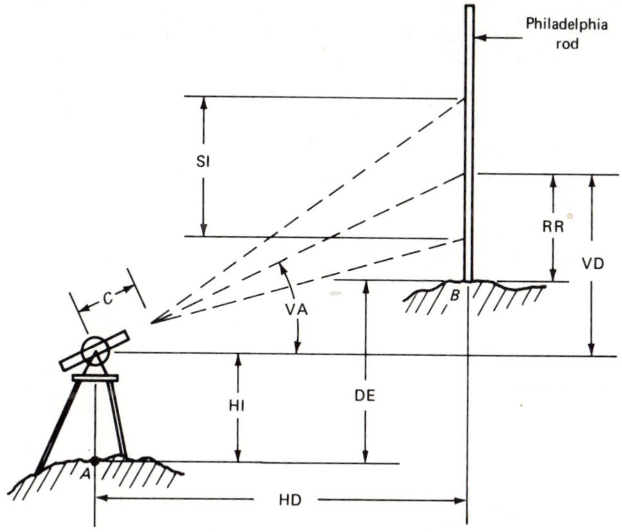

Then the horizontal distance HD and the difference in elevation DE between points *A* and *B* can be calculated. Write a program that will read in VA, RR, SI, HI, and *C* for any number of readings, and then calculate HD and DE. The output should show VA, RR, SI, HI, *C*, HD, and DE. The formulas for the calculations are:

$$\text{HD} = 1\text{Ø}\text{Ø}\text{SI} \cos^2 (\text{VA}) + C \cos \text{VA}$$

$$\text{VD} = 5\text{Ø}\text{SI} \sin^2 (\text{VA}) + C \sin \text{VA}$$

$$\text{DE} = \text{HI} + \text{VD} - \text{RR}$$

Note that the vertical angle VA is read in degrees and minutes and may be either positive or negative. The program must be able to handle any number of data sets. Prepare a data file with appropriate values for the variables to test the program.

6-21 If $24ØØ is invested at 1Ø percent, compounded annually, determine how many years it will take to accumulate at least $15 million if the interest is allowed to accumulate as principal and on each anniversary date an additional $24ØØ is added to the principal. Print the amount accumulated after every five years until the amount equals or exceeds the desired value.

$$A = P\left(1 + \frac{i}{n}\right)^n$$

where A = amount at the end of a year
P = principal
i = interest rate (decimal)
n = number of compounding periods in a year

6-22 Section 1-4 discussed how numbers are expressed in binary form. Write a program to perform the conversion of integer numbers from Ø to 127 to binary form. Test the program with the integer numbers Ø, 5, 1Ø, 25, 56, and 93. The output should show both the original integer and its binary equivalent. Integer numbers are used to simplify the program. Can you alter this program to handle real values?

6-23 A common method of repaying a loan is to make constant monthly payments of the largest amount convenient for you. This means that the number of monthly payments must be determined as a result of month-by-month calculations. Most often the last month's payment is less than the constant payment. You need to borrow $2Ø,5ØØ and have decided you can make monthly payments of $25Ø.ØØ. A bank is found that will lend you the money at an annual interest rate of 1Ø.5 percent.

Write a program that will determine month by month the amount of each payment that will go toward interest based on the unpaid balance at the start of the month, the amount that will be applied toward the repayment of the loan, and the amount of the unpaid balance after that payment. At the same time keep track of the total amount that has been paid, the total amount applied toward the loan, and the total amount that has gone toward interest.

Print the results every 12 months, showing the payment number, the total paid to date, the cumulative interest paid, the total amount paid on the loan, and the remaining balance due as of that month. When the balance due is less than the constant payment, determine the amount of the final payment and print the payment number and the final summation of the transaction. Be sure to print the amount of the final payment.

6-24 Revise Prob. 4-7 so that if a triangle can be formed, the program will determine whether the triangle is a scalene, isosceles, equilateral, or right triangle. Since an isosceles triangle can also be a right triangle, include this case in the test for isosceles triangles. Include a provision that in the case of right triangles, testing is limited to a precision of Ø.ØØ1. Use the data listed below:

A	B	C
1Ø.ØØØØ	7.Ø711	7.Ø711
1Ø.5ØØØ	3.525Ø	6.333Ø
8.66Ø3	1Ø.ØØØØ	5.ØØØØ
9.675Ø	8.125Ø	14.375Ø
4.ØØØØ	1Ø.ØØØØ	1Ø.ØØØØ
5.5ØØØ	5.5ØØØ	5.5ØØØ

CHAPTER **7**

THE DO STATEMENT

7-1 INTRODUCTION

The previous chapters provided sufficient information for the beginning programmer to prepare programs that include iteration routines using the transfer statements discussed in Chap. 4. Controlled iteration can also be achieved through an instruction that causes the repetition of a group of consecutive statements a specified number of times. This instruction is the DO statement. It is called a control statement since the number of iterations is controlled by how the statement is written.

7-2 THE EXPLICIT DO STATEMENT

The explicit DO statement is an executable statement which causes a portion of the program to be repeated a given number of times—a procedure called *looping*. The statements repeatedly executed during the looping procedure are referred to as the DO loop. The DO loop is initiated and controlled by a DO statement, which must be immediately followed by an executable statement, and is terminated with an allowable executable statement (Sec. 7-3) designated by a statement label in the DO statement. All statements following the DO statement, to and including the *terminal* statement, are defined as being within the *range* of the DO loop. The number of repetitions of the loop is established by the specified initial and limiting values of an automatically incremented integer-index variable. The general form for the explicit DO statement is:

DO *i j=k, m, n*

where *i* represents a statement label identifying the terminal statement (always an integer constant)
j represents an integer-variable name called the *index*
k and *m* represent, respectively, the initial and limiting integer values to be assigned to the index *j*
n represents the integer increment of the index (other than zero)

The index *j* is *always* an integer-variable name. The initial and limiting values *k* and *m* may be integer constants, integer-variable names, or integer-arithmetic expressions evaluated positive, negative, or zero. The increment *n* may be an integer constant, an integer-variable name, or an integer-arithmetic expression, evaluated positive or negative, but *not* zero. When the DO statement is written with variable names for the initial or limiting values *k* or *m*, or the increment *n*, values *must* have been *previously* assigned to these names. If arithmetic expressions are used for *k, m,* or *n,* all variables within the expression must have previously been defined. Variable names *k, m,* and *n,* which are parameters of the DO statement, may be used in computations within the range of the DO loop; however, these variable names must not be used in the loop in any way that could change their value (Fig. 7-1).

It is essential that the programmer know how many times a loop will be repeated. In any iterative process involving incrementation, the number of iterations will be one greater than the number of increments. The number of increments is the difference between the limiting value *m* and the initial value *k* divided by the increment *n*, truncated to integer form. Therefore,

$$\text{NR} = \frac{m - k}{n} + 1$$

where NR = number of repetitions (or iterations) of the DO statement
k = initial value specified in the DO statement
m = limiting value specified in the DO statement
n = increment specified in the DO statement

A common DO statement error is to repeat a loop by one iteration more or less than required.

Figure 7-2 illustrates the principal elements of the DO statement and shows how a DO loop is represented in a flowchart. Note the PREPARATION symbol

FIGURE 7-1 Nonpermissible statements within DO loops.

```
      DO 10 J=K,M,N
      J=15
      J=A
      READ(*,*)J
      K=2
      K=B
      READ(*,*)K
      M=10
      M=C
      READ(*,*)M
      N=4
      N=D
      READ(*,*)N
   10 CONTINUE
```

Statements that could change the value of the index, its initial or limiting value, or increment must not be used within the range of a DO loop.

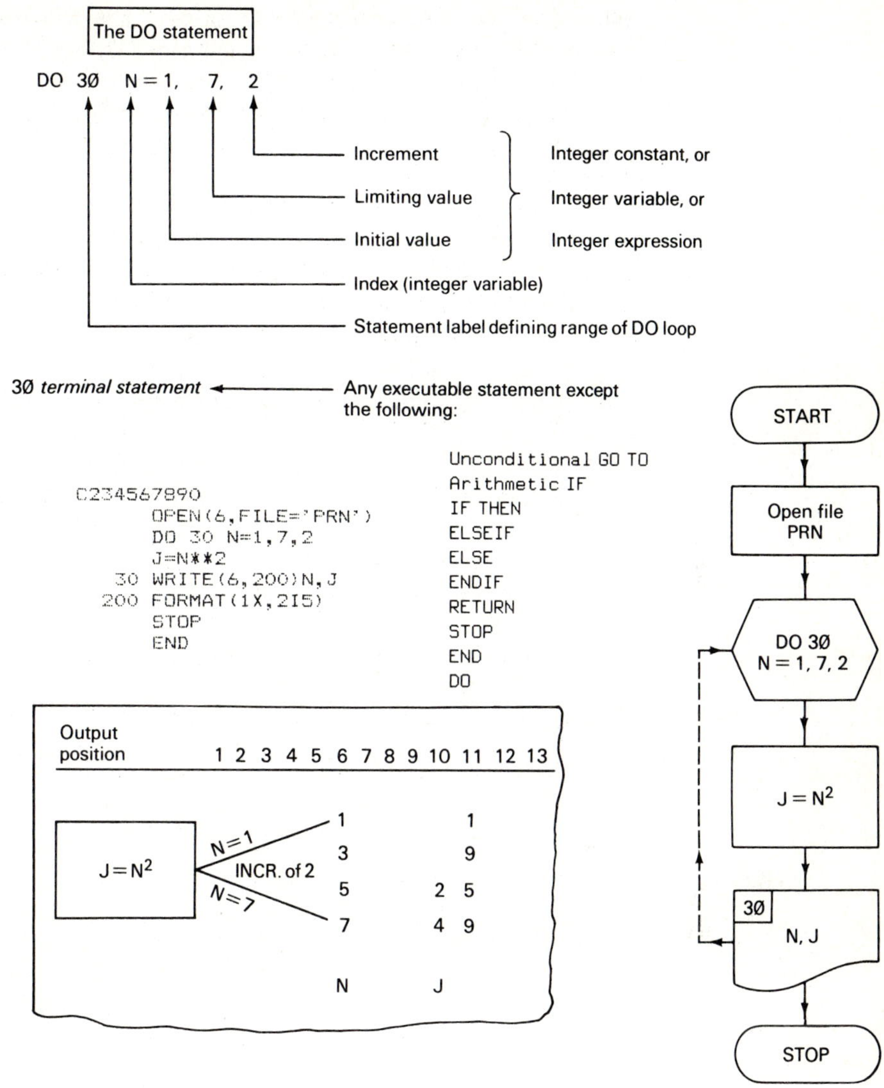

FIGURE 7-2 Elements of an explicit DO loop.

initiating the DO loop and the dashed lines defining the range of the DO loop. The range of the DO loop includes the executable statement J = N**2 and the executable terminating statement 3Ø WRITE(6,2ØØ) N,J. Initally, the index N is assigned a value of 1. This value of N is compared to 7, the limiting value of the index, and since N is less than 7, the loop is initiated. The index N is available for use as an integer variable within the loop with the value of N controlled by the DO statement. The value N^2 is assigned to J, and the values of both N^2 and J (1 and 1) are printed according to the specification of the associated FORMAT statement. This FORMAT statement (a nonexecutable statement) may be either inside or outside the loop, but it must not immediately follow the DO statement or be the terminal statement.

Following execution of statement 3Ø—the terminal statement—the value of index N is incremented by 2, and 3 is assigned to N. The value of N is automatically compared with the limiting value of N (7) specified in the DO statement. N is less than 7, so the loop is repeated. The value of N^2 (9) is assigned to J, and the values of both N and J (3 and 9) are printed. The index is again incremented by 2, making N = 5. Since N is still less than 7, the loop is repeated. The value of N^2 (25) is assigned to J, and the values of N and J (5 and 25) are printed. Once again, the index is incremented by 2, making N = 7. Since N is equal to but not greater than the limiting value, the loop is again repeated. When the index is next incremented, the value assigned to N is 9, which is greater than the limiting value 7; the DO loop is satisfied, and the program execution continues with the next executable statement following the terminating statement of the loop. The last value assigned to the index is one increment greater (or less when the increment is negative) than the limiting value defined in the DO statement. In the above example, the value assigned to N when the loop is satisfied is the value of the limiting value, 7, plus the increment 2. The last value of the index (N = 9, in this example) is retained and is available for subsequent use.

The index of a DO statement may or may not be assigned its limiting value due to the relationship of the increment to the initial and limiting values. For example, the DO statement

```
DO 5Ø I=1,1Ø,2
```

assigns only odd values to the index I. The limiting value of the index, the even number 1Ø, will never be assigned to I. Although this incrementation example may appear different from previous examples, the principle is the same. The index will have an initial value of 1, which is less than the limiting value, thus allowing loop initiation. After executing the statements in the range of the loop, the index will be incremented to a value of 3. This new index value will be compared to the limiting value. Since it is smaller than the limiting value 1Ø, the statements in the range of the loop will be executed a second time. This procedure continues until the index is incremented from a value of 9 to a value of 11. Since 11 is beyond the limiting value of 1Ø, the DO loop is satisfied and control is transferred to the next executable statement following the terminating statement of the DO loop. The value of the index when the DO loop is satisfied will be 11, and this value will be available for subsequent use outside the range of the DO loop.

The DO statement is frequently written to increment the index by 1. When the increment is 1, it need not be explicitly stated; the absence of an increment in the DO statement implies an increment of +1. For example:

```
DO 2Ø J=1,1Ø
```

Here the loop through statement 2Ø will be repeated for J = 1, 2, 3, 4, 5, 6, 7, 8,

9, 1Ø. When J becomes 11, the program continues with the next executable statement following statement 2Ø.

The DO statement may also be used to decrement. Consider the case where a variable must decrement from an initial value of +7 to a limiting value of −3 in increments of −2. This can be accomplished by using negative parameters in the DO statement as shown in Fig. 7-3. Note that again the value of the index is printed after the loop is completed, and that it is one increment less than the limiting value possible within the range of the loop.

It is permissible to transfer out of a DO loop before the loop has been satisfied:

```
      DO 4Ø K=1,15
      VAL=VAL**K
      IF(VAL.GT.1ØØØ.Ø) GOTO 6Ø
4Ø    ABLE=X+VAL
      ----------
      ----------
6Ø    CAN=K
```

In this case, the DO loop through the statement labeled 4Ø is to be executed 15 times. However, since the variable VAL comes from an earlier part of the program, it may be uncertain what the value of VAL will be after exponentiation. The DO loop will be iterated normally unless and until the result of the logical expression in the logical IF statement is true. This occurs when the value assigned to VAL is greater than 1ØØØ.Ø. Transfer will then be made to the statement labeled 6Ø, which is outside the range of the DO loop, and execution of the DO statement will cease. When a transfer out of a DO loop is made before the loop is

FIGURE 7-3 Decrementing with a DO loop.

```
C234567890
      OPEN(9,FILE='PRN')
      WRITE(9,100)
  100 FORMAT(5X,'N   NSQ',/)
      DO 10 N=7,-3,-2
      NSQ=N**2
      WRITE(9,200)N,NSQ
  200 FORMAT(1X,2I5)
   10 CONTINUE
      WRITE(9,300)N
  300 FORMAT(/,1X,I5)
      STOP
      END
```

```
    N   NSQ

    7    49
    5    25
    3     9
    1     1
   -1     1
   -3     9

   -5
```

satisfied, the last value assigned to the index is retained and is available for subsequent use. In this example, statement 6Ø, which is outside the range of the loop, will assign the last integer value of the index K of the DO statement to the real-variable name CAN as a real value.

7-3 THE CONTINUE STATEMENT

Remember that the terminal statement of a DO loop must be an executable statement; however, it cannot be an unconditional GOTO, arithmetic IF, IF THEN, ELSEIF, ELSE, ENDIF, RETURN, STOP, END, or another DO statement. (The RETURN statement will be discussed in Chap. 9.) It may be necessary to use one of these statements as the last "effective statement" in the loop. This can be accomplished by using a CONTINUE statement as the terminal statement. This statement, written simply CONTINUE, is a dummy executable statement that results in no action but allows the last effective executable statement to be one that is not permitted as a terminal statement. The CONTINUE statement has no specific flowchart symbol. However, as illustrated in Fig. 7-9, a circle, indicating the end of the range of the DO loop, may be used to represent the CONTINUE statement. This symbol should include the statement label referenced in the DO statement.

The CONTINUE statement also provides a way to interrupt the programmed iteration of the loop when a given condition occurs and to continue the loop for subsequent iterations. Consider the following simple example:

```
1Ø DO 2Ø N=K,M
   IF(N.LT.L) GOTO 2Ø
   SUM=SUM+FLOAT(N)
   - - - - - - - - - - - - -
   - - - - - - - - - - - - -
2Ø CONTINUE
```

The values of K, M, L, and SUM were assigned by either READ, assignment, or DATA (Sec. 10-4) statements preceding the DO statement. In this example, the initial value is the value previously assigned to K; the limiting value is the value previously assigned to M. The increment (implied) is 1.

As long as the value of the index N is greater than or equal to the value of the variable L, the statements in the loop are sequentially executed. If the value of the index becomes less than the value of L, a transfer is made to the CONTINUE statement, which bypasses the intervening statements and allows the execution of the loop to continue. However, transfer directly from the IF statement to the DO statement reinitiates the DO loop with N = K. This will result in an endless loop, which obviously is undesirable.

Figure 7-4 shows how identical results can be obtained by looping under control of both a logical IF statement and a DO statement. The first six statements in each program are identical, printing the column headings and setting values for the initial and limiting values and the increment for a variable to be used in both

```
C234567890
      OPEN(7,FILE='PRN')
      WRITE(7,100)
  100 FORMAT(5X,'N    NSQ',/)
      INIT=1
      LIMIT=10
      INC=2
      N=INIT
   10 NSQ=N**2
      WRITE(7,200)N,NSQ
  200 FORMAT(1X,2I5)
      N=N+INC
      IF(N.LE.LIMIT)GO TO 10
      WRITE(7,300)N
  300 FORMAT(/,1X,I5)
      STOP
      END
```

```
    N    NSQ

    1    1
    3    9
    5   25
    7   49
    9   81

   11
```

(a)

```
C234567890
      OPEN(8,FILE='PRN')
      WRITE(8,100)
  100 FORMAT(5X,'N    NSQ',/)
      INIT=1
      LIMIT=10
      INC=2
      DO 10 N=INIT,LIMIT,INC
      NSQ=N**2
      WRITE(8,200)N,NSQ
  200 FORMAT(1X,2I5)
   10 CONTINUE
      WRITE(8,300)N
  300 FORMAT(/,1X,I5)
      STOP
      END
```

```
    N    NSQ

    1    1
    3    9
    5   25
    7   49
    9   81

   11
```

(b)

FIGURE 7-4 Comparison of (*a*) IF and (*b*) DO loops.

programs. In the example with the IF loop, Fig. 7-4(*a*), the variable N is set to the initial value N = 1, and the value NSQ is calculated as 1. The values of N and NSQ are printed, and the value of N is incremented (N = 1 + 2 = 3). Then the new value of N is tested by the IF statement to see whether it is less than or equal to the limiting value 1Ø. Since it is less, transfer is made to the statement labeled 1Ø and the loop is repeated, resulting in printing the new values of N and NSQ, 3 and 9, and in the next incrementation of N (N = 3 + 2 = 5). Again the comparison test of N with 1Ø is made, and the loop is repeated since N = 5 is less than the limiting value 1Ø. This iteration continues until the incrementation of N results in a value larger than 1Ø and control is transferred to the WRITE statement where the last value of N (11) is printed.

Compare the above sequence with the DO loop in Fig. 7-4(*b*). Here the DO statement is, in effect, DO 1Ø N=1,1Ø,2, when the values assigned are substituted for the variable names. The value of N is set to 1, which is compared to the limiting value 1Ø. Since N is less than the limiting value, the value of NSQ is calculated, and the values of N and NSQ (1 and 1) are printed. The value of N is incremented (N = 1 + 2 = 3). Since this value is not greater than the limiting value 1Ø, the loop is repeated and the new values of N and NSQ (3 and 9) are printed. This sequence is repeated until the last incrementation of N results in a value of 11 (N = 9 + 2). Since this value is greater than the limiting value 1Ø, the DO statement is satisfied and the program continues with the first executable statement following the CONTINUE statement. This statement requires printing the value of N, and 11 is printed. This demonstrates that when the DO loop is satisfied, the final value assigned to the index, N = 11 in this example, is available for subsequent use and is one increment greater than the limiting value possible within the range of the loop.

7-4 FRACTIONAL INCREMENTATION AND DECREMENTATION

The index of a DO statement may be used to control incrementation or decrementation in fractional increments. Suppose variable A is to be incremented from an initial value of Ø.Ø to a final value of 1.Ø in increments of Ø.1, and a variable B is to be incremented from an initial value of Ø.Ø to a final value of 5.Ø in increments of Ø.5. Since the number of increments in each case is the same, and although real values are not valid parameters of the DO statement, the required fractional incrementations can be accomplished by using integer values for the parameters of the DO statement as shown in Fig. 7-5. As the index increments from Ø to 1Ø in increments of 1, A will increment (as a function of N) from Ø.Ø through 1.Ø in increments of Ø.1, and B will increment (as a function of N) from Ø.Ø through 5.Ø in increments of Ø.5. Note that the statements calculating the values of A and B could have been coded:

```
A=REAL (N) *Ø. 1
B=REAL (N) *Ø. 5
```

Fractional decrementation can be accomplished in the same manner by using a

FIGURE 7-5 Fractional incrementation with a DO loop.

```
C234567890
      OPEN(6,FILE='PRN')
      WRITE(6,100)
  100 FORMAT(1X,4X,'N     A      B',/)
      DO 20 N=0,10
      A=FLOAT(N)/10.0
      B=FLOAT(N)/2.0
      WRITE(6,200)N,A,B
  200 FORMAT(1X,I5,2F6.1)
   20 CONTINUE
      STOP
      END
```

```
    N     A     B

    0    .0    .0
    1    .1    .5
    2    .2   1.0
    3    .3   1.5
    4    .4   2.0
    5    .5   2.5
    6    .6   3.0
    7    .7   3.5
    8    .8   4.0
    9    .9   4.5
   10   1.0   5.0
```

```
C234567890
      OPEN(7,FILE='PRN')
      WRITE(7,100)
  100 FORMAT(4X,'N     A',/)
      DO 10 N=75,0,-15
      A=FLOAT(N)/10.0
      WRITE(7,200)N,A
  200 FORMAT(1X,I4,F6.1)
   10 CONTINUE
      STOP
      END
```

```
    N     A

   75   7.5
   60   6.0
   45   4.5
   30   3.0
   15   1.5
    0    .0
```

FIGURE 7-6
Fractional decrementation with a DO loop.

```
C234567890
      OPEN(8,FILE='PRN')
      WRITE(8,100)
  100 FORMAT(4X,'K     L')
      DO 10 K=0,20,2
      L=100-K*2
      WRITE(8,200)K,L
  200 FORMAT(1X,I4,I6)
   10 CONTINUE
      STOP
      END
```

```
    K     L
    0   100
    2    96
    4    92
    6    88
    8    84
   10    80
   12    76
   14    72
   16    68
   18    64
   20    60
```

FIGURE 7-7
Incrementing and decrementing with a DO loop.

negative increment as in Fig. 7-6. Here a value A is to be decremented from a value of 7.5 to a value of Ø.Ø in increments of −1.5. Again note that the statement calculating the value of A could have been coded:

```
A=REAL(N)*Ø.1
```

It is possible to both increment and decrement in the same DO loop. Suppose that a variable K is to be incremented from Ø to 2Ø in increments of 2, and L is to be decremented from 1ØØ to 6Ø in decrements of 4. The same number of decrements as increments is required, and the decrement is a multiple of the increment. Figure 7-7 shows such a program. Note the calculations for the values of L.

7-5 NESTED DO LOOPS

DO loops may be nested one within the other as illustrated by the program in Fig. 7-8 (see p. 198) and graphically shown in Fig. 7-9 (see p. 199). The DO 2Ø loop is called the *outer loop;* the DO 1Ø loop is called the *inner loop*. When the index J of the outer DO statement is set to the initial value, 3, the inner loop is executed with the index K assigned the values 2, 4, and 6. J is then incremented to 6 and the inner loop is executed again with K = 2, 4, and 6. This repetition continues until both loops have been satisfied. The assignment statement L=J+K simply illustrates how the index variable of a DO statement can be used as a working variable within the loop without violating any of the following rules.

```
C234567890
      OPEN(6,FILE='PRN')
      WRITE(6,100)
  100 FORMAT(3X,'J  K    L')
      DO 20 J=3,12,3
      DO 10 K=2,6,2
      L=J+K
      WRITE(6,200)J,K,L
  200 FORMAT(1X,2I3,I4)
   10 CONTINUE
   20 CONTINUE
      STOP
      END
```

```
  J  K   L
  3  2   5
  3  4   7
  3  6   9
  6  2   8
  6  4  10
  6  6  12
  9  2  11
  9  4  13
  9  6  15
 12  2  14
 12  4  16
 12  6  18
```

FIGURE 7-8 Nested DO loops.

7-6 RULES FOR DO LOOPS

1 The first statement in the range of a DO loop (the statement immediately following the DO statement) must be an executable statement. A specification statement, such as a FORMAT statement, cannot immediately follow a DO statement.

2 The last statement within the range of a DO loop (the terminal statement) must be an executable statement, but it cannot be an unconditional GOTO, arithmetic IF, IF THEN, ELSEIF, ELSE, ENDIF, RETURN, STOP, END, or another DO statement. The CONTINUE statement, always a suitable terminal statement, is recommended.

3 It is *not permissible* for any statement within the range of a DO loop to assign in any way a value to the index, the initial or limiting values, or the increment. It is permissible to use the index within the loop in an arithmetic or logical expression, in a computed GOTO statement, or in an output statement, or to assign its value to another variable name, as long as its value (assigned in the DO statement) is not altered.

4 In nesting DO loops, the range of the inner loop *must* be completely within the range of the outer loop. Nested DO loops may share the same terminal statement (e.g., CONTINUE), or a different allowable executable statement may be used to terminate each DO statement.

5 Transfer may be made from inside a DO loop to a statement outside the DO loop. With nested DO loops, transfer may be made from an inner loop to a statement within the outer loop. Transfer between statements within the range of a given loop is always permissible.

6 It *is not permissible* to transfer from outside a DO loop to a statement inside

Nested DO loops

```
C234567890
      OPEN(6,FILE='PRN')
      DO 20 J=3,12,3
      DO 10 K=2,6,2
      L=K+J
      WRITE(6,200)J,K,L
  200 FORMAT(1X,2I3,I4)
   10 CONTINUE
   20 CONTINUE
      STOP
      END
```

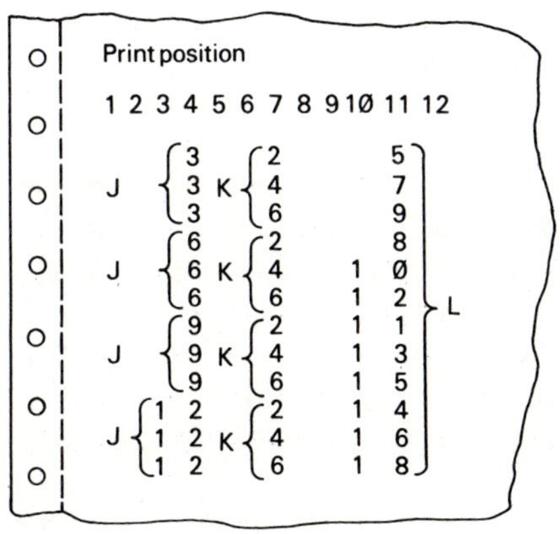

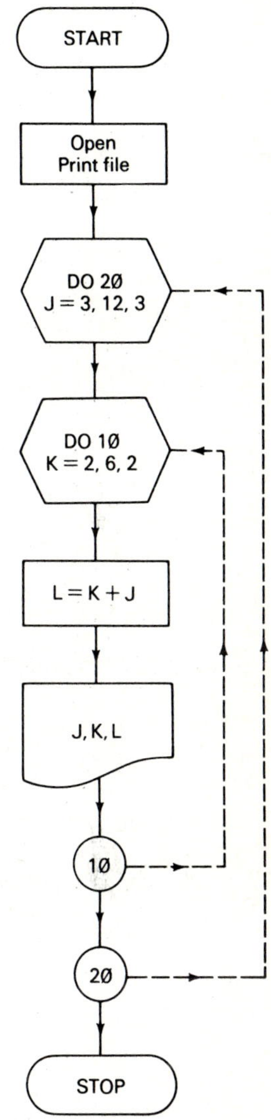

FIGURE 7-9 Elements of nested DO loops.

the loop. Entry into a loop must always be through the DO statement. Rules 4, 5, and 6 are illustrated schematically in Fig. 7-10 (see p. 200).

7-7 THE IMPLIED DO LOOP

The defining statements of the explicit DO statement as just described may be combined with input/output statements in an *implied* DO loop. The implied DO

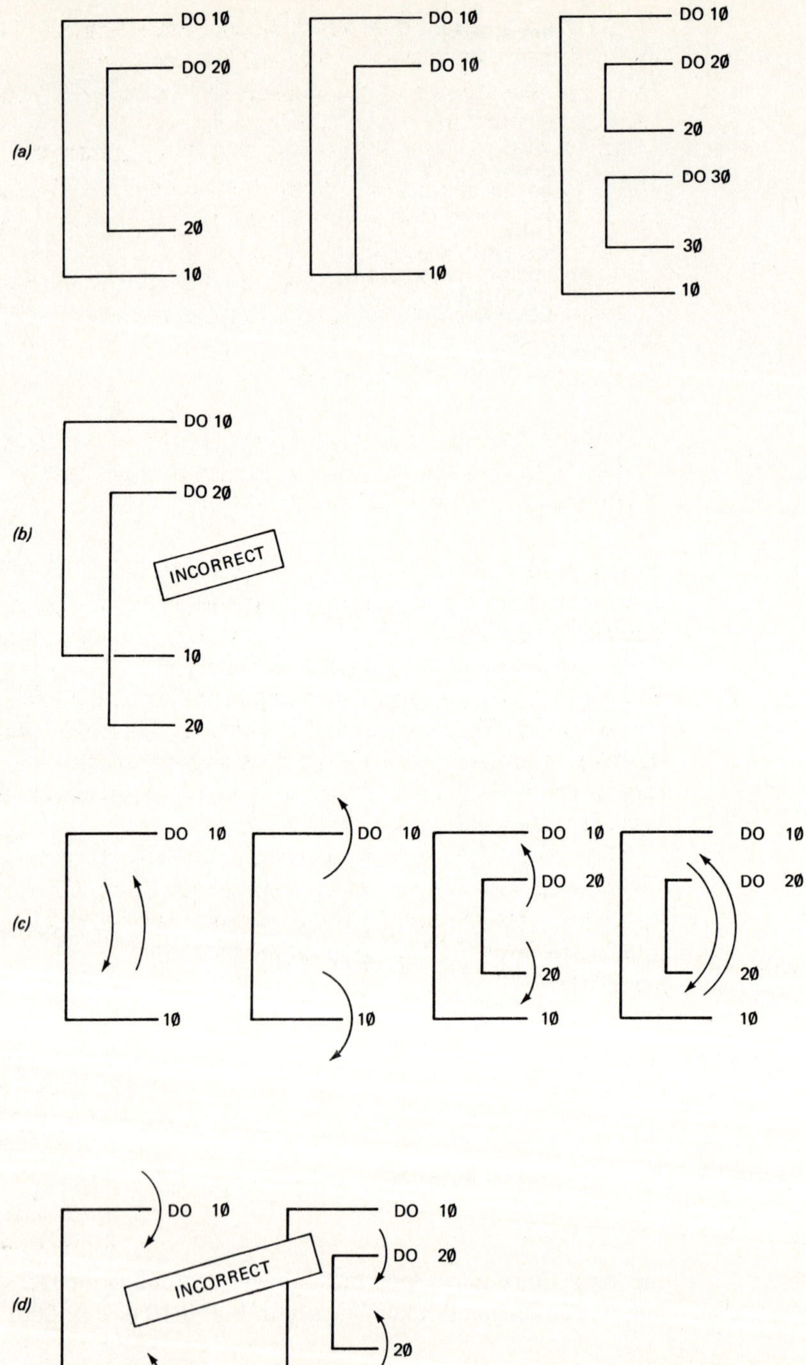

FIGURE 7-10 (*a*) Permissible and (*b*) nonpermissible nesting of DO loops; (*c*) permissible and (*d*) nonpermissible transfers in DO loops.

loop assigns a series of incremental values to a single variable name in a READ or WRITE list without the additional statements needed to construct an explicit DO loop. (Discussion of the implied DO in the READ statement as applied to subscripted variables appears in Chap. 8.)

The use of the implied DO in the WRITE statement is illustrated in Fig. 7-11. The WRITE statement is combined with an implied DO which assigns five values to N, in turn, beginning with N=2 (the initial value) and continuing through N=1Ø (the limiting value) in increments of 2 (the increment). The associated FORMAT statement provides five I edit descriptors for the five integer values—2, 4, 6, 8, and 1Ø—assigned to N. Note the use of parentheses (essential) in the WRITE list.

Rule 2 of Sec. 6-13 stated that:

> If there are more variable names in the READ or WRITE list than edit descriptors in the associated FORMAT specification, the descriptors are repeated until the READ or WRITE list is satisfied.

Now consider the third WRITE statement of Fig. 7-11. As in the first WRITE statement, five integer values—2, 4, 6, 8, and 1Ø—are assigned in turn to N; however, the associated FORMAT statement provides only one I edit descriptor. Rule 2 applies, and this single I edit descriptor will be repeated (5 times) until the five values assigned to N by the implied DO in the WRITE statement have been printed. (The WRITE statement is satisfied.) Since the output control will be indexed to column 1 each time the closing (right) parenthesis in the FORMAT specification is encountered and a *blank* (vertical-control character) is specified, the five values of N will be printed on successive lines.

The two WRITE statements are identical except for the edit descriptors in the associated FORMAT statement. The specification for the first WRITE statement results in a row of printed values; the specification for the third WRITE statement results in a column of printed values.

FIGURE 7-11 Implied DO loops.

```
C234567890
      OPEN(7,FILE='PRN')
      WRITE(7,100)(N,N=2,10,2)
  100 FORMAT(1X,5I5)
      WRITE(7,200)
  200 FORMAT('0')
      WRITE(7,300)(N,N=2,10,2)
  300 FORMAT(1X,I5)
      STOP
      END
```

```
    2    4    6    8   10


    2
    4
    6
    8
   10
```

```
C234567890
      OPEN(8,FILE='PRN')
      WRITE(8,100)(6-K,K=1,5)
  100 FORMAT(1X,5I3)
      WRITE(8,200)
  200 FORMAT(' ')
      WRITE(8,300)(6-L,L=1,5)
  300 FORMAT(1X,I3)
      STOP
      END
```

```
  5  4  3  2  1

  5
  4
  3
  2
  1
```

FIGURE 7-12 Decrementing with implied DO loops.

The implied DO can be combined with the WRITE statement to decrement successively the value assigned to a single variable name from a given initial value to a given limiting value. In Fig. 7-12 the index in each implied DO is incremented from an initial value of 1 through a limiting value of 5 in increments of 1. Each time the loops are repeated, the value assigned to the index (K or L) is subtracted from a constant (6) which is one increment of 1 greater than the given limiting value 5, resulting in decrementing values of 5, 4, 3, 2, and 1. Since no increment is specified for either implied DO loop, the increment is 1 by default. The values from the loop having K as the index are printed in a row; the values from the loop having L as the index are printed in a column. The two WRITE statements are identical in form but reference different FORMAT statements. Note that the same results may be obtained from implied DOs coded with a negative increment.

```
WRITE(8,1ØØ) (K,K=5,1,-1)
WRITE(8,3ØØ) (L,L=5,1,-1)
```

Implied DO loops can be nested, as shown in Fig. 7-13. Note the parentheses nesting in the WRITE list. The value of J, the index of the outer loop, is incremented from 1 through 3, while the value of K, the index of the inner loop, is incremented from 1 through 5, each in increments of 1. Rule 2 of Sec. 6-13 applies to the first edit descriptor of the 2ØØ FORMAT statement (the descriptor applying to the index J of the outer loop); hence, there are three lines of output, one for each value of J.

7-8 APPLICATIONS

Example 7-1

Knowledge of the DO statement provides yet another technique for solving the circle problem presented in Secs. 3-20, 4-8, and 6-16. This time, assume that

```
C234567890
      OPEN(9,FILE='PRN')
      WRITE(9,100)
  100 FORMAT(1X,'  J    K    K    K    K    K',/)
      WRITE(9,200) (J, (K,K=1,5),J=1,3)
  200 FORMAT(1X,I3,5I5)
      STOP
      END
```

```
  J    K    K    K    K    K

  1    1    2    3    4    5
  2    1    2    3    4    5
  3    1    2    3    4    5
```

FIGURE 7-13 Nesting of implied DO loops.

the radius is to vary from 5.ØØ to 7.ØØ in increments of Ø.25 and that two lines are to be skipped after each four lines of output. Figure 7-14 (see p. 204) shows the flowchart, and Fig. 7-15 (see p. 205) shows the program. Note the use of the DO statement and the FLOAT function to define successive real values for the radius. Note also the use of the IF statement to skip the two lines and the use of the repetition number in the 2ØØ FORMAT statement.

Example 7-2

In this example the problem is to compute and print the rectangular X and Y coordinates of all points whose polar coordinates R and θ are shown on the polar grid in Fig. 7-16 (see p. 205), where the radius R varies from 1 through 5 in increments of 2, and the angle θ varies from Ø to 36Ø° in increments of 15°. Observe that angles increase counterclockwise (Sec. 5-7). The logic of the solution is shown in the flowchart of Fig. 7-17 (see p. 206). Note the decision sequence between the inner and outer loops, which provides for either single-spacing the lines of output or double-spacing to set off Ø, 9Ø, 18Ø, 27Ø, or 36Ø°, as appropriate.

The program listing is shown in Fig. 7-18 (see p. 207). Note the use of the implied DO loop in the WRITE statement (second statement of the program) to provide the three values of the radius for the column headings. Next observe the computed GOTO. This is used to compute the three sets of X and Y coordinates for the three radial points along each radius line (angle). However, since the limiting value of the radius, used as the numerical indicator IR, will be 5, there must be five statement labels included in the list. Statements 1Ø, 2Ø, and 3Ø are the statements that compute the desired X and Y coordinates. Statement 4Ø, the CONTINUE statement, provides a convenient dummy statement label to use so that statements 1Ø, 2Ø, and 3Ø will be the first, third, and fifth labels in the required list of five statement labels. (The dummy statement label must be an actual statement label used in the program or a compiler error will prevent execution of the program, as described in Sec. 3-21 and App. E-6.) Fi-

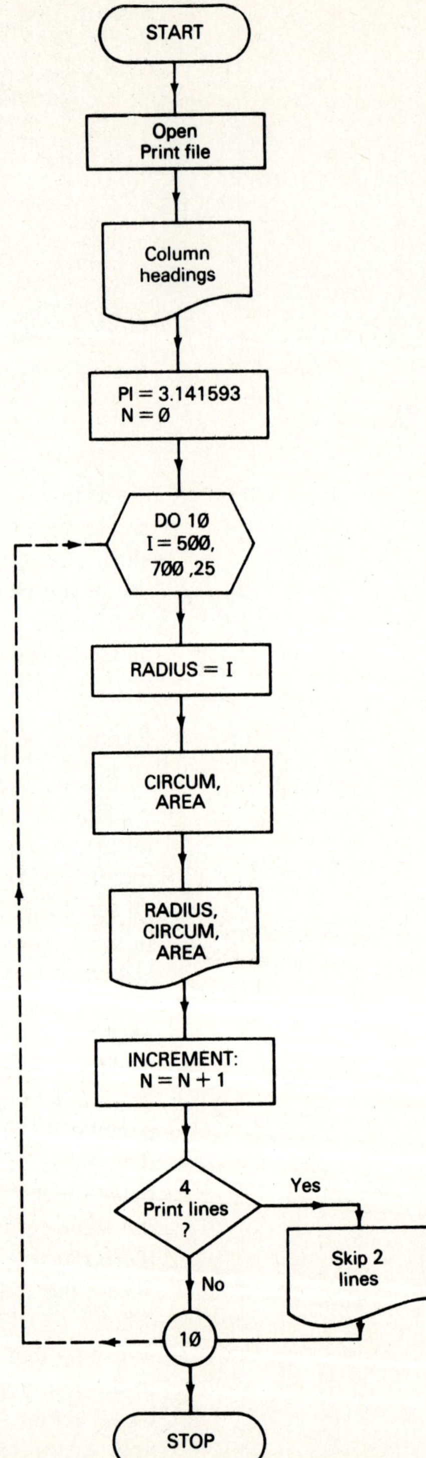

FIGURE 7-14 Flowchart for the circle problem with a DO loop.

```
C234567890
      OPEN(6,FILE='PRN')
      WRITE(6,100)
  100 FORMAT(7X,'RADIUS',6X,'CIRCUMFERENCE',7X,'AREA',/)
      PI=3.141593
      N=0
      DO 10 I=500,700,25
      RADIUS=FLOAT(I)/100.0
      CIRCUM=PI*RADIUS*2.0
      AREA=PI*RADIUS**2
      WRITE(6,200)RADIUS,CIRCUM,AREA
  200 FORMAT(6X,F8.5,2(6X,F10.6))
      N=N+1
      IF(N/4*4.EQ.N)WRITE(6,300)
  300 FORMAT('0')
   10 CONTINUE
      STOP
      END
```

```
      RADIUS       CIRCUMFERENCE       AREA

      5.00000       31.415930        78.539830
      5.25000       32.986720        86.590160
      5.50000       34.557520        95.033190
      5.75000       36.128320       103.868900


      6.00000       37.699120       113.097400
      6.25000       39.269910       122.718500
      6.50000       40.840710       132.732300
      6.75000       42.411510       143.138800


      7.00000       43.982300       153.938000
```

FIGURE 7-15 Program for the circle problem with a DO loop.

FIGURE 7-16 Polar versus rectangular coordinates.

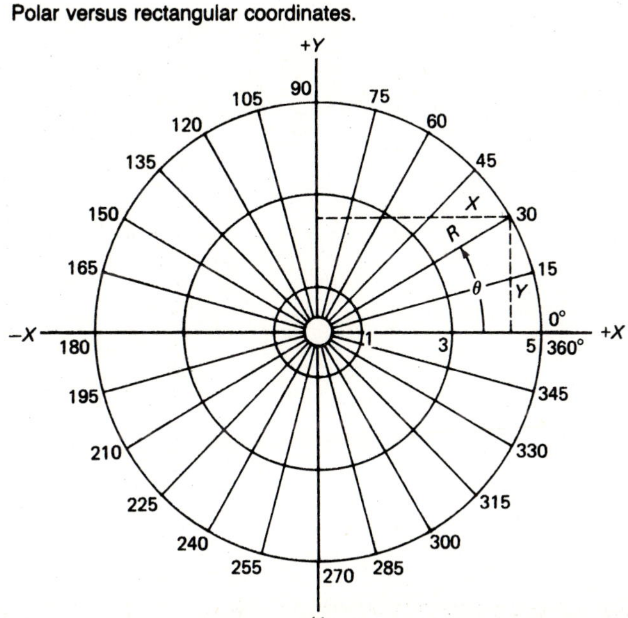

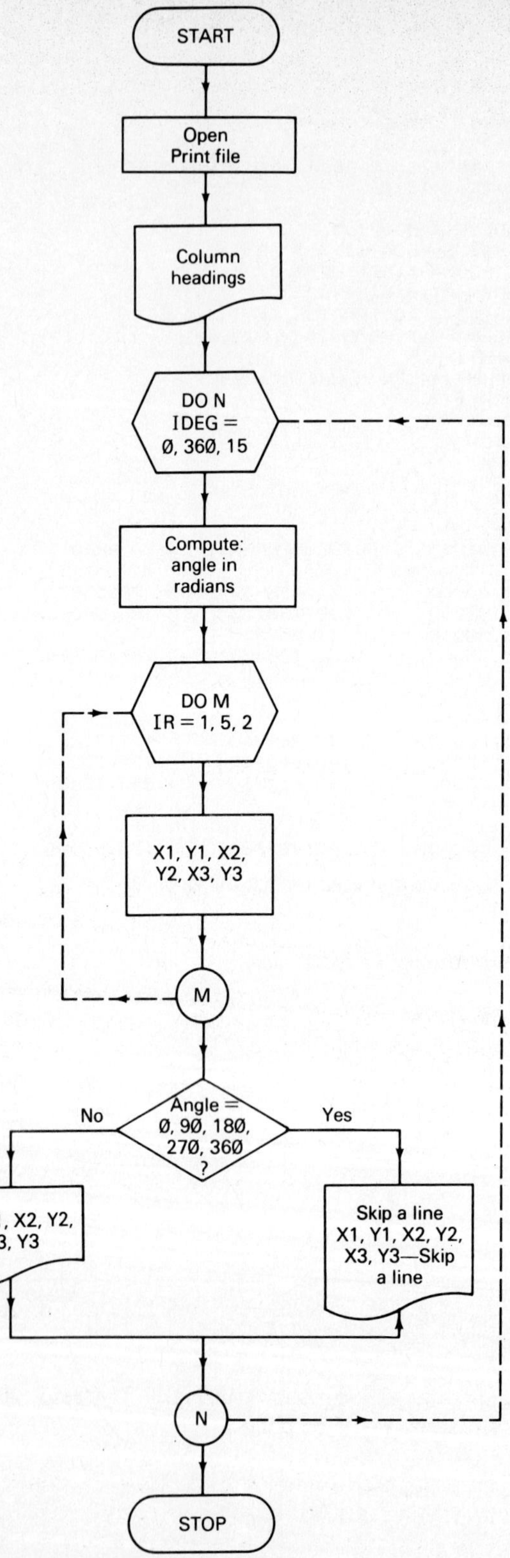

FIGURE 7-17 Flowchart for polar-coordinate conversion.

```
C234567890
      OPEN(7,FILE='PRN')
      WRITE(7,100) (J,J=1,5,2)
  100 FORMAT('1RADIUS',I11,2I18)
      WRITE(7,150)
  150 FORMAT(12X,'X',7X,'Y',9X,'X',7X,'Y',9X,'X',7X,'Y')
      WRITE(7,200)
  200 FORMAT(1X,'ANGLE')
      DO 60 NDEG=0,360,15
      RAD=FLOAT(NDEG)*3.141593/180.0
      DO 40 IR=1,5,2
      GO TO(10,40,20,40,30)IR
   10 X1=FLOAT(IR)*COS(RAD)
      Y1=FLOAT(IR)*SIN(RAD)
      GO TO 40
   20 X2=FLOAT(IR)*COS(RAD)
      Y2=FLOAT(IR)*SIN(RAD)
      GO TO 40
   30 X3=FLOAT(IR)*COS(RAD)
      Y3=FLOAT(IR)*SIN(RAD)
   40 CONTINUE
      IF(NDEG.EQ.0.OR.NDEG.EQ.90)GO TO 50
      IF(NDEG.EQ.180.OR.NDEG.EQ.270.OR.NDEG.EQ.360)GO TO 50
      WRITE(7,300)NDEG,X1,Y1,X2,Y2,X3,Y3
  300 FORMAT(I5,3X,3(2F8.3,2X))
      GO TO 60
   50 WRITE(7,400)NDEG,X1,Y1,X2,Y2,X3,Y3
  400 FORMAT(/,I5,3X,3(2F8.3,2X),/)
   60 CONTINUE
      STOP
      END
```

FIGURE 7-18 Program for polar-coordinate conversion.

nally, note the last logical IF and the WRITE statement to which transfer is made when the logic is true. These statements, and the associated FORMAT statement, provide for skipping a line before and after each quadrant break (Ø, 9Ø, 18Ø, 27Ø, and 36Ø°).

Figure 7-19 (see p. 208) shows the output resulting from the program. Observe that the signs of the *X* and *Y* values of the coordinates agree with the signs described in Fig. 5-2. The output is printed on the page following the program listing because of the vertical-control character (a 1 in the character constant '1RADIUS') placed in the first output column.

Since a DO statement may be applied so many ways, DO loops usually merit an explanatory comment in a documented program.

PROBLEMS

7-1 Study the program shown in Fig. 7-20 (see p. 208) and determine the numerical values that would be printed.

7-2 Study the program shown in Fig. 7-21 (see p. 208) and determine the numerical values that would be printed.

7-3 This problem demonstrates the DO loop and how its index can be used as a function for determining other values. Using only a DO loop, where the index varies from 1 to 1Ø, calculate the square roots of numbers 1 through 5Ø. Remember that the argument of a square-root function must be real. Print the results in five pairs of

```
RADIUS          1                3                5
           X         Y       X        Y       X        Y
ANGLE

   0     1.000      .000   3.000     .000   5.000     .000

  15      .966      .259   2.898     .776   4.830    1.294
  30      .866      .500   2.598    1.500   4.330    2.500
  45      .707      .707   2.121    2.121   3.536    3.536
  60      .500      .866   1.500    2.598   2.500    4.330
  75      .259      .966    .776    2.898   1.294    4.830

  90      .000     1.000    .000    3.000    .000    5.000

 105     -.259      .966   -.776    2.898  -1.294    4.830
 120     -.500      .866  -1.500    2.598  -2.500    4.330
 135     -.707      .707  -2.121    2.121  -3.536    3.536
 150     -.866      .500  -2.598    1.500  -4.330    2.500
 165     -.966      .259  -2.898     .776  -4.830    1.294

 180    -1.000      .000  -3.000     .000  -5.000     .000

 195     -.966     -.259  -2.898    -.776  -4.830   -1.294
 210     -.866     -.500  -2.598   -1.500  -4.330   -2.500
 225     -.707     -.707  -2.121   -2.121  -3.536   -3.536
 240     -.500     -.866  -1.500   -2.598  -2.500   -4.330
 255     -.259     -.966   -.776   -2.898  -1.294   -4.830

 270      .000    -1.000    .000   -3.000    .000   -5.000

 285      .259     -.966    .776   -2.898   1.294   -4.830
 300      .500     -.866   1.500   -2.598   2.500   -4.330
 315      .707     -.707   2.121   -2.121   3.536   -3.536
 330      .866     -.500   2.598   -1.500   4.330   -2.500
 345      .966     -.259   2.898    -.776   4.830   -1.294

 360     1.000      .000   3.000     .000   5.000     .000
```

FIGURE 7-19 Output for polar-coordinate conversion.

columns with 1Ø values in each column. The first value in each pair should be the integer number and the second value should be its square root. Include appropriate column headings.

FIGURE 7-20
Problem 7-1.

```
C   PROB 7-1
C234567890
      OPEN(6,FILE='PRN')
      N=0
      DO 10 J=9,45,9
      DO 10 K=2,10,2
      N=N+1
      IF(J.EQ.K**2)WRITE(6,100)N,J,K
  100 FORMAT(3I3)
   10 CONTINUE
      WRITE(6,200)N,J,K
  200 FORMAT('+',8X,3I3)
      STOP
      END
```

FIGURE 7-21
Problem 7-2.

```
C   PROB 7-2
C234567890
      OPEN(6,FILE='PRN')
      N=0
      DO 10 J=10,30,5
      DO 10 K=1,9,2
      N=N+1
      IF(J.NE.K**2)GO TO 10
      WRITE(6,100)J,K,N
  100 FORMAT(3I3)
   10 CONTINUE
      WRITE(6,200)J,K,N
  200 FORMAT('0',3I3)
      STOP
      END
```

7-4 The compound interest formula is:

$$A = P\left(1 + \frac{i}{m}\right)^{nm}$$

where A = amount at end of n years
n = number of years
P = original principal invested
i = annual interest rate (expressed as a decimal)
m = number of times per year that interest is compounded

Prepare a table showing the amount at the end of each year for 1Ø years for an original principal of $1ØØ.ØØ invested in a savings account at 8 percent annual interest, compounded quarterly. Single-space the data, but skip a line after the fifth year. Include appropriate headings.

7-5 Revise the above problem to print successive tables showing the effect of varying the annual interest from 9 to 12 percent in increments of 1 percent.

7-6 The increase with time in the number of bacteria in a culture is directly proportional to the number of bacteria at the start of the time interval. Mathematically, the number of bacteria can be expressed as:

$$P_t = P_0\left[1 + \frac{Ø.Ø54t}{1!} + \frac{(Ø.Ø54t)^2}{2!} + \frac{(Ø.Ø54t)^3}{6!} + \cdots + \frac{(Ø.Ø54t)^n}{n!}\right]$$

where P_t = number of bacteria at time t, hours
P_0 = number of bacteria at some initial time
t = time in hours after the initial time

Write a program that will compute and print the multiplying factor (the value of the terms within the brackets) for time from 1 to 5 hours. Use only the first 11 terms of this series.

7-7 Your company has been using engineering drawings dimensioned in decimal inches. To meet international standards the company has decided to convert all drawings to the metric system (1 in = 25.4ØØ1 mm). You decide to write a program, using DO loops, that will print a table of conversions to millimeters of inch lengths from Ø.1 to 1.Ø in steps of Ø.1, from 1.Ø to 1Ø.Ø in steps of 1.Ø, and from 1Ø.Ø to 1ØØ.Ø in steps of 1Ø.Ø. You further decide to print the metric results to the nearest Ø.ØØ1 in two columns so that, for example, the conversions of Ø.1 and Ø.6 in are printed on the same line. You also decide to single-space the lines within each interval and double-space between intervals. Write the program that will accomplish the conversion and print the results in the required tabular form.

7-8 The graph of $I_X^2 + J_Y^2 = K^2$ is a circle whose radius is K and whose center is at the origin. Determine and print the integer rectangular coordinates (I_X, J_Y) of all points that lie on circles whose radii vary from 1 to 5 in increments of 1. It should be obvious that for a circle of a given radius, the values of I and J cannot exceed the value of K. Since the center of the circle is at the origin, a number of the values of I and J will be negative. Analyze this problem carefully before starting the flowchart and writing the program.

7-9 Using a DO loop, tabulate the values of X and Y for the function:

$$Y = X^5 + 3X^3 - 1ØX - 6$$

for values from $X = -3$ through $X = 3$, where X varies in increments of Ø.5. Include appropriate headings.

7-10 Many values in engineering, science, and mathematics are defined by a series, and often the signs alternate from term to term of the series. Evaluating such a series provides a stimulating programming problem. Write a program that will evaluate the sum of the series below through the twentieth term.

$$1 - \frac{1}{2} + \frac{1}{3} - \frac{1}{4} + \cdots + \frac{1}{N}$$

7-11 Prime numbers are those integer values greater than 1 that cannot be divided evenly by any integer value other than themselves and 1. Write a program that will generate, determine, and print all prime numbers N between 1 and 1ØØ. (*Note*: No trial divisor will be larger than $N/2$.)

7-12 Write a program that will read in an integer value N and then determine all its divisors (factors) other than 1 and N. If there are no such divisors, print the integer and a statement that the integer is a prime number. If there are such divisors, print the integer and all its divisors in a column under the integer. Note that if the integer is not a prime number, it will have a divisor less than or equal to $N/2$. (*Hint*: Think of the results of integer arithmetic. The integers used should be greater than 1 and less than 1ØØ. Use as test values the integers 18, 31, 57, 83, and 96.)

7-13 In 1984, January 1 fell on Sunday. If Sunday is considered as day 1 of the week and Saturday as day 7, write a program that will determine the day upon which January 1 falls for the succeeding 1Ø years. Remember that a leap year (a year whose number is exactly divisible by 4) contains 366 days.

7-14 Write a program that will compute various functions of numbers from 1 through 25. The functions desired are the square, cube, square root, cube root, and reciprocal. Determine the cube root by the method discussed in Sec. 5-6. Plan the output to skip a line after every five numbers, but do not use an IF statement to do so. Include appropriate column headings.

7-15 Businesses commonly write off the cost of new equipment by depreciating its initial cost over a given number of years. One method used to calculate depreciation is the sum-of-years method, in which the number of years over which the equipment is to be depreciated is determined. The sum of years is calculated by the formula:

$$\text{SUMYR} = 1 + 2 + 3 + 4 + \cdots + i = \frac{i(i + 1)}{2}$$

where i represents the number of years of depreciation. The depreciation at the end of the first year is i/SUMYR times the initial cost; at the end of the second year it is $(i - 1)$/SUMYR times the initial cost; at the end of the third year it is $(i - 2)$/SUMYR times the initial cost; etc. Note that at the end of year K the depreciation is $(i - K + 1)$/SUMYR times the initial cost.

Your company has just purchased a piece of equipment costing $37,5ØØ, which is to be depreciated over a span of 15 years. Write a program that will calculate and print a table showing the depreciation at the end of each year and the remaining value of the equipment. Plan the output to skip a line after every 5 years. Include proper column headings. Ensure that the remaining value at the end of the last year will be $Ø.ØØ.

7-16 In these days when banks advertise various methods of compounding interest, it is difficult to understand the actual, or effective, rate of interest. The effective interest rate ER depends on the number of compounding periods C and the nominal rate of interest R. The effective rate can be calculated by:

$$\mathrm{ER} = \left(1 + \frac{R}{C}\right)^{C} - 1$$

Determine the effective rate of interest when compounded daily, monthly, quarterly, and semiannually for nominal rates of from 8 to 12 percent in increments of 1 percent.

7-17 Write a program to compute the rectangular coordinates (X, Y) for each point in the polar grid shown in Fig. 7-22. Print the values for the radius, angle (in degrees), X, and Y such that they are centered under appropriate column headings at the top of the page following the program listing. Print all the conversions for the angles of 15, 3Ø, 45°, etc., skipping a line between each group.

FIGURE 7-22 Problem 7-17.

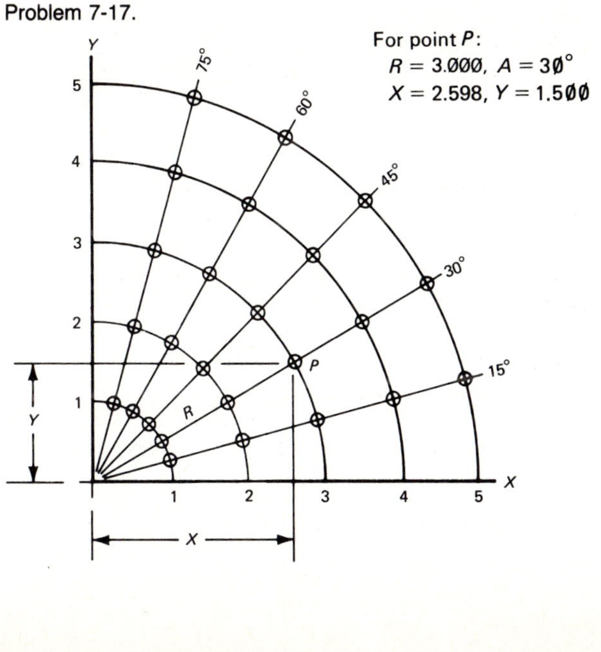

7-18 For a beam fixed at one end and supported at the other end, with a uniformly distributed load, as shown in Fig. 7-23, the reactions at the ends are:

$$R_A = \frac{3W\ell}{8} \qquad R_B = \frac{5W\ell}{8}$$

The shear, moment, and deflection equations for the beam are:

$$(\mathrm{VS})_X = R_A - WX$$

$$(\mathrm{BM})_X = R_A X - \frac{WX^2}{2}$$

$$(\mathrm{DE})_X = \frac{WX(\ell^3 - 3\ell X^2 + 2X^3)}{48EI}$$

where $(\mathrm{VS})_X$ = vertical shear at X, lb
$(\mathrm{BM})_X$ = bending moment at X, lb·in
$(\mathrm{DE})_X$ = deflection at X, in
ℓ = length, in
E = modulus of elasticity, lb/in^2
I = moment of inertia, in^4

The uniform load is W lb/in, and the distance from the supported end is X in. Write a program that will read in the initial data and then calculate and print in tabular form the results of the given equations for uniform intervals along the beam. The length of the beam is 96 in; the uniform load is 5Ø lb/in; the modulus of elasticity is 3Ø × 1Ø^6 lb/in^2; and the moment of inertia is 625 in^4. Use an interval of 3 in and print appropriate column headings.

7-19 Most people at some time purchase a high-cost item on a time-payment plan. There are two methods of computing periodic payments for such plans. In the constant-payment plan, the monthly payment can be computed by:

$$\mathrm{PAY} = iA\frac{(1 + i)^n}{(1 + i)^n - 1}$$

FIGURE 7-23 Problem 7-18.

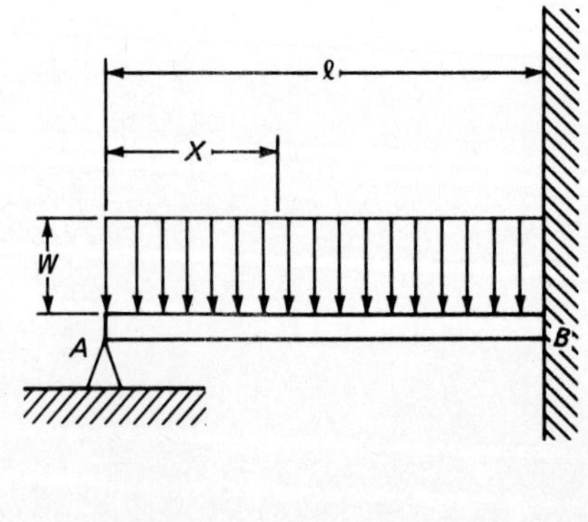

where PAY = constant monthly payment
A = total amount of money to be paid
i = monthly interest in decimal form
n = number of monthly payments due

The amount of money that goes toward interest can be computed by:

$$\text{TOINT} = i(\text{BAL})$$

where BAL is the remaining balance after the previous payment. Obviously the amount of the payment that goes for decreasing the balance is the payment less the interest. In this method the final payment may be less than the periodic payment. Your program must account for this possibility. Assume that you owe \$6ØØØ and are to repay this in monthly installments over a 2-year period. The annual rate of interest is 12 percent. Compute and show the payment number, the monthly payment, the monthly interest, the cumulative interest paid, the amount of the payment that goes toward the balance, and the balance after each payment.

7-20 Another method of computing periodic payments is the decreasing-payment method where a constant amount is paid toward decreasing the balance. This is calculated simply by dividing the amount of the loan by the number of monthly payments. But interest must be paid each month, and this can be computed by:

$$\text{TOINT} = i(\text{BAL})$$

as in Prob. 7-19. This time, however, the total monthly payment is the sum of the constant payment plus the monthly interest. The balance is decreased each payment by the amount of the constant payment. Assume the same loan, interest rate, and duration of loan as in Prob. 7-19. Compute and show the payment number, the monthly payment, the monthly interest, the cumulative interest paid, and the balance after each payment.

7-21 The natural logarithm of X (when X > Ø) can be approximated by the series:

$$\ln X \approx 2\left[\frac{X-1}{X+1} + \frac{1}{3}\left(\frac{X-1}{X+1}\right)^3 + \frac{1}{5}\left(\frac{X-1}{X+1}\right)^5 + \cdots + \frac{1}{n}\left(\frac{X-1}{X+1}\right)^n\right]$$

where X is positive and n is odd. Write a program that compares the natural logarithm of numbers from 2 through 1Ø (in intervals of 2) with the corresponding library function. Use the first 2Ø terms of the series. Also show the difference between the two values.

7-22 A projectile fired at a vertical angle of $\theta°$ with an initial velocity of V meters per second (m/s) will travel a horizontal distance (range) of R m and reach a height of H m. This flight will last T seconds. Using the formulas below, compute these factors. Use angles varying from 3Ø to 6Ø° in increments of 5° with an initial velocity of 2ØØ, 3ØØ, and 4ØØ m/s. Print the results such that for each initial velocity, the corresponding R, H, and T values are shown for each angle.

$$R = \frac{V^2 \sin 2\theta}{g} \qquad H = \frac{V^2 \sin^2 \theta}{2g} \qquad T = \frac{2V \sin \theta}{g}$$

where g = 9.8Ø665 m/s².

CHAPTER **8**

SUBSCRIPTED VARIABLES AND ARRAYS

8-1 INTRODUCTION

It is often necessary to work with numerical quantities that are elements of an associated group called an *array*. Arrays may also be referred to as *matrices* or *vectors,* depending on their form. An array is a family of related *elements,* or quantities, all assigned to the same variable name, each element of the array being identified by a different subscript. Variables that are elements of an array are known as *subscripted variables*. (Variables without subscripts are referred to as *simple variables*.)

Consider a program to solve three simultaneous equations with three unknowns, *X, Y,* and *Z*. Three different coefficients of *X*, three different coefficients of *Y*, three different coefficients of *Z*, and three different constants (sums) are involved:

$$2.\text{Ø}X + 3.\text{Ø}Y + 4.\text{Ø}Z = 49.\text{Ø}$$
$$4.\text{Ø}X + 3.\text{Ø}Y + 2.\text{Ø}Z = 41.\text{Ø}$$
$$X + Y + Z = 15.\text{Ø}$$

Each coefficient and each sum could be assigned a different simple-variable name:

$$AX + BY + CZ = R$$
$$DX + EY + FZ = S$$
$$GX + HY + PZ = T$$

This would require inventing, remembering, and accounting for a large number of variable names (12 in this example). The number of statements in the program can be significantly reduced and much of the remembering and accounting chore can be shifted from the programmer to the computer if the three coefficients of each unknown *X, Y,* and *Z* are elements of three arrays *A, B,* and *C*, respectively, and the three sums are elements of a fourth array, SUM:

$$A_1X + B_1Y + C_1Z = \text{SUM}_1$$
$$A_2X + B_2Y + C_2Z = \text{SUM}_2$$
$$A_3X + B_3Y + C_3Z = \text{SUM}_3$$

The nine coefficients might also be assigned to a single array name, such as C (for coefficient), with nine elements:

$$C_{1,1}X + C_{1,2}Y + C_{1,3}Z = \text{SUM}_1$$
$$C_{2,1}X + C_{2,2}Y + C_{2,3}Z = \text{SUM}_2$$
$$C_{3,1}X + C_{3,2}Y + C_{3,3}Z = \text{SUM}_3$$

The first subscript of each element of C refers to the equation (row), first, second, or third; the second subscript refers to the unknown (column), first (X), second Y), or third (Z). SUM, with one subscript, is a *one-dimensional array*. C, with two subscripts, is a *two-dimensional array*.

Through the knowledgeable use of subscripted variables the programmer can write relatively short programs that take full advantage of the computer's capacity to process large quantities of numerical data efficiently. This chapter will describe arrays, as defined in FORTRAN, and explain how the fundamental statements associated with arrays are written and applied.

8-2 ARRAYS

Arrays in FORTRAN may range from one- to seven-dimensional, meaning that a subscripted variable that is an element of that array will have from one to seven subscripts, respectively. Discussion in this text will be limited to one- and two-dimensional arrays, with variables of one and two subscripts, respectively.

a One-Dimensional Arrays

A one-dimensional array is written in mathematical notation as follows:

$$x_1 \; x_2 \; x_3 \cdot \cdot \cdot x_n$$

where the small numbers 1, 2, 3, . . . , n, printed slightly below the line, are known as *subscripts*. Since the subscript form is not available in the FORTRAN character set, other symbols must be used. In FORTRAN the subscript is identified by enclosing the subscript in parentheses. The example above, rewritten with FORTRAN subscripted variables, is:

```
X(1)  X(2)  X(3)  X(4)  · · ·  X(N)
```

The variable X(N) is a real one-dimensional subscripted variable with one subscript, N. The single subscript in a one-dimensional array element specifies the position of that element in the array. For example, X(3) is the third element; X(4) is the fourth element; and X(N) is the Nth element in the N-element real array X.

b Two-Dimensional Arrays

A two-dimensional array is written in mathematical notation as follows:

$$
\begin{matrix}
n_{1,1} & n_{1,2} & n_{1,3} & n_{1,4} & \cdots & n_{1,k} \\
n_{2,1} & n_{2,2} & n_{2,3} & n_{2,4} & \cdots & n_{2,k} \\
n_{3,1} & n_{3,2} & n_{3,3} & n_{3,4} & \cdots & n_{3,k} \\
\cdot\cdot & \cdot\cdot & \cdot\cdot & \cdot\cdot & \cdots & \cdot\cdot \\
n_{j,1} & n_{j,2} & n_{j,3} & n_{j,4} & \cdots & n_{j,k}
\end{matrix}
$$

The same array expressed in FORTRAN is:

	Column					
Row	**1**	**2**	**3**	**4**		**K**
1	N(1,1)	N(1,2)	N(1,3)	N(1,4)	. . .	N(1,K)
2	N(2,1)	N(2,2)	N(2,3)	N(2,4)	. . .	N(2,K)
3	N(3,1)	N(3,2)	N(3,3)	N(3,4)	. . .	N(3,K)
	. . .	. . .	. . .	. . .	. . .	. . .
J	N(J,1)	N(J,2)	N(J,3)	N(J,4)	. . .	N(J,K)

The variable N(J,K) is an integer, two-dimensional subscripted variable with two subscripts, J and K. The first subscript specifies the row; the second subscript specifies the column. For example, the element N(2,3) is located in the second row (from the top), third column (from the left), of the two-dimensional integer array N(J,K).

c Rules for Subscripted Variables

1 A subscripted variable may be either integer or real. Since every element of the array is assigned to the same variable (array) name, it is obvious that there can be no mixed modes among the array elements. All the elements in a given array are either integer or real, as specified by the first-letter designator of the array name. The rules that govern simple-variable names (Sec. 3-4) apply to all subscripted-variable names.

2 Subscripts follow the variable name and are enclosed by parentheses.

3 Dual subscripts are separated by a comma.

4 Subscripts must be positive-integer values other than zero. A subscript may be an integer constant, an integer-variable name, or an integer expression (Table 8-1).

5 Subscript variables must be assigned an integer value before the subscripted variable is used in an executable statement. Care must be taken to ensure that subscripts whose values are assigned as the result of calculation or iteration are not assigned a zero or a negative value or a value larger than the size of the array specified by the DIMENSION statement (Sec. 8-3).

The combinations described in Table 8-1 on p. 218 represent the subscript forms generally acceptable to most FORTRAN compilers. Other forms may be permitted by some compilers.

TABLE 8-1 PERMITTED FORMS OF SUBSCRIPTS

Subscripted Variable	Subscript
ARRAY (5)	Integer constant
ARRAY (N)	Integer variable
ARRAY (N+5) or (N−5)	Variable plus a constant or a variable minus a constant
ARRAY (5∗N)	Constant times a variable
ARRAY (5∗N+3) or (5∗N−3)	Constant times a variable plus a constant or a constant times a variable minus a constant

8-3 THE DIMENSION STATEMENT

Before a subscripted variable can be used in any way in a program, the array of which it is an element must first be established by a DIMENSION statement. DIMENSION statements *must* appear in the program *before* any executable statement. As a general rule, the DIMENSION statement should be the first statement in any program where subscripted variables are used. The DIMENSION statement is a nonexecutable declaration statement that:

1 Establishes the array by name and number of subscripts (one- or two-dimensional)
2 Sets the maximum numerical value of each subscript
3 Reserves sufficient storage locations to accommodate each element (subscripted variable) in the array

The general form for the DIMENSION statement is:

```
DIMENSION a(n), b(m,n), k(i,j)
```

where *a, b,* and *k* represent array names (variables to be subscripted) and (*n*), (*m,n*), and (*i,j*) represent constants that set the maximum value of each subscript. There is no flowchart symbol or indication of dimensioning in a flowchart. When a variable has been declared as an array name (subscripted variable) in a DIMENSION statement, that name *must never* be used in that program as a simple variable (a variable without subscripts).† When more than one array is included in a single DIMENSION statement, array names are separated by a comma. A comma is also placed between the first and second subscript of a two-dimensional array. Any number of arrays may be declared in a single DIMENSION statement. Three arrays declared in a single DIMENSION statement of the general form above could also have been declared with three separate DIMENSION statements:

```
DIMENSION A(5)
DIMENSION B(3,5)
DIMENSION K(5,4)
```

†Exceptions to this generalization may occur when the array name is included in a type-declaration statement, in an input/output list, or as an argument of a subprogram (Secs. 8-9 and 9-4).

Integer variables *cannot* be used to define the maximum numerical value of a subscript. Since the DIMENSION statement must appear in the program before any executable statements, the value of an integer variable is necessarily undefined. Hence integer constants must be used in the DIMENSION statement. An exception to this rule occurs when the DIMENSION statement is used in a subprogram (Sec. 9-4).

In the above examples, array A is a one-dimensional (one-subscript) real array where the largest subscript value is 5 and the array contains not more than five real-subscripted variables (elements) designated:

```
A(1)  A(2)  A(3)  A(4)  A(5)
```

Array B is a two-dimensional (two-subscript) real array where the largest value of the first subscript is 3, the largest value of the second subscript is 5, and the array contains not more than 15 (3 × 5) real-subscripted variables (elements) ordered in 3 rows and 5 columns:

```
B(1,1)  B(1,2)  B(1,3)  B(1,4)  B(1,5)
B(2,1)  B(2,2)  B(2,3)  B(2,4)  B(2,5)
B(3,1)  B(3,2)  B(3,3)  B(3,4)  B(3,5)
```

Array N is a two-dimensional (two-subscript) integer array where the largest value of the first subscript is 5, the largest value of the second subscript is 4, and the array contains not more than 2Ø (5 × 4) integer-subscripted variables ordered in 5 rows and 4 columns:

```
N(1,1)  N(1,2)  N(1,3)  N(1,4)
N(2,1)  N(2,2)  N(2,3)  N(2,4)
N(3,1)  N(3,2)  N(3,3)  N(3,4)
N(4,1)  N(4,2)  N(4,3)  N(4,4)
N(5,1)  N(5,2)  N(5,3)  N(5,4)
```

The following program segment shows how a one-dimensional real array of five elements can be established and numerical values assigned to each element of the array named A:

```
DIMENSION A(5)
A(1)=Ø.5
A(2)=1.Ø
A(3)=1.5
A(4)=2.Ø
A(5)=2.5
```

The use of five separate assignment statements may be acceptable if only a few subscripted variables are to be assigned values. If 5Ø or 5ØØ or 5ØØØ values must be assigned, a more efficient technique for assigning the incremented array values is indicated in the following program segment:

```
      DIMENSION A(5)
      N=Ø
      X=Ø.Ø
   1Ø N=N+1
      X=X+Ø.5
      A(N)=X
      IF(N.LT.5)GOTO 1Ø
   2Ø ----------
```

The DIMENSION statement declares A to be a real-subscripted variable with one subscript. Five storage locations are reserved for the array A. The integer value of a subscript may be 1, 2, 3, 4, or 5 but must not exceed 5. The subscript variable is N, and the value assigned to each successive element of the real array is X. As N increments from 1 through 5 in increments of 1, and X increments from Ø.5 through 2.5 in increments of Ø.5, the consecutive elements of A are assigned values as follows:

```
A(1)=Ø.5    A(2)=1.Ø    A(3)=1.5    A(4)=2.Ø    A(5)=2.5
```

The logical IF statement prevents the value of the subscript N from exceeding the maximum value 5 specified in the DIMENSION statement. By increasing the size of the array in the DIMENSION statement to A(5Ø) and by changing the 5 in the logical IF statement to 5Ø, the same sequence of statements can be used to assign values to 5Ø subscripted variables of the array A.

It is important to distinguish between the number assigned to the subscript variable (always a positive integer other than zero) and the value assigned to the array name. In the example above, A(3), for instance, is the third element in the array; the value assigned to A(3) is 1.5.

Consider a similar example with the same DIMENSION statement:

```
      DIMENSION A(5)
      N=1
      X=Ø.Ø
   10 X=X+Ø.5
      A(N)=X
      IF(X.GE.2.5)GOTO 2Ø
      N=N+2
      GOTO 1Ø
   2Ø ----------
```

In this case, as in the first example, five storage locations are reserved for the five elements of the one-dimensional array A. Five real values from Ø.5 through 2.5 in increments of Ø.5 are to be assigned, through five incrementations of X, to the five subscripted variables (elements) in array A. The condition of the logical expression in the IF statement now depends on the real value assigned to the array element rather than the integer value assigned to the subscript variable. The logical IF statement prevents the value of X (and presumably the value of A) from exceeding 2.5—the value desired for the fifth element of A. However, this program segment *will not* execute to completion; there is a problem. The subscript variable N in five iterations is assigned five successive integer values from 1 through 9 in increments of 2. If all statements are properly executed, the subscripts of A and the values assigned to A should be:

```
A(1)=Ø.5     A(3)=1.Ø     A(5)=1.5     A(7)=2.Ø     A(9)=2.5
```

But the DIMENSION statement not only limits the number (count) of elements in array A to five but also declares the maximum subscript value to be 5. When the integer assigned to the subscript N exceeds 5 and execution of the statement A(7)=X is attempted, an error will result. It is not necessary to use all the storage locations reserved by the DIMENSION statement, but the subscript-integer number must never exceed the number specified.

In the previous example, changing the DIMENSION statement to DIMENSION A(9) will permit the program to be executed to completion without error. Storage locations for A(2), A(4), A(6), and A(8) will not be used. The DIMENSION statement not only reserves enough storage locations to accommodate all the array elements but also specifies the largest subscript integer needed. When the maximum subscript cannot be predicted exactly, it is advisable to "overdimension," i.e., specify a subscript in the DIMENSION statement sufficiently large to accommodate the maximum subscript anticipated.

The two type-declaration statements introduced in Sec. 3-6 can also be used to declare an array. For example, the statements:

```
INTEGER A,B(1Ø),C(3,4)
REAL L,J(6,9),K(8)
```

declare A to be a simple integer variable, B to be a one-dimensional integer array, C to be a two-dimensional integer array, L to be simple real variable, J to be a two-dimensional real array, and K to be a one-dimensional real array.

When a type-declaration statement is used to declare an array, no additional DIMENSION statement is needed. When either the INTEGER or REAL declaration statement is used with an array name, the declaration statement defines not only the type of the elements but the size of the array as well. Repeating this information in a DIMENSION statement will result in a compilation error. However, both a DIMENSION statement and a declaration statement referring to the same array are acceptable when used as follows:

```
DIMENSION B(1Ø),C(3,4),J(6,9),K(8)
INTEGER A,B,C
REAL L,J,K
```

This arrangement is useful if the array type already established by a DIMENSION statement in an existing program needs to be changed. Since the size of the array has already been specified by the DIMENSION statement, it should not be repeated in the type-declaration statement.

8-4 GENERATING ARRAY VALUES WITH THE DO LOOP

Arrays, either integer or real, in which the values assigned each successive subscripted-variable element increase or decrease uniformly may have the values of the elements defined as a function of the subscript. Consider a one-dimensional real array with five elements named A. The five values assigned to the five subscripted variables progress from 1.ØØ to 3.ØØ in increments of Ø.5Ø as follows:

```
A(1)=1.ØØ   A(2)=1.5Ø   A(3)=2.ØØ   A(4)=2.5Ø   A(5)=3.ØØ
```

Either of the following program segments will generate this array:

(*a*)

```
      DIMENSION A(5)
      N=1
      DO 1Ø J=1Ø,3Ø,5
      A(N)=FLOAT(J)/1Ø.Ø
      N=N+1
   1Ø CONTINUE
```

(*b*)

```
      DIMENSION A(5)
      DO 1Ø N=1,5
      A(N)=REAL(N+1)/2.Ø
   1Ø CONTINUE
```

Note that solution (*b*) defines the value of each array element as a function of the subscript.

Now consider a two-dimensional real array with 12 elements named B. The 12 elements are to be ordered in 3 rows and 4 columns with the values assigned to the 12 subscripted variables decrementing, in row order, from 7.ØØ through 1.5Ø in decrements of Ø.5Ø as follows:

```
B(1,1)=7.ØØ   B(1,2)=6.5Ø   B(1,3)=6.ØØ   B(1,4)=5.5Ø
B(2,1)=5.ØØ   B(2,2)=4.5Ø   B(2,3)=4.ØØ   B(2,4)=3.5Ø
B(3,1)=3.ØØ   B(3,2)=2.5Ø   B(3,3)=2.ØØ   B(3,4)=1.5Ø
```

Either of the following program segments will generate this array:

(*a*)

```
      DIMENSION B(3,4)
      M=1
      DO 2Ø L=1,41,2Ø
      N=1
      J=L+15
      DO 1Ø K=L,J,5
      I=71-K
      B(M,N)=FLOAT(I)/1Ø.Ø
      N=N+1
   1Ø CONTINUE
      M=M+1
   2Ø CONTINUE
```

(*b*)

```
      DIMENSION B(3,4)
      C=15.Ø
      DO 1Ø M=1,3
      DO 1Ø N=1,4
      C=C-1.Ø
      B(M,N)=C/2.Ø
   1Ø CONTINUE
```

The program segments in each of the foregoing examples should be carefully studied and analyzed line by line, statement by statement, with the result of each repetition of the loop(s) compared with the value of each successive subscripted variable in the array the program was written to generate. In each pair of program segments, solution (*b*) is shorter, but solution (*a*) illustrates several statements that can be modified and applied with advantage in appropriate situations.

The values assigned to the successive elements of an array usually do not progress in uniform increments. The DO loop can still be used to uniformly increment the integer subscript(s), but when the values of the array elements are random, they must be assigned in some other manner, usually by a READ statement indicating input from a data file.

8-5 INPUT AND OUTPUT OF ONE-DIMENSIONAL ARRAYS USING THE FORMAT-DIRECTED READ AND WRITE STATEMENTS WITH DO LOOPS

When the values assigned to subscripted variables are read from a record in a data file, the programmer must know how the values are entered in the record and the order in which these values are read and assigned to each element in the array. The READ and associated FORMAT statements can then be coded and the record(s) organized to effect the desired assignments.

Consider a one-dimensional real array with five elements named X. If the five values are listed in five consecutive records:

FILEONE.DAT
1.5 2.Ø 3.Ø 5.5 6.Ø

the following program segment can be used to assign the five values, in order, to the five elements of the subscripted variable:

```
      DIMENSION X(5)
      OPEN(3,FILE='FILEONE.DAT')
      READ(3,1ØØ)X(1),X(2),X(3),X(4),X(5)
1ØØ   FORMAT(F3.1)
```

In the above example, there are five (subscripted) variables in the READ list and only one edit descriptor in the FORMAT statement. This descriptor is repeated (5 times) until the READ list is satisfied. Each time the edit descriptor is repeated, a new record is read, hence there must be five records with one value per record. Assignment of values is X(1) = 1.5, X(2) = 2.Ø, X(3) = 3.Ø, X(4) = 5.5, and X(5) = 6.Ø. Review Sec. 6-13 and Rule 2 as applied to satisfying the READ list. Rule 2 (repeated here) states:

If there are more variable names in the READ or WRITE list than edit descriptors in the associated FORMAT specification, the specification is repeated until the READ or WRITE list is satisfied.

The same results are obtained by placing all five data values in a single record:

FILETWO.DAT
1.5 2.Ø 3.Ø 5.5 6.Ø

and rewriting the FORMAT specification with a repetition number ahead of the edit descriptor:

```
      DIMENSION X(5)
      OPEN(5,FILE='FILETWO.DAT')
      READ(5,2ØØ)X(1),X(2),X(3),X(4),X(5)
2ØØ   FORMAT(5F4.1)
```

Listing each element in the array in the READ statement is inefficient and unnecessary. An explicit DO loop can be used to increment the subscript of X(N) from N = 1 through N = 5 in increments of 1:

```
      DIMENSION X(5)
      OPEN(3,FILE='FILEONE.DAT')
      DO 1Ø N=1,5
      READ(3,1ØØ)X(N)                    (with five records, one
1ØØ   FORMAT(F4.1)                       value per record)
 1Ø   CONTINUE
```

By combining the DO statement with the READ statement an implied DO loop (Sec. 7-7) is formed, and an even simpler way of incrementing the subscript and reading and assigning values in order to the five elements of the subscripted variable is possible:

```
      DIMENSION X(5)
      OPEN(3,FILE='FILETWO.DAT')
      READ(3,2ØØ) (X(N),N=1,5)           (with five values in a
2ØØ   FORMAT(5F4.1)                      single record)
```

It is generally better to place the five values in a single record and repeat the edit descriptor 5 times as just illustrated. Note that with the explicit DO loop each value must be in a separate record, while the implied DO loop permits several values to be in one record. The execution of the explicit DO statement causes the READ statement to be executed 5 times. Each time the READ statement is executed one value will be read. Hence five records with one value per record are required. But the READ statement with an implied DO loop is executed only once. Thus one record with five values is indicated.

Several techniques, in a variety of formats, are available for printing the values assigned to the subscripted variables of an array. Consider the five-element, one-dimensional real array called X, as read above, with values assigned as follows: X(1) = 1.5, X(2) = 2.Ø, X(3) = 3.Ø, X(4) = 5.5, and X(5) = 6.Ø. The most straightforward procedure is to list each subscripted variable separately in the WRITE statement. The statements:

```
    WRITE(*,2ØØ)X(1),X(2),X(3),X(4),X(5)
2ØØ FORMAT(5F5.1)
```

will display the five values in a row on a single line:

```
  1.5  2.Ø  3.Ø  5.5  6.Ø
```

The five values will be right-justified in output columns 5, 1Ø, 15, 2Ø, and 25. Other arrangements of the values can be specified with different edit descriptors in the FORMAT specification.

The five values can be displayed in a single column, one value per line, by changing the edit descriptor in the FORMAT specification to:

```
2ØØ FORMAT(F5.1)
```

The value in each line will be right-justified in output column 5. In the above example, there are five (subscripted) variables in the WRITE list and only one edit descriptor in the FORMAT statement. This single descriptor is repeated (5 times) until the WRITE list is satisfied. Each time the descriptor is repeated, the output control is returned to column 1, and the leading *blank* provided by the extended field width (a field of five with only three characters in the output) advances the display to the next line. Review Sec. 6-13 and Rule 2 as applied to satisfying the WRITE list. Rule 2 (repeated here) states:

> If there are more variable names in the READ or WRITE list than edit descriptors in the associated FORMAT specification, the specification is repeated until the READ or WRITE list is satisfied.

A more efficient way to display this array uses an explicit DO loop to increment the subscript of X(N) from N = 1 through N = 5 in increments of 1. Thus:

```
    DO 2Ø N=1,5
    WRITE(*,2ØØ)X(N)
2ØØ FORMAT(F5.1)
 2Ø CONTINUE
```

will display the five values, in a column, on five successive lines:

```
1.5
2.Ø
3.Ø
5.5
6.Ø
```

The DO statement can be combined with the WRITE statement to form an implied DO loop (Sec. 7-7):

```
    WRITE(*,2ØØ) (X(N),N=1,5)
2ØØ FORMAT(5F5.1)                    (for a row format)
```

or

```
2ØØ FORMAT(F5.1)                     (for a column format)
```

Figure 8-1 demonstrates reading and printing an array, first using explicit DO loops and then using implied DO loops. The data for both parts of the program are as shown in the records of the data file printed immediately following the END statement.

An advantage of using DO loops is that a DIMENSION statement can be set for the maximum number of elements (the subscript) that might be needed in a general problem. Then, if the specific application of the general problem requires fewer elements, an integer number can be read from an input record and assigned to the variable that defines the limiting value of the DO statement (the maximum subscript number); for example:

```
    DIMENSION J(15)
    OPEN(3,FILE='EXAM.DAT')
    READ(3,1ØØ)K
1ØØ FORMAT(I5)
    READ(3,2ØØ) (J(N),N=1,K)
2ØØ FORMAT(15I3)
    WRITE(*,3ØØ) (J(N),N=1,K)
3ØØ FORMAT(1X,15I5)
```

If K is assigned a value of 5 by the first READ statement, for example, the second READ statement will read only five values and the unused edit descriptors will be ignored. Only five values will be displayed, and the unused edit descriptors will be ignored.

8-6 INPUT AND OUTPUT OF ONE-DIMENSIONAL ARRAYS USING THE FORMAT-DIRECTED READ AND WRITE STATEMENTS WITHOUT DO LOOPS

One-dimensional arrays can also be read without DO loops, either explicit or implied. The following statements accomplish the same result as the reading exam-

```
C234567890
      DIMENSION A(5),X(5)
      OPEN(3,FILE='FIG8-1.DAT')
      OPEN(6,FILE='PRN')
C  THIS PART OF THE PROGRAM READS AND PRINTS
C  AN ARRAY USING EXPLICIT DO LOOPS.
      DO 10 J=1,5
      READ(3,100)A(J)
  100 FORMAT(F4.1)
   10 CONTINUE
      DO 20 K=1,5
      WRITE(6,200)A(K)
  200 FORMAT(10X,F5.1)
   20 CONTINUE
      WRITE(6,300)
  300 FORMAT(' ')
C  THIS PART OF THE PROGRAM READS AND PRINTS
C  AN ARRAY USING IMPLIED DO LOOPS.
      READ(3,400)(X(J),J=1,5)
  400 FORMAT(5F4.1)
      WRITE(6,500)(X(K),K=1,5)
  500 FORMAT(10X,5F5.1)
      STOP
      END
```

```
1.5
2.0
3.0
5.5
6.0
1.5 2.0 3.0 5.5 6.0
```

```
          1.5
          2.0
          3.0
          5.5
          6.0

          1.5  2.0  3.0  5.5  6.0
```

FIGURE 8-1 Reading and printing one-dimensional arrays with formatted READ and WRITE statements and DO loops.

ples shown in Sec. 8-5; but, with this method there *must be exactly* the same number of values in the record(s) as are specified by the DIMENSION statement.

```
      DIMENSION X(5)
      READ(3,1ØØ)X
1ØØ   FORMAT(5F4.1)
```

If the DIMENSION statement specifies a five-element array (as in this example), five data values must be provided. Providing fewer than the number of data values required can create problems. If there are other data values, intended to be read later in the program, those values will also be read until the required number of values are assigned and the READ list is satisfied. This results in unexpected values in the array; the READ statement(s) later in the program will have no values (or the wrong values) to read. If there are fewer data values than required by

```
C234567890
      DIMENSION A(5)
      OPEN(3,FILE='FIG8-2.DAT')
      OPEN(6,FILE='PRN')
      READ(3,100)A
  100 FORMAT(5F4.1)
      WRITE(6,200)A
  200 FORMAT(10X,5F5.1)
      STOP
      END
```

```
1.5 2.0 3.0 5.5 6.0
```

```
          1.5  2.0  3.0  5.5  6.0
```

FIGURE 8-2 Reading and printing a one-dimensional array with formatted READ and WRITE statements without DO loops.

the array and no other subsequent data values, the execution of the program will terminate for lack of data with an error message. If more data values are provided than required, the excess data values will be ignored.

The array can also be displayed without DO loops:

```
      DIMENSION A(5)
      OPEN(3,FILE='EXAM.DAT')
      READ(3,1ØØ)A
 1ØØ  FORMAT(5F4.1)
      WRITE(*,2ØØ)A
 2ØØ  FORMAT(5F5.1)
```

as illustrated in Fig. 8-2. The input record for the READ statement is similar to the sixth record of Fig. 8-1.

8-7 INPUT AND OUTPUT OF TWO-DIMENSIONAL ARRAYS USING THE FORMAT-DIRECTED READ AND WRITE STATEMENTS WITH DO LOOPS

The reason for establishing an array is to have the values assigned to the elements of that array available for subsequent calculations. To do that, the programmer must know the order in which the values are assigned to each element. The examples of reading and displaying one-dimensional arrays have shown that there is no problem in reading and assigning each value to the proper element as long as all values are provided in the proper order.

Two-dimensional arrays are more complicated. Two-dimensional arrays should always be ordered as described in Sec. 8-2*b*, where N(J,K) is in row J and column K. The following discussions demonstrate format-directed input and output statements that will ensure the assignment of each numerical value to the array element in its proper row-column position and provide an array output in predictable row-column order.

Both the explicit and implied DO loops can be nested to increment the two subscripts of a two-dimensional array while reading or displaying that array. Consider a two-dimensional integer array called N, consisting of 3 rows and 4 columns:

ROW (First subscript)	Column (Second subscript) 1	2	3	4
1	$n_{1,1}$	$n_{1,2}$	$n_{1,3}$	$n_{1,4}$
2	$n_{2,1}$	$n_{2,2}$	$n_{2,3}$	$n_{2,4}$
3	$n_{3,1}$	$n_{3,2}$	$n_{3,1}$	$n_{3,4}$

There are 12 elements (3 × 4) in this array. The values to be assigned to each element are placed in 12 records, 1 integer value per record. The array can be read and stored with the following statements:

```
      DIMENSION N(3,4)
      OPEN(5,FILE='EX1.DAT')
      DO 1Ø J=1,3
      DO 1Ø K=1,4
      READ(5,1ØØ) N(J,K)
1ØØ   FORMAT(I5)
 1Ø   CONTINUE
```

The outer DO loop increments the first (row) subscript J from 1 through 3. For each value of the first subscript, the inner DO loop increments the second (column) subscript K from 1 through 4. The READ statement is thus executed 12 times, assigning the single value in each record to the appropriate array element.

Using an explicit and an implied DO loop as shown below:

```
      DIMENSION N(3,4)
      OPEN(4,FILE='EX2.DAT')
      DO 1Ø J=1,3
      READ(4,2ØØ) (N(J,K),K=1,4)
2ØØ   FORMAT (4I5)
 10   CONTINUE
```

permits the data to be read from 3 records of 4 values per record:

```
    1    2    3    4
   1Ø   2Ø   3Ø   4Ø
  1ØØ  2ØØ  3ØØ  4ØØ
```

Here the READ statement is executed 3 times (once for each row), and each time 4 values (1 for each column) are read. Notice that the FORMAT specification was changed to permit the reading of 4 values from each record. However, if the FORMAT statement had not been changed, but left as:

```
100 FORMAT(I5)
```

then a data file of 12 records with 1 value per record is applicable.

The use of nested implied DO loops:

```
      DIMENSION N(3,4)
      OPEN(3,FILE='EX3.DAT')
      READ(3,100)((N(J,K),K=1,4),J=1,3)
100   FORMAT(12I5)
```

permits the data to be read from 1 record of 12 values. To read the data values from a data file of 3 records with 4 values per record, change the FORMAT specification to:

```
100   FORMAT(4I5)
```

To read the data values from a data file of 12 records with 1 value per record, change the FORMAT specification to:

```
100   FORMAT(I5)
```

This array can be displayed by adding appropriate WRITE/FORMAT statements to the various program segments; for example:

```
      DIMENSION N(3,4)
      OPEN(2,FILE='EX1.DAT')
      DO 10 J=1,3
      DO 10 K=1,4
      READ(2,100)N(J,K)
100   FORMAT(I5)
      WRITE(*,200)N(J,K)
200   FORMAT(1X,I5)
 10   CONTINUE
```

The I5 edit descriptor in the 200 FORMAT statement will be repeated 12 times (each time the WRITE statement is encountered), returning the output control to column 1 each time and displaying the 12 values on 12 successive lines, right-justified in output column 6:

$$\left.\begin{matrix} n_{1,1} \\ n_{1,2} \\ n_{1,3} \\ n_{1,4} \end{matrix}\right\} \text{(row 1)}$$

$$\left.\begin{matrix} n_{2,1} \\ n_{2,2} \\ n_{2,3} \\ n_{2,4} \end{matrix}\right\} \text{(row 2)}$$

$$\left.\begin{matrix} n_{3,1} \\ n_{3,2} \\ n_{3,3} \\ n_{3,4} \end{matrix}\right\} \quad \text{(row 3)}$$

Note that the array was stored and displayed in row order: row 1—columns 1, 2, 3, and 4; row 2—columns 1, 2, 3, and 4; row 3—columns 1, 2, 3, and 4. Since the subscripts in the READ list and the subscripts in the WRITE list were incremented identically, the output is displayed in the same order in which the values were read and stored.

The elements of the array can be displayed in 3 rows and 4 columns by moving the WRITE statement outside both DO loops and listing each subscripted variable separately, in the order in which they are to be displayed:

```
      -----------
      -----------

   1Ø CONTINUE
      WRITE(*,2ØØ) (N(1,1),N(1,2),N(1,3),N(1,4),N(2,1),
     $......,N(3,4)
  2ØØ FORMAT(1X,4I5)
```

The displayed array will look like this:

$$\begin{matrix} n_{1,1} & n_{1,2} & n_{1,3} & n_{1,4} \\ n_{2,1} & n_{2,2} & n_{2,3} & n_{2,4} \\ n_{3,1} & n_{3,2} & n_{3,3} & n_{3,4} \end{matrix}$$

which is the same as the given array.

Listing each subscripted variable separately is cumbersome, leads to error, and defeats the purpose of the subscripted-variable capability. A simpler way to display the elements in 3 rows and 4 columns is to use two CONTINUE statements, placing the WRITE statement between the two, i.e., outside the inner loop and inside the outer loop, as below:

```
      DIMENSION N(3,4)
      OPEN(6,FILE='EX2.DAT')
      DO 2Ø J=1,3
      DO 1Ø K=1,4
      READ(6,1ØØ)N(J,K)
  1ØØ FORMAT(I5)
      -----------
      -----------
   1Ø CONTINUE
      WRITE(*,2ØØ)N(J,1),N(J,2),N(J,3),N(J,4)
  2ØØ FORMAT(1X,4I5)
   2Ø CONTINUE
```

This way the first (row) subscript remains constant, while the second (column) subscript is incremented from 1 through 4 by the inner explicit DO loop. Each time the inner loop is satisfied, a row of four values is displayed.

The same 3-row, 4-column output can be obtained by placing the WRITE statement with two nested implied DO loops outside both explicit DO loops. The implied DO loops will call each element of the array by subscript number and will display it according to the edit descriptors of the associated FORMAT specification:

```
      -----------
      -----------

  1Ø  CONTINUE
      WRITE(*,2ØØ) ((N(J,K),K=1,4),J=1,3)
 2ØØ  FORMAT(1X,4I5)
```

A more efficient procedure for reading and displaying the 12 elements of this 3-row, 4-column array is to place the 12 values on a single record, read with two nested implied DO loops in the READ statement, and display with similar nested implied DO loops in the WRITE statement. That is:

```
      DIMENSION N(3,4)
      OPEN(3,FILE='EXAMPLE.SIX')
      READ((3,1ØØ) ((N(J,K),K=1,4),J=1,3)
 1ØØ  FORMAT(12I5)
      WRITE(*,2ØØ) ((N(J,K),K=1,4),J=1,3)
 2ØØ  FORMAT(1X,4I5)
```

will result in the same 3-row, 4-column output.

Changing the output FORMAT to:

```
 2ØØ  FORMAT(1X,12I5)
```

will display the 12 values with row 1, row 2, and row 3 in a single line:

$$\underbrace{n_{1,1}\ n_{1,2}\ n_{1,3}\ n_{1,4}}_{\text{row 1}}\ \underbrace{n_{2,1}\ n_{2,2}\ n_{2,3}\ n_{2,4}}_{\text{row 2}}\ \underbrace{n_{3,1}\ n_{3,2}\ n_{3,3}\ n_{3,4}}_{\text{row 3}}$$

Changing the output FORMAT statement to:

```
 2ØØ  FORMAT(1X,I5)
```

will display the 12 values in a single column:

$$\left.\begin{array}{l} n_{1,1} \\ n_{1,2} \\ n_{1,3} \\ n_{1,4} \end{array}\right\} \text{row 1}$$

$$\left.\begin{array}{l} n_{2,1} \\ n_{2,2} \\ n_{2,3} \\ n_{2,4} \end{array}\right\} \text{row 2}$$

$$\left.\begin{array}{l} n_{3,1} \\ n_{3,2} \\ n_{3,3} \\ n_{3,4} \end{array}\right\} \text{row 3}$$

Figure 8-3 illustrates the statements and data file needed to read and assign values to the 48 elements of a two-dimensional integer array (6 rows and 8 columns) with nested implied DO loops in the READ statement using a data file with 6 records with 8 values in each record.

By changing the FORMAT statement to:

```
100 FORMAT(24I2)
```

the same values can be read from 2 records:

```
b1b2b3b4b5b6b7b8b9101112131415161718192021222324
252627282930313233343536373839404142434445464748
```

FIGURE 8-3 Reading a two-dimensional array with nested implied DO loops.

```
*****************************************
*      DIMENSION K(6,8)                 *
*      READ(3,100)((K(J,L),L=1,8),J=1,6) *
* 100  FORMAT(8I4)                      *
*****************************************
```

```
                COL COL COL COL COL COL COL COL
                 1   2   3   4   5   6   7   8

DATA LINE 1      1   2   3   4   5   6   7   8
DATA LINE 2      9  10  11  12  13  14  15  16
DATA LINE 3     17  18  19  20  21  22  23  24
DATA LINE 4     25  26  27  28  29  30  31  32
DATA LINE 5     33  34  35  36  37  38  39  40
DATA LINE 6     41  42  43  44  45  46  47  48

                         1         2         3
                123456789012345678901234567890123
                      DATA COLUMN NUMBER
```

Values 1 through 24 occupy the first 48 columns of the first record; values 25 through 48 occupy the first 48 columns of the second record.

The two-dimensional 6 × 8 integer array whose values are read and assigned from the data file of Fig. 8-3 can be printed with nested implied DO loops in the WRITE statement, as shown in Fig. 8-4.

Since the values assigned to the 48 subscripted variables in this array increase by uniform increments from 1 to 48, both the array values and the subscript integer can be generated by nesting explicit DO loops within the program as follows:

```
    DIMENSION K(6,8)
    N=Ø
    DO 1Ø J=1,6
    DO 1Ø L=1,8
    N=N+1
    K(J,L)=N
 1Ø CONTINUE
    WRITE(*,1ØØ)((K(J,L),L=1,8),J=1,6)
1ØØ FORMAT(1X,8I4)
```

Once an array has been established, each element in the array can be used as a variable in an arithmetic expression by using the array name in the same way that a simple-variable name might be used and incrementing the subscript(s) under the control of appropriate explicit DO statements.

Figure 8-5 illustrates the use of the above program segment in generating the 48-element array K and then creating a new array KSQ, in which each element is

```
*****************************************
*     DIMENSION K(6,8)                  *
*     WRITE(6,200)((K(J,L),L=1,8),J=1,6) *
* 200 FORMAT(8I4)                       *
*****************************************
```

```
          COL COL COL COL COL COL COL COL
            1   2   3   4   5   6   7   8

ROW 1       1   2   3   4   5   6   7   8
ROW 2       9  10  11  12  13  14  15  16
ROW 3      17  18  19  20  21  22  23  24
ROW 4      25  26  27  28  29  30  31  32
ROW 5      33  34  35  36  37  38  39  40
ROW 6      41  42  43  44  45  46  47  48

                   1         2         3
          123456789012345678901234567890123
                   PRINT POSITION
```

FIGURE 8-4 Printing a two-dimensional array with a nested implied DO loop.

```
C234567890
      DIMENSION K(6,8),KSQ(6,8)
      OPEN(6,FILE='PRN')
      N=0
C
C  GENERATE ARRAY K
      DO 10 J=1,6
      DO 10 L=1,8
      N=N+1
      K(J,L)=N
   10 CONTINUE
C
C  PRINT ARRAY K:
      WRITE(6,50)
   50 FORMAT(1X,'THIS IS ARRAY K :')
      WRITE(6,100)((K(J,L),L=1,8),J=1,6)
  100 FORMAT(1X,8I6)
      WRITE(6,200)
  200 FORMAT('0')
C
C  GENERATE NEW ARRAY KSQ:
      DO 20 J=1,6
      DO 20 L=1,8
      KSQ(J,L)=K(J,L)**2
   20 CONTINUE
C
C  PRINT ARRAY KSQ:
      WRITE(6,150)
  150 FORMAT(1X,'THIS IS ARRAY KSQ :')
      WRITE(6,100)((KSQ(J,L),L=1,8),J=1,6)
      WRITE(6,200)
      STOP
      END
```

```
THIS IS ARRAY K :
     1     2     3     4     5     6     7     8
     9    10    11    12    13    14    15    16
    17    18    19    20    21    22    23    24
    25    26    27    28    29    30    31    32
    33    34    35    36    37    38    39    40
    41    42    43    44    45    46    47    48

THIS IS ARRAY KSQ :
     1     4     9    16    25    36    49    64
    81   100   121   144   169   196   225   256
   289   324   361   400   441   484   529   576
   625   676   729   784   841   900   961  1024
  1089  1156  1225  1296  1369  1444  1521  1600
  1681  1764  1849  1936  2025  2116  2209  2304
```

FIGURE 8-5 Program to generate a two-dimensional array, square each element, and print both arrays.

the square of the corresponding element in array K. Both arrays are printed. By the same technique, the elements of one array can be multiplied or divided (or otherwise manipulated) by the corresponding elements of another array.

Although knowledgeable application of nested implied DO loops in the READ and WRITE statements often saves both programming and computer time, there are situations where the explicit DO loop must be used. Consider a case where a program is written to process any two-dimensional array with subscripts less than or equal to a specified maximum. Figure 8-6 illustrates a program intended to read and print the element values of any two-dimensional real array up to and including a 1Ø × 1Ø array. The DIMENSION statement sets the maximum subscript size, A(1Ø,1Ø). The program is tested by using a 6 × 6 array which must also be called A, to correspond to the name established by the DIMENSION statement. The data records, printed following the program listing, show the data values and organization of data. A data record is required to provide values declaring the actual subscript values to be used. These values, 6 for the first (row) subscript and 6 for the second (column) subscript, are read and assigned to the corresponding variable names N and M by the first READ and FORMAT statements of the program. Six records are required, with 6 values per record, representing, respectively, the 6 rows and 6 columns of the array. The array records are read and printed with the next READ and WRITE statements. The associated FORMAT statements must provide edit descriptors for the maximum number of values (1Ø) that could be listed in a single record or printed on one row of the array; otherwise, the program could not be used with a 1Ø × 1Ø array, its maximum design capacity. Note the order of the values and the values themselves in the printed output and compare with the values listed in the printed records. The output is not ordered in 6 rows and 6 columns corresponding to the 6 records and the values listed on each record. What happened? Where did the extraneous zeros

```
C234567890
      DIMENSION A(10,10)
      OPEN(3,FILE='FIG8-6.DAT')
      OPEN(6,FILE='PRN')
      READ(3,100)N,M
  100 FORMAT(2I5)
      READ(3,200)((A(J,K),K=1,M),J=1,N)
  200 FORMAT(10F7.2)
      WRITE(6,*)
      WRITE(6,250)
  250 FORMAT(1X,'THIS IS THE ATTEMPTED PRINTING OF THE ARRAY :')
      WRITE(6,400)((A(J,K),K=1,M),J=1,N)
  400 FORMAT(1X,10F7.2)
      STOP
      END
```

```
    6    6
 1.00   0.01   0.02   0.03   0.04   7.00
 0.05   2.00   0.06   0.07   8.00   0.08
 0.09   0.10   3.00   9.00   0.11   0.12
 0.13   0.14  10.00   4.00   0.15   0.16
 0.17  11.00   0.18   0.19   5.00   0.20
12.00   0.21   0.22   0.23   0.24   6.00
```

```
THIS IS THE ATTEMPTED PRINTING OF THE ARRAY :
   1.00    .01    .02    .03    .04   7.00    .00    .00    .00    .00
    .05   2.00    .06    .07   8.00    .08    .00    .00    .00    .00
    .09    .10   3.00   9.00    .11    .12    .00    .00    .00    .00
    .13    .14  10.00   4.00    .15    .16
```

FIGURE 8-6 Incorrectly reading and printing a two-dimensional array when the size of the array is variable.

come from, and how can they be purged? When J (the row subscript in the implied DO loop in the READ statement) is set at 1 and K (the column subscript) is cycled from 1 through 6, the 6 values listed in the first record are assigned, in turn, to A(1,1), A(1,2), A(1,3), A(1,4), A(1,5), and A(1,6). The reading should then advance to the second record and assign the first value to A(2,1), the second value to A(2,2), etc. However, the right parenthesis of the 200 FORMAT statement (the signal for the reading to advance to the next record) has not yet been encountered, and four specifications have not been used. The nested implied DO loops in the READ statement continue to cycle, and four *blank* fields of the first record are read, assigning a value of zero to A(2,1), A(2,2), A(2,3), and A(2,4). The second record is now read and the first value is assigned to A(2,5), the second value to A(2,6), the third value to A(3,1), etc. The well-ordered array is now hopelessly disorganized. Since the 6 × 6 subscript limit permits array A only 36 elements, the 12 values on the last two records remain unread—forced out by the 12 zeros—and the last records are lost.

What can be done to align the values in 6 rows and 6 columns? Figure 8-7 provides a solution. The program and data files are identical in Figs. 8-6 and 8-7 ex-

```
C234567890
      DIMENSION A(10,10)
      OPEN(3,FILE='FIG8-6.DAT')
      OPEN(6,FILE='PRN')
      READ(3,100)N,M
  100 FORMAT(2I5)
      DO 10 J=1,N
   10 READ(3,200)(A(J,K),K=1,M)
  200 FORMAT(10F7.2)
      WRITE(6,*)
      WRITE(6,250)
  250 FORMAT(1X,'THIS IS THE CORRECT PRINTING OF THE ARRAY :')
      DO 20 J=1,N
   20 WRITE(6,300)(A(J,K),K=1,M)
  300 FORMAT(1X,10F7.2)
      STOP
      END
```

```
    6    6
 1.00   0.01   0.02   0.03   0.04   7.00
 0.05   2.00   0.06   0.07   8.00   0.08
 0.09   0.10   3.00   9.00   0.11   0.12
 0.13   0.14  10.00   4.00   0.15   0.16
 0.17  11.00   0.18   0.19   5.00   0.20
12.00   0.21   0.22   0.23   0.24   6.00
```

```
THIS IS THE CORRECT PRINTING OF THE ARRAY :
   1.00    .01    .02    .03    .04   7.00
    .05   2.00    .06    .07   8.00    .08
    .09    .10   3.00   9.00    .11    .12
    .13    .14  10.00   4.00    .15    .16
    .17  11.00    .18    .19   5.00    .20
  12.00    .21    .22    .23    .24   6.00
```

FIGURE 8-7 Correctly reading and printing a two-dimensional array when the size of the array is variable.

cept that now the data file is read by a single implied DO loop in the READ statement, which controls the second (column) subscript inside an explicit DO loop, which controls the first (row) subscript. The explicit DO statement will set J at 1, and the implied DO loop will read the six (the value assigned to M) values listed in the second record (the first record sets the size of the array) according to the first six descriptors in the associated 2ØØ FORMAT statement. When the inner (implied) DO loop is satisfied with the six iterations, the four extra edit descriptors in the 2ØØ FORMAT specification are ignored (Sec. 6-13, Rule 1). Control then reverts to the outer (explicit) DO loop, and its index (J) increments to 2. Then the READ statement with its implied DO loop is again encountered, and the sequence of reading is repeated with the six values in the third record assigned to the second row of the array. The extra descriptors are again ignored. This sequence is repeated until all six (the value assigned to N) records have been read. Note that each time the explicit DO loop cycles, the READ statement is executed according to its associated FORMAT specification and only the required number of descriptors, as specified by the second subscript number, are used, thus avoiding the problem that plagued the program in Fig. 8-6. The printed output follows the same logic. The two-dimensional array A has now been read, assigned, and printed in *row order*. The printed output is ordered in 6 rows and 6 columns with the first (row) and second (column) subscripts correctly locating each subscripted variable by its row and column position in the array.

8-8 INPUT AND OUTPUT OF TWO-DIMENSIONAL ARRAYS USING FORMAT-DIRECTED READ AND WRITE STATEMENTS WITHOUT DO LOOPS

Two-dimensional arrays can also be read and displayed (printed) without using DO loops—either explicit or implied—by using the READ and WRITE statements as described in Sec. 8-6. The DIMENSION statement in the following example establishes a two-dimensional array of 3 rows and 5 columns (3 × 5):

```
      DIMENSION N(3,5)
      OPEN(3,FILE='EXAMPLE.DAT')
      READ(3,1ØØ)N
1ØØ   FORMAT(15I3)
      WRITE(*,2ØØ)N
2ØØ   FORMAT(1X,5I5)
```

The number of data values required to satisfy the READ statement (the number specified in the DIMENSION statement) *must* be provided. The 3 × 5 array in the above example requires 15 data values. When using this method of input/output, it is important to understand that the sequence of reading and displaying two-dimensional arrays is in *column order* rather than row order as in the previous examples of two-dimensional array input/output. This variation is inherent in the internal programming of the compiler.

The following integer array N is to be read and printed:

	Column				
Row	**1**	**2**	**3**	**4**	**5**
1	11	12	13	14	15
2	21	22	23	24	25
3	31	32	33	34	35

The two-dimensional arrays discussed in Sec. 8-7 were all read and displayed in row order. Figure 8-8 shows the results of reading and printing the above array when the element values are arranged sequentially in row order as shown in the record printed after the END statement of the program listing. The array, as read, is then printed by the first WRITE/FORMAT statements and appears as the first array in the output. The first array *looks* exactly like the given array as shown above, and listed in the record, because the element values are printed in the same (column) order in which they were read. But when the array is printed by the WRITE statement with the nested implied DO loops, where the loops are ar-

```
C234567890
      DIMENSION N(3,5)
      OPEN(3,FILE='FIG8-8.DAT')
      OPEN(6,FILE='PRN')
      READ(3,100)N
  100 FORMAT(15I3)
      WRITE(6,200)N
  200 FORMAT(10X,5I5)
      WRITE(6,300)
  300 FORMAT(//)
      WRITE(6,200)((N(J,K),K=1,5),J=1,3)
      WRITE(6,300)
      WRITE(6,400)N(1,5),N(2,3),N(3,1)
  400 FORMAT(15X,3I5)
      STOP
      END
```

```
 11 12 13 14 15 21 22 23 24 25 31 32 33 34 35
```

```
           11   12   13   14   15
           21   22   23   24   25
           31   32   33   34   35


           11   14   22   25   33
           12   15   23   31   34
           13   21   24   32   35


                33   23   13
```

FIGURE 8-8 Incorrectly reading a two-dimensional array without DO loops.

ranged to print the array in row order, the second array in the output shows the values ordered differently from the given array. The values of the specific elements of the array *are not* the values shown in the given array. This is further demonstrated by the next WRITE/FORMAT statements, which call for printing a few specific elements, shown in the last line of output. From the given array it can be seen that N(1,5) = 15, N(2,3) = 23, and N(3,1) = 31. The values printed for these elements are 33, 23, and 13, respectively. Obviously the values were not stored as intended.

What went wrong? A study of the first and second arrays in the output of Fig. 8-8 reveals that the READ(3,1ØØ)N and the WRITE(6,2ØØ)N statements caused the values, as listed in the record, to be read and printed in column order rather than in row order. This column-row sequence of input/output is, as stated earlier, inherent in the internal programming of the compiler. A programmer accustomed to reading and storing two-dimensional arrays in row order, as discussed in Sec. 8-7, may find the column order of reading and storing annoying.

Figure 8-9 illustrates a procedure for taking advantage of these obviously simpler input/output statements (and circumventing the inherent column-order assignment) by reordering the data values in column rather than row order, as shown in the record printed following the END statement of the program listing.

```
C234567890
      DIMENSION N(3,5)
      OPEN(3,FILE='FIG8-9.DAT')
      OPEN(6,FILE='PRN')
      READ(3,100)N
  100 FORMAT(15I3)
      WRITE(6,200)N
  200 FORMAT(10X,5I5)
      WRITE(6,300)
  300 FORMAT(//)
      WRITE(6,200)((N(J,K),K=1,5),J=1,3)
      WRITE(6,300)
      WRITE(6,400)N(1,5),N(2,3),N(3,1)
  400 FORMAT(15X,3I5)
      STOP
      END
```

```
11 21 31 12 22 32 13 23 33 14 24 34 15 25 35
```

```
          11   21   31   12   22
          32   13   23   33   14
          24   34   15   25   35


          11   12   13   14   15
          21   22   23   24   25
          31   32   33   34   35


               15   23   31
```

FIGURE 8-9 Correctly reading a two-dimensional array without DO loops.

(Compare the sequence of values with the given array.) The programs of Figs. 8-8 and 8-9 are otherwise identical. The first array of the output, printed by the first WRITE/FORMAT statements, shows the values assigned to each element printed in the order read. But this may not, of itself, demonstrate that the values have been stored in the desired elements. However, the second array of the output, printed by the WRITE statement with the nested implied DO loops, results in the given array order. Since this output was under the control of the implied DO loops arranged to print the array in row order, it is apparent that arranging the data in column order and reading the array by the READ(3,1ØØ)N statement results in the assignment of the values to the desired elements. This is further demonstrated by the last line of output, where the values of the same three elements as in Fig. 8-8 are printed, with predictable results, from the given row-column order.

Reading and printing subscripted variables in a two-dimensional array without using DO loops can reduce programming time, but this method must be applied with understanding and caution. It is important that the numerical values of a two-dimensional array be predictably assigned in the correct row-column order. Otherwise, computations involving the elements of the arrays will yield incorrect results. This problem does not exist with one-dimensional arrays.

8-9 INPUT AND OUTPUT OF ARRAYS USING LIST-DIRECTED READ AND WRITE STATEMENTS

a One-Dimensional Arrays

The list-directed READ and WRITE statements provide a simple way to read and/or display one-dimensional arrays, in a manner similar to the statements discussed in Sec. 8-6. In the statements:

```
DIMENSION K(5)
OPEN(3,FILE='EXAMPLE.DAT')
READ(3,*)K
WRITE(*,*)K
```

the input statement READ(3,*)K will read five integer values from any combination of records—i.e., five values from one record, two values from one record and three from another, one value from each of five records, etc.—without regard to format. The values may be listed in any field position in the record, provided that multiple values in a single record are separated by a comma or one or more *blanks*. The only requirement is that there be at least five values (the number specified as the largest subscript value in the DIMENSION statement). Providing less than five values to the READ statement results in an execution error. If more than five values are provided, the additional values, after the READ list has been satisfied, will be ignored. The data file shown below:

```
Record 1:         6ØØ
Record 2:    25         75Ø          5
Record 3:                      1Ø
```

will be read, and values assigned as follows:

```
K(1)=6ØØ     K(2)=25     K(3)=75Ø     K(4)=5     K(5)=1Ø
```

The output statement WRITE(*,*)K will display the five values in the order in which they were read and assigned in a single line (row) from left to right:

```
 6ØØ          25          75Ø          5          1Ø
```

The list-directed WRITE statement will display all values according to the specifications described in Sec. 3-12 for list-directed output. If there are more values to be displayed than will fit on a single line, a second line will be started when the number of output columns remaining on the first line is insufficient to accommodate the next value. Values are thus displayed on successive lines until all values have been displayed. When the list-directed WRITE statement is used, the programmer has no control over the output format. The only difference between the pair of statements READ(3,1ØØ)A and WRITE(*,2ØØ)A and the pair of statements READ(3,*)A and WRITE(*,*)A is that in the first pair the programmer controls the input/output formats, and in the second pair the programmer does not control the input/output formats.

b Two-Dimensional Arrays

The list-directed READ and WRITE statements can also be used to read and display two-dimensional arrays in a manner similar to the READ(3,1ØØ)N and WRITE(*,2ØØ)N statements discussed in Sec. 8-8. The array:

$$\begin{matrix} n_{1,1} & n_{1,2} & n_{1,3} \\ n_{2,1} & n_{2,2} & n_{2,3} \end{matrix}$$

can be read and displayed by the statements:

```
DIMENSION N(2,3)
OPEN(3,FILE='EXAMPLE.DAT')
READ(3,*)N
WRITE(*,*)N
```

It is important to know that the same column order of reading and displaying two-dimensional values inherent in the READ(3,1ØØ)N and WRITE(*,2ØØ)N statements (Sec. 8-8) also applies to the list-directed READ(3,*)N and WRITE(*,*)N statements. These last two statements read and display values for two-dimensional arrays in column order rather than row order. Therefore, if the array shown above is to be stored in mathematically correct order, with each value in its given row-column location, the data must be provided in column order.

Figure 8-10 shows the list-directed reading and printing of a two-dimensional array. The data were read from a data file of one record, as shown immediately following the END statement. Note that the data are arranged in column order. The data can be listed on several different records and randomly spaced. There must be at least six values provided, with the values given in the proper sequence (column order) for correct row-column assignment and separated by at least one *blank* or comma. The list-directed printing of the array is controlled by the compiler.

The first line of output is the result of the WRITE(6,*)N statement. Here the six array values are printed on one line. Note that the values are printed in the order read. (If there are, say, 12 values to print, printing will continue until the output columns remaining on that line are insufficient to accommodate the next value. Then a second line of print will be started for the remaining values.) The second group of output is the result of the WRITE statement under the control of the nested explicit DO loops. Here the explicit DO loops control row, then column, order, with the result that the 1Ø WRITE(6,*)N(J,K) was encountered 6 times. The result is a column of values, indicating that each value has been assigned to the proper element. The last line of output is the result of the WRITE statement with the implied DO loop under the control of an explicit DO loop. This line is printed in the same manner as the first line, but in row order as specified by the loops. This line of data demonstrates that the proper values are located in the desired array elements.

FIGURE 8-10 Reading and printing a two-dimensional array using list-directed input/output statements.

```
C234567890
      DIMENSION N(2,3)
      OPEN(3,FILE='FIG8-10.DAT')
      OPEN(6,FILE='PRN')
      READ(3,*)N
      WRITE(6,*)N
      WRITE(6,*)
      DO 10   J=1,2
      DO 10 K=1,3
   10 WRITE(6,*)N(J,K)
      WRITE(6,*)
      WRITE(6,*)((N(J,K),K=1,3),J=1,2)
      STOP
      END
```

```
11 21 12 22 13 23
```

```
11            21            12            22            13            23

11
12
13
21
22
23

11            12            13            21            22            23
```

The statements READ(3,1ØØ)N and READ(3,*)N both indicate input in column order. The statements WRITE(3,2ØØ)N and WRITE(*,*)N both indicate output in column order. If these facts are remembered and the data are correspondingly arranged, the array values can be read and correctly assigned to the correct array element. Failure to arrange the data in the order in which it will be read results in values assigned to the wrong array element.

8-10 APPLICATIONS OF THE SUBSCRIPTED VARIABLE

Example 8-1

The circle problem, which calculates the circumference and area from given radius values, can be revised with the radius values read from a data file and assigned as elements of a one-dimensional array named RADIUS. Since the maximum number of subscripts (elements in the array) must be specified at the beginning of the program, the number of radii read (size of the array) will be arbitrarily limited to 1ØØ. If the properties of more than 1ØØ circles need to be calculated, the program must be repeated with additional data.

The first step is to develop a flowchart (Fig. 8-11) for the solution. The integer variable K will be used both as a counter to count the number of radius values read and as the subscript of the subscripted variable RADIUS. The initial value assigned to K will be 1. The value of π is defined as 3.141593. The first radius value is read from the first record and assigned to the subscripted variable RADIUS(1). The first subscript is 1; therefore, the value assigned to K must be set at 1 before the READ statement in the program is executed for the first time.

Since the maximum value of the subscript is 1ØØ, a check must be made each time the subscript is incremented and another radius value read to ensure that the subscript has not exceeded the maximum allowed (1ØØ). If the value of the subscript does exceed 1ØØ, transfer is made to a print instruction that will print a message to the effect that 1ØØ values have been assigned, and continue the program outside the reading loop.

A check must also be made after each record is read to determine whether that was the last record in the file. If so, transfer is made out of the reading loop, and calculation can begin.

A print instruction is included in the flowchart to print identifying column headings. This print instruction could as well have been placed at the beginning of the sequential steps but must be located before the repetitive print instructions for printing the numerical values, and outside both the READ loop and the DO loop to avoid repetitive printing of the headings.

Note the ONPAGE CONNECTOR symbol—a numeral 1 inside a circle, indicating continuation of the flowchart from the bottom of the left side of the figure to the top of the right side. All calculations and printing of the values are performed under control of the DO statement, recalling in turn the value assigned to each subscripted variable of array RADIUS, i.e., RADIUS(1), RADIUS(2), RADIUS(3), etc. The subscript is J, the index

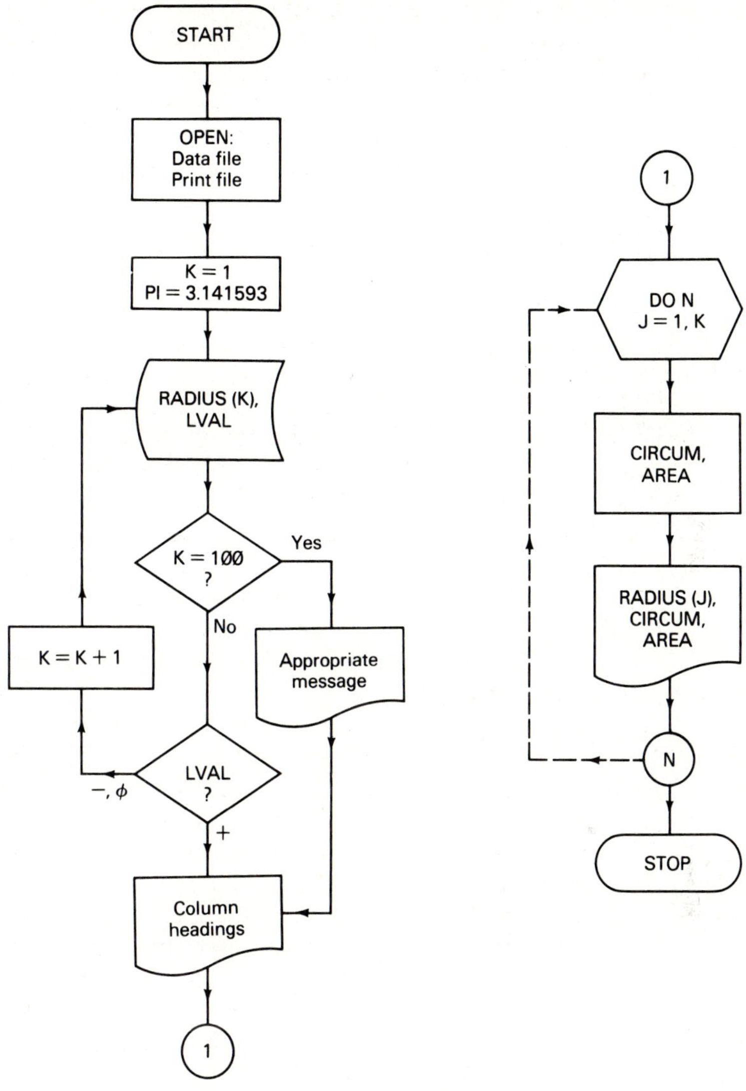

FIGURE 8-11 Flowchart of the circle problem using subscripted variables.

of the DO statement. The index is incremented in increments of 1, from an initial value of 1 through the limiting value K, thus controlling the number of records read and the maximum subscript value of RADIUS. Values for circumference and area are calculated for each element of the array RADIUS and printed—one line of output for each repetition of the DO loop—beneath appropriate headings (which have already been printed). The program terminates when the DO loop is satisfied, the DO loop being satisfied when the value of the index variable J is greater than K, the number of data records read. Note that a letter N is placed in the PREPARATION symbol and in the circle indicating the end of the DO loop. This letter represents a statement number which will be given to the CONTINUE statement in the program.

The flowchart is implemented with the program of Fig. 8-12. Note that fewer than 100 records (radius values) were supplied to the READ statement. Transfer out of the READ loop occurs when the last record has been read rather than after the maximum capacity of 100 records of the array RADIUS has been reached.

Example 8-2

Figure 8-13 is the flowchart for a sorting problem, in which a specified number of integer values arranged in random order are to be read from a data file and assigned as elements of a one-dimensional integer array. The values are ordered in decreasing numerical value and assign these ordered

FIGURE 8-12 Program for the circle problem using subscripted variables.

```
C234567890
      DIMENSION RADIUS(100)
      OPEN(3,FILE='FIG8-12.DAT')
      OPEN(6,FILE='PRN')
      K=1
      PI=3.141593
   10 READ(3,100)RADIUS(K),LVAL
  100 FORMAT(F10.3,I4)
      IF(K.EQ.100)GO TO 30
      IF(LVAL)20,20,40
   20 K=K+1
      GO TO 10
   30 WRITE(6,200)
  200 FORMAT(1X,'READING HALTED SINCE 100 CARDS READ')
   40 WRITE(6,300)
  300 FORMAT(10X,'RADIUS',5X,'CIRCUMFERENCE',6X,'AREA',/)
      DO 50 J=1,K
      CIRCUM=PI*RADIUS(J)*2.0
      AREA=PI*RADIUS(J)**2
   50 WRITE(6,400)RADIUS(J),CIRCUM,AREA
  400 FORMAT(1X,3F15.3,/)
      STOP
      END
```

```
    1.000   0
    4.750   0
   10.333   0
   25.468   1
```

```
         RADIUS     CIRCUMFERENCE      AREA

          1.000          6.283          3.142

          4.750         29.845         70.882

         10.333         64.924        335.431

         25.468        160.020       2037.697
```

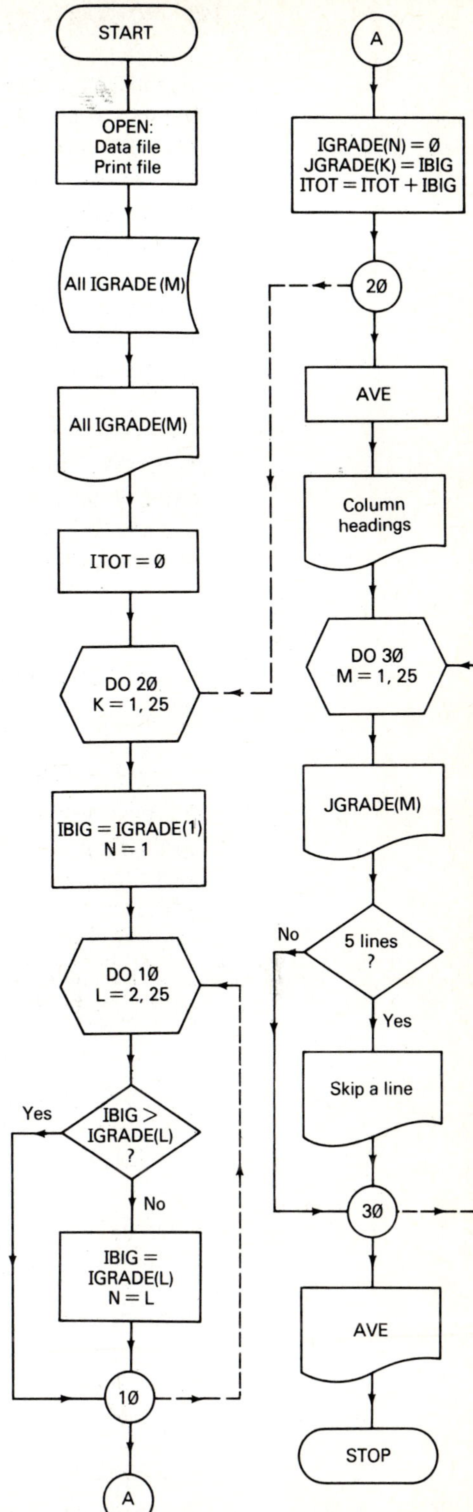

FIGURE 8-13 Flowchart of the grade averaging and ordering problem.

values, in turn, to the first, second, third, etc., subscripted variables of another one-dimensional array. The values are totaled and averaged. The ordered values and the average are then printed.

The integer values in this example represent student test grades in a class of 25 students. There will always be 25 grades, ranking in value from a maximum of 1ØØ down to Ø. The 25 grades are listed in two records (of a data file) in the (random) order in which the test papers were submitted. The records are read and the values assigned to the 25-element integer array IGRADE. The subscript M is incremented from 1 through 25 by an implied DO loop in the READ statement.

After the randomly ordered grades have been assigned to array IGRADE, they must be sorted, totaled, and averaged. Sorting the grades in descending numerical order can be accomplished by comparing each grade with the value of a simple variable, IBIG. For comparison purposes, IBIG is assigned an initial value equal to the first grade, IGRADE(1), each time the outer loop of the two nested DO loops is repeated. The remaining 25 grades are compared, one at a time, with IBIG in the inner DO loop. As long as IBIG is greater than the succeeding grades, the comparison continues. When a grade appears that is greater than IBIG, its value is assigned to IBIG, and the comparison continues with this new value of IBIG. When the inner loop is satisfied the first time, the last value assigned to IBIG is the largest numerical value of the 25 grades. This value is then assigned to the first subscripted variable of the 25-element integer array, JGRADE(1). As each largest grade is determined, it must be eliminated from further comparison. After each largest value is assigned to IBIG, the program must keep track of the subscript of the IGRADE from which the value was transferred to IBIG. This is done by introducing a subscript variable N whose value will always be equal to the subscript of the largest value of IGRADE. Thus when the inner DO loop is satisfied, the value of N will be the subscript of the largest value of IGRADE. Therefore, making IGRADE(N) = Ø removes that particular IGRADE element from further consideration.

The comparisons continue until both nested DO loops have been satisfied. JGRADE has now been assigned the grade values in descending numerical order from JGRADE(1) through JGRADE(25).

To determine the sum of the grades, an integer variable, ITOT, is given an initial value of zero. As each greatest value of IBIG is determined, that value is added to the value of ITOT. The value of ITOT is always the cumulative sum of the values assigned to the consecutive elements of JGRADE. The last value of ITOT is the sum of the 25 values. The average can be calculated by dividing the sum ITOT by the number of grades (25). To achieve a real value for the average, the value of ITOT must be temporarily changed to a real value.

Printing the 25 grades in a column of descending numerical values, printing the average, and printing appropriate annotation completes the solution. Figure 8-14 lists the program that implements the flowchart of Fig. 8-13. Figure 8-15 (see p. 250) shows the printed output with the grades, first in their

```
C234567890
      DIMENSION IGRADE(25),JGRADE(25)
      OPEN(3,FILE='FIG8-14.DAT')
      OPEN(6,FILE='PRN')
      READ(3,100)(IGRADE(M),M=1,25)
  100 FORMAT(13I3,/,12I3)
      WRITE(6,200)
  200 FORMAT(2X,'ORIGINAL LIST OF GRADES:',/)
      WRITE(6,300)(IGRADE(M),M=1,25)
  300 FORMAT(2X,13I4,/,2X,12I4,//)
      ITOT=0
      DO 20 K=1,25
      IBIG=IGRADE(1)
      N=1
      DO 10 L=2,25
      IF(IBIG.GT.IGRADE(L))GO TO 10
      IBIG=IGRADE(L)
      N=L
   10 CONTINUE
      IGRADE(N)=0
      JGRADE(K)=IBIG
   20 ITOT=ITOT+IBIG
      AVE=FLOAT(ITOT)/25.0
      WRITE(6,400)
  400 FORMAT(4X,'ORDER OF GRADES',/)
      DO 30 M=1,25
      WRITE(6,500)JGRADE(M)
  500 FORMAT(10X,I3)
      IF(M/5*5-M.EQ.0)WRITE(6,600)
  600 FORMAT(' ')
   30 CONTINUE
      WRITE(6,700)AVE
  700 FORMAT(1X,'THE AVERAGE GRADE =',F6.2)
      STOP
      END
```

```
72 85100 98 76100 99 73 74 65 54 93 85
70 86 87 89 72 90 63 79 78 91 88 75
```

FIGURE 8-14 Program for the grade averaging and ordering problem.

original random order as received and listed in data records, then in descending numerical order in column form.

Example 8-3

The theorem of Pythagoras is used in this example:

$$C = \sqrt{A^2 + B^2}$$

where C is the hypotenuse of a right triangle and A and B are the legs of the triangle. The values of the leg A are to vary from 1 through 1Ø, inclusive, in increments of 1, and the values of leg B are to vary from 2 through 2Ø, inclusive, in increments of 2. The resulting values of C are calculated and placed in a two-dimensional array where A controls the column order and B controls the row order. Since the logic of these calculations is well known, a flowchart is not shown. Figure 8-16 (see p. 251) shows the program. Note the statements

```
ORIGINAL LIST OF GRADES:

  72  85 100  98  76 100  99  73  74  65  54  93  85
  70  86  87  89  72  90  63  79  78  91  88  75


  ORDER OF GRADES
        100
        100
         99
         98
         93

         91
         90
         89
         88
         87

         86
         85
         85
         79
         78

         76
         75
         74
         73
         72

         72
         70
         65
         63
         54

THE AVERAGE GRADE =  81.68
```

FIGURE 8-15 Output for the grade averaging and ordering problem.

that provide the column headings, and the first part of the WRITE statement with the implied nested DO loops, which provides the row headings. This example is shown, not because of its complexity, but to give a simple example of a problem involving a two-dimensional array and to show how column and row headings can be included in the output.

PROBLEMS

8-1 Study the program shown in Fig. 8-17 and determine the numerical values that would be printed.

8-2 Study the program shown in Fig. 8-18 and determine the numerical values that would be printed.

8-3 Study the program shown in Fig. 8-19 (see p. 252) and determine the numerical values that would be printed.

```
C234567890
      DIMENSION C(20,10)
      OPEN(6,FILE='PRN')
      WRITE(6,100)
  100 FORMAT(27X,'THEOREM OF PYTHAGORAS',/)
      WRITE(6,200)(N,N=1,10)
  200 FORMAT(3X,'A',I3,9I7,/)
      DO 10 J=2,20,2
      DO 10 K=1,10
      C(J,K)=SQRT(FLOAT(J)**2+FLOAT(K)**2)
   10 CONTINUE
      WRITE(6,300)
  300 FORMAT(2X,'B')
      WRITE(6,400)(J,(C(J,K),K=1,10),J=2,20,2)
  400 FORMAT(1X,I2,F6.2,9F7.2,/)
      STOP
      END
```

```
                           THEOREM OF PYTHAGORAS

   A  1      2      3      4      5      6      7      8      9     10

  B
  2  2.24   2.83   3.61   4.47   5.39   6.32   7.28   8.25   9.22  10.20

  4  4.12   4.47   5.00   5.66   6.40   7.21   8.06   8.94   9.85  10.77

  6  6.08   6.32   6.71   7.21   7.81   8.49   9.22  10.00  10.82  11.66

  8  8.06   8.25   8.54   8.94   9.43  10.00  10.63  11.31  12.04  12.81

 10 10.05  10.20  10.44  10.77  11.18  11.66  12.21  12.81  13.45  14.14

 12 12.04  12.17  12.37  12.65  13.00  13.42  13.89  14.42  15.00  15.62

 14 14.04  14.14  14.32  14.56  14.87  15.23  15.65  16.12  16.64  17.20

 16 16.03  16.12  16.28  16.49  16.76  17.09  17.46  17.89  18.36  18.87

 18 18.03  18.11  18.25  18.44  18.68  18.97  19.31  19.70  20.12  20.59

 20 20.02  20.10  20.22  20.40  20.62  20.88  21.19  21.54  21.93  22.36
```

FIGURE 8-16 Program for the theorem of Pythagoras.

FIGURE 8-17
Problem 8-1.

```
C   PROB 8-1
C234567890
      DIMENSION K(6)
      OPEN(6,FILE='PRN')
      DO 10 N=1,6
      K(N)=7-N
   10 CONTINUE
      WRITE(6,100)(K(J),J=1,6)
  100 FORMAT(3I2,/,2I2,/,I2)
      WRITE(6,*)
      STOP
      END
```

FIGURE 8-18
Problem 8-2.

```
C   PROB 8-2
C234567890
      DIMENSION K(6)
      OPEN(6,FILE='PRN')
      DO 10 N=1,6
      K(N)=(2*N)-1
   10 CONTINUE
      WRITE(6,100)(K(L),L=1,6)
  100 FORMAT(I3,/,2I3,/,3I3)
      WRITE(6,*)
      STOP
      END
```

```
C   PROB 8-3
C234567890
      DIMENSION J(6,9)
      OPEN(6,FILE='PRN')
      DO 10 L=2,6,2
      DO 10 M=1,9,2
      J(L,M)=L+M
   10 CONTINUE
      WRITE(6,100)((J(L,M),M=1,9,2),L=2,6,2)
  100 FORMAT(5I3)
      WRITE(6,*)
      STOP
      END
```

FIGURE 8-19 Problem 8-3.

8-4 Study the program shown in Fig. 8-20 and determine the numerical values that would be printed.

8-5 Generate a multiplication table for numbers from 1 to 1Ø. Provide for row and column headings (number of row or column). (*Hint:* Each value in the table will equal its row multiplied by its column.)

8-6 Generate a table of volumes in gallons for right circular tanks whose radii vary from 1 to 1Ø ft in increments of 1 ft, and whose heights vary from 1 to 9 ft in increments of 2 ft, where 1 ft^3 = 7.481 gal. Provide column headings and titles.

8-7 The area of an ellipse is determined by the formula: $A = \pi R_1 R_2$, where R_1 and R_2 are one-half of the major and minor axes, respectively. Write a program to compute the areas of all ellipses where R_1 varies from 1 through 3 in increments of 1 and R_2 varies from 2 through 1Ø in increments of 2. After all calculations are completed, print the area as a two-dimensional array. Have R_1 control the rows and R_2 the columns. Include appropriate column headings.

8-8 Given a right triangle with sides *A* and *B* and hypotenuse *C*, write a program to compute and print as a two-dimensional array the values of the hypotenuse for all odd values of *A* from 1 through 9 and all even values of *B* from 2 through 18. The values for *A* indicate the column, the values for B indicate the row. Print the values for *C* to the nearest hundredth. Include appropriate column headings.

FIGURE 8-20 Problem 8-4.

```
C   PROB 8-4
C234567890
      DIMENSION J(4,6)
      OPEN(6,FILE='PRN')
      DO 10 L=1,4
      DO 10 M=2,6,2
      J(L,M)=L*M
   10 CONTINUE
      WRITE(6,100)((J(L,M),M=2,6,2),L=1,4)
  100 FORMAT(3I3)
      WRITE(6,*)
      STOP
      END
```

8-9 Write a program that will read one integer value from each record of a 15-record data file and arrange the values (left to right) in a 3 × 5 array such that the first five values are the values of the first row, the next five values are the values of the second row, and the last five values are the values of the third row. Sum the values in each row and print the sum at the right end of the row. Sum the values in each column and print the sum at the bottom of the column. It is suggested that the values 1 through 15 be sequentially listed in the 15 records.

8-10 Refer to Prob. 8-9. Use the same data file but arrange the values in a 5 × 3 array. The first five values are to be the values in the first column (top to bottom), the second five values are to be the values in the second column, and the last five values are to be the values in the third column. Again sum each row and column, and print as in Prob. 8-9.

8-11 This problem demonstrates array manipulation. Write a program to read in a 6 × 4 array. The values of the elements are the positive integer numbers from 1 through 24 inclusive, arranged in random order. Reorder that array into a new array, where the first column contains the largest values arranged in descending order, the second column contains the remaining largest values arranged in descending order, etc., until the bottom value in the fourth column is 1. Print the original random array and the numerical decrementing array.

8-12 Given a 1Ø × 1Ø array whose elements are randomly ordered integer numbers between Ø and 1Ø, inclusive, determine the sum of the elements of the odd-numbered columns in the odd-numbered rows and the elements of the even-numbered columns in the even-numbered rows. Print the given array and the required sum. Prepare a suitable data file.

8-13 Write a program that will search an $N \times M$ array for the value of the largest element. The maximum array will be 1Ø × 1Ø. Have the array printed as well as its maximum element. The program should handle any number of arrays. Assume that all values in the array are integers. Search through at least two different $N \times M$ arrays.

8-14 In surveying, one type of closed traverse starts and ends at a given point of known X and Y coordinates. When the azimuth (angle measured clockwise from north) and the distance of each leg of the traverse are known, the X and Y coordinates of the endpoint of each leg can be computed. This is done by calculating the change in the X value (*departure*) and the change in the Y value (*latitude*) along the leg. The algebraic signs of the changes must be considered in determining the coordinates of the endpoint. For a closed traverse the coordinates of the endpoint of the final leg should be the same as for the initial point. Usually they are not exactly the same. Then an *error of closure* is calculated. The error of closure is the straight-line distance between the coordinates of the initial point and the calculated coordinates of the endpoint of the final leg. Write a program that will read in the X and Y coordinates of the initial point, the number of legs in the traverse, and the azimuth and distance along each leg. Calculate and print the coordinates of each endpoint. Calculate and print the error of closure. The program should be capable of reading up to 5Ø legs. For test data, assume that the coordinates of the initial point are 1Ø,ØØØ.ØØ and 5Ø,ØØØ.ØØ. The azimuth and distances for each leg are:

Azimuth	Distance
26.17°	285.1Ø
1Ø4.58	61Ø.45
195.5Ø	72Ø.48
358.3Ø	2Ø3.ØØ
3Ø6.9Ø	647.Ø2

Note that no units are shown for the distance as the units are immaterial; they could be either feet or meters.

8-15 Another type of closed traverse is one that starts at one known point and ends at a second known point. Revise the program of Prob. 8-14 so that it will solve both types of closed traverses. Note that a recognition signal must be made so that the program can identify the type of traverse; the output should identify the type of traverse by name. The program should be written so that it can handle any number of traverses.

Use the data of Prob. 8-14 to test the program for that type of traverse. For the second type described above, assume that the coordinates of the initial point are 1Ø,ØØØ.ØØ and 5Ø,ØØØ.ØØ. The coordinates of the second known point are 1Ø,367.ØØ and 49,161.ØØ. The azimuths and distances for each leg are:

Azimuth	Distance
33.8°	215.5
138.3	472.4
73.5	38Ø.3
196.6	895.1
297.1	163.3

8-16 It is desired to calibrate a dipstick to measure the number of gallons remaining in a cylindrical storage tank that is positioned with the axis horizontal. The diameter of the tank is 6 ft, and the length of the tank is 1Ø ft. The dipstick should be marked as close as possible to increments of 2ØØ gal. Distances from the bottom of the dipstick to each graduation are to be determined to Ø.ØØ1 ft (Ø.Ø12 in). (*Caution:* Be careful in calculating the volumes and distances for the upper half of the tank.)

8-17 A square array has two diagonals. Write a program to interchange the values along these two diagonals, leaving the remaining elements unchanged in position. Write the program to handle any $N \times N$ array up to a 1Ø × 1Ø array, and test at least two different sizes of arrays. The first record should contain the value of N, and then the next N records should contain the array values with N values per record. The second array is arranged in like manner. Print the original and the final arrays. Prepare a suitable data file to test your program.

8-18 Two-dimensional arrays, or matrices, are used in matrix algebra. One of the operations in matrix algebra is generating the transpose of a given matrix. The *transpose* is made by interchanging the rows and columns of a given array to yield a new matrix. For example:

$$\begin{bmatrix} 1 & 4 & 7 \\ 2 & 5 & 8 \\ 3 & 6 & 9 \end{bmatrix} \quad \begin{bmatrix} 1 & 2 & 3 \\ 4 & 5 & 6 \\ 7 & 8 & 9 \end{bmatrix} \qquad \text{or} \qquad \begin{bmatrix} 1 & 5 & 9 \\ 2 & 6 & 10 \\ 3 & 7 & 11 \\ 4 & 8 & 12 \end{bmatrix} \quad \begin{bmatrix} 1 & 2 & 3 & 4 \\ 5 & 6 & 7 & 8 \\ 9 & 10 & 11 & 12 \end{bmatrix}$$

Matrix Transpose Matrix Transpose

Write a program that will generate the transpose of any matrix up to a maximum of 1Ø rows and 1Ø columns. For simplicity, use integers for the values in the matrices. Print both the given matrix and its transpose. Test the program with at least two different matrices, one of which is not square.

8-19 Matrix algebra provides for the addition of two conformable matrices. Matrices are *conformable* when they have the same number of rows and columns. The addition of matrices follows the rule:

$$c_{i,j} = a_{i,j} + b_{i,j}$$

For example, if the two matrices are:

$$\begin{bmatrix} 1 & 4 & 7 \\ 2 & 5 & 8 \\ 3 & 6 & 9 \end{bmatrix} \quad \text{and} \quad \begin{bmatrix} 10 & 13 & 16 \\ 11 & 14 & 17 \\ 12 & 15 & 18 \end{bmatrix}$$

their sum will be:

$$\begin{bmatrix} 11 & 17 & 23 \\ 13 & 19 & 25 \\ 15 & 21 & 27 \end{bmatrix}$$

Write a program to add any two conformable matrices of up to 1Ø rows and 1Ø columns. For simplicity, use integer values. Print both given matrices and the new matrix created by addition. Test the program with at least two different pairs of given matrices, one of which is not a square. Include a test to determine whether the two given matrices are conformable.

8-20 In Prob. 8-18 the transpose of a matrix was determined, and in Prob. 8-19 two matrices were added. Since subtraction is the reverse of addition, it is possible to express any square matrix as the sum of a symmetric matrix and a skew-symmetric matrix, where the *symmetric matrix* is one-half the sum of the given matrix and its transpose, and the *skew-symmetric matrix* is one-half the difference when the transpose is subtracted from the given matrix.

Write a program that will determine the symmetric and skew-symmetric matrices for any given square matrix up to 1Ø rows and 1Ø columns. Print the given matrix and the two required matrices. Test the program with at least one matrix using real values.

8-21 A common problem in matrix algebra is to multiply a matrix (multiplicand) by a vector (multiplier) to obtain a new vector. A *vector* is a one-dimensional array. The rule governing this operation is that the *number of elements (columns) in the given vector must be the same as the number of rows in the matrix.* The number of elements in the *product vector* are the same as the number of columns in the given matrix. The value of each element in the product vector will be the sum of the products of each element in the given vector times the corresponding element in a column of the matrix. In other words, if the given vector and matrix are:

$$[a_1 \quad a_2 \quad a_3 \quad a_4] \quad \text{and} \quad \begin{bmatrix} b_{1,1} & b_{1,2} & b_{1,3} \\ b_{2,1} & b_{2,2} & b_{2,3} \\ b_{3,1} & b_{3,2} & b_{3,3} \\ b_{4,1} & b_{4,2} & b_{4,3} \end{bmatrix}$$

the product vector will be:

$$[c_1 \quad c_2 \quad c_3]$$

where $c_1 = a_1b_{1,1} + a_2b_{2,1} + a_3b_{3,1} + a_4b_{4,1}$
$c_2 = a_1b_{1,2} + a_2b_{2,2} + a_3b_{3,2} + a_4b_{4,2}$
$c_3 = a_1b_{1,3} + a_2b_{2,3} + a_3b_{3,3} + a_4b_{4,3}$

Write a program that will read in a vector of up to 1Ø elements and a matrix of up to a 1Ø × 1Ø array. Then calculate the values of each element of the product vector. Print and identify the given vector and matrix and the product vector. The program should be able to handle any number of such problems. Note that certain vectors cannot be used in the multiplication of a particular matrix. The rule stated above must be followed. Include a test to determine whether the required vector multiplication can be performed.

8-22 Another matrix-algebra operation is determining the matrix that is the product of two other matrices. This is a more challenging extension of the previous problem. The rule governing matrix multiplication is: *Two matrices can be multiplied if the number of columns in the first matrix is equal to the number of rows in the second.* The first matrix is the multiplier and the second matrix is the multiplicand. The number of rows in the *product matrix* equals the number of rows in the multiplier, and the number of columns in the product matrix equals the number of columns in the multiplicand. Stated mathematically:

$$\text{If } A = [a_{i,j}] \text{ and } B = [b_{j,k}], \text{ then } AB = C = [c_{i,k}]$$

where brackets indicate matrices. For example, if the two given matrices are:

$$\begin{bmatrix} a_{1,1} & a_{1,2} & a_{1,3} & a_{1,4} \\ a_{2,1} & a_{2,2} & a_{2,3} & a_{2,4} \\ a_{3,1} & a_{3,2} & a_{3,3} & a_{3,4} \end{bmatrix} \quad \text{and} \quad \begin{bmatrix} b_{1,1} & b_{1,2} & b_{1,3} & b_{1,4} & b_{1,5} \\ b_{2,1} & b_{2,2} & b_{2,3} & b_{2,4} & b_{2,5} \\ b_{3,1} & b_{3,2} & b_{3,3} & b_{3,4} & b_{3,5} \\ b_{4,1} & b_{4,2} & b_{4,3} & b_{4,4} & b_{4,5} \end{bmatrix}$$

the product matrix is:

$$\begin{bmatrix} c_{1,1} & c_{1,2} & c_{1,3} & c_{1,4} & c_{1,5} \\ c_{2,1} & c_{2,2} & c_{2,3} & c_{2,4} & c_{2,5} \\ c_{3,1} & c_{3,2} & c_{3,3} & c_{3,4} & c_{3,5} \end{bmatrix}$$

The values of each element in the product matrix are determined by summing the products of the elements in a row of the multiplier matrix times the corresponding elements in a column of the multiplicand matrix; for example:

$$c_{1,1} = a_{1,1}b_{1,1} + a_{1,2}b_{2,1} + a_{1,3}b_{3,1} + a_{1,4}b_{4,1}$$
$$c_{1,5} = a_{1,1}b_{1,5} + a_{1,2}b_{2,5} + a_{1,3}b_{3,5} + a_{1,4}b_{4,5}$$
$$c_{2,1} = a_{2,1}b_{1,1} + a_{2,2}b_{2,1} + a_{2,3}b_{3,1} + a_{2,4}b_{4,1}$$

Write a program that will read the values for any two matrices up to a 1Ø × 1Ø array and determine the product matrix. Both the given matrices and the product matrix should be printed. For simplicity, use integer elements and plan the program so that the matrix with the fewer rows is read first. Notice that the operation of multiplication is not necessarily reversible; i.e., B can be multiplied by A, but A cannot be multiplied by B. Include a test to determine whether the two matrices can be multiplied.

8-23 An instructor in a mechanics class gives six examinations during the term. The first three each count as 1Ø percent of the final grade, the next two each count as 2Ø percent, and the last one counts as 3Ø percent of the final grade. Design a program that will read in each student's social security number (SSN) and examination grades and then compute the final grade. After reading in all students' SSNs and grades, compute the class average for each of the six examinations and the term grade for each student. The program should permit the number of students to vary from term to term. Use the data below:

	Examination					
Student SSN	**1**	**2**	**3**	**4**	**5**	**6**
123-45-6789	45	5Ø	1Ø	7Ø	9Ø	9Ø
234-56-7891	95	9Ø	8Ø	95	85	8Ø
345-67-8912	5Ø	45	42	55	65	6Ø
456-87-9123	8Ø	7Ø	84	85	65	7Ø
567-89-1234	1ØØ	94	92	98	1ØØ	1ØØ

Thought must be given as to how to read in the SSNs and in what form to read the exam grades.

8-24 Determine the largest size loan that is possible for 2Ø-year loans where the monthly payments may range from $1ØØ through $5ØØ in $5Ø increments, and the annual interest varies from 1Ø to 16 percent in 2 percent increments. Print the results so that each monthly payment line shows the size of the loan possible for each interest rate. Refer to Prob. 7-19 for appropriate equations.

8-25 Problem 7-11 required the determination of the prime numbers between 1 and 1ØØ. Note that no even number can be a prime number as all even numbers are divisible by 2. Any number that is not a prime number is called a *composite number* since it must have two or more factors. One factor of any composite number will be a number equal to or less than one-half the composite number. This fact can be used to reduce the quantity of trial divisors when attempting to determine whether a given number is prime or composite.

Successive prime numbers separated by a difference of 2 are called *twin primes*. The primes 3 and 5 are twin primes, as are 5 and 7. The number 5 is the twin of 3; 7 is the twin of 5. Write a program that will determine the primes between 5 and 5ØØ. Test each successive prime to determine whether it is the twin of the previous prime. If it is, save these two prime numbers (twins). After all primes are determined, print out all twin primes. Arrange the output in four columns so that the first column shows the prime, the second column its twin, the third column shows the next prime, and the fourth column its twin. Use appropriate column headings. The number of twin primes occurring between 5 and 5ØØ will not exceed 25. A flowchart of the logic will prove to be a great help.

8-26 An engineer is approached by a daredevil who needs help in planning a stunt. She proposes to ride a rocket-powered skateboard on a leap over a nearby river. Her weight is 147 lb, and the skateboard, when emptied of fuel, weighs 13 lb. The terrain at the jump site is level, and the river is 275 ft wide. The stunt woman wants to know the minimum takeoff velocity necessary to make the leap. Assuming the pull of gravity to be 32 ft/s^2, determine the velocity required for different angles of the takeoff ramp. Start with an angle of 3Ø° and increase to 6Ø° in increments of 5°. If the jump is to be made with no wind, the formula for V is (neglecting air friction):

$$V^2 = \frac{gd}{\sin 2A}$$

where g = acceleration due to gravity
d = horizontal distance covered
A = ramp angle

Determine the minimal velocity and the corresponding ramp angle.

8-27 Many problems require the use of random numbers. There are many random-number generators possible, but most have a common problem in that the numbers generated start repeating or are not uniformly distributed. Thus the randomness may soon be lost. Hence all random-number generators should be checked for repetition and distribution.

One method that yields reasonable results uses a four-digit integer value that is odd and does not end in 5. This starting value is multiplied by a two-digit integer constant. The four rightmost digits of the product are saved to become the next starting value. The leftmost two digits of the four saved digits become the integer random number. For example, the value 155519 is the result of multiplying 17Ø9 and 91. The digits 5519 are saved as the next starting number, and the digits 55 are saved as the first integer random number. Then 5519 is multiplied by 91, and the sequence repeated. Note that integer values can be converted into decimal values, if required.

Write a program to generate 5ØØ two-digit integer random numbers with 17Ø9 as the starting value and 91 as the constant. When all numbers are generated, run a check to see how many are between Ø and 9, 1Ø and 19, 2Ø and 29, etc. If these counts are fairly uniform, the generator is acceptable. Now pick a starting value and constant and try again.

CHAPTER **9**

SUBPROGRAMS

9-1 INTRODUCTION

The principal reason for using the computer in problem solving is to reduce the time required for making repetitive calculations. Planning and writing a computer program is often a laborious and time-consuming task requiring careful attention to every detail of every statement in the program. The more statements in the program, the more opportunity for error. Anything that can be done to eliminate unnecessary statements or avoid writing the same lengthy statement more than once is worth considering.

The common mathematical functions (Chap. 5) which are used frequently in the solution of a wide variety of problems have already been introduced. These intrinsic functions are actually subprograms of a type to be described in this chapter. The convenience and ease of use of these functions disguise the sophisticated programming techniques used but clearly indicate the advantage of subprogram usage.

Many programs contain either single-statement calculations or calculations requiring a program segment of many statements to be repeated in that program and/or in related programs. Such repetitive routines can be removed from the main program and written separately as *subprograms*. These subprograms can then be called individually by a simple statement placed appropriately in the main program whenever needed. The programmer-developed subprogram serves the same purpose for limited applications as the more generally applicable intrinsic functions and can be saved for subsequent use in other programs (App. E-7).

This chapter introduces the preparation and use of three forms of subprograms which can be written to suit the programmer's unique requirements: the *statement-function statement,* the *FUNCTION* subprogram, and the *SUBROUTINE* subprogram.

9-2 THE STATEMENT-FUNCTION STATEMENT

When a single arithmetic expression is used repeatedly in a program, it can be defined in a statement-function statement, commonly referred to as simply a *statement function*. An evaluation of the statement function can be accomplished whenever required by referring to the function name (*calling* the statement function) in an arithmetic expression. The statement function is not a true subprogram since it is located in the main program, but for simple calculations it serves the same purpose. The statement function consists of a single, nonexecutable defining statement placed in the program before the first executable statement.

The general form for the statement function is:

```
name(a,b,j)=arithmetic expression
```

where *name* is the name given to the statement function by the programmer, and *a, b,* and *j* represent dummy arguments (Sec. 9-4) corresponding to the variable names used in the arithmetic expression. The *arithmetic expression* establishes the mathematical relationship existing between the dummy arguments. The rules for composing the statement function's name are the same as those that apply in forming any variable name (Sec. 3-4). The value assigned to the name of the statement function can be either integer or real, the first letter of the statement function's name designating the type.

The dummy arguments, listed in an arbitrary order in parentheses following the statement function's name, identify the variables used in the calculations. These dummy arguments must be used in the arithmetic expression that establishes the mathematical relationship of the variables. When the statement function is subsequently used (called) later in the program, other variable names, the *actual* arguments (not necessarily the dummy-argument names of the defining statement) are listed. The actual arguments listed in the calling statement must agree in number, type, and relative position with the dummy arguments listed in the defining statement. When the calling statement is executed, the values of the variable names listed as actual arguments in the calling statement are assigned, on a one-to-one basis, to the variable names listed as dummy arguments in the defining statement. These values, assigned from the actual-argument values, are then used in evaluating the arithmetic expression in the defining statement. The value of the arithmetic expression is assigned to the statement-function name and returned to the calling statement.

As a simple example, suppose that the relationship of the Pythagorean theorem must be evaluated repeatedly in several different locations in a given program. A statement function with the real-name HYP identifying an arithmetic expression describing the mathematical relationship between the two sides of a right triangle represented by *dummy* arguments A and B and the hypotenuse could be written as:

```
HYP(A,B)=SQRT(A**2+B**2)
```

This statement function is then placed in the program *before* any executable statement. Note that this example employs a system-supplied intrinsic function SQRT in the arithmetic expression defining the statement function HYP.

The statement function can then be called in the executable portion of the program when needed by using it in an arithmetic expression such as:

```
R=HYP(X,Y)
```

The variable names X and Y represent actual arguments with assigned values. When the statement containing HYP is executed, the assigned values of the actual arguments, X and Y, will be assigned to the dummy arguments A and B in the order listed, and the arithmetic expression in the defining statement will be evaluated. This value will be assigned to the statement-function name HYP and returned to the statement calling HYP for further use. In this example, the value of HYP is assigned to the variable name R.

Since a two-dimensional subscripted variable and the statement-function name of this example are identical in appearance, how does the compiler distinguish between a statement-function name and a subscripted variable? When HYP(X,Y) appears in an executable statement, a comparison is made to determine whether HYP has been declared a subscripted variable with two subscripts in a DIMENSION statement. If no such variable exists, a second comparison is made to determine whether HYP is stored as an intrinsic function. Finally, a third comparison is made to determine whether there is either a statement-function statement or a subprogram named HYP. If the name HYP is used in more than one context, i.e., used as both an array name and a function name, execution will abort with an error message. Also, if HYP(X,Y) is used without having been previously specified as a subscripted variable or defined as a statement function or subprogram, execution will abort with an error message.

The flowchart symbol for the statement-function statement is the PREDEFINED PROCESS symbol (Fig. 2-6). It should be placed in the main program, as illustrated in the example in Fig. 9-1.

For another example of the statement function, suppose that the roots of a quadratic equation are required frequently in a program. Statement functions defining the two roots could be written:

```
ROOT1 (A, B, C) = (-B+SQRT (B**2-4.Ø*A*C) ) / (2.Ø*A)
ROOT2 (A, B, C) = (-B-SQRT (B**2-4.Ø*A*C) ) / (2.Ø*A)
```

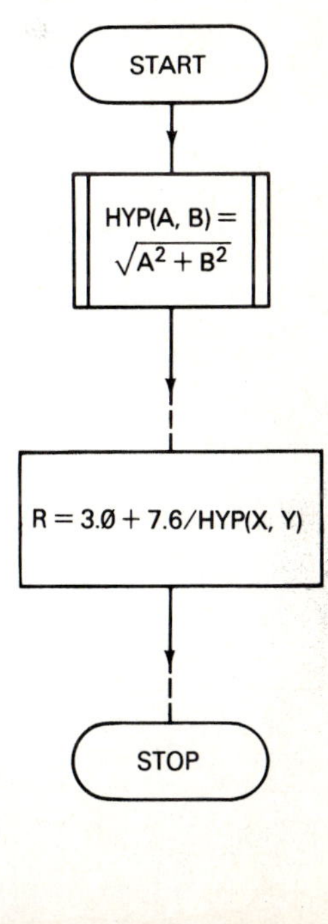

FIGURE 9-1 Flowchart illustrating the statement-function statement.

(It must be assumed that the argument of SQRT will never be negative.) With these statement functions so defined, the following might be used as calling statements:

```
VAL=X*ROOT1(T, (S-R), 1.34)
POWER=ROOT2(U, DELTA(1), DELTA(K))**4.5
```

The value assigned to VAL will be the value of X multiplied by the value of ROOT1. The value of ROOT1 is calculated by substituting the value of T for A, S−R for B, and 1.34 for C in the arithmetic expression of the statement function defining ROOT1. The value assigned to POWER will be the value of ROOT2 raised to the 4.5 power. The value of ROOT2 is calculated by substituting the value of U for A, DELTA(1) for B, and DELTA(K) for C in the statement function defining ROOT2. Of course, all variable names used in the calling statements, including the subscript variable, must have an assigned numerical value before their appearance in the calling statements. The array name DELTA must have been specified as a subscripted variable in a DIMENSION statement at the beginning of the program.

Table 9-1 provides a brief summary description of the statement function.

9-3 SUBPROGRAMS DEFINED

A subprogram is a complete program initiated with a defining statement, followed by whatever FORTRAN statements are needed to perform the calculations for which it is written, and terminated with an END statement. A subprogram usually receives one or more values from, and returns one or more values to, the main

TABLE 9-1 THE STATEMENT-FUNCTION STATEMENT

1. A single statement-function statement within the calling program defines the relationship of a set of variables.
2. The defining statement must appear before the first executable statement in the calling program or subprogram.
3. Example of the defining statement in mathematical form:

$$f(x, y, z) = x^3 + x^2y + xy^2z + y^3z^2 + z^3$$

and in FORTRAN notation:

```
VALUE(X, Y, Z)=X**3+X**2*Y+X*Y**2*Z+Y**3*Z**2+Z**3
```

4. The function is called in an arithmetic statement:

```
ALPHA=VALUE(23.2,15.6,35.2)    or
ALPHA=VALUE(A,B,C) if A, B, C previously defined, or
ALPHA=3.7+2.6/VALUE(1.Ø,2.Ø,3.Ø)
```

5. The variables in the actual argument list must agree in number, type, and relative position with the dummy arguments in the defining statement.

program. Normally these values are interchanged through the actual arguments and dummy arguments used with the calling and defining statements. Another method of transferring values is through the use of the COMMON statement, discussed in Sec. 9-7.

A subprogram follows the END statement of the main program. When more than one subprogram follows a main program, their order of placement is arbitrary. When the main program includes statements that call subprograms, compilation continues until the END statement in the last subprogram indicates that compilation of the subprogram is complete. A subprogram can call another subprogram, but a subprogram cannot call itself; and if subprogram A calls subprogram B, then B cannot call A. A subprogram that has been prepared for one main program can be used with other main programs (or subprograms) where the calculation unique to that subprogram is needed. Subprograms on one diskette can be copied to another diskette to be used with another main program (App. E-7).

There are two forms of *true* subprograms: the *FUNCTION* subprogram and the *SUBROUTINE* subprogram (Secs. 9-5 and 9-6). They are indicated in a flowchart with the PREDEFINED PROCESS symbol.

9-4 ACTUAL VERSUS DUMMY ARGUMENTS

The use of *actual* arguments in the calling statement and *dummy* arguments in the *defining* statement was covered in the explanation of the statement function (Sec. 9-2). Both the FUNCTION and SUBROUTINE subprograms also require the use of actual and dummy arguments.

The arguments listed in the calling statement must be variables to which values have been previously assigned or, as in the case of the SUBROUTINE subprogram, that will be calculated in the subprogram for return to the calling program. They may also be constants. Hence, they are called *actual arguments*. The arguments listed in the defining statement of the subprogram are dummy arguments because they have no value assigned at the point in the program where they first appear (the defining statement).

The following rules apply to the actual and dummy arguments used in calling and defining statements:

1 The actual arguments in the calling statement *must* agree with the dummy arguments in the defining statement in number, order, and type.

2 The actual arguments may be constants, simple-variable names, array names, or arithmetic expressions. A function name (an intrinsic function, a statement function, or a FUNCTION subprogram) is also permissible as an actual argument.

3 Whatever the form of the actual argument, all variable names used to transfer data to the subprogram *must* have a numerical value assigned before the calling statement is executed and *must* be of the same type (integer or real) as the corresponding dummy arguments in the defining statement.

4 The dummy arguments in the defining statement *must* be simple-variable (nonsubscripted) names or array names (written without a subscript), either integer or real, as appropriate.

5 Dummy arguments *cannot* be constants, other function names, or arithmetic expressions.

6 If an array name is used as a dummy argument, a DIMENSION statement must immediately follow the defining statement in the subprogram. The number and maximum value of the subscripts defined for that array must be the same as those specified for the corresponding actual array in the calling program. The subscript of the array in the DIMENSION statement may be an integer-variable name, provided the variable name has been included as a dummy argument in the defining statement and supplied a value from the calling program.

9-5 THE FUNCTION SUBPROGRAM AND THE RETURN STATEMENT

A FUNCTION subprogram is similar in some respects to the statement function. The calling statement is identical in form with that of the statement function, and only a single value is calculated and available to the calling program. However, the FUNCTION subprogram is a true subprogram, compiled after the main program, and consists of several statements instead of a single statement (as many as are needed to evaluate a given condition). The first statement of a FUNCTION subprogram is the nonexecutable defining statement, which specifies the type of subprogram, names it, and lists the variables whose values are to be received from the calling program.

The general form for the defining statement of a FUNCTION subprogram is:

```
FUNCTION name (a, b, j)
```

The FORTRAN term FUNCTION defines the type of subprogram; *name* is the name given to the function by the programmer; and *a, b,* and *j* represent a list of dummy arguments. The rules for composing the function name are the same as those which apply in forming any variable name (Sec. 3-4). The value assigned to the name of the FUNCTION subprogram can be either integer or real, the first letter of the function name designating the type. The rules outlined in Sec. 9-4 regarding actual and dummy arguments must be observed. The statements that constitute the subprogram follow the defining statement. One statement in the subprogram must assign a value to the function name, i.e., the function name must appear at least once on the left side of the assignment symbol, since the value assigned to *name* is the value returned to the main program. In other words, a statement of the form:

```
name=arithmetic expression
```

must appear at least once in the FUNCTION subprogram.

When the required calculations are completed and a value has been assigned to *name,* an executable RETURN statement is used to return control to the calling statement in the calling program. The RETURN statement consists of the single FORTRAN term RETURN. The last statement in a FUNCTION subprogram is an END statement. A FUNCTION subprogram is usually terminated by the statements:

```
RETURN
END
```

The FUNCTION subprogram is called in the same manner as the statement function by using the *name* of the FUNCTION subprogram—*name*—with the actual arguments in an arithmetic expression in the calling program when the value of *name* is needed.

The Pythagorean theorem example of Sec. 9-2 written as a FUNCTION subprogram might look like this:

```
OPEN(3,FILE='PYTH.DAT')
OPEN(6,FILE='PRN')
READ(3,*)X,Y
R=HYP(X,Y)
WRITE(6,*)X,Y,R
STOP
END
FUNCTION HYP(A,B)
HYP=SQRT(A**2+B**2)
RETURN
END
```

Values assigned to X and Y by the READ statement in the main program are read from a record in a data file named PYTH.DAT. The next statement, R=HYP(X,Y), includes the calling term for the FUNCTION subprogram HYP. Execution of this statement in the main program is interrupted when the function name HYP is encountered, and control is transferred to the defining statement of the FUNCTION subprogram. Values assigned to the actual arguments X and Y in the calling program are substituted in the order listed for the dummy arguments A and B in the defining statement of the FUNCTION subprogram. The necessary calculations are then performed in one or more executable statements, and a single value is assigned to the function name HYP. Execution of the RETURN statement returns control to the statement containing HYP in the calling program, where the value assigned to HYP in the subprogram is substituted for the function name HYP in the arithmetic expression, and execution of the calling statement is completed by assigning the value of HYP to the variable R. Execution of statements in the calling program then continues in order. The subprogram can be called as often as needed. Note the placement of the subprogram, immediately following the END statement of the main program.

The flowchart for this example appears as illustrated in Fig. 9-2 (see p. 266). Note the independence of the main program and the subprogram, as well as the use of the TERMINAL, INTERRUPT symbol for the RETURN statement.

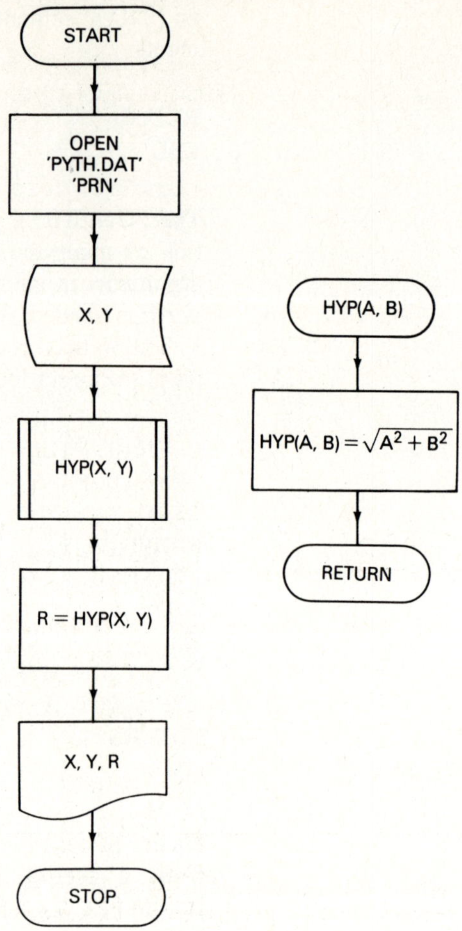

FIGURE 9-2 Flowchart for a FUNCTION subprogram.

The only values supplied to the subprogram are the values assigned to the actual arguments listed in the statement calling the FUNCTION subprogram. These values are then assigned, on a one-to-one basis, to the dummy arguments listed in the defining statement of the FUNCTION subprogram. The value returned to the main program from the FUNCTION subprogram is the value assigned to the function name HYP by an assignment statement in the subprogram. This value is then available in the calling program through the statement calling HYP.

The programmer must remember that the values of the real and dummy arguments are passed to and from the calling program and the subprogram. If new values are assigned to the dummy arguments in the subprogram, the new values of the dummy arguments will return to the calling program as new values for the actual arguments. This is illustrated in Fig. 9-3, where actual arguments X and Y are assigned the values 3.Ø and 4.Ø. After HYP is determined in the FUNCTION

```
234567890
      OPEN(7,FILE='PRN')
      X=3.0
      Y=4.0
      R=HYP(X,Y)
      WRITE(7,100)X,Y,R
  100 FORMAT(1X,3F10.1)
      STOP
      END
      FUNCTION HYP(A,B)
      HYP=SQRT(A**2+B**2)
      A=10.0
      B=20.0
      RETURN
      END
```

```
      10.0      20.0       5.0
```

FIGURE 9-3 Interchange of arguments between main programs and subprograms.

subprogram, the dummy arguments are assigned the values 1Ø.Ø and 2Ø.Ø. When the WRITE statement in the main program is executed, the value of R is printed as 5.Ø, which is correct, but the values of the actual arguments are printed as 1Ø.Ø and 2Ø.Ø, the new values assigned to the dummy arguments in the subprogram and returned to the calling program.

Another example of a FUNCTION subprogram is provided in Fig. 9-4. In this illustration, more than one RETURN statement is needed in the subprogram. The value of VAL depends on the value assigned to another variable, DISP. When DISP is negative, VAL is equal to DISP squared; when DISP is zero, VAL is equal to zero; and when DISP is positive, VAL is equal to the square root of DISP. At any point in the FUNCTION subprogram after a value has been assigned to the function name (VAL in this example), control can be returned to the calling statement in the main program by a RETURN statement in the subprogram. For these three conditions, with three possible values for the function name VAL, three RETURN statements are required.

Table 9-2 (see p. 268) provides a brief summary of the FUNCTION subprogram.

```
------------------
------------------
Y = 3.Ø*VAL(DISP)*S
------------------
------------------
------------------
```

Main program

(*a*)

```
      FUNCTION VAL (A)
      IF (A) 1Ø, 2Ø, 3Ø
   1Ø VAL = A**2
      RETURN
   2Ø VAL = Ø
      RETURN
   3Ø VAL = SQRT (A)
      RETURN
      END
```

Subprogram

(*b*)

FIGURE 9-4 (*a*) Main program and (*b*) FUNCTION subprogram.

TABLE 9-2 THE FUNCTION SUBPROGRAM

1. A program compiled after the calling program and referred to by a single name.
2. Only one new value (the FUNCTION's *name*) is returned to the calling program.
3. FUNCTION subprograms are placed separately, following the END statement of the calling program.
4. A FUNCTION subprogram is called by referring to it by name in a single arithmetic statement in the calling program, for example:

   AREA=ALPHA(X, Y) *or* AREA=3.6+7.2*ALPHA(X, Y)

5. The defining statement is the first statement of the FUNCTION subprogram, for example:

   FUNCTION ALPHA(A, B)

6. The dummy arguments in the defining statement must agree with the actual arguments in the calling statement in number, order, and type.
7. A value must be assigned to the FUNCTION name by a statement in the FUNCTION subprogram, for example:

   ALPHA=*arithmetic expression*

8. The first letter of the FUNCTION subprogram name commits the FUNCTION's name to type real or type integer.
9. The FUNCTION subprogram is terminated and control returned to the calling statement with:

   RETURN
   END

9-6 THE SUBROUTINE SUBPROGRAM: THE CALL AND RETURN STATEMENTS

A SUBROUTINE subprogram is similar to a FUNCTION subprogram; it is compiled after the main program, begins with a defining statement, and terminates with an END statement. There are, however, four basic characteristics, significantly different from the FUNCTION subprogram, that make the SUBROUTINE subprogram a more versatile subprogram.

1 A SUBROUTINE subprogram can receive the value of any number of variables from the calling program and return the value of *any number* of variables to the calling program, provided that these variables are included as actual arguments in the calling statement in the calling program and listed as corresponding dummy arguments in the defining statement of the SUBROUTINE subprogram.

2 The name of the SUBROUTINE subprogram has no assigned value; therefore, no type (integer or real) is associated with the first letter of the name. The name given to the SUBROUTINE subprogram may be composed of any combination of not more than six letters or digits, provided that the first character of the name is a letter.

3 Since the name of a SUBROUTINE subprogram has no value assigned, it cannot be called simply by using the name in an arithmetic expression in the calling program. A *CALL* statement is required in the calling program to transfer control to the defining statement of the SUBROUTINE subprogram.

4 When control is returned to the calling program, it returns to the *first* executable statement *following* the CALL statement.

The general form for the executable CALL statement is:

```
CALL name (x, y, n)
```

where *name* is the name of the SUBROUTINE subprogram given by the programmer and *x, y,* and *n* represent the list of *actual* arguments whose values are supplied to or received from the corresponding dummy arguments in the defining statement of the subprogram.

The first statement of the SUBROUTINE subprogram is a nonexecutable defining statement. The general form for the defining statement of the SUBROUTINE subprogram is:

```
SUBROUTINE name (a, b, j)
```

where SUBROUTINE is a FORTRAN term defining the type of subprogram; *name* is the name given to the subprogram by the programmer; and *a, b,* and *j* represent the list of *dummy* arguments whose values are received from or returned to the corresponding actual arguments in the CALL statement in the calling program. The rules listed in Sec. 9-4 must be observed for the actual and dummy arguments. The statements required for the calculations of the subprogram then follow the defining statement. The SUBROUTINE subprogram is usually terminated by the statements:

```
RETURN
END
```

Execution of the RETURN statement returns control to the first executable statement following the CALL statement in the calling program.

A variable name used in the calling program and not included in either argument list can also be used independently in the subprogram. The value assigned to that variable name in the subprogram *will not* be returned to the calling program. Only values assigned to the dummy arguments are returned through the corresponding actual arguments in the CALL statement to the calling program. However, if a dummy argument is assigned a new value in the subprogram different from the value assigned to it by the corresponding actual argument, that new value *will* be returned to the CALL statement as the new (changed) value of the actual argument, as discussed in Sec. 9-5. This can lead to unexpected errors. *It must be remembered that the only values exchanged between the calling program and the subprogram are the values assigned to the corresponding actual and dummy arguments in the CALL and defining statements, respectively.*

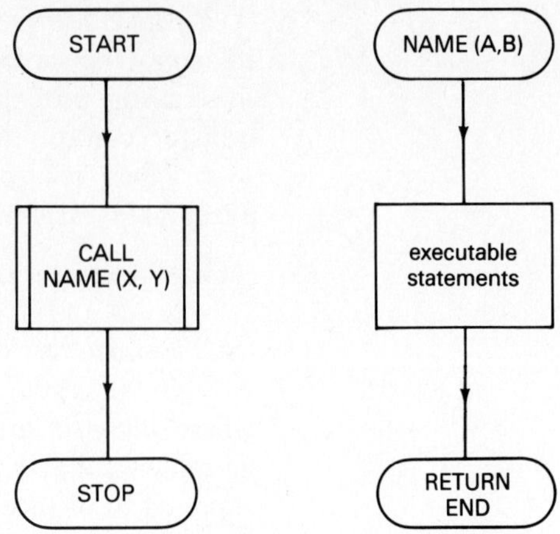

FIGURE 9-5 Flowchart for a SUBROUTINE subprogram.

The flowchart for a SUBROUTINE subprogram is similar to that for a FUNCTION subprogram as illustrated in Fig. 9-5. Table 9-3 provides a brief summary of the SUBROUTINE subprogram.

9-7 THE COMMON STATEMENT

The calling and defining statements of both the FUNCTION and SUBROUTINE subprograms as described in Secs. 9-5 and 9-6 required a list of actual and dummy arguments, respectively. Instead of using argument lists, it may be advantageous to use a COMMON statement that can be employed to replace the lists of arguments and also may be used to replace any required DIMENSION statements in both the calling program and the subprogram. The COMMON statement is a nonexecutable definition statement that must appear in *both* the calling program and the subprogram *before* the first executable statement of each. The COMMON statement lists the names of the variables used as arguments and specifies the subscript(s) for the variables (arguments) that are array names. The COMMON statement provides a common storage location available to both the calling program and subprogram for both the actual and dummy variables (arguments). The general form for the COMMON statement is:

COMMON *x*, *y*, *z* (*m*, *n*)

listing *x*, *y*, and the two-dimensional $m \times n$ element array name *z* as variables. If this COMMON statement is used in the calling program, the variables are the actual variables (arguments). Then the COMMON statement in the subprogram could be:

COMMON *a*, *b*, *c* (*j*, *k*)

listing *a*, *b*, and the two-dimensional $j \times k$ element array name *c* as dummy vari-

TABLE 9-3 THE SUBROUTINE SUBPROGRAM

1. A program compiled after the calling program and referred to by a single name.
2. More than one value can be returned to the calling program, provided those values are listed as arguments.
3. SUBROUTINE subprograms are placed separately, following the END statement of the calling program.
4. SUBROUTINE subprograms are called by a CALL statement in the calling program, for example:

```
CALL ALPHA(X, Y, Z)
```

5. The defining statement is the first statement of a SUBROUTINE program, for example:

```
SUBROUTINE ALPHA(A, B, C)
```

6. The dummy arguments in the defining statement must agree with the actual arguments in the calling statement in number, order, and type.
7. The first letter of the name of the SUBROUTINE subprogram does not determine the type.
8. The SUBROUTINE subprogram is terminated and control returned to the first executable statement following the CALL statement in the calling program with:

```
RETURN
END
```

ables (arguments). Common storage is accomplished in the order listed. The variable names *x* and *a,* and *y* and *b,* and the elements of the arrays *z* and *c* share, respectively, the same storage locations. The values assigned are available in either the calling program or the subprogram when referred to by either the actual-variable (argument) name or the dummy-variable (argument) name. Note that when array values are available in both the calling program and subprogram, the array size may be specified in the COMMON statement, eliminating the need for a DIMENSION statement in both the calling program and subprogram. Declaring a given array in both a COMMON and a DIMENSION statement results in an error, but declaring the size of an array in a DIMENSION statement followed by a COMMON statement including the array name only is acceptable. For example:

```
DIMENSION A(5,3)
COMMON A
```

is allowed. There is no flowchart symbol for the COMMON statement.

In a SUBROUTINE subprogram, the COMMON statement is placed *before* the first executable statement in the calling program and *immediately following* the defining statement of the subprogram. Both the CALL statement in the calling program and the defining statement of the subprogram are written without a list of arguments, the variable names of the argument list being part of the COMMON statement. For example:

```
COMMON D,E,M,N(1Ø)
---------
---------
CALL NAME
---------
---------
STOP
END
SUBROUTINE NAME
COMMON R,S,K,L(1Ø)
---------
---------
RETURN
END
```

When the COMMON statement is used, fewer storage locations are required, and, since storage locations specified in the COMMON statement are assigned during compilation, execution time is reduced. In a long, complex program with several subprograms and many simple-variable names and array names, use of the COMMON statement can effect a significant saving in storage and in execution time.

The COMMON statement can also be used with a FUNCTION subprogram *provided* at least *one actual* argument and its corresponding *dummy* argument are included in the argument list. Otherwise, the compiler will not recognize the set of statements as a FUNCTION subprogram, and an error will result. However, all other variables to be transferred from the main program to the FUNCTION subprogram, and vice versa, can be listed in a COMMON statement. For example:

```
COMMON X,Y,Z(3,5)
---------
---------
L=NAME(N)
---------
---------
STOP
END
FUNCTION NAME(K)
COMMON A,B,C(3,5)
---------
NAME=arithmetic expression
RETURN
END
```

9-8 ILLUSTRATIVE EXAMPLES OF SUBPROGRAMS

Example 9-1: The Statement Function

Consider the program of computing the volume V of a truncated right circular cone (a pail) using the relationship:

$$V = \frac{\pi H}{3} (R_1^2 + R_1 R_2 + R_2^2)$$

where H = height
R_1, R_2 = radii of the two bases

Figure 9-6 illustrates a statement function named VTRCN using this equation to compute the volume (VOL) from the values for R_1, R_2, and H read from data records in a data file named FIG9-6.DAT. The statement function is defined on the third line of the program and called by use of an arithmetic expression as indicated by the appropriate comment statement.

Example 9-2: The FUNCTION Subprogram

$$V = \frac{H}{3} (A_1 + A_2 + \sqrt{A_1 \; A_2})$$

where H = height
A_1, A_2 = areas of the two bases

FIGURE 9-6 Truncated-cone problem with statement-function statement.

```
C   STATEMENT-FUNCTION STATEMENT
C23456789
      VTRCN(R1,R2,H)=3.141593*H/3.0*(R1**2+R1*R2+R2**2)
C
      OPEN(3,FILE='FIG9-6.DAT')
      OPEN(6,FILE='PRN')
      WRITE(6,100)
  100 FORMAT(18X,'R1',8X,'R2',9X,'H',7X,'VOL',/)
   10 READ(3,200,END=20)R1,R2,H
  200 FORMAT(3F6.2)
C
C   THIS STATEMENT CALLS THE STATEMENT-FUNCTION STATEMENT
      VOL=VTRCN(R1,R2,H)
      WRITE(6,300)R1,R2,H,VOL
  300 FORMAT(F21.2,3F10.2)
      GO TO 10
   20 STOP
      END
```

```
 1.00  2.00  1.00
 1.50  2.00  1.25
 2.00  2.50  1.50
 2.50  3.00  1.75
 3.00  3.50  2.00
```

```
                  R1        R2         H       VOL

                1.00      2.00      1.00      7.33
                1.50      2.00      1.25     12.11
                2.00      2.50      1.50     23.95
                2.50      3.00      1.75     41.69
                3.00      3.50      2.00     66.50
```

Figure 9-7 uses a FUNCTION subprogram called VTRCN and the above equation to compute the volume (VOL). Note the subprogram location following the END statement of the main program, the assignment of a value to VTRCN, and the RETURN and END statements in the subprogram. Values for R1, R2, and H used in the subprogram were assigned by the READ statement in the main program. The subprogram was called by referring to it in an arithmetic expression in the main program. The RETURN statement returned control to the main program and assigned one value, the value of VTRCN, to the variable VOL.

FIGURE 9-7 Truncated-cone problem with FUNCTION subprogram.

```
C  FUNCTION SUBPROGRAM
C234567890
      OPEN(2,FILE='FIG9-7.DAT')
      OPEN(7,FILE='PRN')
      WRITE(7,100)
  100 FORMAT(18X,'R1',8X,'R2',9X,'H',7X,'VOL',/)
   10 READ(2,200,END=20)R1,R2,H
  200 FORMAT(3F6.2)
C
C  THIS STATEMENT CALLS THE FUNCTION SUBPROGRAM
      VOL=VTRCN(R1,R2,H)
C
      WRITE(7,300)R1,R2,H,VOL
  300 FORMAT(F21.2,3F10.2)
      GO TO 10
   20 STOP
      END
      FUNCTION VTRCN(R1,R2,H)
C  THE ABOVE STATEMENT DEFINES THE FUNCTION SUBPROGRAM
C
      A1=3.141593*R1**2
      A2=3.141593*R2**2
      VTRCN=H/3.0*(A1+A2+SQRT(A1*A2))
      RETURN
      END
```

```
1.00  2.00  1.00
1.50  2.00  1.25
2.00  2.50  1.50
2.50  3.00  1.75
3.00  3.50  2.00
```

```
                  R1        R2         H       VOL

                1.00      2.00      1.00      7.33
                1.50      2.00      1.25     12.11
                2.00      2.50      1.50     23.95
                2.50      3.00      1.75     41.69
                3.00      3.50      2.00     66.50
```

Example 9-3: The SUBROUTINE Subprogram

A SUBROUTINE subprogram named VTRCN using the equation of Example 9-2 to compute the volume is illustrated in Fig. 9-8. Note the similarities and differences in the SUBROUTINE and FUNCTION subprograms. Both are located following the END statement of the main program; both terminate with RETURN and END statements. But the FUNCTION subprogram returns only one value (the name of the FUNCTION subprogram) to the main program, while the SUBROUTINE subprogram returns more than one value (provided the associated variables are listed as arguments or in a COMMON statement) to the main program. The calling statement of the SUBROUTINE subprogram is indicated by the comment statement in the main program; the defining statement of the SUBROUTINE subprogram follows the END statement of the main program. Note the list of arguments given in both

FIGURE 9-8 Truncated-cone problem with SUBROUTINE subprogram.

```
C   SUBROUTINE SUBPROGRAM
C234567890
      OPEN(2,FILE='FIG9-8.DAT')
      OPEN(7,FILE='PRN')
      WRITE(7,100)
  100 FORMAT(18X,'R1',8X,'R2',9X,'H',8X,'A1',8X,'A2',7X,'VOL',/)
   10 READ(2,200,END=20)R1,R2,H
  200 FORMAT(3F6.2)
C
C   THE STATEMENT BELOW CALLS THE SUBROUTINE SUBPROGRAM
      CALL VTRCN(R1,R2,H,A1,A2,VOL)
      WRITE(7,300)R1,R2,H,A1,A2,VOL
  300 FORMAT(F21.2,5F10.2)
      GO TO 10
   20 STOP
      END
      SUBROUTINE VTRCN(R1,R2,H,A1,A2,VOL)
C   THE ABOVE STATEMENT DEFINES THE SUBROUTINE SUBPROGRAM
C
      A1=3.141593*R1**2
      A2=3.141593*R2**2
      VOL=H/3.0*(A1+A2+SQRT(A1*A2))
      RETURN
      END
```

```
1.00  2.00  1.00
1.50  2.00  1.25
2.00  2.50  1.50
2.50  3.00  1.75
3.00  3.50  2.00
```

R1	R2	H	A1	A2	VOL
1.00	2.00	1.00	3.14	12.57	7.33
1.50	2.00	1.25	7.07	12.57	12.11
2.00	2.50	1.50	12.57	19.63	23.95
2.50	3.00	1.75	19.63	28.27	41.69
3.00	3.50	2.00	28.27	38.48	66.50

the calling and defining statements. The list contains both the variables whose values are read and assigned in the main program (R1, R2, H) and the variables whose values are computed and assigned in the subprogram (A1, A2, VOL). When execution of the subprogram is completed, the RETURN statement transfers control to the first executable statement following the CALL statement.

For comparison, the same SUBROUTINE subprogram is shown in Fig. 9-9, this time using the COMMON statement to replace the lists of arguments in the calling and defining statements. Note the use of the COMMON statement in the main program and in the SUBROUTINE subprogram. Whether to list the arguments or to use COMMON statements is a decision the programmer must make.

It is conceded that writing a subprogram for the simple calculations in Examples 9-1 to 9-3 hardly saves time and effort for either the programmer

FIGURE 9-9 Truncated-cone problem with SUBROUTINE subprogram and a COMMON statement.

```
C   SUBROUTINE SUBPROGRAM USING THE COMMON STATEMENT
C234567890
      COMMON R1,R2,H,A1,A2,VOL
      OPEN(2,FILE='FIG9-8.DAT')
      OPEN(7,FILE='PRN')
      WRITE(7,100)
  100 FORMAT(18X,'R1',8X,'R2',9X,'H',8X,'A1',8X,'A2',7X,'VOL',/)
   10 READ(2,200,END=20)R1,R2,H
  200 FORMAT(3F6.2)
      CALL VTRCN
      WRITE(7,300)R1,R2,H,A1,A2,VOL
  300 FORMAT(F21.2,5F10.2)
      GO TO 10
   20 STOP
      END
      SUBROUTINE VTRCN
      COMMON R1,R2,H,A1,A2,VOL
      A1=3.141593*R1**2
      A2=3.141593*R2**2
      VOL=H/3.0*(A1+A2+SQRT(A1*A2))
      RETURN
      END
```

```
  1.00  2.00  1.00
  1.50  2.00  1.25
  2.00  2.50  1.50
  2.50  3.00  1.75
  3.00  3.50  2.00
```

R1	R2	H	A1	A2	VOL
1.00	2.00	1.00	3.14	12.57	7.33
1.50	2.00	1.25	7.07	12.57	12.11
2.00	2.50	1.50	12.57	19.63	23.95
2.50	3.00	1.75	19.63	28.27	41.69
3.00	3.50	2.00	28.27	38.48	66.50

or the computer, but these examples demonstrate how subprograms are used and include the basic elements of each of the three forms.

Example 9-4: The Grade-Sorting Program Revised

The grade-sorting problem in Example 8-2 is revised here to include a SUBROUTINE subprogram. The largest segment of the original program is devoted to sorting and rearranging data, and, since a data-sorting routine may be applicable to a variety of situations, a subprogram performs the sorting task in this program. The logic expressed in the left portion of the flowchart shown in Fig. 8-13 can be used with slight modifications for the SUBROUTINE subprogram. The name of the subprogram is SORT. J, K, and L are dummy arguments, where J is an array name representing the array of original (unsorted) data, K is an array name representing the data arranged (sorted) in descending numerical order, and L represents the number of data items to be sorted and serves as the integer-variable subscript for both integer array J and integer array K. The value assigned to L establishes the maximum number of data items. This is a sort routine for integer numbers; a similar sort routine can be written for real numbers by changing the integer array names J and K to real.

The revised program can read any number of data (grades) between 1 and 1ØØ inclusive. When the last data have been read (if the data count is less than or equal to 1ØØ), a transfer out of the READ loop occurs and the main program continues to completion. When the number of repetitions of the READ loop exceeds 1ØØ, the loop is terminated, a message is printed indicating that the capacity of the array has been exceeded, and the main program continues to completion. Observe that the value of the counter J is decremented by 1 before the calculations are started. The value of the counter J, which is also the value of the subscript of IGRADE, must vary from 1 through 1ØØ, inclusive, in increments of 1. If fewer than 1ØØ data are provided, the END=3Ø option in the READ statement will transfer control out of the READ loop (to statement 3Ø) when an attempt is made to read another data record. Since the attempt to read an invalid data record will be counted, the value assigned to J at the time of transfer out of the READ loop will be greater by 1 than the number of data records from which data have been read and assigned to the elements of the array IGRADE. Subsequent incrementations of the subscript from 1 to J specify an array element of IGRADE to which no value has been assigned. Therefore, the last value of J must be reduced by 1 (3Ø J=J−1), before any further calculations can be made. If more than 1ØØ values are provided, execution of the IF statement will transfer control out of the READ loop when J is greater than 1ØØ, i.e., 1Ø1. After the one-hundredth value has been read and a value assigned to IGRADE(1ØØ), J is incremented to 1Ø1. Transfer is made to the WRITE statement, which prints the message: READING HALTED; 1ØØ GRADES READ. The next statement in sequence, 3Ø J=J−1, reduces J by 1, back to 1ØØ, the largest permissible subscript of IGRADE.

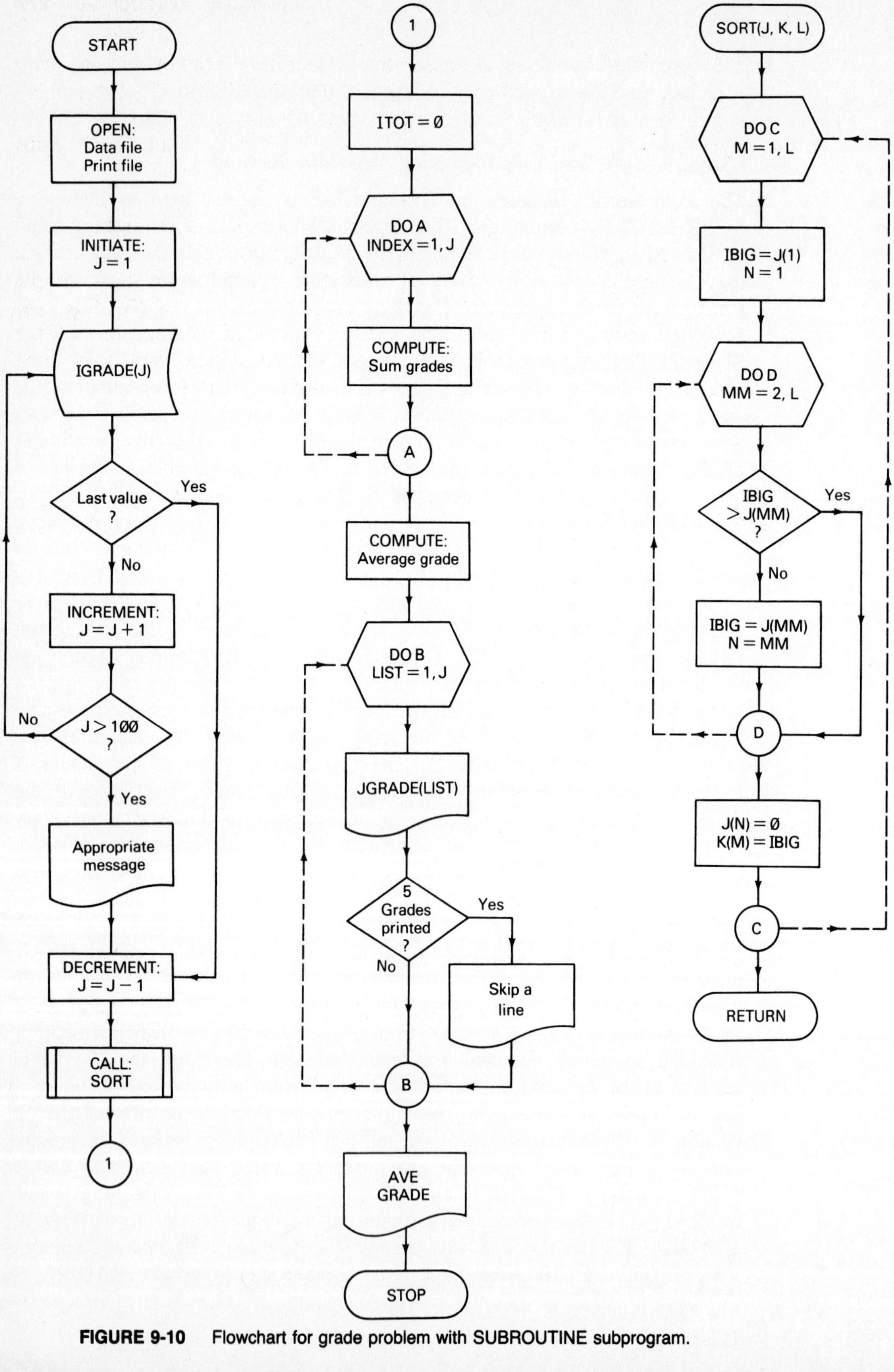

FIGURE 9-10 Flowchart for grade problem with SUBROUTINE subprogram.

Figure 9-10 shows the flowchart outlining the logic of this program solution. Note the symbol used for the box labeled CALL SORT. This symbol represents the subprogram called at this point in the flowchart. The subprogram name appears again in the TERMINAL, INTERRUPT symbol which begins the subprogram. RETURN is used in the TERMINAL, INTERRUPT symbol which terminates the subprogram.

Figure 9-11 is the program listing; Fig. 9-12 (see p. 280) is the printed output. Since the same data are used in this program as in Example 8-2, the results (Figs. 8-15 and 9-12) are identical except for the listing of the initial data shown in Fig. 8-15. Note that the array names IGRADE and JGRADE, listed as actual arguments in the CALL statement, and the corresponding array names J and K, listed as dummy arguments in the defining statement of SUBROUTINE SORT, are listed *without* subscripts.

FIGURE 9-11 Program for grade averaging and ordering problem with SUBROUTINE subprogram.

```
C234567890
      DIMENSION IGRADE(100),JGRADE(100)
      OPEN(3,FILE='FIG9-11.DAT')
      OPEN(6,FILE='PRN')
      J=1
   10 READ(3,100,END=30)IGRADE(J)
  100 FORMAT(I3)
      J=J+1
      IF(J.GT.100)GO TO 20
      GO TO 10
   20 WRITE(6,200)
  200 FORMAT(1X,'READING HALTED; 100 GRADES READ.')
   30 J=J-1
      CALL SORT(IGRADE,JGRADE,J)
      ITOT=0
      DO 40 INDEX=1,J
   40 ITOT=ITOT+JGRADE(INDEX)
      AVE=FLOAT(ITOT)/FLOAT(J)
      WRITE(6,300)
  300 FORMAT(4X,'ORDER OF GRADES',/)
      DO 50 LIST=1,J
      WRITE(6,400)JGRADE(LIST)
  400 FORMAT(10X,I3)
      IF(LIST/5*5-LIST.EQ.0)WRITE(6,500)
  500 FORMAT(' ')
   50 CONTINUE
      WRITE(6,600)AVE
  600 FORMAT(1X,'THE AVERAGE GRADE =',F6.2)
      STOP
      END
      SUBROUTINE SORT(J,K,L)
      DIMENSION J(L),K(L)
      DO 20 M=1,L
      IBIG=J(1)
      N=1
      DO 10 MM=2,L
      IF(IBIG.GT.J(MM))GO TO 10
      IBIG=J(MM)
      N=MM
   10 CONTINUE
      J(N)=0
   20 K(M)=IBIG
      RETURN
      END
```

```
ORDER OF GRADES

  100
  100
   99
   98
   93

   91
   90
   89
   88
   87

   86
   85
   85
   79
   78

   76
   75
   74
   73
   72

   72
   70
   65
   63
   54

THE AVERAGE GRADE =  81.68
```

FIGURE 9-12 Printout of grade problem.

Note the DIMENSION statement in the SUBROUTINE. The variable L specifies the maximum value for the subscripts of arrays J and K. The rules governing a DIMENSION statement (Sec. 8-3) declare that the maximum value for a subscript must be specified by an integer constant. This rule is true and inviolable when the DIMENSION statement is in the main program, where it precedes any executable statement. However, when the DIMENSION statement is in a subprogram, a subscript may be specified by an integer variable whose value has been assigned to an actual argument (J) in the main program and supplied to a corresponding dummy argument (L) listed in the defining statement in the subprogram. Note also that the simple variable J in the main program is different from, and bears no relationship to, the integer array name J in the subprogram. The value assigned to J in the main program is the value supplied for L, the subscript of J (and K) in the subprogram. The values assigned to the actual arguments in the CALL statement are substituted for the dummy arguments in the defining statement for the subprogram in the order of listing: IGRADE for J, JGRADE for K, and J for L.

Example 9-5: Playing the Probability Game with Random Numbers

In this example the computer will be used to simulate the economic aspects of an oil-well-drilling operation and to try to determine the probability of making a \$2 million net profit with a number of different (and increasing) initial investments. A FUNCTION subprogram will be used to supply the random numbers needed for playing the probability game. Begin with the following assumptions. It costs $1ØØ,ØØØ to drill one oil well. If the well produces oil, a net profit of $1 million will be realized. If the well does not produce oil, the total initial investment is lost. Only one well out of three can be expected to produce oil. A FUNCTION subprogram that generates random real numbers greater than zero and less than 1.Ø will be used to simulate the one out of three probability of striking oil. For each well assumed drilled, a random value can be called. If that value is Ø.3333333 or less, we have struck oil. A (random) value greater than Ø.3333333 indicates a dry hole.

With all the assumptions stated, the probability game can begin. Starting with an initial investment of $1ØØ,ØØØ, the first assumed well is drilled. If the first well is a dry hole, the total initial investment, and the game, are lost. If we strike oil with this first well, a net profit of $1 million is made, and another assumed well can be drilled. If the second well also produces oil, another net profit of $1 million is made, and the game is won; we have realized the $2 million net profit, the object of the game. If the second well produces no oil, we take a loss of $1ØØ,ØØØ; but, since there is still some capital left from the profit on the first well, another well can be drilled. This process is repeated until the game is either won ($2 million or more net profit is made) or lost (initial investment of $1ØØ,ØØØ is gone). If the game is repeated, say, 5ØØ times for each initial investment, and the number of wins and losses counted, the probability of winning can be computed. The initial investment is then incremented by $1ØØ,ØØØ and the cycle repeated. This is continued through an initial investment of $1 million.

Figure 9-13 (see p. 282) shows the flowchart outlining the logic of this problem. The random number is supplied by a FUNCTION subprogram. Note that the initial value of the constant supplied to the FUNCTION subprogram is assigned in the main program. There are a number of variations of algorithms used to compute random numbers, and most computing centers can provide such programs.

Figure 9-14 (see p. 283) shows the program listing, and the results are shown in Fig. 9-15 (see p. 284), with initial investments ranging from $1ØØ,ØØØ through $1,ØØØ,ØØØ, inclusive, in increments of $1ØØ,ØØØ. Note that all money values are in units of $1 million (1.Ø=1,ØØØ,ØØØ). The solution to this problem clearly demonstrates that "it takes money to make money." It is also far easier and much cheaper to play the probability game by computer simulation than it is to invest real money and drill real oil wells (but no thrill).

The FUNCTION subprogram used here to generate random real numbers can be changed to generate random integer numbers from Ø through 9 by changing the name from RAND to IRAND and changing the arithmetic assignment statement that assigns the function name its value to:

```
IRAND=FLOAT(J)/4Ø96.Ø*1Ø.Ø
```

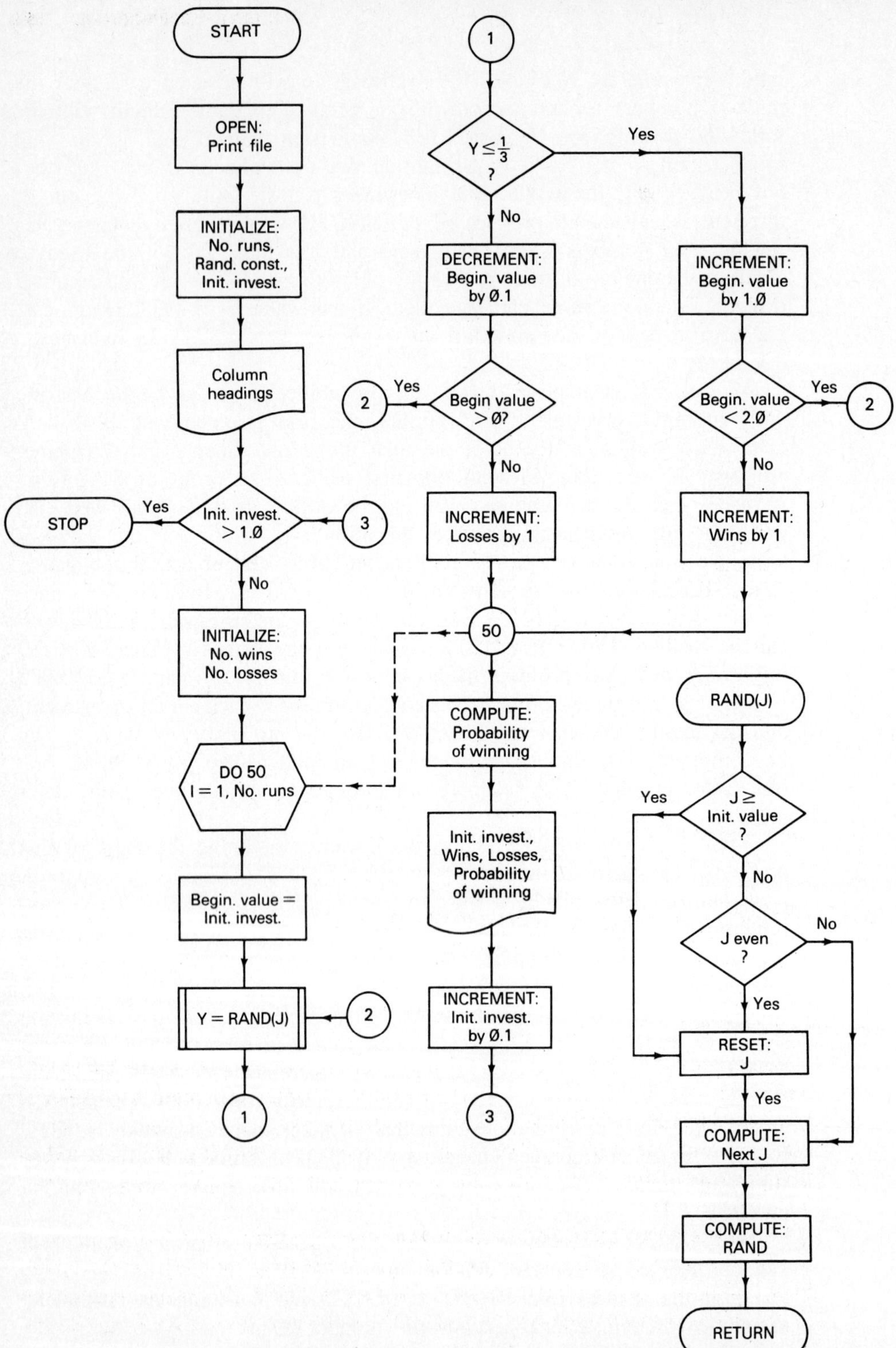

FIGURE 9-13 Flowchart of probability problem with FUNCTION subprogram.

```
C234567890
      OPEN(6,FILE='PRN')
      N=500
      J=4096
      V=0.1000000
      WRITE(6,100)N
  100 FORMAT(25X,'NO. SIMULATED RUNS =',I4,/)
      WRITE(6,200)
  200 FORMAT(17X,'INITIAL     NUMBER     NUMBER       PROBABILITY')
      WRITE(6,300)
  300 FORMAT(15X,'INVESTMENT     WINS      LOSSES      OF WINNING')
      WRITE(6,400)
  400 FORMAT(15X,'(MILLIONS)')
   10 IF(V.GT.1.000005)STOP
      IWIN=0
      LOSE=0
      DO 40 I=1,N
      BV=V
   20 Y=RAND(J)
      IF(Y.LE.0.3333333)GO TO 30
      BV=BV-0.1000000
      IF(BV.GT.0.0000000)GO TO 20
      LOSE=LOSE+1
      GO TO 40
   30 BV=BV+1.0000000
      IF(BV.LT.2.0000000)GO TO 20
      IWIN=IWIN+1
   40 CONTINUE
      PRWIN=FLOAT(IWIN)/FLOAT(N)
      WRITE(6,500)V,IWIN,LOSE,PRWIN
  500 FORMAT(18X,F3.1,I12,I10,F13.4)
      WRITE(6,600)
  600 FORMAT(' ')
      V=V+0.1000000
      GO TO 10
      END
      FUNCTION RAND(J)
      IF(J.GE.4096)GO TO 10
      IF(J/2*2.NE.J)GO TO 20
   10 J=1535
   20 J=1003*J-1003*J/4096*4096
      RAND=FLOAT(J)/4096.0
      RETURN
      END
```

FIGURE 9-14 Program for probability problem with FUNCTION subprogram.

9-9 STRUCTURED PROGRAMMING

Now that the elementary aspects of programming with subprograms have been described, the procedure for the development of larger and more sophisticated programs should be introduced. This procedure is normally referred to as *structured programming*. It is applicable at all levels of programming, but its introduction has been delayed until this point because it is most useful when employed with subprograms.

Throughout the preceding chapters, an orderly, logical organization of steps has been emphasized to ensure that the logic of the program could be easily followed and that detailed, but necessary, steps are included. Comments were sometimes included to separate one segment of the program from another and to describe what is to be done in each segment of the program. As programs become larger, with more statements of a more complex nature, the compilation of pro-

NO. SIMULATED RUNS = 500

INITIAL INVESTMENT (MILLIONS)	NUMBER WINS	NUMBER LOSSES	PROBABILITY OF WINNING
.1	156	344	.3120
.2	275	225	.5500
.3	420	80	.8400
.4	436	64	.8720
.5	460	40	.9200
.6	461	39	.9220
.7	481	19	.9620
.8	488	12	.9760
.9	497	3	.9940
1.0	494	6	.9880

FIGURE 9-15 Printout of probability problem.

grams undoubtedly becomes more troublesome. More than likely, numerous error messages referring to statements throughout the program make debugging a tedious, time-consuming task requiring cross referencing of all program segments. To shorten and simplify this procedure, large programs (and for that matter, small ones too) are often written in modules, each of which is then coded as a subprogram and compiled independently of the main program. The independent compilation of the various subprograms then allows a less tedious, less time-consuming debugging of problems.

As a result, the main program is composed primarily of statements calling the various subprograms. Thus, the main program may be quite short. The beauty of this simplification is that no new FORTRAN statements need be introduced; those statements and techniques previously illustrated are as applicable as always. The only new material to be learned consists of additional DOS commands and strategies, described in App. E.

As an example of how a program may be written with and without the use of structured programming techniques, consider the problem of the multiplication of any two matrices having ten or less rows and columns. Without the use of structured programming, the program might appear as illustrated in Fig. 9-16. Although the problem is neither difficult nor lengthy, it does lend itself to structured programming techniques. From an analysis of the steps of the program, three distinct sections may be identified. The first section which might be isolated consists of reading values of the elements of the two matrices. The second section involves the arithmetic operation of multiplying the two matrices, and the third section controls the display of the elements of the product of the two matrices. Each of these sections may be written as a separate subroutine and compiled as a separate program. A main program could then be written which would call each of the three subroutines in the appropriate order.

```
C234567890
      DIMENSION A(10,10),B(10,10),C(10,10)
C   READ IN MATRIX ELEMENT VALUES
      OPEN(5,FILE='MATA.DAT')
      OPEN(7,FILE='MATB.DAT')
      READ(5,*)IRA,ICA
      READ(5,*)((A(I,J),J=1,ICA),I=1,IRA)
      READ(7,*)IRB,ICB
      READ(7,*)((B(I,J),J=1,ICB),I=1,IRB)
C   CALCULATE PRODUCT OF THE TWO MATRICES
      C(1,1)=0.0
      DO 10 I=1,IRA
      DO 10 J=1,ICB
      DO 10 K=1,ICA
   10 C(I,J)=C(I,J)+A(I,K)*B(K,J)
C   DISPLAY ELEMENTS OF PRODUCT IN MATRIX FORM
      OPEN(6,FILE='PRN')
      DO 20 I=1,IRA
   20 WRITE(6,100)(C(I,J),J=1,ICB)
  100 FORMAT(10(F7.2,2X))
      STOP
      END
```

FIGURE 9-16 An unstructured program.

Figure 9-17(*a*) through (*d*) (see p. 286) illustrates the problem described above, structured so that distinct operations are executed by individual subroutines. As indicated in Fig. 9-17(*a*), the main program serves solely as a controller, calling the various subroutines in the proper order. The operation of reading the values of the matrix elements is performed by the SUBROUTINE READ, shown in Fig. 9-17(*b*). This subprogram is written in a somewhat general form so that matrices having up to 10 rows and up to 10 columns may be handled. Multiplication of the two matrices is executed by the SUBROUTINE MULT, illustrated in Fig. 9-17(*c*). This subprogram is also written in a general form so that multiplication of compatible matrices may occur. Figure 9-17(*d*) illustrates the SUBROUTINE DISPL used to write the elements of the product matrix in matrix form, also written in a general manner.

It should be emphasized that each of the four segments of Fig. 9-17 represents an independently compiled program segment. Obviously the SUBROUTINE structures could not be executed as independent programs, but when linked with the main program structure, as explained in App. E, the same results will be obtained by using the formally structured program as with using the "unstructured" program. Although not obviously apparent from this simple example, the advantage of eliminating syntax errors from each subprogram, independently of the main program and other subprograms, is especially useful when subprograms are long and tedious.

Writing all programs in independently compiled subprogram form for future use is another advantage. If a sufficiently large library of such subprograms is developed, it is entirely possible that only a short main program, calling the appropriate error-free subprograms, need be developed to solve typical problems. The time savings could be enormous.

Various BLOCK IF structures are often used in structured programming because of their power. However, neither BLOCK IF structures nor structured programming is an essential part of the other. Structured programming refers only to

```
C234567890     MAIN PROGRAM
      COMMON A(10,10),B(10,10),C(10,10),IRA,ICA,IRB,ICB
      CALL READ
      CALL MULT
      CALL DISPL
      STOP
      END
```

(a)

```
C234567890
      SUBROUTINE READ
      COMMON A(10,10),B(10,10),C(10,10),IRA,ICA,IRB,ICB
      OPEN(5,FILE='MATA.DAT')
      OPEN(7,FILE='MATB.DAT')
      READ(5,*)IRA,ICA
      READ(5,*)((A(I,J),J=1,ICA),I=1,IRA)
      READ(7,*)IRB,ICB
      READ(7,*)((B(I,J),J=1,ICB),I=1,IRB)
      RETURN
      END
```

(b)

```
C234567890
      SUBROUTINE MULT
      COMMON A(10,10),B(10,10),C(10,10),IRA,IRC,IRB,ICB
      DO 10 I=1,IRA
      DO 10 J=1,ICB
      C(I,J)=0.0
      DO 10 K=1,ICA
   10 C(I,J)=C(I,J)+A(I,K)*B(K,J)
      RETURN
      END
```

(c)

```
C234567890
      SUBROUTINE DISPL
      COMMON A(10,10),B(10,10),C(10,10),IRA,IRC,IRB,ICB
      OPEN(6,FILE='PRN')
      DO 10 I=1,IRA
   10 WRITE(6,100)(C(I,J),J=1,ICB)
  100 FORMAT(10(F7.2,1X))
      RETURN
      END
```

(d)

FIGURE 9-17 Elements of a structured program.

the concept of programming in modules that can be individually tested and debugged.

No specific problems given at the end of this chapter require the use of structured programming. However, experience may be obtained by working any or all of the previous problems in the text, as well as those at the end of this chapter, using the structured programming technique.

PROBLEMS

9-1 Using a statement-function statement to define the calculations necessary to determine the area of a trapezoid, write a program that will read in the values for the two parallel bases and the altitude of any number of trapezoids, determine the area of each, and print values for the two bases, the altitude, and the area for each trapezoid. The area of the trapezoid is:

$$\text{AREA} = \frac{H(A + B)}{2}$$

where H is the length of the altitude and A and B are the lengths of the parallel bases.

9-2 In scientific work the area under a curve must often be computed. One method for doing so uses Simpson's rule. Figure 9-18 illustrates Simpson's rule, where the area under the curve between the limits x_1 and x_n is to be determined. The area is divided into any even number of intervals. After the value of each ordinate has been determined, the value of the area is found by the formula:

$$A = \frac{\Delta x}{3}[(y_1 + y_n) + 4(y_2 + y_4 + \cdots + y_{n-1}) + 2(y_3 + y_5 + \cdots + y_{n-2})]$$

Note that since the distance between x_1 and x_n is divided into an even number of intervals, the number of ordinates will always be 1 more than the number of intervals and therefore the value of n in y will always be an odd number.

Write a program to compute the area under any curve. Use a statement function to define the curve. The next two statements should specify the value of the initial x and final x ordinates. Divide the distance between these two ordinates into an even number of intervals such that the maximum value of the interval is less than Ø.Ø2. The remaining portion of the main program should calculate the values of all the resulting ordinates and print the value of the area. Use a FUNCTION subprogram to

FIGURE 9-18 Simpson's rule.

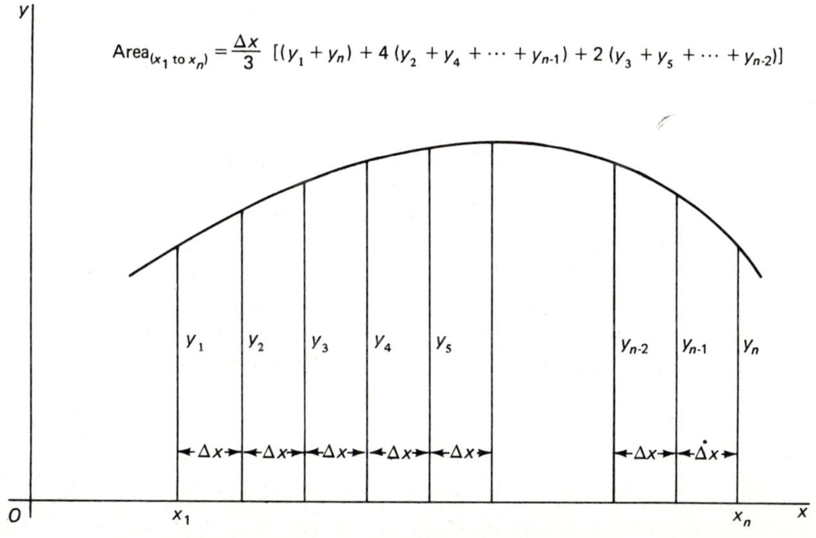

calculate the area. Then determine the area under a sine curve between $x_1 = Ø$ and $x_n = \pi$. Note that by changing only three statements (the statement function and the two statements specifying values of the initial and final ordinates) the program can be used to determine the area under any curve. Students who have studied calculus will recognize this as a computerized approximation of integration.

9-3 The trapezoidal rule is another mathematical procedure for approximating the integral (area under a curve). It is similar to Simpson's rule except that since each interval (Fig. 9-18) is considered as a small trapezoidal area, the final formula for the area becomes:

$$A = \frac{\Delta x}{2}(y_1 + 2y_2 + 2y_3 + \cdots + y_n)$$

Write a SUBROUTINE subprogram to calculate the area under a curve by using the trapezoidal rule. Use a statement function to define the curve in the SUBROUTINE subprogram. Compute successive approximations starting with two trapezoidal areas and doubling the number of trapezoidal areas for each successive approximation until two successive approximations agree within a given limit. If this limit has not been attained by the use of 256 zones, stop the approximations at that point but provide a way of warning the main program that the given limit has not been attained. Have the subprogram print each successive calculation of area, together with the number of zones used, so that the effect of doubling the zones can be appraised visually. Then solve the following problem:

A boat weighing 322 lb moves with a velocity that varies with time according to:

$$V = 7.5(1 - e^{0.2T})T$$

where V is the velocity in feet per second and T is the time in seconds. Inasmuch as distance is the integral of velocity, determine the distance the boat moves in the first 1Ø s, and then calculate the average velocity during that time period. Use a limit of Ø.Ø5.

9-4 Revise Prob. 8-13 so that the minimum element value as well as the maximum element value of the matrix is found by using a SUBROUTINE subprogram.

9-5 Write a program that will read a table of up to 25 pairs of values, representing respectively X's and the corresponding function of X, $f(X)$, from records in a data file. Then the program should return any other intermediate value of X and determine the value of the corresponding function of X, $f(X)$, by linear interpolation from the table. The output should show the table of X and $f(X)$ values, then the various intermediate X's and their corresponding $f(X)$ values. The program should be able to read any number of intermediate X values.

Use a SUBROUTINE subprogram to perform the linear interpolation. The SUBROUTINE subprogram should include a test to determine whether the X value lies within the limits of the table and, if so, to find the linearly interpolated value of $f(X)$. If the value of X lies outside the range of the table, an appropriate message should be printed by the main program.

Use a table of values for X and $f(X)$ as supplied by your instructor, or create one of your own. A suggestion in this case is to use values from a table of logarithmic or trigonometric values.

Use the intermediate values for X assigned by your instructor, or set your own values. These should include the first and the last value of X in the table, and one value should be outside the range of the table so that your subprogram will be completely tested.

9-6 A system of simultaneous equations can be solved by using Cramer's rule, which involves the use of determinants. In a system of three linear equations with three unknown variables, such as:

$$\begin{aligned} A_{1,1}X_1 + A_{1,2}X_2 + A_{1,3}X_3 &= B_1 \\ A_{2,1}X_1 + A_{2,2}X_2 + A_{2,3}X_3 &= B_2 \\ A_{3,1}X_1 + A_{3,2}X_2 + A_{3,3}X_3 &= B_3 \end{aligned}$$

A and B are sets of constants and X is the set of variables. With such a system Cramer's rule becomes:

$$X_1 = \frac{\begin{matrix} B_1 & A_{1,2} & A_{1,3} \\ B_2 & A_{2,2} & A_{2,3} \\ B_3 & A_{3,2} & A_{3,3} \end{matrix}}{\begin{matrix} A_{1,1} & A_{1,2} & A_{1,3} \\ A_{2,1} & A_{2,2} & A_{2,3} \\ A_{3,1} & A_{3,2} & A_{3,3} \end{matrix}} \qquad X_2 = \frac{\begin{matrix} A_{1,1} & B_1 & A_{1,3} \\ A_{2,1} & B_2 & A_{2,3} \\ A_{3,1} & B_3 & A_{3,3} \end{matrix}}{\begin{matrix} A_{1,1} & A_{1,2} & A_{1,3} \\ A_{2,1} & A_{2,2} & A_{2,3} \\ A_{3,1} & A_{3,2} & A_{3,3} \end{matrix}} \qquad X_3 = \frac{\begin{matrix} A_{1,1} & A_{1,2} & B_1 \\ A_{2,1} & A_{2,2} & B_2 \\ A_{3,1} & A_{3,2} & B_3 \end{matrix}}{\begin{matrix} A_{1,1} & A_{1,2} & A_{1,3} \\ A_{2,1} & A_{2,2} & A_{2,3} \\ A_{3,1} & A_{3,2} & A_{3,3} \end{matrix}}$$

Note that the three numerators are different, but the three denominators are identical.

If you are not familiar with the evaluation of determinants, the evaluation of the denominator's determinant follows the pattern:

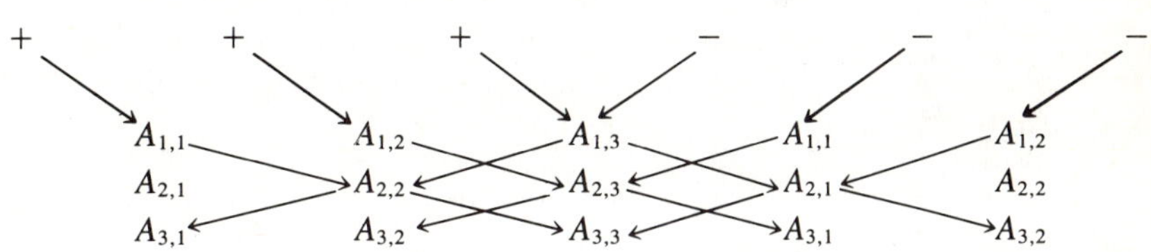

where each line of arrows represents the multiplication of the three indicated constants with the given algebraic sign. The evaluation of the determinant is the summation of all six multiplications. The numerator's determinants are evaluated similarly.

With a FUNCTION subprogram to set up the solution of a general 3×3 determinant, write a program that will read the values of the four constants for a system of three linear simultaneous equations, and then solve for and print the values of the three variables.

9-7 An artillery-gun position and potential targets are located by rectangular coordinates. A table of powder charges to be used for various ranges is given, as are the minimum and maximum azimuths defining the safety limits for firing the gun at that position. The maximum range of the gun is also given. Gun and target coordinates are given as eight-digit integer numbers, where the first four digits are the X coordinates to the nearest 1Ø m and the second four digits are the Y coordinates to the nearest 1Ø m. Azimuth is defined as a clockwise angle measured from the north and can vary from Ø to 36Ø°.

Write a program to determine the range in meters and azimuth in degrees from the gun position to the target and the appropriate charge to use. Check the azimuth against the safety limits and the range against the maximum range. Use a SUBROUTINE subprogram to calculate the range and azimuth, and use a FUNCTION subprogram to determine the charge.

The coordinates of the gun position are 3ØØØ5ØØØ. The minimum safe azimuth is 42°, and the maximum safe azimuth is 235°. The maximum range is 15,ØØØ m. The table of ranges and charges is:

Range, m	Charge
Ø–3,ØØØ	1
3,ØØ1–6,ØØØ	2
6,ØØ1–9,ØØØ	3
9,ØØ1–12,ØØØ	4
Over 12,ØØØ	5

The possible targets are at coordinates 3741531Ø, 32255ØØØ, 33834Ø32, 38733925, 3ØØØ4525, 345Ø5515, 25354715, and 38633675.

Be careful when calculating azimuths since in some cases the determination of the size of the angle may result in division by zero. If this occurs, an execution error will halt the program. Since coordinates are given only to the nearest 1Ø m, the range calculations cannot have a greater precision. However, the printout of the range should show the range to the nearest meter.

9-8 Engineers and scientists frequently must evaluate series of observed data by using statistical operations. Some of the statistical measures used are the average (or mean) value, the median value, and the standard deviation of the series. The *average* is simply the sum of the data divided by the number of data, or:

$$A = \frac{\Sigma X}{n}$$

The *median,* on the other hand, is the midpoint value of the data and often is different from the average. For data arranged in increasing (or decreasing) order, the median is the middle value when the number of data is odd, and the average of the two middle values when the number of data is even.

The standard deviation of the data is determined from the formula:

$$S = \sqrt{\frac{\Sigma(X - A)^2}{n - 1}}$$

where n is the number of data values and X represents each data value. Without being concerned with how these values are used in statistical operations, write a program that will read any number of data up to a maximum of 5Ø. Ensure that no more than 5Ø values can be read. Compute and print values of the average, the median, and the standard deviation. Be careful when determining the median since the individual values may come in any order. A subprogram to rearrange the data may be desirable. The program must also be able to handle any number of records. Use the following two sets of data to test the program. The data are to be read in the order given.

Set 1	Set 2
5ØØ.ØØ	2215.12
57Ø.75	2242.57
52Ø.66	225Ø.92
6ØØ.ØØ	222Ø.56
5Ø5.45	226Ø.8Ø
	223Ø.ØØ

9-9 It is important for all drivers to understand the safe distance between moving cars. Assume that there are 2Ø cars moving in a single lane. All are traveling at 55 mi/h with 4Ø ft between cars. An unexpected danger appears in the road ahead, and the first driver applies the brakes for an emergency stop. Each succeeding driver seeing the brake lights of the car ahead reacts and applies the brakes. Assume that the average braking distance to a full stop from 55 mi/h is 2ØØ ft and that all cars are capable of stopping in that distance once the brakes are applied. Also assume that the reaction time between seeing the danger signal and applying the brakes varies from 1.25 to Ø.75 s. Then the reaction time for each driver can be determined by the equation:

$$\text{RT} = 1.25 - \frac{\text{RAND(J)}}{2.\text{Ø}}$$

where RAND(J) is a random-number generator giving real numbers greater than Ø.Ø and less than 1.Ø.

Write a program that will determine the distance traveled by each car before it comes to a stop and whether any car will collide with the car ahead. If a collision occurs, further assume that the impact of the colliding car will move the final stopping point 2 ft forward from the point of impact. Print out the number of collisions that occur with the given distance between cars. Then increase the distance between cars by 1Ø ft and repeat the program. Do this until there are no collisions. The distance between cars is the safe distance between cars for the conditions of this problem. Write your own real-random-number generator as a FUNCTION subprogram.

To gain understanding of the effect of speed, change the rate of speed to 65 mi/h with 6Ø ft between cars. Assume the average braking distance to a full stop from 65 mi/h is 26Ø ft. Repeat the problem for these conditions.

9-10 Write a program where the main program reads in integer numbers and prints the number and its factorial, which has been computed in a subprogram. Ensure that only integers whose factorials can be computed by your computer are acceptable.

9-11 Revise Prob. 4-16 so that the "bubble sort" is performed by a SUBROUTINE subprogram. Provide your own data or use the data of Prob. 4-16.

9-12 Change Prob. 9-11 so that real values can be sorted, but this time have them arranged from the largest to the smallest. Provide your own data.

CHAPTER **10**

ADDITIONAL FORTRAN TECHNIQUES

10-1 INTRODUCTION

The first nine chapters introduced and explained the fundamental statements and techniques of the FORTRAN language. These statements and techniques constitute a working knowledge of the FORTRAN language and should provide sufficient information for the beginning programmer to write and evaluate programs and apply programming techniques to the solution of problems in a variety of scientific and engineering disciplines. Many statements, functions, edit descriptors, and acceptable shortcuts not previously discussed are available with most FORTRAN compilers. This chapter presents a few of the more generally useful statements and techniques in the "nice-to-know" category. These additional FORTRAN routines certainly do not represent a complete or comprehensive description of the remainder of the FORTRAN 77 capability. The beginner should be aware that there is much, much more and that this introductory text simply opens the door to computer programming.

10-2 THE CHARACTER STATEMENT

The CHARACTER statement is a nonexecutable *type-declaration* statement that declares that a single variable, or several variables, is to be assigned a character constant consisting of one or more characters. These characters include not only digits, but also letters, the *blank,* and all other keyboard characters. For example, the variable *A* may be assigned the alphanumeric value: STREET #, consisting of eight characters, S, T, R, E, E, T, a *blank,* and #, if a CHARACTER statement first indicates that the variable *A* is to be assigned such a value.

The general form for the CHARACTER statement is:

CHARACTER $a*n_1, b*n_2, j*n_3$

where CHARACTER is the FORTRAN term identifying the type-declaration statement, and n_1, n_2, and n_3 are integer constants specifying the number of characters in a string of characters (the *character constant*) to be assigned to *a, b,* and *j*. The CHARACTER statement should follow any DIMENSION and DOUBLE PRECISION (Sec. 11-4) statements but must be placed *before* any executable statements in the program. A real or integer variable listed in a CHARACTER statement may be assigned a character constant with an assignment statement, with a READ statement, or with a DATA statement (Sec. 10-4). A character constant assigned to a variable with an assignment statement must be enclosed by apostrophes, as illustrated in the following program segment:

```
CHARACTER A*8
------------
A='STREET #'
------------
```

A character constant assigned to a variable by a READ statement (or displayed by a WRITE statement) must be specified with an A edit descriptor (Sec. 10-3) in the associated FORMAT statement. A character constant assigned with a DATA statement (Sec. 10-4) must also be enclosed by apostrophes.

When more than one variable declared in a single CHARACTER statement contains the same number of characters in their character constants, the statement can be written:

```
CHARACTER*n a,b,j
```

meaning that the character constants to be assigned to a, b, and j each contain *n* characters. There is no flowchart symbol for the CHARACTER statement.

When the character constant consists of only one character, the integer constant specifying the number of characters may be omitted. This means that:

```
CHARACTER A*1,B*1,J*1      or      CHARACTER*1 A,B,J
```

can both be coded:

```
CHARACTER A,B,J
```

When the actual arguments in a calling program have been declared type character in the calling program, the corresponding dummy arguments in the subprogram must also be declared type character by a CHARACTER statement.

10-3 THE A EDIT DESCRIPTOR

When a character variable is included in a READ/WRITE list, the A edit descriptor must be used to specify the character variable in the associated FORMAT statement. The A edit descriptor permits the input, manipulation, and output of any character variable recognized by the compiler. With the A edit descriptor it is possible to sort words alphabetically, compare words and/or numbers, and branch to specific statements depending on the comparison.

The general form for the A edit descriptor is:

*r*A*w*

where *r* is the repetition number, A is the edit descriptor, and *w* is the number of characters to be stored in a given WORD. As an example of the use of the A edit descriptor with a CHARACTER statement, assume that the first record in the file TEST.DAT contains the characters + * $ in the first three columns. The program segment:

```
     CHARACTER J,K,L
     OPEN(2,FILE='TEST.DAT')
     READ(2,1ØØ)J,K,L
1ØØ  FORMAT(3A1)
     WRITE(*,2ØØ)J,K,L
2ØØ  FORMAT(2X,A1,2X,A1,2X,A1)
```

reads and stores the three characters, respectively, in the three variables, and displays on the screen:

bb+*bb***bb*$

Care should be taken to ensure that the number of characters defined by the CHARACTER statement for a particular variable and specified by the A edit descriptor for that variable are the same. Figure 10-1 illustrates what happens when this relationship is not observed. Two identical records were provided in the data file FIG10-1.DAT, each record being:

*b*COMPUTER*b*GRAPHICS

FIGURE 10-1 Reading and printing with the A edit descriptor.

```
C234567890
      CHARACTER*4 J,K,L,M,JJ,KK,LL,MM,NN
      CHARACTER*2 N
      OPEN(3,FILE='FIG10-1.DAT')
      OPEN(6,FILE='PRN')
      READ(3,100)J,K,L,M,N
  100 FORMAT(4A4,A2)
      READ(3,200)JJ,KK,LL,MM,NN
  200 FORMAT(5A4)
      WRITE(6,300)J,K,L,M,N
  300 FORMAT(10X,4A4,A2,'END')
      WRITE(6,400)JJ,KK,LL,MM,NN
  400 FORMAT(10X,5A4,'END')
      WRITE(6,*)
      WRITE(6,400)J,K,L,M,N
      WRITE(6,300)JJ,KK,LL,MM,NN
      STOP
      END
```

```
 COMPUTER GRAPHICS
 COMPUTER GRAPHICS
```

```
          COMPUTER GRAPHICSEND
          COMPUTER GRAPHICS  END

          COMPUTER GRAPHI  CSEND
          COMPUTER GRAPHICSEND
```

The first READ statement assigns *b*COM to J, PUTE to K, R*b*GR to L, APHI to M, and CS to N. Note that J, K, L, and M are specified in the CHARACTER statement as having four characters and are read with A4 edit descriptors, while N was specified as having two characters and read with an A2 edit descriptor. The output FORMAT was arranged, in each case, so the the word END would follow the letter S in the output in order to clearly identify the end of each output example. The first line of output was specified by using the same edit descriptors as in the READ statement. The first two lines of output are exactly as expected. However, the third line of output was specified with an A4 edit descriptor for N as well as for J, K, L, and M. Remember that N was specified as having two characters and was read with an A2 edit descriptor. The third line of output shows that when the output edit descriptor for N was increased to A4, two *blanks* were printed *preceding* the characters CS.

The program of Fig. 10-1 further defines the variables JJ, KK, LL, MM, and NN as having four characters, and they are read from the second record with A4 edit descriptors. Thus, *b*COM is assigned to JJ, PUTE to KK, R*b*GR to LL, APHI to MM, and CS*bb* to NN. The second line of output was specified using A4 edit descriptors and the presence of the two *blanks* in NN confirmed. The last line of output was printed using an A2 edit descriptor for NN. The result was the truncation of the last two characters in NN (the *blanks*). This demonstrates that if a CHARACTER-defined variable is printed with edit descriptors larger than that with which it was read, leading *blanks* will be added to the characters of the variable. If the variable is printed with an edit descriptor smaller than that with which it was read, the rightmost characters will be truncated as required. Thus it is apparent that the best procedure is for the READ and WRITE specifications to be consistent with the number of characters for each variable as specified by the CHARACTER statement.

FIGURE 10-2 Manipulating alphanumeric variables.

```
C234567890
      CHARACTER J,K,L,M
      OPEN(3,FILE='FIG10-2.DAT')
      OPEN(6,FILE='PRN')
      READ(3,100)J,K,L,M
  100 FORMAT(4A1)
      WRITE(6,200)M,L,J,K
  200 FORMAT(5X,4A1)
      WRITE(6,200)L,J,K
      WRITE(6,200)K,J,L,M
      WRITE(6,*)
      WRITE(6,300)J,K,L,M
  300 FORMAT(5X,4A4,'END')
      STOP
      END
```

```
INPS
```

```
     SPIN
     PIN
     NIPS

        I   N   P   SEND
```

Figure 10-2 shows that characters can be read, manipulated, and printed. Here the CHARACTER statement defines J, K, L, and M as variables having one character. The record of the data file FIG10-2.DAT provided for the program contains the letters I, N, P, and S in the first four columns. When read by the READ statement, I is assigned to J, N to K, P to L, and S to M. The first three WRITE statements demonstrate that, by rearranging the order of the variables in the WRITE list, various words can be formed. The last line of output was made with A4 edit descriptors for all variables. As suggested in the previous discussion, three leading *blanks* have been inserted before each character constant.

When the A edit descriptor is used without first declaring the string of characters in a CHARACTER statement or a DATA statement (Sec. 10-4), the string must be assigned to variables (input) or written (output) in blocks of four characters or less (including *blanks*). The field width *w* when the descriptor is used in this manner may be 1, 2, 3, or 4, but must not exceed 4. For example, the A edit descriptor might be applied as follows to read character constants from a data file, assign variable names, and then display the characters with appropriate output statements:

```
      OPEN(3,FILE='FILE.DAT')
      READ(3,1ØØ)A,E,I,M,N,R,V,Z
1ØØ   FORMAT(3A4,A1,/,3A4,A1)
      WRITE(*,2ØØ)A,E,I,M,N,R,V,Z
2ØØ   FORMAT(1X,A4)
```

FILE.DAT
ABCDEFGHIJKLM NOPQRSTUVWXYZ

These statements display:

```
ABCD
EFGH
IJKL
M
NOPQ
RSTU
VWXY
Z
```

In the above example, the READ and its associated 1ØØ FORMAT statement (with the A edit descriptors in the specification) assign the characters in the first four columns of the first record of the data file (ABCD) to the first variable (A) in the input list, the characters in the next four columns (EFGH) to the second variable (E), etc. The last character in the first record (M) occupies a one-column field and is assigned by the A1 descriptor to the fourth variable (M). The characters in the second record of the data file are assigned in a like manner to the last four variables in the input list. The 200 FORMAT specification is written to display the characters assigned to each variable on successive lines of output. Note that the characters on lines 4 and 8 (M and Z, respectively) are left-justified in the four-column field by the A4 edit descriptor.

The following example illustrates what will happen when an attempt is made to assign, without a CHARACTER statement, the entire 13-character record to a single variable name with an A13 descriptor:

```
      OPEN(3,FILE='FILE.DAT')
      READ(3,100)A,N
100   FORMAT(A13,/,A13)
      WRITE(*,200)A,N
200   FORMAT(1X,A13)
```

FILE.DAT
ABCDEFGHIJKLM NOPQRSTUVWXYZ

The above program segment would display:

```
         JKLM
         WXYZ
```

where the characters JKLM and WXYZ are right-justified in output column 13. Since the maximum field width allowed is 4, the last four characters in the 13-column field read in the first record (JKLM) are assigned to A, and the last four characters in the 13-column read in the second record (WXYZ) are assigned to N. The A13 edit descriptor in the output specification right-justifies each block of four characters in the thirteenth column of the 13-column output field.

10-4 THE DATA STATEMENT

The DATA statement is a nonexecutable *definition* statement used to assign character constants or numerical values to variables during compilation. It is advisable to place the DATA statement in the program *before* the first executable statement. The general form for the DATA statement is:

DATA *a*, *b*, *k*/*x*, *y*, *n*/

where DATA is the FORTRAN term identifying the statement
a, b, k represent a list of variable names to which constants are to be assigned
x, y, n represent a list of numerical constants to be assigned, in order, to the variable names

Both the variable names and the constants are separated by commas, and the list of constants begins and ends with a slash. The list of constants *must* agree in number, type, and relative position with the list of variable names to which they are assigned. Real constants may be expressed in exponential form. If any or all of the variable names in the list are DOUBLE PRECISION (Sec. 11-4), the corresponding real constant must be expressed in double-precision form. The flowchart symbol for the DATA statement is the parallelogram (Fig. 2-2).

An example of the DATA statement is:

```
DATA A,B,K/1.5,2.5,3/
```

This statement will assign 1.5 to A, 2.5 to B, and 3 to K. The DATA statement of the above example might also have been coded:

```
DATA A/1.5/,B/2.5/,K/3/
```

with the same assignment: 1.5 to A, 2.5 to B, and 3 to K.

An asterisk may be used in the DATA statement to indicate multiple assignment of the same constant to successive variable names in the list. In the statement:

```
DATA A,B,M,N,J,K/2*1.5,4*3/
```

the constant 1.5 is used twice (2*1.5) and is assigned to both A and B, the first two variable names in the list. The constant 3 is used 4 times (4*3) and is assigned to M, N, J, and K, the next four variable names in the list. The repetition numbers (2 and 4) ahead of the asterisks indicate how many times the constant following each asterisk is to be used. This number must always be an integer constant. Notice that the asterisk as used in the DATA statement does not indicate multiplication.

If values defined in a DATA statement are also declared by a DIMENSION, INTEGER, REAL, CHARACTER, DOUBLE PRECISION (Sec. 11-4), or any other type-declaration statement, the DATA statement must follow the type-declaration statement(s).

The compiler does not permit the use of implied DO loops in the DATA statement for assigning values to dimensioned variables; however, the following statements can be used to assign values to a small array:

```
DIMENSION K(2,2)
DATA K(1,1),K(1,2),K(2,1),K(2,2)/11,12,21,22/
```

In addition, values may be assigned to the elements of both one- and two-dimensional arrays as illustrated in the following two examples:

(a)
```
DIMENSION K(5)
DATA K/1,2,3,4,5/
```

(b)
```
DIMENSION K(2,5)
DATA K/1,1Ø,2,2Ø,3,3Ø,4,4Ø,5,5Ø/
```

In the last example, the values are assigned to the two-dimensional array in column order.

The following examples illustrate how the DATA statement can be used with the CHARACTER statement for assigning character constants to variable names. In these examples, character constants are used as column headings to annotate columns of output. The statements:

```
      CHARACTER*1Ø KOLHD1,KOLHD2
      DATA KOLHD1,KOLHD2/'CURRICULUM','bbCLASSbbb'/
      WRITE(*,1ØØ)KOLHD1,KOLHD2
1ØØ   FORMAT(2X,2A1Ø)
```

will display:

```
bbCURRICULUMbbCLASSbbb
```

If several column headings are required, it may be more efficient to assign each heading as an element of an array. The statements:

```
      CHARACTER*1Ø KOLHD(4)
      DATA KOLHD/'bbbNAMEbbb','bbIDbNO.bb','CURRICULUM',
     $'bbCLASSbbb'/
      WRITE(*,1ØØ) (KOLHD(N),N=1,4)
1ØØ   FORMAT(2X,4A1Ø)
```

will display:

```
bbbbbNAMEbbbbbIDbNO.bbCURRICULUMbbCLASSbbb
```

Rearranging the order of the headings in the output can be accomplished by changing the order of the subscripted variables in the WRITE list.

The variable names to which character constants are assigned may be either real or integer. In most cases it makes little difference. However, when a character constant is assigned to a real-variable name and the contents of that real-variable name are later assigned to an integer-variable name, problems may occur when the contents of the integer-variable name are displayed. It is recommended that character constants be assigned to integer-variable names.

Figure 10-3 shows another example of the use of the CHARACTER and DATA statements to assign and print character constants as column headings.

10-5 THE EQUIVALENCE STATEMENT

The EQUIVALENCE statement is a nonexecutable *declaration* statement that declares all the variables in a given list to be equivalent. Assignment, by any means, of a value to one of the variable names in the list will assign the same value to all the variable names in the list.

```
C234567890
      CHARACTER*3 L
      CHARACTER*4 M
      CHARACTER*6 N
      DATA L,M,N/'RED','BLUE','YELLOW'/
      OPEN(6,FILE='PRN')
      WRITE(6,100)L,M,N
  100 FORMAT(5X,A3,2X,A4,2X,A6)
      STOP
      END
```

FIGURE 10-3 Example of an A edit descriptor using the DATA statement for input.

```
     RED  BLUE  YELLOW
```

The general form for the EQUIVALENCE statement is:

EQUIVALENCE (*a*, *b*, *c*), (*j*, *k*, *l*)

where EQUIVALENCE is the FORTRAN term identifying the declaration statement
(*a*,*b*,*c*) represents a list of real-variable names whose values are to be equivalent
(*j*,*k*,*l*) represents a list of integer-variable names whose values are to be equivalent

Note that the equivalent variable names, grouped by parentheses, are all of the same type. Integer variables *must not* be declared equivalent to real variables. The EQUIVALENCE statement *must be placed before* the first executable statement in the program.

The following program segment illustrates the effects of the EQUIVALENCE statement:

```
    EQUIVALENCE (A,B,C), (J,K,L)
    A=1.5
    K=3
    WRITE(*,1ØØ)A,B,C,J,K,L
1ØØ FORMAT(1X,3F4.1,3I3)
```

These statements will display:

*bb*1.5*b*1.5*b*1.5*bb*3*bb*3*bb*3

Assignment of 1.5 to A is equivalent to assigning 1.5 to A, 1.5 to B, and 1.5 to C. All three real variables declared in the EQUIVALENCE statement have the same value. Likewise, assignment of 3 to K is equivalent to assigning 3 to J, 3 to K, and 3 to L. All three integer variables declared in the EQUIVALENCE statement have the same value.

The program segment below illustrates another important fact:

```
      EQUIVALENCE (A,B,C), (J,K,L)
      OPEN(6,FILE='PRN')
      A=1.5
      B=2.Ø
      C=2.5
      J=1
      L=5
      K=3
      WRITE(6,1ØØ)A,B,C,J,K,L
1ØØ   FORMAT(1X,3F4.1,3I3)
```

The above program segment will print:

```
bb2.5b2.5b2.5bb3bb3bb3
```

The *last* value assigned to a variable name in each group of equivalent variables is the value assigned to each variable in each group. C = 2.5 and K = 3, in this example, are the values assigned, respectively, to the equivalent real-variable names A, B, C and the equivalent integer-variable names J, K, L when the WRITE statement is executed.

The EQUIVALENCE statement can be used to associate more than one variable name with the same value in an existing program. Suppose that in a long and involved program the variable names AREA, A, AERA, and AR are all used carelessly and indiscriminately as storage locations for the value of the area. The first variable name used is AREA in an assignment statement where the correct value is assigned. Subsequent mistakes using A, AERA, and AR can be easily corrected by adding one EQUIVALENCE statement at the beginning of the program:

```
EQUIVALENCE (AREA,A,AR,AERA)
```

All three incorrect variable names are declared equivalent to AREA, the correct variable name. The value assigned to AREA is now assigned to A, AR and AERA wherever they appear in the program.

The EQUIVALENCE statement can also be applied to reduce the number of storage locations required in a given program by reusing storage locations assigned early in the program but no longer needed. When two large arrays are used in the same program, the second array, if used late in the program, can be assigned the same storage location reserved for the first array used early in the program, provided the values assigned to its elements are no longer needed. For example:

```
DIMENSION X(1ØØØ),Y(5ØØ)
```

will reserve 1ØØØ storage locations for array X and 5ØØ storage locations for array Y. Then:

```
EQUIVALENCE (X(1),Y(1))
```

declares the 5ØØ elements of array Y and the first 5ØØ elements of array X to be equivalent and share the same storage locations. The storage locations required will be reduced by one-third; 5ØØ fewer storage locations will be needed. Note that only the first element of each array, X(1) and Y(1), is listed in the EQUIVALENCE statement. Since successive elements in an array are always stored in successive storage locations, only the first element of each array is listed. The equivalent relationship of the following 499 elements of each array is automatically established by the compiler. It is important to remember that when values are assigned to the 5ØØ elements of array Y later in the program, they replace the first 5ØØ elements of array X. The first, and original, 5ØØ elements of array X, namely X(1) through X(5ØØ), are lost. However, the last 5ØØ original values, X(5Ø1) through X(1ØØØ), are still unchanged and available.

Two elements of the same array *cannot* be related in an EQUIVALENCE statement. The statements:

```
DIMENSION A(1Ø)
EQUIVALENCE (A(1),A(1Ø))
```

are *incorrect*. But individual elements of an array can be declared equivalent to other simple-variable names if desired:

```
DIMENSION Y(1Ø)
EQUIVALENCE (Y(1),YONE), (Y(5),YFIVE), (Y(1Ø),YTEN)
```

10-6 THE G EDIT DESCRIPTOR

The generalized, or G, edit descriptor can be used to specify any real value (single- or double-precision). The general form for the G edit descriptor is:

*r*G*w*.*d*

where *r* represents a repetition number
- G indicates a type-real decimal or exponential form; single- or double-precision or complex
- *w* represents the field width
- *d* specifies the number of significant digits following the decimal point

In reading real values, G*w*.*d* has the same meaning as F*w*.*d* and E*w*.*d* according to how the value read is expressed in the data record. It is in the output of real values that significant advantages of the G edit descriptor become apparent. If the absolute value of the integer portion to the left of the decimal point is *less than or equal to* 1Ø***d*, the value is displayed as though the edit descriptor were F*w*.*d*. In this case the value is printed right-justified in a field width of $w-4$ output columns. A peculiarity in the application of the *d* portion of the G descriptor in the output of these values will be discussed later when examples of the use of the G edit descriptor in the output specification are shown.

If the absolute value of the integer portion to the left of the decimal point is *greater than* 1Ø***d*, the value is displayed as though the edit descriptor were E*w*.*d*. In this case the output columns required for the value are right-justified in the field width of *w* output columns. This possibility makes it necessary to have *w* greater or equal to $d + 7$ in order to provide sufficient field width to display the value with its exponent, as discussed in Sec. 6-8*b*. When the value to be read or displayed is type complex (Sec. 10-10), two edit descriptors must be provided.

Figure 10-4 illustrates the printing of various sizes of single-precision values using the G edit descriptor. Observe how the various values are printed according to the *d* part of the descriptor. Note the alignment of the values simulating the

FIGURE 10-4 Examples of G edit descriptors for single-precision values.

```
C234567890
      OPEN(6,FILE='PRN')
      X=.1234567
      DO 10 J=1,4
      WRITE(6,100)X
  100 FORMAT(1X,'THE VALUE:',F15.7,' IS PRINTED AS:')
      WRITE(6,200)X
  200 FORMAT(1X,G17.7,' WHEN THE SPECIFICATION IS G17.7')
      WRITE(6,300)X
  300 FORMAT(1X,G17.5,' WHEN THE SPECIFICATION IS G17.5')
      WRITE(6,400)X
  400 FORMAT(1X,G17.3,' WHEN THE SPECIFICATION IS G17.3')
      WRITE(6,500)X
  500 FORMAT(1X,G17.1,' WHEN THE SPECIFICATION IS G17.1',//)
      X=X*100.0
   10 CONTINUE
      STOP
      END
```

```
THE VALUE:       .1234567 IS PRINTED AS:
      .1234567     WHEN THE SPECIFICATION IS G17.7
        .12346     WHEN THE SPECIFICATION IS G17.5
          .123     WHEN THE SPECIFICATION IS G17.3
            .1     WHEN THE SPECIFICATION IS G17.1


THE VALUE:     12.3456700 IS PRINTED AS:
      12.34567     WHEN THE SPECIFICATION IS G17.7
        12.346     WHEN THE SPECIFICATION IS G17.5
          12.3     WHEN THE SPECIFICATION IS G17.3
            .1E+02 WHEN THE SPECIFICATION IS G17.1


THE VALUE:   1234.5670000 IS PRINTED AS:
      1234.567     WHEN THE SPECIFICATION IS G17.7
        1234.6     WHEN THE SPECIFICATION IS G17.5
          .123E+04 WHEN THE SPECIFICATION IS G17.3
            .1E+04 WHEN THE SPECIFICATION IS G17.1


THE VALUE: 123456.7000000 IS PRINTED AS:
      123456.7     WHEN THE SPECIFICATION IS G17.7
        .12346E+06 WHEN THE SPECIFICATION IS G17.5
          .123E+06 WHEN THE SPECIFICATION IS G17.3
            .1E+06 WHEN THE SPECIFICATION IS G17.1
```

F*w*.*d* or E*w*.*d* edit descriptors. An examination of the values printed according to the F*w*.*d* descriptor reveals the peculiarity mentioned previously. When so used, the *d* in the G*w*.*d* descriptor does not control the number of decimal places; it controls the number of significant digits in the total value.

Figure 10-5 illustrates the printing of a double-precision value. Note that the manner of printing is the same as for single-precision values except that more significant digits are available. The *d* still controls the number of significant digits and not the number of decimal places.

The principal advantage of the G edit descriptor is that it can handle any real value and ensure that a value will be displayed since the G edit descriptor will display in decimal or exponential form as appropriate. It is an advantage to use the G edit descriptor for the first run of a program when the range of resulting values is uncertain. After the first run, the descriptor can be changed to the F or E, as appropriate, if that output form or positioning of the printed value is desired.

10-7 THE SCALE-FACTOR EDIT DESCRIPTOR

Section 6-8*b* states that the stored value 123.4567 displayed with the edit descriptor E13.7 will appear as:

b.1234567E+Ø3

Some programmers prefer to see exponential values displayed with a leading integer between 1.Ø and 1Ø.Ø. This can be accomplished by using the scale-factor edit descriptor together with an E edit descriptor. The general form for the scale-factor edit descriptor is: *n*P

FIGURE 10-5 Examples of G edit descriptors for double-precision values.

```
C234567890
      DOUBLE PRECISION X
      OPEN(6,FILE='PRN')
      X=123456789.0D0
      WRITE(6,100)X
  100 FORMAT(1X,'THE VALUE :',D20.9,' IS PRINTED AS :',/)
      WRITE(6,200)X
  200 FORMAT(5X,G20.9,' WHEN THE SPECIFICATION IS G20.9')
      WRITE(6,300)X
  300 FORMAT(5X,G20.7,' WHEN THE SPECIFICATION IS G20.7')
      WRITE(6,400)X
  400 FORMAT(5X,G20.5,' WHEN THE SPECIFICATION IS G20.5')
      WRITE(6,500)X
  500 FORMAT(5X,G20.3,' WHEN THE SPECIFICATION IS G20.3')
      STOP
      END
```

```
THE VALUE :         .123456789D+09 IS PRINTED AS :

          123456789.       WHEN THE SPECIFICATION IS G20.9
            .1234568E+09 WHEN THE SPECIFICATION IS G20.7
              .12346E+09 WHEN THE SPECIFICATION IS G20.5
                .123E+09 WHEN THE SPECIFICATION IS G20.3
```

where *n* is an integer number indicating the number of times the value of the variable is to be multiplied by 10, and P indicates the type of edit descriptor.

Coding the combined edit descriptor as 1PE13.7 causes the above value to be displayed as:

```
1.2345670E+02
```

Note that there are eight digits in the value and that the power of 10 has been reduced by 1. The 1P is the scale-factor edit descriptor. Its effect, when used with the E edit descriptor in an output FORMAT, is to multiply the value by a factor of 10 and reduce the value of the exponent by 1. The actual value is unchanged. Note that the complete edit descriptor provides no space for the minus sign if the value is negative. Hence, the field width of the E edit descriptor should be changed to 1PE14.7. Other scale-factor edit descriptors such as 2P or 3P can be used. When using the scale-factor edit descriptor, a FORMAT statement to print three values in exponential form can be written:

```
200 FORMAT(1X,1P3E14.7)
```

Note that the scale-factor edit descriptor is written first, then the repetition number, and then the E edit descriptor.

The effects of a scale-factor edit descriptor are illustrated in Fig. 10-6, where the values of A, B, C, and J are assigned by four assignment statements and then printed by four different WRITE/FORMAT statements. The 100 FORMAT statement prints the values normally. In the 200 FORMAT statement a scale-factor

FIGURE 10-6 Effects of the scale-factor edit descriptor in printing.

```
C234567890
      OPEN(6,FILE='PRN')
      A=12.34567
      B=789.1234
      C=56.78901
      J=5
      WRITE(6,100)A,B,C,J
  100 FORMAT(1X,E15.7,E20.7,F20.7,I4,/)
      WRITE(6,200)A,B,C,J
  200 FORMAT(1X,1PE15.7,E20.7,F20.7,I4,/)
      WRITE(6,300)A,B,C,J
  300 FORMAT(1X,1PE15.7,OPE20.7,F20.7,I4,/)
      WRITE(6,400)A,B,C,J
  400 FORMAT(1X,1PE15.7,E20.7,OPF20.7,I4)
      STOP
      END
```

```
  .1234567E+02         .7891234E+03          56.7890100   5

 1.2345670E+01        7.8912340E+02         567.8901000   5

 1.2345670E+01         .7891234E+03          56.7890100   5

 1.2345670E+01        7.8912340E+02          56.7890100   5
```

edit descriptor of 1P is used with the first E15.7 edit descriptor to print the value of A. The remaining descriptors are written without the scale-factor descriptor. Compare the values printed on the second line of output with the first-line values. The effect of the scale-factor descriptor used with the E15.7 descriptor to print the value A is also applied to the descriptors to print values for B and C. The result is correct values for A and B, but the value for C is incorrect (increased by a power of 10). The value for J is not affected.

In the 3ØØ FORMAT statement, a scale-factor edit descriptor is again used with the E descriptor to print the value of A, but a scale-factor edit descriptor of ØP is used with the E2Ø.7 edit descriptor (ØPE2Ø.7) to print the value of B. The remaining descriptors are now correct. Compare the values now in the third printed line with the previous lines. The value for A is as before, but then the effect of the first scale-factor descriptor is canceled by the second scale-factor descriptor, and the values of B and C are correctly printed. The value of J is again correct.

In the 4ØØ FORMAT statement of Fig. 10-6, a scale-factor edit descriptor of 1P is again used with the E descriptor to print the value of A; no scale-factor edit descriptor is used with the E descriptor for B, but a scale-factor edit descriptor of ØP is used with the F descriptor (ØPF2Ø.7) to print the value of C. Again compare the values in the fourth printed line with the previous lines. The values for A and B are both printed with the effect of the first scale-factor edit descriptor, but its effect is canceled by the second scale-factor descriptor and C is printed correctly. J is still not affected.

To sum up the above discussions, if a scale-factor edit descriptor is used with another edit descriptor to display any real value, its effect in that FORMAT statement is canceled or changed *only* by the use of another scale-factor edit descriptor used with a following edit descriptor, or by reaching the end of the FORMAT specification. In no case will a scale-factor edit descriptor change the value of an integer value. If for some reason a scale-factor edit descriptor greater than 1P is desired, say 2P, the programmer must be aware that this will add digits to be printed to the left of the decimal point and that the field width of the associated edit descriptor must be increased correspondingly.

10-8 THE POSITIONAL T EDIT DESCRIPTOR

The positional T edit descriptor, used in a FORMAT statement associated with a READ or WRITE statement, designates the starting column for reading the record or the starting column for displaying the output field specified by the I, F, E, A, H, or apostrophe edit descriptor immediately following the T edit descriptor. The general form for the T edit descriptor is:

T*n*

where T identifies the positional edit descriptor and *n* represents an integer constant designating the *starting* column of the input or output field. A repetition number is *never* used with the T edit descriptor.

This is illustrated in Fig. 10-7, where the READ statement and its associated FORMAT statement reference the indicated record 123456789Ø and assign the sequence of digits in columns 1 through 5 (12345) to N, the sequence of digits in columns 7 through 9 (789) to K, the sequence of digits in columns 2 through 5 (23.45) to A, and the sequence of digits in columns 8 through 1Ø (89.Ø) to B. Note that the T edit descriptor can designate the starting column of the specified data field, moving either forward or backward along the record. This property of the T edit descriptor permits any left-to-right sequence of characters in the record to be read as many times as desired.

In Fig. 10-7 the values assigned to N, K, A, and B are then printed by the two WRITE statements and their associated FORMAT statements. In the first WRITE and its associated 2ØØ FORMAT statement, the five-print-position field occupied by 12345—the value assigned to N—begins (T3) in output column 3; the three-print-position field occupied by 789—the value assigned to K—begins (T15) in output column 15; the five-print-position field occupied by 23.45—the value assigned to A—begins (T2Ø) in output column 2Ø; and the four-print-position field occupied by 89.Ø—the value assigned to B—begins (T27) in output column 27.

In the second WRITE and its associated FORMAT statement, the values assigned to N and K (12345 and 789, respectively) are printed exactly as before, beginning in output columns 3 and 15 as specified by the T3 and T15 edit descriptors. However, the value assigned to A (23.45) occupies a five-print-position field that begins in output column 9, specified by the T9 edit descriptor, placing the value assigned to A between the values assigned to N and K. The value assigned to B (89.Ø) occupies a four-print-position field that begins in output column 2Ø, designated by the T2Ø edit descriptor. The left-to-right order of variable values in the second line of output is N, A, K, B, rather than the order of the variable names in the WRITE list, N, K, A, B.

FIGURE 10-7 Effects of the positional T edit descriptor.

```
C234567890
      OPEN(2,FILE='FIG10-7.DAT')
      OPEN(6,FILE='PRN')
      READ(2,100)N,K,A,B
  100 FORMAT(T1,I5,T7,I3,T2,F4.2,T8,F3.1)
      WRITE(6,200)N,K,A,B
  200 FORMAT(T3,I5,T15,I3,T20,F5.2,T27,F4.1,/)
      WRITE(6,300)N,K,A,B
  300 FORMAT(T3,I5,T15,I3,T9,F5.2,T20,F4.1)
      STOP
      END
```

```
1234567890
```

```
  12345         789  23.45  89.0

  12345 23.45 789  89.0
```

The T edit descriptor permits the values assigned to the variable names in the WRITE list to be displayed in any desired order by designating the starting output column, either forward or backward, along the output line. When used in the input FORMAT specification, the value of the integer constant *n* in the T edit descriptor must be between 1 and the maximum number of columns in a record (8Ø) less the field width covered by the edit descriptor immediately following plus 1. For example, with an 8Ø-column record and an edit descriptor of F5.2, the starting column designated in the related T edit descriptor can be no greater than 8Ø − 5 + 1, or T76. If the maximum permissible value of the integer constant *n* in the T edit descriptor is exceeded, execution will terminate with an error message when execution of the associated READ statement is attempted.

When used in the output FORMAT specification, the value of the integer constant *n* in the T edit descriptor must be between 1 and the maximum number of output columns available (usually 8Ø for the personal computer printers) less the field width covered by the edit descriptor immediately following plus 1. For example, with 8Ø output columns available and an edit descriptor of I1Ø, the output column designated in the related T edit descriptor can be no greater than 8Ø − 1Ø + 1, or T71. If the maximum permissible value of the integer constant *n* in the T edit descriptor is exceeded, execution will terminate with an error message when execution of the associated WRITE statement is attempted.

When using the T edit descriptor in the WRITE/FORMAT statement, designating an output column to the left of output columns already specified creates the possibility of having two or more characters located in the same output column. This situation is illustrated in Fig. 10-8. There should be no problem in understanding the output produced by the 1ØØ FORMAT statement. But what happened to the line of output resulting from the 2ØØ FORMAT statement? Execution of the WRITE statement according to the 2ØØ FORMAT statement holds in temporary storage, beginning in output column 11, the digits 123456789Ø—the value assigned to N. Output columns 11 through 2Ø are occupied by these characters, but

FIGURE 10-8 Effect of overlapping output with the positional T edit descriptor.

```
C234567890
      OPEN(5,FILE='PRN')
      N=1234567890
      K=92
      WRITE(5,100)N,K
  100 FORMAT(T11,I10,/,T13,'ABCDEF',/,T15,I2,/)
      WRITE(5,200)N,K
  200 FORMAT(T11,I10,T13,'ABCDEF',T15,I2)
      STOP
      END
```

```
          1234567890
            ABCDEF
              92

          12AB92EF90
```

nothing is printed because execution is not yet complete. Then the T13, 'ABCDEF' edit descriptor requires that the character constant ABCDEF occupy output columns 13 through 18, inclusive, replacing the digits 345678. The final two edit descriptors T15,I2 require that the value assigned to K, the digits 92, occupy output columns 15 and 16, replacing the character constant CD. Execution being complete, the final line of output is printed in columns 11 through 2Ø as 12AB92EF9Ø. Note that there is no overprinting. The entire line of output is held in temporary storage before printing occurs, with each subsequent character specified in a given output column, replacing the character previously specified in that column. The final arrangement of characters at the end of the execution of the second WRITE using the associated 2ØØ FORMAT statement is what is actually printed. There is no difference in the results when the output is displayed.

There are two additional positional edit descriptors: TL*n* and TR*n*. They accomplish little that cannot be accomplished by the T edit descriptor, but they do provide additional versatility. The TL*n* edit descriptor specifies that the starting column of the output field allocated by the edit descriptor immediately following is *n* columns to the left (backward) from the current position. TR*n* specifies the same positional relationship to the right (forward) from the current position. However, the programmer must be aware, when using these two additional edit descriptors, of the "*current position*." In either input or output, the current position is one column to the right of (past) the column from which data have just been read or the column that has just been printed. This is illustrated in Fig. 10-9. Note the first record of the data file. This record was set up to indicate column numbers for the following records. The first READ statement is a dummy statement to get past this first record. The second READ, using the associated 1ØØ FORMAT statement, causes the reading of the second record. The T9,I3 causes the reading for the value of J to start in column 9 and continue through column 11, assigning 987 to J. Note that the reading continues *through* column 11; there-

FIGURE 10-9 Effects of the TR and TL positional edit descriptors.

```
C234567890
      OPEN(3,FILE='FIG10-9.DAT')
      OPEN(7,FILE='PRN')
      READ(3,*)
      READ(3,100)J,K,L,M,N
  100 FORMAT(T9,I3,TL6,I3,TL6,I3,TR3,I3,TR2,I3)
      WRITE(7,200)J,K,L,M,N
  200 FORMAT(1X,5I5)
      READ(3,300)JJ,KK,LL,MM,NN
  300 FORMAT(T9,I3,TL7,I3,TL5,I3,TR4,I3,TR3,I3)
      WRITE(7,200)JJ,KK,LL,MM,NN
      STOP
      END
```

```
12345678901234567890
12345678987654321234
12345678987654321234
```

```
  987  678  345  987  432
  987  567  345  876  212
```

fore the current column is column 12. The TL6,I3 causes the reading for the value of K to start in column 6 (12 − 6), and the reading continues *through* column 8, assigning 678 to K. The current column is now column 9. The TL6,I3 is used again for the value of L. Columns 3 (9 − 6) through 5 are read, assigning 345 to L, and the current column is now column 6. Now TR3,I3 is used for the value of M. The reading starts in column 9 (6 + 3) and continues through column 11, assigning 987 to M. The current column is now column 12. Finally, TR2,I3 is used for the value of N. The reading starts in column 14 (12 + 2) and continues through column 16, assigning 432 to N. The values are printed by the first WRITE and 2ØØ FORMAT statements and confirm the above analysis. The last record is read by the third READ and 3ØØ FORMAT statements. It is left to the reader to check out the assignment of the indicated values to JJ, KK, MM, and NN. Obviously the use of the TL*n* and TR*n* edit descriptors requires more attention to detail than the use of the basic T*n* edit descriptor.

10-9 ADDITIONAL EDIT DESCRIPTORS

The edit descriptors previously discussed are the most useful in programming solutions for most science and engineering problems. However, there are other edit descriptors available that are of value in special conditions.

a The H Edit Descriptor

As with apostrophe editing, the H, or Hollerith,[†] edit descriptor can also be used for including character constants in the output. These character constants, like those resulting from apostrophe editing, are literally displayed or printed as part of the output. The general form for the H edit descriptor is:

*n*H *list of characters*

where *n* represents an integer constant corresponding to the number (count) of characters, including *blanks,* in the *list of characters* immediately following the letter H, which indicates a character constant. An example of the use of the H edit descriptor is:

```
    WRITE(*,1ØØ)
1ØØ FORMAT(3X,23HDIA.bCIRCUMFERENCEbAREA)
```

These statements will display:

```
bbbDIA.bCIRCUMFERENCEbAREA
```

[†]Named after Herman Hollerith of the U.S. Census Bureau, who developed a punched-card system for mechanically processing large volumes of statistical data. Hollerith's punched-card system was first used on a large scale to compile the census of 1890.

The 3X edit descriptor causes the skipping of the first three output columns; the 23H descriptor causes the character constant (the 23 characters following the H) to be printed just as listed, in the next 23 output columns, columns 4 through 26. When using the H edit descriptor, care must be exercised to make *n* equal the number of characters (including *blanks*) following the H. An error in counting will result in an execution error.

Another example of the use of the H edit descriptor is:

```
      X=3.75
      Y=25.50
      WRITE(*,100)X,Y
100   FORMAT(1X,7HWHENbX=,F6.2,8HbTHENbY=,F6.2)
```

The above program segment will display:

```
bWHENbX=bb3.75bTHENbY=b25.50
```

The single line of output is in sentence form with the numerical values assigned to X and Y displayed as specified by the F6.2 edit descriptor following each character constant specified by an H descriptor.

b Optional-Plus Editing

As has been stated, the positive algebraic sign is omitted from the output of positive values. There may be situations when the programmer desires positive algebraic signs to be included in the output. The SS and SP edit descriptors are used for this purpose. The SP edit descriptor causes the plus sign to be displayed for all subsequent positive values in that specification, and the SS edit descriptor causes the suppression of the plus sign for all subsequent positive values in that specification. These two edit descriptors obviously apply only to FORMAT statements associated with WRITE statements. The SS descriptor is the default condition in all output FORMAT statements.

The use of these edit descriptors is illustrated in Fig 10-10. The record of data file FIG10-10.DAT provides four real values (two in decimal form and two in exponential form). Since no negative signs are included, all values are read as positive values. The first line of output is printed under the control of the 200 FORMAT statement, where the four values are printed in the usual manner—without plus signs.

The second line of output is printed under the control of the 300 FORMAT statement. Note the SP edit descriptor associated with the 2F10.3 edit descriptor. Also note that the plus sign is printed for *all four* values. Therefore, the effect of the SP edit descriptor is applied to all subsequent edit descriptors.

The third line of output is printed under the control of the 400 FORMAT statement. Note that the SP and SS edit descriptors are alternated with the other edit descriptors. This line of output illustrates the result of the SP and SS edit descriptors in the output FORMAT specification.

```
C234567890
      OPEN(3,FILE='FIG10-10.DAT')
      OPEN(6,FILE='PRN')
      READ(3,100)A,B,C,D
  100 FORMAT(2F10.3,2E10.3)
      WRITE(6,200)A,B,C,D
  200 FORMAT(1X,2F10.3,2E15.7)
      WRITE(6,300)A,B,C,D
  300 FORMAT(1X,SP2F10.3,2E15.7)
      WRITE(6,400)A,B,C,D
  400 FORMAT(1X,SPF10.3,SSF10.3,SPE15.7,SSE15.7)
      STOP
      END
```

```
1234.567    56.789    4.321E1    0.789E6
```

```
 1234.567    56.789    .4321000E+02    .7890000E+06
+1234.567   +56.789   +.4321000E+02   +.7890000E+06
+1234.567    56.789   +.4321000E+02    .7890000E+06
```

FIGURE 10-10 Effects of optional-plus (SS and SP) editing.

c Blank-Interpretation Editing

Blanks occurring within the field width of a numerical value in an input record are interpreted as zeros. The BN edit descriptor in the FORMAT specification causes *blanks* in subsequent input fields to be ignored. The BZ edit descriptor equates *blanks* other than leading *blanks* to zero. The BZ edit descriptor is the default condition of all input FORMAT specifications.

The use of the BN and BZ edit descriptors is illustrated by Fig. 10-11 (see p. 314). The data file FIG1Ø-11.DAT is printed below the program and contains three identical records of integer data and three identical records of real data. The first record is established to provide column numbers in the data file and is read by the dummy READ (3,*) statement so that subsequent READ statements will read the actual records. Note the *blanks* in each record.

The first line of output shows the values read from the second record by the READ(3,1ØØ)I,J statement. Here the first two *blanks* of the first value in the record are ignored (because they are leading *blanks*), and the *blanks* in columns 6 and 7 are treated as zeros. The first three leading *blanks* of the second value are ignored, and the *blanks* in columns 17, 18, and 19 are treated as zeros.

The second line of output shows the values read from the third record by the READ(3,2ØØ)K,L statement. Here the first two leading *blanks* of the first value are ignored; the *blanks* in columns 6 and 7 are also ignored. The three leading *blanks* of the second value are ignored; the *blanks* in columns 17 and 18 are also ignored. Since the 2ØØ FORMAT statement contains the BN edit descriptor, its ability to ignore *blanks* is demonstrated. Note the difference in values resulting from reading the second record and the third record.

The third line of output shows the values read from the fourth record by the READ(3,3ØØ)M,N statement. The first value is read under the control of a BN edit descriptor and the resulting value is the same as in the second line of output.

```
C234567890
      OPEN(3,FILE='FIG10-11.DAT')
      OPEN(6,FILE='PRN')
      READ(3,*)
      READ(3,100)I,J
  100 FORMAT(2I10)
      READ(3,200)K,L
  200 FORMAT(BN2I10)
      READ(3,300)M,N
  300 FORMAT(BNI10,BZI10)
      READ(3,400)A,B
  400 FORMAT(F10.3,E10.3)
      READ(3,500)C,D
  500 FORMAT(BNF10.3,E10.3)
      READ(3,600)E,F
  600 FORMAT(BNF10.3,BZE10.3)
      WRITE(6,700)I,J
  700 FORMAT(2I15)
      WRITE(6,700)K,L
      WRITE(6,700)M,N
      WRITE(6,800)
  800 FORMAT('0')
      WRITE(6,900)A,B
  900 FORMAT(F20.7,E20.7)
      WRITE(6,900)C,D
      WRITE(6,900)E,F
      STOP
      END
```

```
12345678901234567890
  123  456    987   6
  123  456    987   6
  123  456    987   6
  20.  123 34.    1E3
  20.  123 34.    1E3
  20.  123 34.    1E3
```

```
       12300456        9870006
         123456           9876
         123456        9870006

     20.0012300     .3400010E+05
     20.1230000     .3410000E+05
     20.1230000     .3400010E+05
```

FIGURE 10-11 Effects of blank-interpretation (BN and BZ) editing.

The second value of the fourth record is read under the control of a BZ edit descriptor and the resulting value in the third line of output is the same as in the first line of output.

The last three records in Fig. 10-11 contain real values read in a similar manner as the first three records. The effects of reading *blanks* as zeros or of ignoring *blanks* is apparent from an examination of the output.

10-10 COMPLEX VALUES

Numbers that can be expressed as the ratio of two integers (3 can be expressed as 3:1, $\frac{1}{2}$ as 1:2, $5\frac{1}{4}$ as 21:4, etc.) are called *rational* numbers. All integers and fractions are rational numbers. When expressed as a decimal fraction, a rational number will either continue indefinitely, periodically repeating the same sequence of digits or terminate. For example, the ratio of 3:2 expressed as a decimal fraction will terminate as 1.5. The ratio of 11:7 expressed as decimal fraction 1.571428571428 . . . , will repeat the six-digit sequence of 571428 indefinitely.

A number that cannot be expressed as the ratio of two numbers is called an *irrational* number. Examples of irrational numbers are 3.141593 . . . , 2.718282 . . . , and 1.414214 . . . , which are the values of π, e, and $\sqrt{2}$, respectively. Square roots of imperfect squares are irrational numbers. When expressed as a decimal fraction, irrational numbers neither terminate nor repeat the same sequence of digits.

The rational and irrational numbers form a set of numbers called the *real-number system*. In the real-number system the product of two positive numbers or two negative numbers is a positive number. The square root of a negative number does not exist in the real-number system.

Computing the square root of a negative number requires an extension of the number system to include a class of numbers called *imaginary* numbers, numbers whose squares are negative. Imaginary numbers are represented by the mathematical symbol i or j, which has the value of $\sqrt{-1}$. (Mathematical discussions use i, while engineering discussions usually use j. In the following discussions i will be used.) The square root of -4, for example, can be written: $\sqrt{-4} = (\sqrt{4})(\sqrt{-1})$, which reduces to $2i$. When $2i$ is squared, the result is $4i^2$ or $4(-1)$ or -4. The square of an imaginary number is a negative number.

The rational and irrational numbers of the real-number system combined with imaginary numbers form the *complex-number* system. Complex numbers include all the rational and irrational numbers, all the imaginary numbers, and combinations of real and imaginary numbers. Complex numbers are written in the form: $a \pm bi$, where a represents a real number and bi an imaginary number.

The FORTRAN techniques previously discussed included calculations with numbers in the real-number system only. Special techniques are required for calculations with complex numbers. The expression $a \pm bi$ is a two-part complex number, with a representing the real part and bi representing the imaginary part. There is no provision in the FORTRAN character set for the imaginary-number symbol i. In FORTRAN, a complex constant is represented by an ordered pair of type-real numbers, the first number of the pair defining the real part and the second number defining the imaginary part. (It should be noted that the term *real* is used here in the mathematical sense to denote the first or nonimaginary part of a complex constant.) A complex value in FORTRAN consists of two type-real numbers. A FORTRAN complex value is written (A,B), the ordered pair of type-real numbers A and B being enclosed by parentheses, with the first—A (real part)—separated from the second—B (imaginary part)—by a comma. Because each complex value is made up of two numbers, two storage WORDs are required for each variable name to which a complex number is assigned. Integer variables declared COMPLEX and integer constants assigned to complex variable names are converted to type real.

Before the two numbers representing a complex constant can be assigned to a (single) variable name, that variable name must be declared complex by an appropriate type-declaration statement. The general form for the nonexecutable complex *type-declaration* statement is:

```
COMPLEX a,b(n),fname
```

where COMPLEX is the FORTRAN term that declares the variable names in the list to be complex, and *a*, *b*(*n*), and *fname* represent, respectively, a variable name, an array name, and a function name to which numerical constants are to be assigned. The COMPLEX declaration statement *must* be placed in the program *before* any executable statement. When a subscripted variable is declared in a COMPLEX statement, as is *b*(*n*) above, no additional DIMENSION statement is required. No flowchart symbol is available for the COMPLEX statement.

Complex constants can be assigned to complex-variable names by any of the applicable statements previously discussed for assigning type-real values to variable names, i.e., the DATA statement, the assignment statement, or the READ statement. The complex number 12.345 ± 67.89Ø*i*, expressed as numerical constants (12.345,67.89Ø) can be assigned to the declared complex variable A by:

(*a*) A DATA statement:

```
      COMPLEX A
      DATA A/(12.345,67.89Ø)/
```

(*b*) An ASSIGNMENT statement:

```
      COMPLEX A
      A=(12.345,67.89Ø)
```

(*c*) A READ statement:

```
      COMPLEX A
      OPEN(3,FILE='TEST.DAT')
      READ(3,1ØØ)A
 1ØØ  FORMAT(F6.3,F8.3)
```

Note the requirement for two edit descriptors, F6.3 and F8.3, in the FORMAT statement to read the two parts of the complex number from a data record (beginning in the first column) as follows:

```
12.345bb67.89Ø
```

The two parts of a complex constant may be written in the form above or in single- or double-precision exponential form (Sec. 11-4). If the complex constant is to be double-precision, the complex-variable name to which it will be assigned may be declared DOUBLE PRECISION as follows:

```
COMPLEX*16 A
DATA A/(Ø.12345D2,Ø.6789ØD2)/
```

If only one number (rather than an ordered pair) is assigned to a complex-variable name:

```
COMPLEX B
B=5.Ø
```

the result is that the single constant, 5.Ø in this case, is assigned as the real part of the complex number with zero implied as the imaginary part. The effect is the same as:

```
COMPLEX B
B=(5.Ø,Ø.Ø)
```

Note that in each of the above examples, a complex constant is assigned to a declared complex-variable name. When a complex number is represented by a variable name, i.e., when the two parts of the complex number are variables (rather than constants), a CMPLX intrinsic function must be used to establish the complex relationship of the two variables. For example:

```
COMPLEX A
X=12.345
Y=67.89Ø
A=CMPLX(X,Y)
```

The same complex value is assigned to the complex-variable name A as in the previous examples. The variable names X and Y are simple type-real variable names to which type-real constants have been assigned. When combined as the arguments of the CMPLX function, they define a complex number.

Complex numbers can be added, subtracted, multiplied, divided, and raised to a power. These arithmetic operations are performed according to the following mathematical relationships. If

$$x = a + bi \qquad \text{and} \qquad y = c + di$$

then

$$x + y = (a + c) + i(b + d)$$

$$x - y = (a - c) + i(b - d)$$

$$xy = (ac - bd) + i(ad + bc)$$

$$\frac{x}{y} = \frac{(ac + bd)}{(c^2 + d^2)} + \frac{i(bc - ad)}{(c^2 + d^2)}, \quad \text{where } y \neq \emptyset$$

$$x^n = (a^2 + b^2)^{n/2}(\cos n\theta + i \sin n\theta), \quad \text{where } \theta = \arctan(a/b)$$

Fortunately, the above equations need not be remembered. FORTRAN arithmetic operations with complex numbers are effected by simply writing appropriate assignment statements specifying the required arithmetic operation, being careful to observe the rules that apply to complex constants and variables. Execution of one of these statements automatically calls a system-supplied subroutine to perform the calculations necessary to evaluate the specified complex-arithmetic operation. The following examples illustrate how assignment statements that include complex numbers can be written:

(a)

```
COMPLEX X,Y,R,S,T,U,V
X=(1.23456,6.54321)
Y=(5.123,8.765)
R=X+Y
S=X-Y
T=X*Y
U=X/Y
V=X**2
```

(b)

```
COMPLEX X,Y,R,S,T,U,V,
A=1.23456
B=6.54321
C=5.123
D=8.765
N=2
X=CMPLX(A,B)
Y=CMPLX(C,D)
R=X+Y
S=X-Y
T=X*Y
U=X/Y
V=X**N
```

Figure 10-12 illustrates a complete program using complex-number calculations, and Fig. 10-13 (see p. 320) illustrates the output of that program.

Certain intrinsic functions described in Chap. 5 can be modified for use with complex numbers, namely, ABS, COS, EXP, LOG, SIN, and SQRT. They are made complex by placing a C before the function name (CABS, CCOS, CEXP, CLOG, CSIN, and CSQRT), as shown in Table 10-1 (see pp. 321–322). Arguments of complex functions must be complex. The following example illustrates the use of a complex variable as the arguments of a complex intrinsic function:

```
COMPLEX X,A
X=(1.23,4.32)
A=CSQRT(X)
```

Complex numbers *cannot* be used in the arithmetic expression of an arithmetic IF statement or in the logical expression of a logical IF statement. Complex numbers *cannot* be used as exponents or subscripts. Any arithmetic expression containing a complex number is called a *complex expression*. The result of a complex expression must be assigned to a complex-variable name.

The values assigned to complex-variable names can be displayed in the same manner as all variables, using either the list-directed WRITE statement or the format-directed WRITE statement with an associated FORMAT statement. Since there are two parts to a complex number, two edit descriptors must be included in the FORMAT specification for each complex variable in the associated WRITE list. The same applies to the READ statement. For example, the program:

```
OPEN(3,FILE='CHAP1Ø.DAT')
COMPLEX A
READ(3,1ØØ)A
```

```
C234567890
      COMPLEX A,B,C
      OPEN(3,FILE='FIG10-12.DAT')
      OPEN(6,FILE='PRN')
      READ(3,100)A
  100 FORMAT(2F10.5)
      WRITE(6,200)
  200 FORMAT(5X,'THE VALUE OF A IS:')
      WRITE(6,300)A
  300 FORMAT(1X,'REAL PART =',F10.5,/,1X,'IMAGINARY PART =',F10.5,//)
      B=(5.123,8.765)
      WRITE(6,400)
  400 FORMAT(5X,'THE VALUE OF B IS:')
      WRITE(6,300)B
      C=A+B
      WRITE(6,500)
  500 FORMAT(5X,'THE VALUE OF A+B IS:')
      WRITE(6,300)C
      C=A-B
      WRITE(6,600)
  600 FORMAT(5X,'THE VALUE OF A-B IS:')
      WRITE(6,300)C
      C=A*B
      WRITE(6,700)
  700 FORMAT(5X,'THE VALUE OF A*B IS:')
      WRITE(6,300)C
      C=A/B
      WRITE(6,800)
  800 FORMAT(5X,'THE VALUE OF A/B IS:')
      WRITE(6,300)C
      C=A**2
      WRITE(6,900)
  900 FORMAT(5X,'THE VALUE OF A**2 IS:')
      WRITE(6,300)C
      STOP
      END
```

```
1.23456   6.54321
```

FIGURE 10-12 Assigning complex values and complex operations.

```
100 FORMAT(F6.3,F8.3)
    OPEN(6,FILE='PRN')
    WRITE(6,200)A
200 FORMAT(2X,F6.3,F7.2)
    END
```

Data File CHAP10.DAT
*bb*12.345*bb*67.89

will print:

*bb*12.345*bb*67.89

```
      THE VALUE OF A IS:
REAL PART =    1.23456
IMAGINARY PART =    6.54321


      THE VALUE OF B IS:
REAL PART =    5.12300
IMAGINARY PART =    8.76500


      THE VALUE OF A+B IS:
REAL PART =    6.35756
IMAGINARY PART =   15.30821


      THE VALUE OF A-B IS:
REAL PART =   -3.88844
IMAGINARY PART =   -2.22179


      THE VALUE OF A*B IS:
REAL PART = -51.02659
IMAGINARY PART =   44.34179


      THE VALUE OF A/B IS:
REAL PART =     .61779
IMAGINARY PART =     .22024


      THE VALUE OF A**2 IS:
REAL PART = -41.28946
IMAGINARY PART =   16.15597
```

FIGURE 10-13 Complex output of Fig. 10-12.

The list-directed WRITE statement may be used to display complex values, as illustrated in the following program segment:

```
COMPLEX A,B
OPEN(6,FILE='PRN')
A=(1.57,Ø.3E-17)
B=(-Ø.13,1.26)
WRITE(6,*)A,B
END
```

will print:

```
(1.57ØØØØØ,3.ØØØØØØE-Ø18)      (-1.3ØØØØØ,1.26ØØØØØ)
```

Figure 10-14 (see p. 322) illustrates other examples of the input and output of complex numbers. Note the list-directed display of the sine of the complex variable A.

10-11 ROUTING PROGRAM OUTPUT TO DISKETTE STORAGE

The results of a FORTRAN program (output) can be displayed on the screen or printed on a sheet of paper, depending on how the OPEN and WRITE statements

TABLE 10-1 INTRINSIC FUNCTIONS WITH CORRESPONDING COMPLEX FUNCTIONS

Definition	Single-precision (Chap.5)	Complex form (Chap. 10)
Square root	SQRT(*a*)	CSQRT(*z*)
Absolute value	ABS(*a*) ABS(*k*) IABS(*k*)	CABS(*z*)
Type conversion:		
Change to integer	INT(*a*) INT(*k*) IFIX(*a*)	
Change to real	REAL(*k*) REAL(*a*) FLOAT(*k*)	
Exponential	EXP(*a*)	CEXP(*z*)
Logarithm:		
Common	LOG1Ø(*a*) ALOG1Ø(*a*)	
Natural	LOG(*a*) ALOG(*a*)	CLOG(*z*)
Trigonometric:		
Sine	SIN(*a*)	CSIN(*z*)
Cosine	COS(*a*)	CCOS(*z*)
Tangent	TAN(*a*)	
Arcsine	ASIN(*s*)	
Arccosine	ACOS(*cs*)	
Arctangent	ATAN(*t*) ATAN2(*y*,*x*)	
Maximum	MAX(*a*,*b*,*c*,...) MAX(*i*,*j*,*k*,...) MAXØ(*i*,*j*,*k*,...) MAX1(*a*,*b*,*c*,...) AMAXØ(*i*,*j*,*k*,...) AMAX1(*a*,*b*,*c*,...)	
Minimum	MIN(*a*,*b*,*c*,...) MIN(*i*,*j*,*k*,...) MINØ(*i*,*j*,*k*,...) MIN1(*a*,*b*,*c*,...) AMINØ(*i*,*j*,*k*,...) AMIN1(*a*,*b*,*c*,...)	
Truncation	AINT(*a*)	
Rounding:		
To real	ANINT(*a*)	
To integer	NINT(*a*)	

TABLE 10-1 INTRINSIC FUNCTIONS (*continued*)

Definition	Single-precision (Chap.5)	Complex form (Chap. 10)
Remainder	MOD(*a*,*b*)	
	MOD(*i*,*j*)	
	AMOD(*a*,*b*)	
Complex:		
Convert to	CMPLX(*x*,*y*)	
	CMPLX(*x*)	
Isolate real part	REAL(*z*)	
Isolate imaginary part	AIMAG(*z*)	
Conjugate	CONJG(*z*)	
Double-precision,convert to	DBLE(*x*)	

FIGURE 10-14 Assigning complex values and complex operations.

```
C234567890
      COMPLEX A,B,C,CMPLX,CSQRT,CSIN
      OPEN(6,FILE='PRN')
      X=3.45
      Y=1.23
      A=CMPLX(X,Y)
      WRITE(6,100)
  100 FORMAT(5X,'THE VALUE OF A IS:')
      WRITE(6,200)A
  200 FORMAT(1X,'REAL PART =',F10.5,/,1X,'IMAGINARY PART =',F10.5,//)
      B=5.0
      WRITE(6,300)
  300 FORMAT(5X,'THE VALUE OF B IS:')
      WRITE(6,200)B
      C=CSQRT(A)
      WRITE(6,400)
  400 FORMAT(5X,'THE VALUE OF THE SQUARE ROOT OF A IS:')
      WRITE(6,200)C
      C=CSIN(A)
      WRITE(6,*)'THE VALUE OF THE SINE OF A IS:',C
      STOP
      END
```

```
     THE VALUE OF A IS:
REAL PART =    3.45000
IMAGINARY PART =    1.23000


     THE VALUE OF B IS:
REAL PART =    5.00000
IMAGINARY PART =     .00000


     THE VALUE OF THE SQUARE ROOT OF A IS:
REAL PART =    1.88583
IMAGINARY PART =     .32612


THE VALUE OF THE SINE OF A IS: (-5.636042E-001,-1.4906540)
```

are coded (Sec. 3-12). Instructions can also be written to route the output directly to an old file (a file already existing on the diskette) or to open and store the results on a new file. It should be noted that columns 1 through 8Ø of the record may be used for storage. Column 1 is not reserved for vertical control.

In Fig. 10-15, PROGRAM ONE generates a 3-row, 5-column integer array called K. The OPEN statement opens a new file, FILEONE.DAT, which did not previously exist on the diskette. The WRITE statements route the output directly into this data file. This file is known as a *sequential-access file*. Data can be read from or written to a sequential-access file in sequential order only. Note the STATUS='NEW' term in the OPEN statement. This indicates that a new file is being opened. A display of the contents of FILEONE.DAT after the execution of the program follows the listing of PROGRAM ONE. FILEONE.DAT now contains the array K.

PROGRAM TWO in Fig. 10-16 (see p. 324) generates a 4-row, 3-column real array called A. The OPEN statement, containing the term STATUS='OLD', indicates that the file to which the output will be routed is an existing file with the filename and extension FILEONE.DAT. Since the new array A is to be added to the file without deleting the old array K (from PROGRAM ONE, Fig. 10-15), the first record of array A must begin following the last record of array K. The IF, READ, and GOTO statements preceding the WRITE statements "read through" the file, assigning the first value in each successive record to X but not changing the records of the existing file in any way. When the end-of-file is reached (the EOF[†] expression in the IF statement is true), control is transferred to the first WRITE statement, and the new values are *added* to FILEONE.DAT beginning with the next data record following the last data record of the existing file. Note

[†]This is a Disk Operating System (DOS) command that is acceptable to FORTRAN. For more information, refer to the DOS Manual.

FIGURE 10-15 Storing generated data in a new file.

```
C234567890
      PROGRAM ONE

      DIMENSION K(3,5)
      DO 10 I=1,3
      DO 10 J=1,5
      K(I,J)=I*J
   10 CONTINUE

      OPEN(6,FILE='FILEONE.DAT',STATUS='NEW')

      WRITE(6,*)
      WRITE(6,100)((K(I,J),J=1,5),I=1,3)
  100 FORMAT(1X,5I5)
      STOP
      END
```

```
    1    2    3    4    5
    2    4    6    8   10
    3    6    9   12   15
```

```
C234567890
      PROGRAM TWO

      DIMENSION A(4,3)
      DO 10 I=1,4
      DO 10 J=1,3
      A(I,J)=REAL(I+J)
   10 CONTINUE

      OPEN(6,FILE='FILEONE.DAT',STATUS='OLD')

   15 IF(EOF(6))GOTO 20
      READ(6,*)X
      GOTO 15

   20 WRITE(6,*)
      WRITE(6,200)((A(I,J),J=1,3),I=1,4)
  200 FORMAT(3X,3F5.1)
      STOP
      END
```

```
   1    2    3    4    5
   2    4    6    8   10
   3    6    9   12   15

   2.0  3.0  4.0
   3.0  4.0  5.0
   4.0  5.0  6.0
   5.0  6.0  7.0
```

FIGURE 10-16 Storing generated data in an old file while saving old data.

that the new data begins with a *blank* record created by the "dummy" WRITE statement. A display of the contents of FILEONE.DAT follows the PROGRAM TWO listing. FILEONE.DAT now contains the array K from PROGRAM ONE, followed by the array A from PROGRAM TWO.

In Fig. 10-17, PROGRAM THREE generates a 2-row, 6-column real array B. FILEONE.DAT, containing both the array K from PROGRAM ONE and the array A from PROGRAM TWO, is reopened as an old file. This time no provision is made for retaining the old files, and the entire contents of the file are replaced with the new data. A display of the contents of FILEONE.DAT follows the PROGRAM THREE listing. Note that the file contains only the array B, the last data written to it. The old files, arrays K and A, have been erased.

In PROGRAM TWO and PROGRAM THREE, the STATUS='OLD' term in the OPEN statement is not necessary since the default condition is 'OLD'. The term was included in these two programs to emphasize the reopening of an existing ('OLD') file.

10-12 THE ASCII CHARACTERS IN FORTRAN

In addition to the characters on the keyboard of the personal computer, the characters of the American Standard Code for Information Interchange (ASCII) may be included in the output of a FORTRAN program. Each character in the ASCII lists (Figs. 10-18 and 10-19, pp. 326, 327) is assigned a code number. The de-

```
C234567890
      PROGRAM THREE

      DIMENSION B(2,6)
      K=0
      DO 10 I=1,2
      DO 10 J=1,6
      K=K+1
      B(I,J)=REAL(K)
   10 CONTINUE

      OPEN(6,FILE='FILEONE.DAT',STATUS='OLD')

      WRITE(6,*)
      WRITE(6,300)((B(I,J),J=1,6),I=1,2)
  300 FORMAT(3X,6F5.1)
      STOP
      END
```

FIGURE 10-17 Storing generated data in an old file and replacing previous data.

```
   1.0  2.0  3.0  4.0  5.0  6.0
   7.0  8.0  9.0 10.0 11.0 12.0
```

sired character can be displayed by using the assigned code number as the argument of a CHAR function in the WRITE list with an A edit descriptor in the specification of the associated FORMAT statement. For example, the Greek letters π, Σ, and θ can be displayed by:

```
    WRITE(*,1ØØ)CHAR(227),CHAR(228),CHAR(233)
1ØØ FORMAT(3A5)
```

where 227, 228, and 233—the arguments of the CHAR function—are the ASCII numbers assigned to the characters π, Σ, and θ, respectively.

The same output can be obtained by:

```
    WRITE(*,2ØØ)
2ØØ FORMAT(4X,'π',4X,'Σ',4X,'θ')
```

where the characters π, Σ, and θ are included as character constants in the FORMAT specification. The characters π, Σ, and θ are created by holding down the Alt key and keying in the ASCII code numbers, 227, 228, and 233, respectively, on the numeric keypad.

The ASCII characters may be assigned to character-variable names by a DATA statement, a READ statement, or an assignment statement by first declaring the variable type in a CHARACTER declaration statement. The ASCII character is then entered as a character constant by enclosing in apostrophes, thus: 'π'. Examples of this are:

```
    CHARACTER I,J,K
    DATA I,J,K/'π','Σ','θ'/
```

FIGURE 10-18 ASCII character codes.

ASCII value	Character	ASCII value	Character	ASCII value	Character
032	(space)	064	@	096	‘
033	!	065	A	097	a
034	’’	066	B	098	b
035	#	067	C	099	c
036	$	068	D	100	d
037	%	069	E	101	e
038	&	070	F	102	f
039	’	071	G	103	g
040	(	072	H	104	h
041	)	073	I	105	i
042	*	074	J	106	j
043	+	075	K	107	k
044	,	076	L	108	l
045	-	077	M	109	m
046	.	078	N	110	n
047	/	079	O	111	o
048	0	080	P	112	p
049	1	081	Q	113	q
050	2	082	R	114	r
051	3	083	S	115	s
052	4	084	T	116	t
053	5	085	U	117	u
054	6	086	V	118	v
055	7	087	W	119	w
056	8	088	X	120	x
057	9	089	Y	121	y
058	:	090	Z	122	z
059	;	091	[	123	{
060	<	092	\	124	¦
061	=	093	]	125	}
062	>	094	∧	126	~
063	?	095	—	127	⌂

FIGURE 10-19 More ASCII character codes.

ASCII value	Character	ASCII value	Character	ASCII value	Character	ASCII value	Character
128	Ç	160	á	192	└	224	α
129	ü	161	í	193	┴	225	β
130	é	162	ó	194	┬	226	Γ
131	â	163	ú	195	├	227	π
132	ä	164	ñ	196	─	228	Σ
133	à	165	Ñ	197	┼	229	σ
134	å	166	ª	198	╞	230	μ
135	ç	167	º	199	╟	231	τ
136	ê	168	¿	200	╚	232	Φ
137	ë	169	⌐	201	╔	233	Θ
138	è	170	¬	202	╩	234	Ω
139	ï	171	½	203	╦	235	δ
140	î	172	¼	204	╠	236	∞
141	ì	173	i	205	═	237	Ø
142	Ä	174	«	206	╬	238	∈
143	Å	175	»	207	╧	239	∩
144	É	176	░	208	╨	240	≡
145	æ	177	▒	209	╤	241	±
146	Æ	178	▓	210	╥	242	≥
147	ô	179	│	211	╙	243	≤
148	ö	180	┤	212	╘	244	⌠
149	ò	181	╡	213	╒	245	⌡
150	û	182	╢	214	╓	246	÷
151	ù	183	╖	215	╫	247	≈
152	ÿ	184	╕	216	╪	248	°
153	Ö	185	╣	217	┘	249	•
154	Ü	186	║	218	┌	250	·
155	¢	187	╗	219	█	251	√
156	£	188	╝	220	▄	252	^{n}
157	¥	189	╜	221	▌	253	^{2}
158	Pt	190	╛	222	▐	254	■
159	ƒ	191	┐	223	▀	255	(blank 'FF')

or:

```
WRITE(*,*)'Key in character constants'
READ(*,*)I,J,K
```

The ASCII characters π, Σ, and θ are created by holding down the Alt key and keying in 227, 228, and 233, respectively, on the numeric keypad, enclosing the character in apostrophes, and separating each character by at least one *blank*, or a comma.

Assignment of ASCII character constants may be made to type-character variables in an assignment statement as follows:

```
CHARACTER I,J,K
I=CHAR(227)
J=CHAR(228)
K=CHAR(233)
```

or:

```
CHARACTER I,J,K
I='π'
J='Σ'
K='θ'
```

The techniques described above and the resulting output are illustrated in Fig. 10-20. Note that the CHAR function cannot be used in the DATA statement or in the READ statement.

The following characters can be combined to form plane geometric figures with horizontal and vertical sides and right-angled corners:

Code	179	196	218	191	192	217	197	193	194	195	180
Character	│	─	┌	┐	└	┘	┼	┴	┬	├	┤

Assuming a dot-matrix printer that prints 10 columns per inch in a horizontal direction and 6 columns per inch in a vertical direction, it is possible to "draw" rectangles with specific linear dimensions. Since the characters shown above are printed in the center of the column-row block, it is necessary to print one more column or row than calculations might indicate to obtain the precise dimension required. For example, 11 columns and 7 rows of characters are required to draw a square 1 by 1 in. Figure 10-21 (see p. 330) lists the FORTRAN source program for drawing a 3-in (wide) by 2-in (high) rectangle divided into four equal quadrants by horizontal and vertical lines. (Note that the rectangle in Fig. 10-21 has been reduced by one-third, since all figures in this text are reduced by that amount from the original size.) Figure 10-22 (see p. 331) lists the FORTRAN source program for drawing a simple bar graph.

```
C234567890
      CHARACTER I,J,K,L,M,N,A,B,C,X,Y,Z
      OPEN(3,FILE='PRN')

      WRITE(3,100)CHAR(224),CHAR(225),CHAR(226)
  100 FORMAT(/,3A5)

      WRITE(3,200)
  200 FORMAT(/,4X,'π',4X,'Σ',4X,'Φ')

      DATA I,J,K /'Ω','ε','μ' /
      WRITE(3,100)I,J,K

      WRITE(*,*)'KEY IN ASCII CHARACTERS 236, 246, 251'
      WRITE(*,*)'AS LITERAL CHARACTER CONSTANTS'
      READ(*,*)L,M,N
      WRITE(3,100)L,M,N

      A=CHAR(241)
      B=CHAR(242)
      C=CHAR(243)
      WRITE(3,100)A,B,C

      X='½'
      Y='¼'
      Z='°'
      WRITE(3,100)X,Y,Z

      STOP
      END
```

```
α    β    Γ

π    Σ    Φ

Ω    ε    μ

∞    ÷    √

±    ≥    ≤

½    ¼    °
```

FIGURE 10-20 Use of ASCII characters.

The ASCII character codes listed in Figs. 10-18 and 10-19 and used in the examples are not interpreted the same way by all computers and printers. Consult the appropriate operations manuals utilizing these character codes.

PROBLEMS

10-1 The professor of Prob. 8-23 now wants to completely computerize her term-end grade computations. She will still give six examinations during the term, but they will be of equal weight. She then wants to drop out the lowest score of the six. The numerical term grade will thus be the average of the five highest examinations. She wants the cutoff scores for the A, B, C, and D grades to be 92, 83, 74, and 65 percent, respectively, of the highest student average.

```
C234567890
      OPEN(3,FILE='PRN')
      WRITE(3,100)CHAR(218),(CHAR(196),I=1,14),CHAR(194),
     $(CHAR(196),I=1,14),CHAR(191)
  100 FORMAT(20X,31A1)
      WRITE(3,200)(CHAR(179),CHAR(179),CHAR(179),I=1,5)
  200 FORMAT(20X,A1,14X,A1,14X,A1)
      WRITE(3,100)CHAR(195),(CHAR(196),I=1,14),CHAR(197),
     $(CHAR(196),I=1,14),CHAR(180)
      DO 10 N=1,5
   10 WRITE(3,300)
  300 FORMAT(20X,'│',14X,'│',14X,'│')
      WRITE(3,400)
  400 FORMAT(20X,'└',14('─'),'┴',14('─'),'┘')
      STOP
      END
```

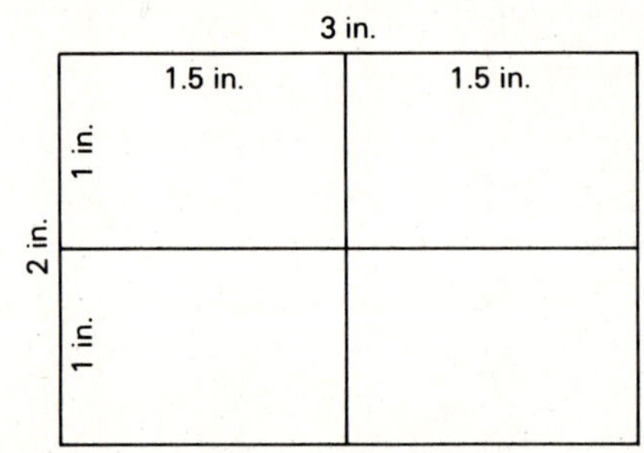

FIGURE 10-21 Use of ASCII characters in constructing a box. (The box is reduced by one-third.)

Write a program that will read up to 100 social security numbers and the scores achieved for each examination by each student. Then determine the numerical term grade and the appropriate letter grade by using the given cutoffs. A grade of F will be given for a term grade below the 65 percent cutoff. The output should give the highest term grade, the cutoff scores, and the average term grade, then print each student's SSN, the scores on each examination, the numerical term grade, and the corresponding letter grade. The SSN should be read as alphanumeric data so that names might be substituted without any change to the program.

10-2 Another teacher also decides to computerize his system of giving final grades. He gives five quizzes, ten homework assignments, and a final examination, all graded on the basis of 100. The quiz average counts 40 percent, the homework average 10 percent, and the final examination 50 percent of the term grade. The grades given are A, B, C, D, and F. There is to be no rounding of averages until the numerical value of the term grade has been determined, and that value will be rounded to the nearest unit value. The grade of A is given for 91 to 100, B for 81 to 90, C for 71 to 80, D for 61 to 70, and F for 60 and below. There will be no more than 35 students in a class.

The term grades are to be printed in order; i.e., all the A's, then all the B's, etc. The grade for each student is to be identified by the student's social security number. Also show the homework average, quiz average, and the final examination grade.

```
C234567890
      OPEN(3,FILE='PRN')
      WRITE(3,100)
  100 FORMAT(///,T32,'BAR GRAPH OF GRADES')
      WRITE(3,150)
  150 FORMAT(T15,'|')
      WRITE(3,200)
  200 FORMAT(T13,'A',1X,'|',22('▓'),1X,'22',13X,'┌',11('─'),'┐')
      WRITE(3,250)
  250 FORMAT(T15,'|',38X,'|',1X,'TOTAL 134',1X,'|')
      WRITE(3,300)
  300 FORMAT(T9,'G',T13,'B',1X,'|',30('▓'),1X,'30',5X,'└',11('─'),'┘')
      WRITE(3,350)
  350 FORMAT(T9,'R',T15,'|')
      WRITE(3,400)
  400 FORMAT(T9,'A',T13,'C',1X,'|',48('▓'),1X,'48')
      WRITE(3,450)
  450 FORMAT(T9,'D',T15,'|')
      WRITE(3,500)
  500 FORMAT(T9,'E',T13,'D',1X,'|',24('▓'),1X,'24')
      WRITE(3,550)
  550 FORMAT(T15,'|')
      WRITE(3,600)
  600 FORMAT(T13,'F',1X,'|',10('▓'),1X,'10')
      WRITE(3,650)
  650 FORMAT(T15,'|')
      WRITE(3,700)
  700 FORMAT(T15,'└',5(9('─'),'┴'))
      WRITE(3,750)
  750 FORMAT(T15,'0',T24,'10',T34,'20',T44,'30',T54,'40',T64,'50')
      WRITE(3,800)
  800 FORMAT(/,T36,'FREQUENCY')
      STOP
      END
```

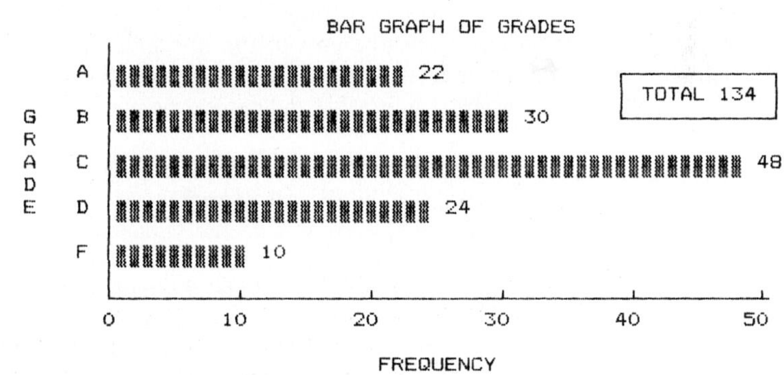

FIGURE 10-22 Use of ASCII characters in constructing a bar graph.

Use a FUNCTION subprogram to determine the term grade, and a SUBROUTINE subprogram to arrange the grades and other required data in order. The record for each student should show the social security number, the five quiz grades, the ten homework grades, and the final examination grade. Prepare a data file for a suitable number of students, and test the program.

10-3 Cryptography is an interesting pastime. Most codes are based on some form of standard shift from the character in the message to be encoded to a corresponding character in the coded message; for example, the letter A is always represented by D. Decoding an encoded message then follows the procedure in reverse. A trained cryptographer can easily discover the encoding process if a number of encoded messages are available by counting the frequency of the use of each character and applying known cryptography tests.

However, if the encoding process uses a random shift (the letter A could be represented by an A, B, C, D, etc.) depending upon a random-number list, the cryptographer would find it difficult to break the code. Write a program that will randomly encode and decode such messages of up to 5Ø characters in length.

To do this you will need your own random-number generator, which should generate the integers from Ø to 9. Use a FUNCTION subprogram for the generator. Then you will need a standard alphabet against which the various characters in a message can be compared. This alphabet should include the 26 alphabetic characters, the digits from Ø to 9, and a *blank* (for the space between words). When a match is found between the character in the message and the character in the standard alphabet, the encoding-decoding shift is determined. Since the encoding shift will be an integer from Ø to 9, the decoding shift must be the same as the encoding shift. This means several things:

(a) The random-number generator must be started with the same initial values when starting the encoding or decoding of each message.

(b) To accommodate both the encoding and decoding processes, the standard alphabet must be extended to repeat the first 9 characters of the alphabet. Then the first 37 characters of the extended alphabet can be used with a plus shift when encoding, and the last 37 characters with a negative shift when decoding.

(c) The storage locations (5Ø) for each original message and the encoded or decoded message should be first loaded with *blanks* to ensure that no characters remain from a previous message.

Use separate SUBROUTINE subprograms for encoding and decoding. Note that some way must be provided to determine which SUBROUTINE is desired. When the program is written, use it to encode several messages. Then store the encoded messages in a data file and decode them.

10-4 This is an extension of the previous problem. The maximum number of characters in a message is now 7Ø. All numerical values are to be spelled out so that a value cannot be completely lost if one character becomes garbled in transmission of the message. On the other hand, in order that every character of a message can be encoded, the character 9 is to be substituted for the space between words during the encoding process. Hence the standard alphabet need contain only the alphabet, a *blank,* and a 9, to be repeated sufficiently to allow for the random shift during encoding and decoding. It is always necessary that *blank* characters end the message; hence, all spaces of a message should be loaded with *blanks* before the reading of each message. This also should be done for the encoded and decoded messages.

The encoding SUBROUTINE must contain a test for one or two *blanks*. If there is only one *blank,* it is the space between words. A 9 should be substituted for the *blank* and then the 9 encoded. If there are two successive *blanks,* it is the end of the message, and encoding should cease. Encoded messages are to be transmitted in groups of five characters. If the message being encoded does not contain a multiple of five characters, the encoding SUBPROGRAM must contain a provision to add sufficient 9s to achieve the required number of characters. The arrangement of the encoded message into groups of five can be done with the FORMAT statement. There must also be a provision for handling any character that is not in the standard alphabet.

The decoding SUBROUTINE must contain a test for one or two *blanks*. If there is only one *blank*, it is the space between groups of five and must be removed from the encoded message. If there are two successive *blanks*, it is the end of the message and decoding should cease. To make the decoded message more readable, all 9s in the decoded message should be changed to *blanks*. Then the decoded message will appear exactly like the original clear text message. There must be a provision for handling any character not in the standard alphabet.

A FUNCTION subprogram should be used to generate the random shift for each character. Write and run such a program. Arrange to test both encoding and decoding SUBROUTINES.

10-5 Write a program that will print the calendar for any year. Revise Prob. 7-13 to be used as a SUBROUTINE for determining the first day of January for the year desired. The year is to be entered via the keyboard. Consider Sunday as day 1 and Saturday as day 7. For each month provide a heading showing the month and year, plus headings for the days of the week. There must be a provision for February to have 29 days if the year is a leap year (divisible by 4 but not by 400).

10-6 An old, but still used, numbering system is the Roman numeral system, which uses letters instead of the common Arabic numerals. In the Roman system, M = 1ØØØ, D = 5ØØ, C = 1ØØ, L = 5Ø, X = 1Ø, V = 5, and I = 1. Numbers are formed by placing the necessary letters in descending order and then adding them. For example, LX = 6Ø and LXXV = 75. There are two important exceptions to this. Multiples of 4 and 9 (4Ø and 9Ø, 4ØØ and 9ØØ, etc.) consist of two letters where the first is subtracted from the second. For example, IV = 4, IX = 9, XL = 4Ø, XC = 9Ø, CD = 4ØØ, and CM = 9ØØ. The concept of zero does not exist in the Roman system.

Write a program that enters Arabic numbers via the keyboard and converts them to Roman numerals. Test the program with 2934, 1984, 9ØØ, 841, 485, 249, 74, and 6Ø.

10-7 There are applications that sometimes call for the manipulation of alphanumeric information. One common application is the comparing of alpha data. For example, one could compare the two words SLIP and LISP and find that each contains the same four letters, or compare the words KEY and LET and find that only one letter is common. Prepare a program that will read two words of up to 1Ø letters and compare the letters of one with the other. Keep a count of the number of common letters, and print. Note that as the number of letters in each word may vary, there must be some way to erase each word after its use.

CHAPTER **11**

COMPUTER ACCURACY

11-1 INTRODUCTION

With the first discovery that the computer is not the unfailingly accurate calculator of all values to any precision, the new programmer discards an illusion common to many people unfamiliar with computer operations. After recovering from this initial shock, the programmer can settle down to the real world of computers with a better appreciation of their actual capabilities and limitations. Some of the limitations in the accuracy of computer calculations and what can be done to identify and correct them will be described in this chapter.

11-2 INCREMENTAL INACCURACIES

In the early descriptions of the capabilities and characteristics of the digital computer (Sec. 1-4) it was noted that only those numbers that can be represented in the binary number system by the presence or absence of a power of 2 can be stored as an exact value. This includes all whole numbers (1, 1.Ø, 3.Ø, 4.Ø, etc.) and such fractional values as one-half (Ø.5), one-fourth (Ø.25), one-eighth (Ø.125), etc., which have a denominator that is a power of 2. All other fractions are stored as a close approximation of their actual value. The values associated with π (3.141593) or one-third (Ø.3333333), for example, are usually defined and stored to a precision of only seven significant digits. When used in repetitive calculations with many iterations, these "approximate" values can lead to significant inaccuracies in the last digits of the resulting value.

Figure 11-1 (see p. 336) shows what happens when a number is incremented by a value such as Ø.Ø1, which is not stored as an exact value. Starting with an initial value of 1.Ø, each successive value of VAR should be Ø.Ø1 greater than its previous value. When the two-hundredth value of VAR is reached, the value should be 2.99; however, the cumulative inaccuracies caused by the approximation of Ø.Ø1 cause the result to have a slightly different value. A programmer unaware of these inaccuracies and expecting the value of the two-hundredth increment to be exactly 2.99 might write a logical IF statement.

```
IF(VAR(I).EQ.2.99)GOTO 6Ø
```

Transfer to statement 6Ø will never occur; the logical expression will always be false because the value of VAR will never be exactly equal to 2.99. With the understanding that the value of VAR might never be exactly 2.99, how can the logical expression be written to be true when the value of VAR is compared with 2.99, the supposed two-hundredth value?

```
C234567890
      DIMENSION VAR(200)
      OPEN(6,FILE='PRN')
      VAR(1)=1.0
      DELTA=0.01
      DO 10 I=2,200
   10 VAR(I)=VAR(I-1)+DELTA
      WRITE(6,100)VAR(200)
  100 FORMAT(5X,'VAR(200) =',F10.7)
      STOP
      END
```

```
     VAR(200) = 2.9899980
```

FIGURE 11-1 Precision loss due to the decimal fraction incrementing value.

The programmer must choose some acceptable range of accuracy. The difference between the exact and calculated values may be positive or negative (the computed value assigned to VAR may be slightly more or slightly less than 2.99) with the magnitude of the difference depending on the WORD size. Since both the algebraic sign and magnitude of the difference are unique to the system, no general rules can be formulated that apply to all situations. In the present example, from the result of Fig. 11-1, it would seem safe to assume that the calculated value of VAR would be within ± Ø.ØØ1 of the mathematically exact value. Thus the following logical expression might be used:

```
IF(VAR(I).GT.2.989.AND.VAR(I).LT.2.991)GOTO 6Ø
```

This expression is written to bracket the mathematically exact value of VAR and is true for no other value assigned to VAR. The GOTO 6Ø statement will be executed, transferring control to statement 6Ø after the two-hundredth value has been calculated and assigned.

11-3 CALCULATION INACCURACIES

When the computer-calculated results do not correspond with anticipated values, the fault is usually in a logic error made by the programmer. However, sometimes the discrepancy is due to the limitations of the calculating capabilities of the computer.

Example 11-1

Assume a flat sheet of thin metal with dimensions *A* and *B*, as shown in Fig. 11-2(*a*). Squares having a side length *X* are removed from each of the four corners of the sheet, forming a pattern which can then be folded into a box [Fig. 11-2(*b*)]. What value of *X* will result in the box of maximum volume? The problem can be solved by applying the calculus or by iteration (trial and error), i.e., assuming different values for *X* over a range of values by bracketing the maximum volume and comparing the results until the largest

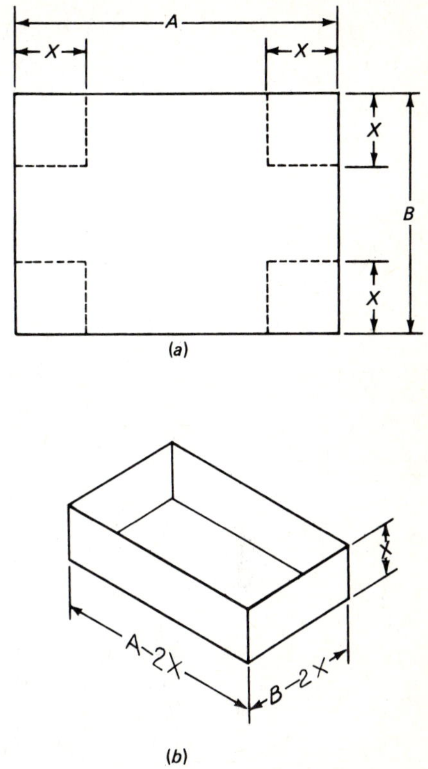

FIGURE 11-2 Physical concept of the maximum-value problem.

volume has been determined. The logic of this iterative method is diagrammed in the flowchart of Fig. 11-3 (see p. 338), and the implementing program and printed results are shown in Fig. 11-4 (see p. 339). If the volume of the first line of the output is calculated by hand, it will be found that when $X = 4.17$, the volume (to five decimal places) should be 1157.4Ø6852 instead of 1157.4Ø7ØØ, the value calculated by the computer.

The difference is not due to incrementing since there are fewer than 2Ø iterations. Nor is the difference caused by an error of logic. The difference occurs because the WORD size of the computer was exceeded during calculations, resulting in a truncation or "cutting down to size" of a value to fit the storage location. The error is quite small, only Ø.ØØØØ128 percent, probably negligible for most purposes.

This type of inaccuracy has appeared in previous illustrative programs in this text. For example, the value shown in Fig. 7-15 for the area of a circle when the radius is 7.Ø is not accurate to nine significant digits. The programmer should be aware of inaccuracies caused by truncation when the result involves six or more significant digits. Incrementation and truncation inaccuracies creep in insidiously, with no warnings to alert the programmer of their presence.

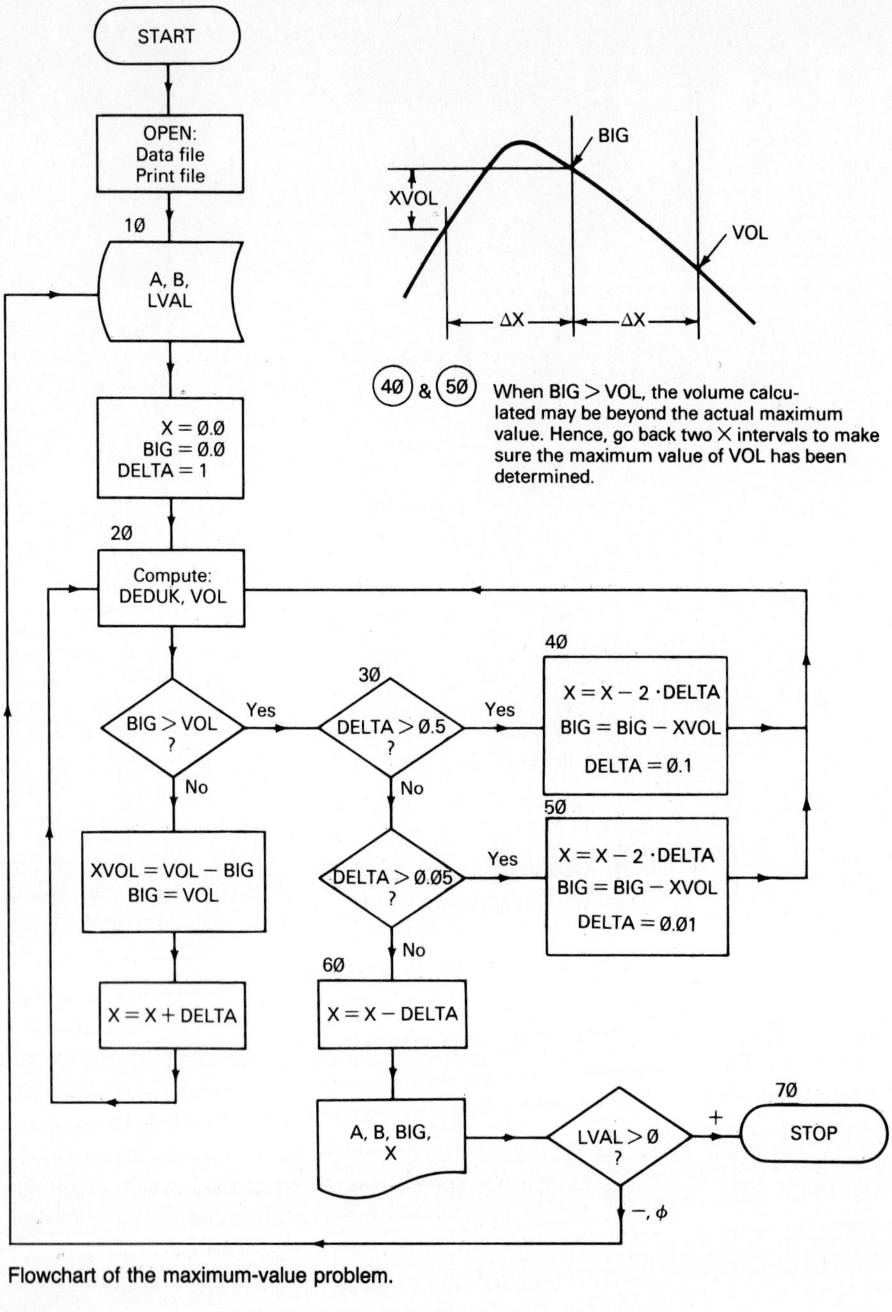

FIGURE 11-3 Flowchart of the maximum-value problem.

11-4 THE DOUBLE PRECISION DECLARATION STATEMENT

If the slight inaccuracies in computer calculations discussed in Sec. 11-3 are not acceptable, a technique called *double-precision* programming is available in FORTRAN to reduce and sometimes eliminate them. The double-precision calcu-

```
C234567890
      OPEN(3,FILE='FIG11-4.DAT')
      OPEN(6,FILE='PRN')
   10 READ(3,100)A,B,LVAL
  100 FORMAT(2F6.2,I3)
      X=0.0
      BIG=0.0
      DELTA=1.0
   20 DEDUK=2.0*X
      VOL=X*(A-DEDUK)*(B-DEDUK)
      IF(BIG.GT.VOL)GO TO 30
      XVOL=VOL-BIG
      BIG=VOL
      X=X+DELTA
      GO TO 20
   30 IF(DELTA.GT.0.5)GO TO 40
      IF(DELTA.GT.0.05)GO TO 50
      GO TO 60
   40 X=X-2.0*DELTA
      BIG=INT(BIG-XVOL)
      DELTA=0.1
      GO TO 20
   50 X=X-2.0*DELTA
      BIG=INT(BIG-XVOL)
      DELTA=0.01
      GO TO 20
   60 X=X-DELTA
      WRITE(6,200)A,B
  200 FORMAT(1X,'IF A =',F7.2,' AND B =',F7.2)
      WRITE(6,300)BIG,X
  300 FORMAT(15X,'THE VOLUME ='F12.5,' WHEN X =',F6.2,/)
      IF(LVAL)10,10,70
   70 STOP
      END
```

```
 25.00 25.00  0
 25.00100.00  0
 50.00 50.00  0
 50.00 75.00  0
 75.00 50.00  0
100.00100.00  5
```

```
IF A =  25.00 AND B =  25.00
               THE VOLUME =  1157.40700 WHEN X =  4.17

IF A =  25.00 AND B = 100.00
               THE VOLUME =  6870.46700 WHEN X =  5.81

IF A =  50.00 AND B =  50.00
               THE VOLUME =  9259.25800 WHEN X =  8.33

IF A =  50.00 AND B =  75.00
               THE VOLUME = 16504.78000 WHEN X =  9.81

IF A =  75.00 AND B =  50.00
               THE VOLUME = 16504.78000 WHEN X =  9.81

IF A = 100.00 AND B = 100.00
               THE VOLUME = 74074.07000 WHEN X = 16.67
```

FIGURE 11-4 Program for the maximum-value problem using single-precision calculations.

lation uses two WORDs to store a given value (instead of one WORD, as with a single-precision calculation), approximately doubling the number of significant digits that can be handled accurately. Actually the number of digits that can be handled is slightly more than doubled. Since a portion of one WORD is occupied by the algebraic sign and the exponent, which need not be repeated in the second WORD, the second WORD is fully occupied by digits. Double-precision calculations are specified by a nonexecutable declaration statement of the general form:

```
DOUBLE PRECISION a, b, n
```

where DOUBLE PRECISION declares that the variables in the list are to be in double precision. The variable names, if there are more than one, are separated in the list by commas. *Integer-variable names in a DOUBLE PRECISION list are type-changed to real variables.* There is no flowchart symbol for the DOUBLE PRECISION statement.

The following rules are applicable to double-precision arithmetic operations:

1 Whenever double precision is used, the DOUBLE PRECISION declaration statement must appear in the program or subprogram *before* any executable statement.

2 If an expression is mixed, with some variables or constants in double precision and others in single precision, the expression will be evaluated in double precision. Thus, the expression 2.Ø*X will be evaluated in double precision if the variable X has been declared double precision in a DOUBLE PRECISION declaration statement. (In this instance, the constant, 2.Ø, is an exact value and need not be written in double-precision form, but if the constant includes a fraction that is not an exact value, say 2.1, the constant should be expressed in double-precision form, as explained in Sec. 11-5.)

3 If the variable name to the left of the assignment symbol (=) has been declared double-precision, the value of the associated expression will be stored as a double-precision value (two WORDs), even if that value is the result of single-precision calculations.

4 If the variable name to the left of the assignment symbol is not declared double precision, the value of the associated expression (if it contains a declared double-precision variable or constant) will be calculated in double precision and the result *rounded* and stored in single precision (one WORD).

The DOUBLE PRECISION declaration statement can be used to declare the maximum size of arrays in double precision, eliminating the need for a DIMENSION statement. For example:

```
DOUBLE PRECISION A(1Ø),X(5,5)
```

declares that the subscripted variables of the arrays A and X are double precision and also specifies that A is a one-dimensional real array with 1Ø elements and X is a two-dimensional real array with 25 elements ordered in 5 rows and 5 columns. Both the DIMENSION and DOUBLE PRECISION statements can be used as follows:

```
DIMENSION A(1Ø),X(5,5)
DOUBLE PRECISION A,X
```

The latter form might be advantageous if it is necessary to declare an array double precision after it has been specified by a DIMENSION statement in an existing program.

11-5 DOUBLE-PRECISION CONSTANTS

Double-precision constants are expressed in exponential form and may contain between 1 and 17 digits. Thus, 123.456789Ø1234, a 14-digit number, represents a double-precision constant, while 123.4567 is interpreted as a single-precision constant. The decimal point may be placed as required in the string of digits. A double-precision constant in exponential form is written in the same manner as the single-precision exponential form (Sec. 3-3) except that a D is used in place of the E. Thus, Ø.3D3 is a double-precision constant in exponential form, while Ø.3E3 is a single-precision constant.

A double-precision constant should be assigned only to a variable name that has been declared in a DOUBLE PRECISION declaration statement. Assigning a double-precision constant to a single-precision variable name results in rounding to seven significant digits.

All double-precision calculations are type real. An integer constant assigned to a declared double-precision variable name will have a decimal point added after the last digit of the value, and a real value will be assigned to the double-precision variable name. The first-letter designator (I, J, K, L, M, or N) no longer applies when the variable is declared double precision. All variable names declared double precision are also declared type real.

Figure 11-5 (see p. 342) shows a double-precision constant that is read and assigned to a declared double-precision variable name. The value in the record is a 15-digit number. Note that a double-precision value can be printed in double-precision exponential form, in single-precision exponential form, or in single-precision decimal form. Note the last line of output resulting from the WRITE (6,*) statement. The value is shown in decimal form, but the number of digits yields a double-precision value rounded to 14 significant digits. The three trailing zeros indicate the use of two WORDs in the double-precision usage.

11-6 DOUBLE-PRECISION INTRINSIC FUNCTIONS

Many of the intrinsic functions described in Chap. 5 are available for double-precision calculations. Intrinsic functions used in double-precision calculations are usually written with a D before the function name, for example: DSQRT(*a*), DSIN(*a*), DCOS(*a*), DTAN(*a*), DASIN(*a*), DACOS(*a*), DATAN(*a*), DATAN2(*a*), DALOG(*a*), DALOG1Ø(*a*), DEXP(*a*), and DABS(*a*) as listed in Table 11-1 (see pp. 343–344). The discussions of intrinsic functions in Chap. 5 pertain also to double-precision intrinsic functions.

```
C234567890
      DOUBLE PRECISION A
      OPEN(3,FILE='FIG11-5.DAT')
      OPEN(6,FILE='PRN')
      READ(3,100)A
  100 FORMAT(D19.15)
      WRITE(6,200)A
  200 FORMAT(4X,D22.15,/)
      WRITE(6,300)A
  300 FORMAT(1X,E17.7,/)
      WRITE(6,400)A
  400 FORMAT(5X,F6.2,/)
      WRITE(6,*)A
      STOP
      END
```

```
0.1234567890123450D3
```

```
    .123456789012345D+03

 .1234568E+03

     123.46

  123.45678901235000
```

FIGURE 11-5 Printing a double-precision value with various edit descriptors.

Figure 11-6 (see p. 345) shows several intrinsic functions used in calculations. Note that only the variables used in the calculations, excluding integer exponents, need to be declared double precision. Also note that the variable N is declared double precision, and when the results are printed the value of N is a real number, not an integer.

11-7 DOUBLE-PRECISION SUBPROGRAMS

Double-precision variable names whose values are supplied to a subprogram or returned to the calling program must be declared in appropriate DOUBLE PRECISION declaration statements in both the calling program (listing the actual arguments) and the subprogram (listing the dummy arguments). Otherwise the double-precision values will be truncated to single-precision when the exchange between the actual and dummy arguments occurs. For example, in a SUBROUTINE subprogram in which double precision is used, the statements required in the calling program and the subprogram are:

```
Calling program: DOUBLE PRECISION X, Y, Z
                 - - - - - - - - - - -
                 - - - - - - - - - - -
                 CALL NAME (X, Y, Z)
                 - - - - - - - - - - -
                 - - - - - - - - - - -
                 END
```

TABLE 11-1 INTRINSIC FUNCTIONS WITH CORRESPONDING DOUBLE-PRECISION FUNCTIONS

Definition	Single-precision (Chap. 5)	Double-precision (Chap. 11)
Square root	SQRT(*a*)	DSQRT(*a*)
Absolute value	ABS(*a*)	DABS(*a*)
	ABS(*k*)	
	IABS(*k*)	
Type conversion:		
Change to integer	INT(*a*)	IDINT(*a*)
	INT(*k*)	
	IFIX(*a*)	
Change to real	REAL(*k*)	DREAL(*k*)
	REAL(*a*)	
	FLOAT(*k*)	
Exponential	EXP(*a*)	DEXP(*a*)
Logarithm:		
Common	LOG1Ø(*a*)	DLOG1Ø(*a*)
	ALOG1Ø(*a*)	
Natural	LOG(*a*)	DLOG(*a*)
	ALOG(*a*)	
Trigonometric:		
Sine	SIN(*a*)	DSIN(*a*)
Cosine	COS(*a*)	DCOS(*a*)
Tangent	TAN(*a*)	DTAN(*a*)
Arcsine	ASIN(*s*)	DASIN(*s*)
Arccosine	ACOS(*cs*)	DACOS(*cs*)
Arctangent	ATAN(*t*)	DATAN(*t*)
	ATAN2(*y*,*x*)	DATAN2(*y*,*x*)
Maximum	MAX(*a*,*b*,*c*,...)	
	MAX(*i*,*j*,*k*,...)	
	MAXØ(*i*,*j*,*k*,...)	
	MAX1(*a*,*b*,*c*,...)	DMAX1(*a*,*b*,*c*,...)
	AMAXØ(*i*,*j*,*k*,...)	
	AMAX1(*a*,*b*,*c*,...)	
Minimum	MIN(*a*,*b*,*c*,...)	
	MIN(*i*,*j*,*k*,...)	
	MINØ(*i*,*j*,*k*,...)	
	MIN1(*a*,*b*,*c*,...)	DMIN1(*a*,*b*,*c*,...)
	AMINØ(*i*,*j*,*k*,...)	
	AMIN1(*a*,*b*,*c*,...)	
Truncation	AINT(*a*)	DINT(*a*)
Rounding:		
To real	ANINT(*a*)	DNINT(*a*)
To integer	NINT(*a*)	IDNINT(*a*)

TABLE 11-1 *(continued)*

Definition	Single-precision (Chap. 5)	Double-precision (Chap. 11)
Remainder	MOD(*a*,*b*) MOD(*i*,*j*) AMOD(*a*,*b*)	DMOD(*a*,*b*)
Complex:		
Convert to	CMPLX(*x*,*y*) CMPLX(*x*)	DCMPLX(*x*,*y*) DCMPLX(*x*)
Isolate real part	REAL(*z*)	DREAL(*z*)
Isolate imaginary part	AIMAG(*z*)	DIMAG(*z*)
Conjugate	CONJG(*z*)	DCONJG(*z*)
Double-precision, convert to	DBLE(*x*)	

Subprogram:

```
SUBROUTINE NAME(A,B,C)
DOUBLE PRECISION A,B,C
-----------
RETURN
END
```

When double-precision calculations are used in a FUNCTION subprogram, the discussion above also applies to the actual and dummy arguments. However, with the FUNCTION subprogram there is one additional requirement. Since the value of the function NAME is the value to be returned to the calling program, the function NAME must also be declared double precision, as shown below:

Calling program:

```
DOUBLE PRECISION NAME,X,Y,Z,R
-----------
-----------
R=NAME(X,Y,Z)
-----------
-----------
END
```

Subprogram:

```
DOUBLE PRECISION FUNCTION NAME(A,B,C)
DOUBLE PRECISION A,B,C
-----------
NAME=arithmetic expression
RETURN
END
```

An existing single-precision FUNCTION subprogram can be converted to double-precision form by adding one statement to the existing FUNCTION subprogram immediately following the defining statement:

```
C234567890
      DOUBLE PRECISION X,Y,N,PI,PISQ,LOG2
      OPEN(6,FILE='PRN')
      X=1.0D0
      Y=1.0D0
      PI=4.0D0*DATAN(Y/X)
      PISQ=PI**2
      N=DSQRT(2.0D0)
      LOG2=DLOG10(2.0D0)
      WRITE(6,*)'          X =',X
      WRITE(6,*)'          Y =',Y
      WRITE(6,*)'         PI =',PI
      WRITE(6,*)'       PISQ =',PISQ
      WRITE(6,*)'          N =',N
      WRITE(6,*)'       LOG2 =',LOG2
      X=LOG2/10.0D0
      WRITE(6,*)
      WRITE(6,*)'      NEW X =',X
      STOP
      END
```

```
      X =          1.00000000000000
      Y =          1.00000000000000
     PI =          3.14159265358980
   PISQ =          9.86960440108940
      N =          1.41421356237310
   LOG2 =   3.01029995663980E-001

  NEW X =   3.01029995663980E-002
```

FIGURE 11-6 Intrinsic functions in double-precision calculations, printed as list-directed values.

```
FUNCTION NAME(A,B,C)
DOUBLE PRECISION NAME,A,B,C
```

The FUNCTION subprogram can then be used as a double-precision subprogram as described above.

The same requirement applies to a statement function. If a statement function is to be evaluated in double precision, both the function name and its dummy arguments, along with the corresponding actual arguments used in the calling statement, must be listed separately in a DOUBLE PRECISION declaration statement that precedes the defining statement. The example from Sec. 9-2, recoded for double-precision calculations, is:

```
DOUBLE PRECISION HYP,A,B,X,Y,R
HYP(A,B)=DSQRT(A**2+B**2)
- - - - - - - - - - -
- - - - - - - - - - -
R=HYP(X,Y)
```

11-8 THE D EDIT DESCRIPTOR IN READING AND PRINTING

Usually the results of double-precision calculations are printed in their full value. The appropriate edit descriptor is similar to the E edit descriptor (Secs. 6-3*b* and 6-8*b*) but with a D substituted for the E. The edit descriptor D2Ø.14 in a FOR-

MAT statement associated with a WRITE statement will cause the value called for to be printed as a number between Ø.1ØØØØØØØØØØØØØ and Ø.99999999999999 (14 decimal places). A double-precision value in storage, such as 123.45678901234 will be displayed (using the edit descriptor D2Ø.14) as *b*.123456789Ø1234D*b*ØØ3, where the *b*'s represent *blanks*. If the number is negative, the first *b* is replaced by a minus sign. If the number is less than Ø.1, the second *b* (after the D) is replaced by a minus sign, indicating a negative power of 1Ø. As with the E edit descriptor, the minimum field width to use in printing double-precision values must be seven output columns wider than the number of decimal places to be printed. However, if that number of decimal digits is not required in the output, the F or E edit descriptors of Secs. 6-8*a* and 6-8*b* can be used.

11-9 DOUBLE-PRECISION CALCULATIONS

The use of double-precision values can increase the precision of calculation but at the expense of programming and computer time. In some cases, double precision is the only programming solution that will provide a correct answer, but before deciding to use double precision, the need for such precision should be carefully weighed against the increased cost and additional time. Double-precision programs must be prepared with considerable care and with the knowledge of how double-precision calculations are performed. Otherwise, the potential precision may be lost due to ignorance or oversight.

A single-precision constant, when used in an expression with a double-precision variable, will be changed to double-precision form during calculations. The compiler accomplishes this enlargement (automatically) by adding sufficient *zeros* to make the number used for calculations double-precision. Its nearness to the mathematically exact value (accuracy) *remains unchanged*. Single-precision constants that are exactly represented in the binary system, i.e., whole numbers and some decimal fractions, can be changed from single- to double-precision form in this manner with no effect on calculation accuracy, since adding zeros does not change their value. However, single-precision constants that cannot be represented in the binary system exactly, i.e., fractions such as Ø.2 and Ø.3, may introduce inaccuracies in double-precision calculation if not initially stored as double-precision values.

Figure 11-7 shows the results of double-precision calculations when not all values used in the calculations are in double-precision form. Note the four calculations following the OPEN statement and the manner in which the constants are expressed. The results of those calculations are first printed with list-directed WRITE statements and then with format-directed WRITE statements. Note the similarities and differences. The first line of output in each group is the true double-precision value. But, although the constants used in the calculations are apparently the same, the results of each calculation are different. A particular oddity is illustrated in the second line of output. This is the result of a single-precision calculation assigned to a double-precision variable (BETA). Theoretically, a seven-digit value when assigned to a double-precision variable should have seven zeros added. From where did the other digits come? Since the single-precision

```
C234567890
      DOUBLE PRECISION ALPHA,BETA,THETA,ZETA
      OPEN(6,FILE='PRN')
      ALPHA=0.2D0/0.3D0
      BETA=0.2/0.3
      THETA=0.2D0/0.3
      ZETA=0.2/0.3D0
      WRITE(6,*)ALPHA
      WRITE(6,*)BETA
      WRITE(6,*)THETA
      WRITE(6,*)ZETA
      WRITE(6,*)
      WRITE(6,100)ALPHA
  100 FORMAT(5X,D22.15)
      WRITE(6,100)BETA
      WRITE(6,100)THETA
      WRITE(6,100)ZETA
      STOP
      END
```

```
6.666666666666667E-001
6.666666501098 2E-001
6.6666664017571E-001
6.6666667660077E-001

     .666666666666667D+00
     .666666650109822D+00
     .666666640175715D+00
     .666666676600774D+00
```

FIGURE 11-7 Effect of mixing single- and double-precision values in calculations.

constant(s) cannot be exactly defined in a single-precision WORD, there are some leftover digits that "tag along" when the result of the single-precision calculation is assigned to a double-precision variable name. Obviously, using these values in further calculation will cause unpredictable inaccuracies in the last digits of the final results.

For another example, in the program segment below neither GAMMA nor DELTA has been declared double precision:

```
GAMMA=Ø.2DØ/Ø.3DØ
DELTA=Ø.2/Ø.3
WRITE(*,*)GAMMA
WRITE(*,*)DELTA
```

Gamma is assigned the result of a double-precision calculation, and DELTA is assigned the result of a single-precision calculation:

```
.6666666EbØØ  (assigned to GAMMA)
.6666666EbØØ  (assigned to DELTA)
```

In both cases a seven-digit single-precision value (note the E form) is assigned to the single-precision variable name.

Changing the output to display 14 decimal places with the WRITE/FORMAT statements:

```
      OPEN(6,FILE='PRN')
      WRITE(6,1ØØ)GAMMA
      WRITE(6,1ØØ)DELTA
1ØØ   FORMAT(E2Ø.14)
```

will add 7 zeros to complete the specified 14 digits, and will assign the following values and print:

```
b.66666660000000EbØØ   (assigned to GAMMA)
b.66666650000000EbØØ   (assigned to DELTA)
```

The added zeros do nothing to increase the precision (over single precision) of the results of further calculations in which these values are used. But why the 5 in the seventh decimal place of the value assigned to DELTA? The values of GAMMA and DELTA are computed differently. Gamma is calculated by truncating a double-precision number developed when one double-precision number was divided by another double-precision number. DELTA, however, is calculated simply by the division of two single-precision numbers. Constants calculated by using double-precision values, even when truncated to single-precision values, are likely to be more precise than constants calculated using corresponding single-precision values. The principles of double-precision calculations are summarized in Table 11-2.

TABLE 11-2 SUMMARY OF DOUBLE-PRECISION PRINCIPLES

1. Whenever any variable is to be double precision, that variable must be declared in a DOUBLE PRECISION declaration statement.
2. The DOUBLE PRECISION declaration statement must appear in the program before any executable statement.
3. A double-precision constant should be written in exponential form, with the letter D used in place of E.
4. An arithmetic expression to be evaluated in double-precision should be written with double-precision terms; i.e., all constants, variables, and function names should be double precision. A double-precision term in an arithmetic expression containing mixed single- and double-precision terms will cause the expression to be evaluated in double precision, but the result probably will not be correct beyond seven digits.
5. If the variable to the left of the assignment symbol (=) has been declared DOUBLE PRECISION, the value of the associated expression will be stored in double precision.
6. If the variable to the left of the assignment symbol has not been declared DOUBLE PRECISION, the value of the associated expression, if evaluated in double precision, will be truncated and stored in single precision.
7. The first-letter integer designators I, J, K, L, M, and N do not apply to double-precision variables. Any integer variable declared double precision becomes type real.

11-10 COMPARISON OF INTEGER, SINGLE-PRECISION, AND DOUBLE-PRECISION CALCULATIONS

The program of Fig. 11-8 (see p. 350) provides a comparison of the degree of precision attainable from calculations with integer values, real single-precision values, and double-precision values. This program calculates the factorials of numbers from 5 through 2Ø in increments of 1, using each of the three types. Note that the value of the factorials from 5! through 12! is the same in all three types. The integer value for 13! and the succeeding integer values in the INTEGER column are set to Ø by the logical IF statement following the 1ØØ FORMAT statement. This is done because the value of 13! is larger than the maximum allowable value of an integer number (Sec. 3-3*a*) and if calculated will cause an execution error. Generally stated, integer calculations are limited to nine significant digits in the results. This limit on the number of significant digits, considered dependable for integer calculations, may differ for different compilers.

Consider the difference between the values printed as the result of single- and double-precision calculations. The single-precision calculation yields a maximum of seven significant digits, the remaining digits (specified in the WRITE/FORMAT statements) being added by the compiler. This severe limitation on the number of available significant digits in single-precision calculations is an important consideration in computer calculations.

The values printed in the column headed DOUBLE PRECISION, the result of double-precision calculations, are precise and accurate through 2Ø!.[†] If the calculated results require a greater precision than seven significant digits, double-precision must be used.

11-11 EXAMPLES OF DOUBLE-PRECISION PROGRAMMING

Example 11-2

The program described in Sec. 11-3, revised with double-precision calculations, is illustrated in Fig. 11-9 (see p. 351). The value for the volume of the box formed by the 25 by 25 sheet now includes 9 significant digits and is accurate to five decimal places.

Example 11-3

In Fig. 11-10 (see p. 352) the statements on program lines 4, 5, and 6 increment the single-precision value 1234567.Ø in increments of Ø.Ø1 for 1Ø,ØØØ incrementations. The last (1Ø,ØØØth) value assigned to the real-variable name X should be 1234667.Ø, but when the value assigned to X is printed, the result is 1234567.Ø, the initial value assigned to X before incrementation. Something odd and unexpected has happened in this single-precision calculation that significantly affects the final result. The inability of single-precision

[†]The exact value of 2Ø! is 2,432,9Ø2,ØØ8,176,64Ø,ØØØ.

```
C234567890
      DOUBLE PRECISION DFACT
      OPEN(6,FILE='PRN')
      WRITE(6,*)'                    INTEGER              SINGLE PRECISION',
     $'             DOUBLE PRECISION'
      WRITE(6,*)'   N        FACTORIAL             FACTORIAL',
     $'                      FACTORIAL'
      WRITE(6,*)
      IFACT=1
      RFACT=1.0
      DFACT=1.0D0
      DO 10 N=1,20
      IFACT=IFACT*N
      RFACT=RFACT*FLOAT(N)
      DFACT=DFACT*FLOAT(N)
      IF(N.LT.5) GOTO 10
      WRITE(6,100)N,IFACT,RFACT,DFACT
  100 FORMAT(I5,I15,E25.14,D26.15,/)
      IF(IFACT.EQ.479001600)IFACT=0
   10 CONTINUE
      STOP
      END
```

N	INTEGER FACTORIAL	SINGLE PRECISION FACTORIAL	DOUBLE PRECISION FACTORIAL
5	120	.12000000000000E+03	.120000000000000D+03
6	720	.72000000000000E+03	.720000000000000D+03
7	5040	.50400000000000E+04	.504000000000000D+04
8	40320	.40320000000000E+05	.403200000000000D+05
9	362880	.36288000000000E+06	.362880000000000D+06
10	3628800	.36288000000000E+07	.362880000000000D+07
11	39916800	.39916800000000E+08	.399168000000000D+08
12	479001600	.47900160000000E+09	.479001600000000D+09
13	0	.62270210000000E+10	.622702080000000D+10
14	0	.87178290000000E+11	.871782912000000D+11
15	0	.13076740000000E+13	.130767436800000D+13
16	0	.20922790000000E+14	.209227898880000D+14
17	0	.35568740000000E+15	.355687428096000D+15
18	0	.64023740000000E+16	.640237370572800D+16
19	0	.12164510000000E+18	.121645100408832D+18
20	0	.24329020000000E+19	.243290200817664D+19

FIGURE 11-8 Comparison of results of computations in integer, real, single-precision, and double-precision modes.

```
C234567890
      DOUBLE PRECISION X,BIG,DELTA,DEDUK,VOL,XVOL
      OPEN(3,FILE='FIG11-9.DAT')
      OPEN(6,FILE='PRN')
   10 READ(3,100)A,B,LVAL
  100 FORMAT(2F6.2,I3)
      X=0.0D0
      BIG=0.0D0
      DELTA=1.0D0
   20 DEDUK=2.0D0*X
      VOL=X*(A-DEDUK)*(B-DEDUK)
      IF(BIG.GT.VOL)GO TO 30
      XVOL=VOL-BIG
      BIG=VOL
      X=X+DELTA
      GO TO 20
   30 IF(DELTA.GT.0.5D0)GO TO 40
      IF(DELTA.GT.0.05D0)GO TO 50
      GO TO 60
   40 X=X-2.0D0*DELTA
      BIG=IDINT(BIG-XVOL)
      DELTA=0.1D0
      GO TO 20
   50 X=X-2.0D0*DELTA
      BIG=IDINT(BIG-XVOL)
      DELTA=0.01D0
      GO TO 20
   60 X=X-DELTA
      WRITE(6,200)A,B
  200 FORMAT(1X,'IF A =',F7.2,' AND B =',F7.2)
      WRITE(6,300)BIG,X
  300 FORMAT(15X,'THE VOLUME =',F12.5,' WHEN X =',F6.2,/)
      IF(LVAL)10,10,70
   70 STOP
      END
```

```
 25.00 25.00  0
 25.00100.00  0
 50.00 50.00  0
 50.00 75.00  0
 75.00 50.00  0
100.00100.00  5
```

```
IF A =  25.00 AND B =  25.00
              THE VOLUME =  1157.40685 WHEN X =  4.17

IF A =  25.00 AND B = 100.00
              THE VOLUME =  6870.46676 WHEN X =  5.81

IF A =  50.00 AND B =  50.00
              THE VOLUME =  9259.25815 WHEN X =  8.33

IF A =  50.00 AND B =  75.00
              THE VOLUME = 16504.77956 WHEN X =  9.81

IF A =  75.00 AND B =  50.00
              THE VOLUME = 16504.77956 WHEN X =  9.81

IF A = 100.00 AND B = 100.00
              THE VOLUME = 74074.07185 WHEN X = 16.67
```

FIGURE 11-9 Program for the maximum-value problem using double-precision variables.

```
C234567890
      DOUBLE PRECISION Y
      OPEN(6,FILE='PRN')
      X=1234567.0
      DO 10 I=1,10000
   10 X=X+0.01
      Y=1234567.0D0
      DO 20 I=1,10000
   20 Y=Y+0.01D0
      WRITE(6,*)'       X =',X
      WRITE(6,*)'       Y =',Y
      STOP
      END
```

```
       X =     1234567.0000000
       Y =     1234667.00000010000000
```

FIGURE 11-10 Computer errors. Example 11-3.

calculation to handle more than seven significant digits implies that when two numbers, such as 1234567.Ø and Ø.Ø1, are added, the result is 1234567.Ø, since the decimal-fraction part of the sum occupies the eighth and ninth significant-figure locations, which are essentially ignored. Thus 1234567. is always assigned to X. However, when the same calculation is done in double-precision form by using the variable Y (program lines 7, 8, and 9), the result is as expected, except that there is a very small, but unexpected, decimal inaccuracy in the result. This unexpected inaccuracy occurs because even in double-precision calculations some values still cannot be stored exactly. Inaccuracies simply occur at a greater significant-figure location.

Example 11-4

Figure 11-11 illustrates another example of computer inaccuracy. The statements on program lines 4 and 5 assign the seven-digit single-precision constants 345678.9 and 345678.8 to the single-precision variable names A and B, respectively. On program line 6 the difference between A and B is evaluated and assigned to the single-precision variable name C. The difference should be Ø.1. But when the value assigned to C is printed, the result is Ø.Ø9375. The same calculations are repeated in program lines 7, 8, and 9 with the same single-precision constants, but this time the values are assigned to double-precision variable names D and E, and the difference to the double-precision variable name F. Again the same printed result—Ø.Ø9375—since the initial constants were single precision. The calculations are repeated a third time on program lines 10, 11, and 12, with double-precision variable names P and Q and the value of the difference assigned to the double-precision variable name R. This time, with the correct use of double-precision calculations, the value printed for R is Ø.1ØØØØØØØØØ3492, the correct value, almost. A little lagniappe from the compiler, perhaps? No, it simply again indicates the inability to store all numbers exactly, even in double precision. Note that both F and R are printed by the list-directed WRITE statements and by format-directed WRITE statements to provide a comparison of the two output forms.

```
C234567890
      DOUBLE PRECISION D,E,F,P,Q,R
      OPEN(6,FILE='PRN')
      A=345678.9
      B=345678.8
      C=A-B
      D=345678.9
      E=345678.8
      F=D-E
      P=0.3456789D6
      Q=0.3456788D6
      R=P-Q
      WRITE(6,*)'      C =',C
      WRITE(6,*)'      F =',F
      WRITE(6,*)'      R =',R
      WRITE(6,100)F
  100 FORMAT(//,6X,'F =',D21.14)
      WRITE(6,200)R
  200 FORMAT(6X,'R =',D21.14)
      STOP
      END
```

```
      C =   9.375000E-002
      F =   9.37500000000000E-002
      R =   1.00000000003492E-001


      F =  .93750000000000D-01
      R =  .10000000003492D+00
```

FIGURE 11-11 Computer errors. Example 11-4.

It is conceded that the single-precision computer mistakes revealed in Figs. 11-10 and 11-11 represent carefully selected examples and that the errors shown are unlikely to occur unless these specific conditions are exactly duplicated. Note that the incrementation in Fig. 11-1—where 1.ØØ was incremented in increments of Ø.Ø1 for 199 iterations—caused no particular problem, while the incrementation in Fig. 11-10—where the single-precision number 1234567.Ø was incremented by Ø.Ø1 for 1Ø,ØØØ iterations—failed to increment.

The point is that sometimes unexpected (and incorrect) results can occur that are not caused by any error in logic or other fault of the programmer. The computer is not the omnipotent oracle of computation it is sometimes represented as being. Every program should be tested with data that will provide known results. These data should include the limiting parameters of the problem and any special cases such as zero or negative conditions, that might be computed differently. Even when the results of the test appear correct, subsequent results should be checked to determine whether they are within reasonable limits of accuracy. It is suggested that less sophisticated hand methods of calculation may be helpful in checking the results of computer calculations. Evaluation of the final results is as important in computer programming as the careful planning of the algorithm.

PROBLEMS

There are no specific problems assigned for this chapter, but many earlier problems lend themselves to double precision.

APPENDIX **A**

THE KEYBOARD

A-1 Introduction

The *keyboard* is the primary input unit through which the human operator supplies information to the central processing unit (CPU) and controls operation of the personal computer. The keyboard of the IBM Personal Computer (Fig. A-1) is divided into three separate areas. A *typewriter keyboard* occupies the center portion, the *numeric keypad* is on the right side, and a bank of *function keys* is arrayed along the left side. Other keys scattered about the keyboard initiate various control functions. The keyboard arrangement of personal computers other than IBM may differ somewhat from that in the illustrations shown here. Refer to the guide to operations for the personal computer being used.

A-2 The Typewriter Keyboard

The typewriter keyboard is used for entering the letters, numerals, and characters that form the words, expressions, and statements which constitute instructions to the computer, a FORTRAN source program, a data file, or some other file. The letters A through Z, the numerals 1 through 9 and Ø, and the characters used for punctuation, i.e., period, comma, apostrophe, question mark, slash, etc., are arranged in standard typewriter-keyboard order. Uppercase (capital) letters and upper-keyboard characters are obtained by depressing one of the two *shift keys,* marked with an open up-pointing arrow (Fig. A-2, p. 356), located at either end of the bottom row of the typewriter keyboard. The *space bar* will create a *blank* character, and the *backspace key* will erase one character at a time (Fig. A-2).

A-3 The Numeric Keypad

The numeric keypad, when activated by depressing the *Num/Lock* key at the top center of the keypad (Fig. A-2), can be used for entering the numerals 1 through 9 and Ø. Either the

FIGURE A-I The keyboard of the IBM Personal Computer.

typewriter keyboard or the numeric keypad may be used, interchangeably, for entering numerals. The algebraic signs, plus (+) and minus (−), may also be entered from the numeric keypad and are located at the extreme right of the keypad.

A-4 The Function Keys

The ten function keys, identified as F1 through F10, can be programmed to perform given tasks depending upon the software and programming language in use. Refer to the guide to operations manual for the personal computer and software being used for detailed information about how the function keys are applied in specific applications.

FIGURE A-2 The keyboard control keys.

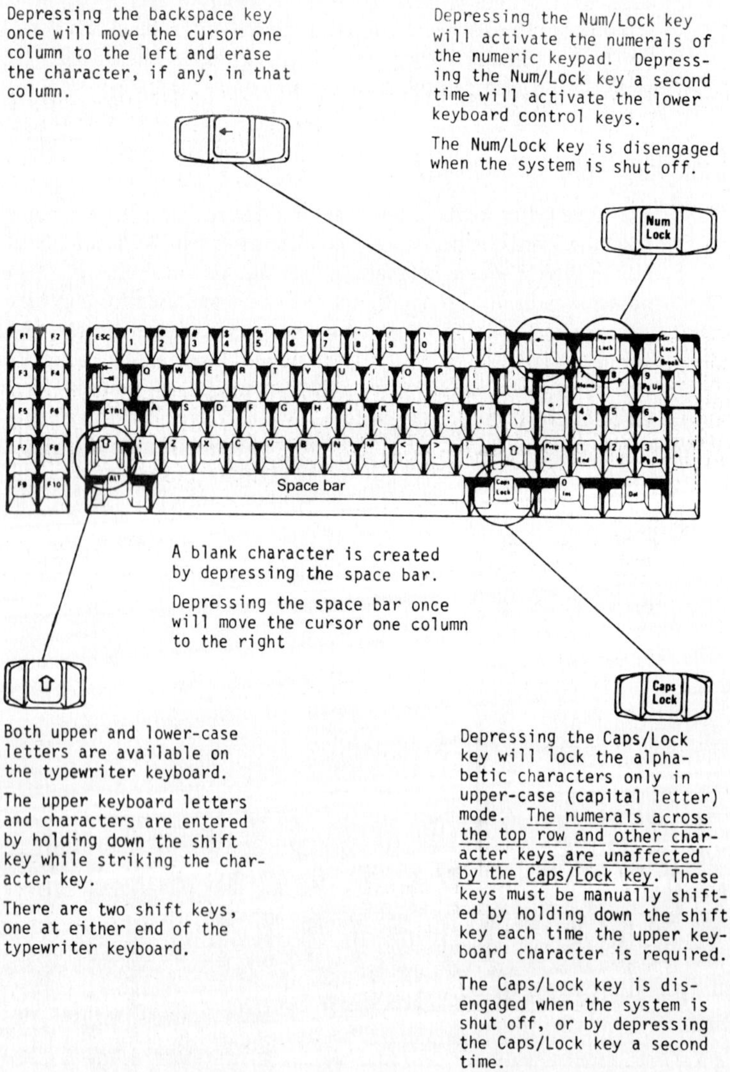

A-5 Control Keys

Other keys (identified as *Ctrl, Alt, Del, Caps/Lock,* etc.), located to the left and right of the typewriter keyboard, perform a variety of control functions when depressed individually or in combination. These control keys are illustrated and their functions described in Figs. A-2, A-3, and A-4 (see p. 358).

FIGURE A-3 The system control keys.

Depressing the Esc (for escape) key will type a backslash (\), scratch the line just typed, and move the cursor back to column one and down one line without returning the default drive prompt (A> or B>) to the screen.

The Esc key provides a means for wiping out an entire mistakenly typed line and starting over.

The enter (or return) key ↵ is used to initiate a command or record a line after it has been typed.

Depressing the ↵ key will move the cursor back to column one and down one line, and, usually, return the default drive prompt (A> or B>) to the screen.

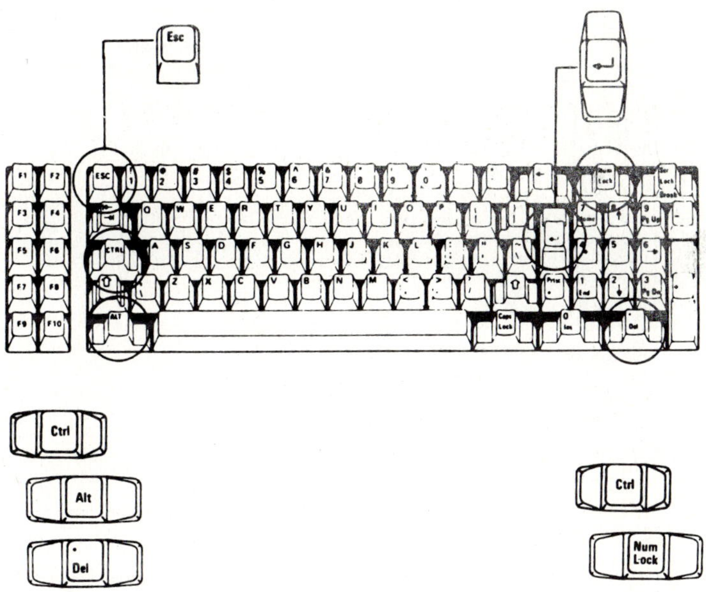

Holding down the Ctrl key and simultaneously depressing the Alt and Del keys will shut off the system and return the cursor to the upper left corner of the screen. The effect is the same as turning the power switch OFF, waiting **4-5 seconds,** and turning the power switch ON.

Holding down the Ctrl key and depressing the Num/Lock key will stop a "scrolling" screen so that portions of it can be read. To restart the "scrolling" screen, strike the ↵ key.

(A program that is too long to fit on the screen, will roll up and off the top of the screen, stopping when the last line appears at the bottom of the screen.)

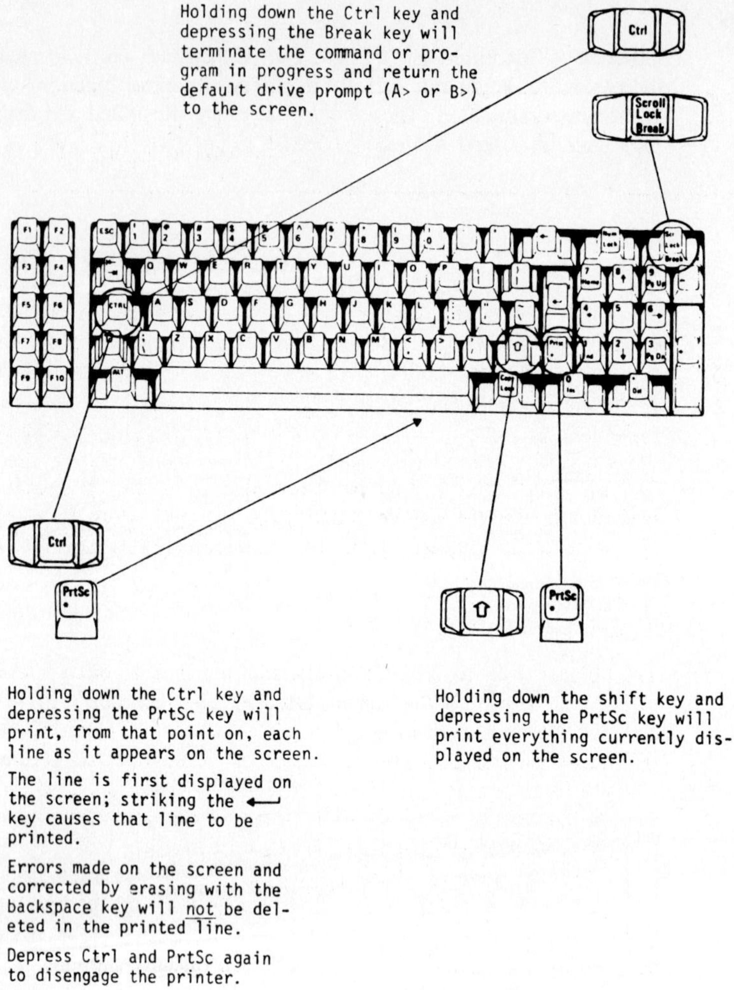

FIGURE A-4 The printer control keys.

APPENDIX **B**

THE 5.25-INCH DISKETTE

B-1 Introduction

Operating instructions and other files for use with the personal computer are recorded on flexible plastic *diskettes* (often referred to as *floppy disks*) and communicated to the central processing unit through a read/write head in a diskette drive. Diskettes containing the operating instructions comprise the *software* required to prepare the personal computer to execute specific instructions. The operating instructions, referred to as the Disk Operating System (DOS), is described in App. C.

FORTRAN main and subprograms, data files, and other files entered into random-access memory (RAM) are irretrievably lost when power to the computer is shut off or when the computer is rebooted. These files may be saved by recording them on a diskette.

B-2 Description of the Diskette

The flexible diskette is a 5.25-in-diameter mylar disk coated with a magnetic substance on which coded information can be electronically recorded (Fig. B-1, p. 360). This mylar disk is encased in a square vinyl protective jacket. A center hole permits the diskette to be mounted on a spindle in the diskette drive. The mylar disk is rotated inside the protective jacket to expose portions of the various sectors and tracks (into which the disk is divided) to the elongated opening or *head slot* in the jacket. Information is recorded on or copied from the diskette by a read/write head, which contacts the disk through the head slot.

A small (0.125 by 0.250 in) rectangular notch is cut about 1 in away from one corner of the protective jacket. This is the *write-protect* notch. The write-protect notch, when open, permits information to be recorded on the diskette. The write-protect notch may be covered by a strip of self-stick metallic foil (usually supplied with a new diskette) which will then prevent any changes in the information recorded on the diskette. A diskette with the write-protect notch covered is said to be *write-protected*. Information can be copied from but no information can be recorded on a write-protected diskette. Diskettes provided as part of a purchased software package may be write-protected by being encased in a jacket having no write-protect notch. Purchased diskettes containing copyrighted information may also be *copy-protected*. Any attempt to copy a copy-protected diskette may destroy or render unusable the information on the original diskette. The documentation accompanying copyrighted diskettes should be carefully studied to determine how the stored information is to be applied.

Diskettes for use with the personal computer (operating on the Disk Operating System) are specified: 5.25-in double-sided, double-density, soft sector diskettes (5.25 DS, DD, SS). The 5.25 refers to the diameter of the disk. *Double-sided* means that information can be recorded on and retrieved from both sides of the diskette. *Double-density* identifies a diskette with 40 tracks per side. *Soft sector* indicates that the number of bytes per sector is defined by the operating system (512 bytes for DOS 2.10). Soft-sector diskettes have one index hole. The index hole in the protective jacket (Fig. B-1) matches a smaller index hole in the mylar disk. The index hole marks the beginning and end of the concentric tracks.

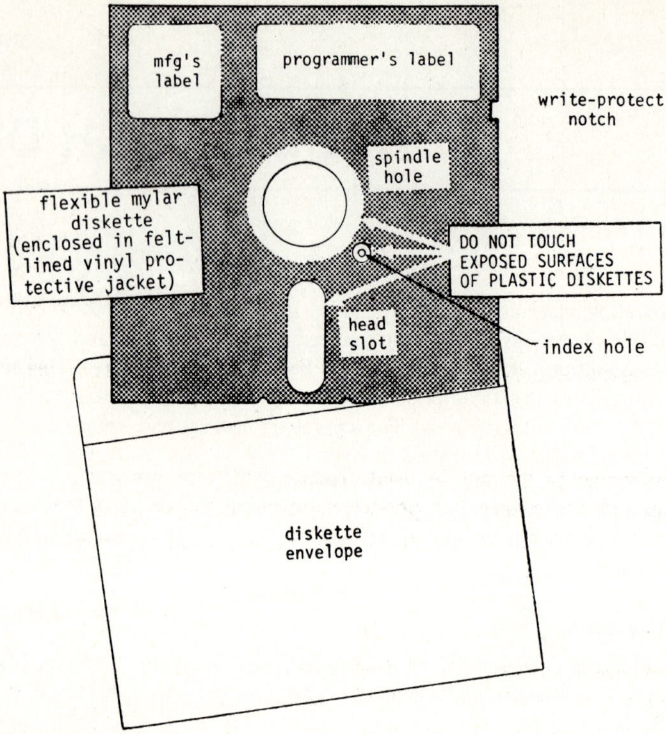

FIGURE B-1 The 5.25-in diskette.

A factory-fresh diskette must be *formatted* before information can be recorded on it. Formatting prepares the diskette for the operating system with which it is to be used by electronically establishing a polar grid of tracks and sectors (Fig. B-2). Diskettes formatted by DOS 2.10 (App. C) are divided into 4Ø concentric tracks, numbered Ø through 39 from the outside in. Each track is divided into 9 sectors, numbered 1 through 9. The sides of the diskette are numbered Ø and 1. Information is recorded on and retrieved from a diskette by side, track, and sector number, i.e., side Ø, track Ø, and sector 1. These "addresses" for specific information storage are "remembered" by the computer and are generally not needed by the personal computer operator.

Storage space on the diskette, like storage space in the computer, is measured in *bytes*. Each character uses 1 byte of storage space. Each sector of each track has a capacity of 512 bytes. Thus the 9 sectors and 4Ø tracks on one side of a single-sided diskette can store up to 184,32Ø bytes (characters). A double-sided diskette can store 368,64Ø bytes (characters) on its two sides. A double-sided diskette can store about 245 double-spaced typewritten pages.

Information stored on diskettes can be erased and the storage space reused for the storage of new information. Existing information can be "overwritten," with the new informa-

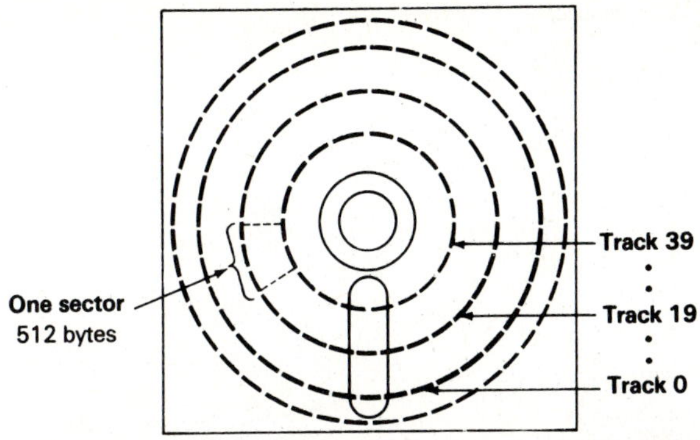

FIGURE B-2 The electronic grid of tracks and sectors on the 5.25-in diskette.

tion replacing the old. A used diskette can be reformatted. *Formatting* a used diskette erases all the information previously recorded and prepares the electronic tracks and sectors to receive new information.

B-3 Care of Diskettes

Diskettes are fragile; the information stored on a diskette may be expensive to obtain and impossible to replace. *Handle diskettes with care!*

Do not fold, bend, sit on, or carry diskettes loose in a flexible bag.

Do not write on a diskette label with a pencil or ballpoint pen. Use a felt-tipped pen and press *lightly,* or write on the self-stick label before placing it on the protective jacket.

Do not touch exposed areas of the mylar disk where it appears through any opening in the jacket. Oily fingerprints may damage the surface of the disk.

Keep diskettes away from heat. Do not leave diskettes on or near a radiator, heater, or sunny window sill, or in an automobile glove compartment, etc.

Keep diskettes away from magnetic fields. Do not place on or near an electric clock, printer, stereo speaker, telephone, or other appliance that may contain a permanent magnet or generate a magnetic field.

Protect diskettes from dust. A tiny particle of dust on the surface of the mylar disk may prevent information from being correctly stored or read.

When not in use diskettes should be returned to the paper envelope provided with each diskette. Diskettes should be stored and transported in a rigid plastic case. Store diskettes vertically. With proper care, a diskette should last indefinitely.

B-4 Diskette Drives

A diskette drive is used to record information on or to read information from a diskette (Fig. B-3, p. 362). A personal computer may be equipped with one drive or two. Two drives are more a matter of convenience than necessity; however, two drives are recommended, and they greatly reduce the time and frustration associated with compiling and running a FORTRAN program. When two drives are installed, they may be mounted side by side or one above the other. When installed side by side, the left drive is designated

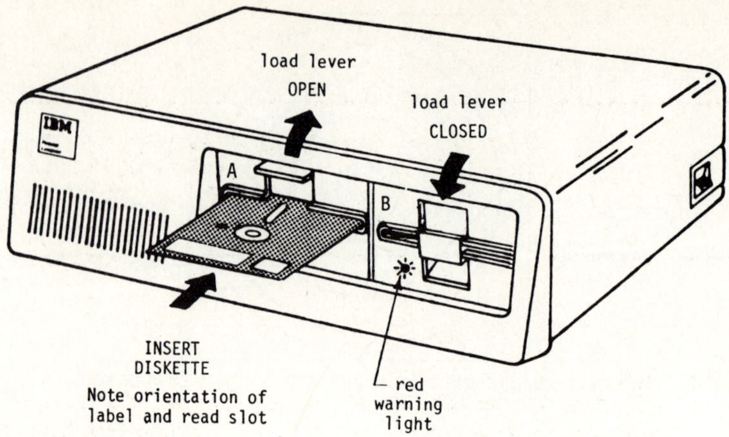

FIGURE B-3 The diskette drives.

drive A and the right drive is designated drive B. When installed one above the other, the upper drive is drive A, while the lower drive is drive B.

To load a diskette into the diskette drive, open the load lever and insert the diskette *label-side up* with the read slot *toward* the opening. Close the load lever (Fig. B-3). Note the red warning light just below and to the left of the load lever. *Do not open the load lever when the red warning light is on.* Opening the load lever when the red warning light is on may result in damage to the diskette or the drive, or in the loss of information on the diskette.

B-5 Other Permanent Storage Devices

Other permanent storage devices which may be available include the fixed disk and tape cassette. These devices will not be discussed in this text. The reader is referred to system manuals and other documentation accompanying the device in question.

APPENDIX **C**

THE DISK OPERATING SYSTEM (DOS)

C-1 Introduction

Information is supplied to and removed from the personal computer's central processing unit through the use of *files* recorded on a 5.25-in diskette (App. B). A FORTRAN source program is an example of information that might be stored as a file. A group of administrative files, known collectively as the *operating system,* is needed to control the operation of the computer and manage the user-generated files. The operating system or *software* most often used with the IBM and IBM-compatible personal computers is the *Disk Operating System* or *DOS*. The version of DOS used in this text is the IBM Personal Computer Disk Operating System Version 2.1Ø, developed by the Microsoft Corporation of Bellevue, Washington, and copyrighted in 1983. DOS files are recorded on a 5.25-in write-protected master diskette supplied with the Disk Operating System manual.

C-2 Files: Filename and Extension

Each file is identified by and referred to by a unique *filename* assigned by the programmer. The filename is used for establishing a new file or recalling an existing file. The filename is used for identification of a particular file for copying, editing, renaming, deleting, displaying on the screen, printing, storing, etc. The filename may or may not have an *extension*.

The general form for the filename with extension is:

```
FILENAME.EXT
```

The filename may be any combination of 1 through 8 letters, numerals, or other acceptable characters assigned by the programmer. The extension may be any combination of 1 through 3 letters, numerals, or other acceptable characters. The filename and extension are separated by a period. The following characters are acceptable in DOS 2.1Ø:

$ # & @ ! % ( ) - { } ' ` _ ; : ¦

Neither the filename nor the extension may contain *blanks*. Truncation of the filename or extension occurs at the first *blank*.

Two other characters, the question mark (?) and the asterisk (*), called *global filename characters* or *wildcard characters,* may be used in place of any character of a filename or extension and may mean *any* character. Specific applications of global filename characters will be described in App. C-10.

The filename and extension chosen should be descriptive of the contents of the file. The following example of a properly identified file might refer to a FORTRAN source program written to calculate hyperbolic functions:

```
HYPFUNC.FOR
```

Within the general rules for composing filenames, the choice of filename and extension is generally left to the programmer. However, certain filenames and extensions have a special meaning either in DOS or to the Microsoft FORTRAN Compiler (App. E) and should not be used out of this context. In the example above, HYPFUNC.FOR, the extension FOR identifies the file to the compiler as a FORTRAN source program. During compilation of the source program, two other files with the filename HYPFUNC are created, with the extensions OBJ and EXE assigned by the compiler. If the file HYPFUNC.FOR is edited using the EDLIN line editor (App. D), the original (unedited) file is saved as HYPFUNC.BAK; the original filename with a new extension, BAK, is supplied by the editor. The edited file is stored under the original filename and extension HYPFUNC.FOR.

The following *reserved extensions* have a special meaning in DOS or to the MS-FORTRAN Compiler and should not be assigned by the programmer out of the intended context:

BAK	BAT	FOR	COM	DOC
BAS	SYS	OBJ	EXE	MAP

In addition, the following *reserved filenames* also have a special meaning in DOS and should not be assigned by the programmer out of the intended context:

Filenames used for controlling devices			**Filenames assigned to DOS system commands**		
AUX	LPT1	CON	DIR	DEL	DISKCOPY
COM1	LPT2	PRN	TYPE	ERASE	DISKCOMP
COM2	LPT3	NUL	RENAME	CLS	CHKDSK
			COPY	FORMAT	EDLIN

C-3 Start-up Procedure

To distinguish the DOS-generated prompts from the user response, user-typed characters are underlined in this and the following appendixes.

To "startup" the personal computer, or, in computer jargon, *boot* the system:

1 Insert a diskette containing the DOS command file COMMAND.COM in drive A, and close the cover by pushing down on the load lever.
2 Turn the system monitor and power switches on.
3 After 15 to 2Ø seconds, the cursor (_) will begin flashing in the upper left corner of the screen, the red drive light on drive A will glow, and about 3Ø seconds later, the following will appear on the screen:

```
Current date is Tue 1-Ø1-198Ø
Enter new date: _
```

4 Respond by keying in the current date (the underlined section below) and striking the ↵ key.

```
Enter new date: 01/05/86_↵
Current time is 0:00:13.56
Enter new time: _
```

5 Respond by keying in the current time (the underlined section below) and striking the ↵ key.

```
Enter new time: 08:30_↵
```

The correct format for entering the current date is:

01/05/86

for January 5, 1986. The digits representing month/day/year are separated by a slash (/). Separation of the month-day-year by a hyphen (-) is also acceptable:

01-05-86

The correct format for entering the current time is:

08:30 and 14:25

for 8:30 A.M. and 2:25 P.M., respectively, using the 24-hour-clock notation. The digits representing hour:minute must be separated by a colon (:). Seconds to the nearest hundredth may also be included, but are not necessary.

Current time and date entries may be bypassed if desired by striking the ↵ key in response to the prompts. Entering the current date and time each time the computer is "booted" will ensure that the directory will record the date and time that each file was entered.

6 Several identification lines similar to the following should now appear:

```
The IBM Personal Computer DOS
Version 2.10 (C)Copyright IBM Corp 1981, 1982, 1983
```

Followed by the default-drive prompt and the flashing cursor:

```
A>_
```

7 The screen should now look like this:

```
Current date is Tue 1-01-1980
Enter new date: 01/05/86
Current time is: 0:00:13.56
enter new time:08:30
```

```
The IBM Personal Computer DOS
Version 2.1Ø (C)Copyright IBM Corp 1981, 1982, 1983

A>_
```

The computer is now ready to receive further instructions. *Note:* Date and time can be entered or updated at any time as shown below.

```
A>date:01/05/86_↵

A>time:08:30_↵
```

C-4 Changing the Default Drive

Unless otherwise directed, either by the programmer from the keyboard or by a programmed instruction, diskette drive A will be engaged, and the A> prompt will appear. All information will be copied from or recorded on the diskette in drive A. Drive A is the *default drive*.

The default drive can be changed from drive A to drive B and back to drive A again as follows:

A>_

A>**B:**_↵ To change the default drive from drive A to drive B, key in **B:** and strike the ↵ key.

B>_

B>**A:**_↵ To change the default drive from drive B to drive A, key in **A:** and strike the ↵ key.

A>_

C-5 The DOS System Commands

The DOS diskette contains a command processor, filed under the filename and extension COMMAND.COM, which controls the computer hardware and manages the software. The COMMAND.COM file can be recorded on a new diskette during the formatting operation described later in this appendix. The COMMAND.COM file includes the following *internal commands,* which are needed by the FORTRAN programmer. These are:

DIR	TYPE	COPY
RENAME	DELETE	ERASE
CLS	VOL	FILENAME.BAT
AUTOEXEC.BAT	ECHO	

In addition to the internal commands included in the COMMAND.COM file, the DOS diskette contains several *external commands,* with the extension COM or EXE, which are needed by the FORTRAN programmer. These are:

FORMAT DISKCOPY DISKCOMP CHKDSK EDLIN SORT MORE

The function of these selected internal and external commands is described in Secs. C-6 through C-21 of this appendix.

The operations described in Secs. C-6 through C-21 require that a diskette containing the command processor COMMAND.COM and the specified DOS external command file be in drive A. Execution of each of the system commands is initiated by striking the ↵ key.

C-6 To Prepare a Diskette to Receive New Information

To prepare a diskette to receive new information (*formatting*), use the (external) FORMAT command:

(*a*) A>**FORMAT B:** ↵ — Erases all the information stored on the diskette in drive B and establishes the electronic grid of tracks and sectors used as "addresses" for the new information.

(*b*) A>**FORMAT B:/S** ↵ — The /S following **FORMAT B:** will automatically copy the DOS command processor file COMMAND.COM and certain "hidden files" required to boot the system from the diskette in drive A to the diskette in drive B.

(*c*) A>**FORMAT B:/V** ↵ — The /V following **FORMAT B:** provides for labeling the diskette with a label (with 11 or less characters) of the programmer's choice. The A> prompt will appear following the formatting, after which the label can be keyed in.

(*d*) A>**FORMAT B:/S/V** ↵ — Both the /S and the /V may be used if desired.

(*e*) A>**VOL B:** ↵ — Displays the label assigned to the diskette in the drive indicated, drive B in this example.

> *Caution:* The FORMAT command will *erase all files* from the diskette being formatted. Any files to be saved *must be copied to another diskette* before formatting.

C-7 To Display a Directory of the Contents of a Given Diskette

To display a directory of the contents of a given diskette, use the (internal) command DIR:

(*a*) A>**DIR** ↵ *or* — Lists the filename and extension, date and time the file was

A>**DIR A:** ↵

(*b*) A>**DIR B:** ↵

entered, and number of bytes used by the file, for each file recorded on the diskette in the drive indicated—the default drive A in example (*a*), drive B in example (*b*). If the directory contains more than 23 files, the list will scroll until the last line of the directory—noting the total bytes remaining on the diskette—appears.

(*c*) A>**DIR B:/P** ↵

The /**P** will stop the scrolling list when the screen is full (23 lines). To display the next 23 lines, strike the ↵ key.

(*d*) A>**DIR B:/W** ↵

The /**W** will list only the filename and extension (without the date, time, and bytes used) of all files recorded on the diskette in the drive indicated, in 5 columns across the screen. This command displays a list of all files on the screen at one time without scrolling.

(*e*) A>**DIR ¦ MORE** ↵

The MORE command will display 23 lines (one screen full) at a time. Striking the ↵ key will display the next 23 lines, etc. The MORE.COM file must be on the diskette whose directory is to be listed. Note the use of the ¦ character.

(*f*) A>**DIR ¦ SORT** ↵

The SORT command will arrange the directory listing in alphabetical order by filename. The SORT.EXE file must be on the diskette whose directory is to be listed. Note the use of the ¦ character.

(*g*) A>**DIR *.FOR ¦ SORT** ↵

Other combinations of the DIR command are possible. For example, DIR *.FOR ¦ SORT will display in alphabetical order all files with the extension FOR.

The above examples show the default (A) drive. This can be changed to drive B as shown in Sec. C-4.

C-8 To Display the Text of a Given File

To display the text of a given file, use the (internal) TYPE command:

(*a*)	A>TYPE FILENAME.EXT=↵ *or* A>TYPE A:FILENAME.EXT=↵	Displays the text of the file recorded under the specified file name and extension on the diskette in the drive indicated—the default drive A in example (*a*), drive B in example (*b*).
(*b*)	A>TYPE B:FILENAME.EXT=↵	

C-9 To Change the Filename and/or Extension of a Given File

To change the filename and/or extension of a given file, use the (internal) command RENAME:

(*a*) A>RENAME OLDNAME.EXT NEWNAME.EXT=↵
or
A>RENAME A:OLDNAME.EXT NEWNAME.EXT=↵

(*b*) A>RENAME B:OLDNAME.EXT NEWNAME.EXT=↵

RENAME changes the filename from the first name listed to the second name listed in the drive indicated, i.e., OLDNAME.EXT to NEWNAME.EXT, in the default drive A, in example (*a*), drive B in example (*b*).

C-10 To Permanently Remove a File from a Diskette

To permanently remove a file from a diskette, use either the (internal) command DEL or the (internal) command ERASE. (Both perform the same function.)

(*a*)	A>DEL FILENAME.EXT=↵ *or* A>ERASE A:FILENAME.EXT=↵	Deletes from the diskette in default drive A the file specified FILENAME.EXT.
(*b*)	A>DEL B:FILENAME.EXT=↵ *or* A>ERASE B:FILENAME.EXT=↵	Deletes from the diskette in drive B the file specified FILENAME.EXT.
(*c*)	A>DEL B:PROGRAM.???=↵ *or* A>DEL B:PROGRAM.*=↵	Use of the "wild-card" character (?) will remove all files with the filename PROGRAM (with any extension) from the diskette in drive B. The other "wild-card" character (*) could also have been used, in which case only one asterisk is required.

(*d*) A>**DEL B:*.BAK**↵ — Use of the "wild-card" character (*) will remove all files with the extension BAK (with any filename) from the diskette in drive B. The other "wild-card" character (?) could have been used; however, 8 question marks, or 1 for each character in the filename, will be required.

or

A>**DEL ????????.BAK**↵

C-11 To Duplicate a Given File and Store under a Different Filename

Use the (internal) COPY command to duplicate a given file and store under a different filename, as follows:

A>**COPY OLDFILE.EXT NEWFILE.EXT**↵

This command copies the text of a specified file (OLDFILE.EXT) to a new file (NEWFILE.EXT). The filename and text of the old file remain unchanged.

NOTE: If a file with the same name as the new file (NEWFILE.EXT) is already stored on the diskette, its contents will be replaced by the contents of the old file (OLDFILE.EXT).

C-12 To Copy a Given File from a Diskette in Drive A to a Diskette in Drive B

Use the (internal) COPY command to copy a given file from a diskette in drive A to a diskette in drive B, as follows:

(*a*) A>**COPY FILENAME.EXT B:**↵ — Copies the text of a specified file (FILENAME.EXT) from the source diskette in drive A to the target diskette in drive B, and assigns the same filename FILENAME.EXT to the copied file.

(*b*) A>**COPY A:OLDNAME.EXT B:NEWNAME.EXT**↵ — Copies the text of a specified file (OLDNAME.EXT) from the source diskette in drive A to the target diskette. Assigns a new filename (NEWNAME.EXT) to the copied file. The filename and text of the old file on the source diskette remain unchanged.

Note: In both (*a*) and (*b*), above, if a file with the same filename (NEWNAME.EXT) is already on the target diskette, its contents will be replaced by the contents of the source diskette.

C-13 To Copy All Files on Diskette from Drive A to Drive B

To copy all the files on the diskette in drive A to the diskette in drive B, one file at a time, use the (internal) COPY command as follows:

```
A>COPY *.* B: ↵
```

Copies the text of each file from the source diskette in drive A to the target diskette in drive B. Files are copied one file at a time and are listed on the screen as they are copied.

C-14 To Enter a File Directly from the Console to a Diskette

To enter a file directly from the console (keyboard) to a diskette, use the (internal) COPY command as follows:

```
A>COPY CON B:FILE.DAT ↵
123.456 ↵  }
987.654 ↵  }  text
1 Ø.123 ↵  }   of
2 1.875 ↵  }  file
3 2.375 ↵  }
^Z          [F6] ↵
```

Copies text directly from the console (keyboard) to the diskette in drive B and assigns the filename FILE.DAT.

Following the last line of the text, strike **F6**, then strike the ↵ key. (Depressing the **F6** key causes the ^Z to appear.)

C-15 To Print the Text of a Given File

Use the (internal) COPY command to print the text of a given file, as follows:

```
A>COPY B:FILENAME.EXT PRN ↵
or
A>COPY B:FILENAME.EXT LPT1 ↵
```

With a printer attached, this command will cause the printer to print the text of the specified file (FILENAME.EXT) from the diskette in drive B.

C-16 To Duplicate a Diskette

To duplicate a diskette, i.e., copy the entire contents of one diskette to another diskette, use the (external) DISKCOPY command. Begin with a diskette containing the DISKCOPY.COM file in drive A.

```
A>DISKCOPY A: B: ↵
```

Respond to prompts by removing the DOS diskette from drive A and inserting the source diskette in drive A and the target diskette in drive B. This command will format the diskette in drive B and copy the entire contents of the diskette in drive A (the source diskette) to the diskette in drive B (the target diskette).

Caution: In DOS 2.10, execution of the DISKCOPY command will automatically format the target diskette. *All information stored on the diskette in drive B will be erased.*

C-17 To Compare and Verify the Contents of Two Diskettes

To compare the contents of two diskettes and verify that they are identical, use the (external) DISKCOMP command. Begin with a diskette containing the DISKCOMP.COM file in drive A.

```
A>DISKCOMP A: B: ↵
```

Respond to prompts by removing the DOS diskette from drive A and inserting the original diskette in drive A and the copy in drive B. This command will compare the files on the diskette in drive B with the files on the diskette in drive A and verify that they are identical.

Note: The DISKCOMP command should be used after duplicating a diskette to ensure that the files on the copy are identical with the files on the original.

C-18 To Check the Status of a Diskette

Use the (external) CHKDSK command to check the status of a diskette:

```
A>CHKDSK B: ↵        Provides a status report on the diskette in
                     the drive indicated. Checks for unusable
                     tracks and sectors; accounts for bytes
                     used; indicates number of bytes of
                     available space remaining on diskette.
```

C-19 To Clear the Screen

Use the (internal) command CLS to clear the screen.

```
A>CLS ↵              Erases the screen and returns A> prompt and
                     the blinking cursor to the upper left
                     corner of the screen.
```

C-20 To Create a Batch File

A *batch* file is a file containing one or more DOS commands which are automatically executed one at a time when the *batch command* is initiated. A batch file can be assigned any suitable filename but must have the extension BAT. A diskette may contain as many batch files as needed, but only one AUTOEXEC.BAT file (App. C-21) per diskette is allowed.

The batch file can be created by copying from the console (keyboard) with the (internal) COPY command (App. C-14) or with the EDLIN line editor (App. D). The following example utilizes the COPY command:

```
A>COPY CON A:FORTRAN.BAT ↵
  ECHO OFF ↵
  CLS ↵
  DIR *.FOR | SORT ↵
  ^Z                    F6 ↵
```

The COPY CON command copies from the console (keyboard) the commands that follow into a batch file called FORTRAN.BAT. The filename, FORTRAN, is assigned by the programmer; the extension, BAT, identifies a batch file.

The batch command is initiated by keying in the filename, FORTRAN, without extension and striking the ↵ key:

```
A>FORTRAN ↵
```

Execution of the batch command in this example will suppress the listing of the commands on the screen as they are executed (ECHO OFF), clear the screen (CLS), and list in alphabetical order all the files with the extension FOR (App. C-7*g*).

C-21 To Create an AUTOEXEC.BAT File

To create a special batch file that will automatically execute a series of commands stored in the file whenever the system is booted, use the internal COPY command (App. C-14) with the AUTOEXEC.BAT file as follows:

```
A>COPY CON A:AUTOEXEC.BAT ↵
DATE: ↵
TIME: ↵
DIR A: ↵
^Z                    F6 ↵
```

When the system is booted, the date and time prompts will appear. After response to date and time prompts, a directory of the files on the diskette in drive A is automatically displayed, followed by the A> prompt.

The COPY CON command copies from the console (keyboard) the commands that follow into a special batch file called AUTOEXEC.BAT. The commands in the AUTOEXEC.BAT file will be executed in the order listed whenever the system is booted.

Note: Any number of commands may be filed in the AUTOEXEC.BAT file, but only *one* AUTOEXEC.BAT file per diskette is permitted.

APPENDIX **D**

THE EDLIN LINE EDITOR

D-1 Introduction

The DOS master diskette contains a line editor stored under the filename and extension EDLIN.COM, which is used for creating, storing, and editing a FORTRAN source program. Although this text is concerned primarily with files that are FORTRAN source programs, subprograms, or data files, the EDLIN line editor can be used for creating and editing any desired file. Some full-screen editors and word processors may also be used for creating, storing, and editing the FORTRAN source program.

The instructions that follow provide sufficient information for the beginning programmer to create, store, and edit any FORTRAN source program, subprogram, or data file by using the EDLIN line editor. For more detailed information consult the Disk Operating System Manual.

D-2 To Create and Store a New File

With the DOS diskette containing the EDLIN.COM file in drive A, the diskette on which the new file will be stored in drive B, and the DOS **A>** prompt displayed, key in EDLIN, the drive designation (**B:**), the filename with extension, and strike the ↵ key.

Note 1: A file cannot be added to a write-protected diskette.

Note 2: The EDLIN.COM file can be copied onto the diskette on which the new file is to be stored. If both EDLIN and the new file are on the same diskette (in drive A), the drive designation may be omitted.

A>**EDLIN B:NEWFILE.FOR** ↵ New file *_	Opens a new file with the file name and extension NEWFILE.FOR to be stored on the diskette in the designated drive (B in this example), and displays the EDLIN prompt * (asterisk).
***1I** ↵	Key the line number (1 for the first line) followed by I (for INSERT, and strike the ↵ key.
1:***C234567** ↵ 2:* **J=3** ↵ 3:* **K=4** ↵ 4:* **N=J+K** ↵	The line number 1 followed by :* will appear. Begin the FORTRAN source program on line 1. The first available column is column 1.

```
5: *      WRITE(*,*)N_↵
6: *      END_↵
7: *^C        [Ctrl]   [C]
```

The comment (C) line is used to identify column numbers. Note that each FORTRAN instruction begins in column 7.

Strike the ↵ key at the end of each line. After the last line of the program has been keyed in, hold down Ctrl and strike C to return the EDLIN prompt to the screen.

Note: If a FORTRAN statement is continued, each line of the continuation requires a new EDLIN line number. Be sure to strike the ↵ key after entering the character in column 72. The cursor automatically indexes to column 1 and advances 1 line; however, it is the return key that enters the new line number.

```
*E_↵
```

To store the FORTRAN source program on the diskette in drive B (the drive specified in the EDLIN initiating instruction), key E (for ENTER) and strike the ↵ key.

```
A>_
```

When the file has been stored on the diskette, the **A>** prompt will return to the screen.

Or to leave the edit mode without storing the file:

```
*Q_↵
Abort edit (Y/N)?Y_↵
A>_
```

To return the A> prompt to the screen without storing the file, key **Q** (for **QUIT**). You may still change your mind. Key Y (for YES) and strike the ↵ key to irrevocably erase this file from memory without storing on the diskette, or key **N** (for **NO**) for another opportunity to store the file.

D-3 To Recall an Existing File for Editing

With the DOS diskette containing the EDLIN.COM file in drive A, the diskette containing the file to be edited in drive B, and the DOS prompt **A>** displayed, key in EDLIN, the drive designation (B:), the filename and extension, and strike the ↵ key.

Note: If the file to be edited and EDLIN.COM are on the same diskette (in drive A), the drive designation may be omitted.

```
A>EDLIN B:OLDFILE.FOR_↵
End of input file

*_
```

This command recalls an existing file with the filename and extension OLDFILE.FOR stored on the diskette in the designated drive (B in this example) and displays the EDLIN prompt * (asterisk).

```
*1L_ ↵
```

Key the line number with which the listing is to begin (1 if from the first line) followed by L (for LIST).

```
1: C234567
2:       J=3
3:       K=4
4:       N=J+K
5:       WRITE(*,*)N
6:       END

*_
```

The first 23 lines of the file (or the 23 lines beginning with the line number indicated) will be listed with the line numbers.

The EDLIN prompt * is displayed following the listing.

D-4 To Delete a Line or Lines from a File

(*a*)

```
*_

*5D_ ↵
```

To delete a single line, key the number of the line to be deleted (5 in this example), followed by **D** (for **DELETE**), and strike the ↵ key. Line 5 will be deleted and the lines renumbered.

(*b*)

```
*_

*3,8D_ ↵
```

To delete several consecutive lines, key inclusive line numbers separated by a comma (3,8 in this example) followed by **D**. Lines 3 through 8, inclusive, will be deleted; the remaining lines will be renumbered.

D-5 To Insert a New Line or Lines

```
*_

*5I_ ↵

   5: *NEW LINE 5_ ↵
   6: *NEW LINE 6_ ↵
   7: *NEW LINE 7_ ↵

   8: *^C      [Ctrl] [C]

*_
```

Key the line number (5 in this example) and **I** (for INSERT) to insert a new line 5 (following existing line 4) and strike the ↵ key. 5:* will appear. Key the text of new line 5 (NEW LINE 5 in this example) and strike the ↵ key.

New lines 6, 7, 8, etc., may be inserted after line 5, if desired, following the appearance of each consecutive line number.

When the last line has been inserted, hold down Ctrl and strike C to return the EDLIN prompt to the screen. Lines 5, 6, and 7 have been added, and the following lines renumbered.

D-6 To Recall and Change an Existing Line

```
*_

*5_↵

5:*OLD LINE 5
5:*_

5:*new line 5_↵
  *_
```

Key the line number (5 in this example) and strike the ↵ key to recall a line for editing.

5:* will appear followed by the text of existing line 5 (OLD LINE 5 in this example) and on the line below 5:* will appear again. Change as desired and strike the ↵ key.

The EDLIN prompt *_ will return to the screen.

Characters requiring no change can be repeated by striking the right-cursor movement key (→) on the numeric keypad.

Note: The file should be listed (Sec. D-3) after each deletion, insertion, or change to ensure that the editing is correct.

D-7 To Move a Line From One Location to Another or Repeat an Existing Line

To move a line or lines from one location to another or repeat an existing line in another location:

```
(a) *_

    *5,8,1M_↵

    *_
```

Key the inclusive numbers of the block of consecutive lines to be moved (lines 5 through 8 in this example), separated by a comma, followed by a comma and the new number for the first line of the block (,1 in this example), then M (for MOVE). Strike the ↵ key.

Lines 5 through 8 are now lines 1 through 4, and the entire file is renumbered with the specified block of lines deleted from the old position and inserted in the new position.

(*b*) *=

***5,8,10C**=↵

*=

Key the inclusive numbers of the block of consecutive lines to be copied (lines 5 through 8 in this example, separated by a comma, followed by a comma and the new number for the first line of the block (,1Ø in this example), then **C** (for **COPY**). Strike the ↵ key.

Lines 5 through 8 are repeated as lines 1Ø through 13, and the entire file is renumbered accordingly.

(*c*) *=
***4,4,1M**=↵
or
***4,4,10C**=↵
*=

If only one line is to be moved or copied, key the line number twice, separated by a comma (4,4 in this example), and proceed as in example (*a*) or (*b*) above.

D-8 To Merge a Stored File with Another File Position

To transfer (merge) a file stored on the (same) diskette to a specified position in a file currently in EDLIN mode:

*=
***17 T FILENAME.EXT**=↵
*=

Key the line number that will be the first line of the transferred file (17 in this example), a *blank*, T (for transfer), another *blank*, and the filename with extension, if any, of the file to be transferred. Strike the ↵ key.

The entire file stored on the diskette as FILENAME.EXT will be copied to the file currently in EDLIN mode beginning with line 17 of the current file. Lines will be renumbered to account for the inserted file.

The original text of FILENAME.EXT remains unchanged on the diskette.

D-9 Editing Shortcuts with the Function Keys

The function keys F1, F2, F3, F4, F5, and F6 may be used to advantage when editing a

	Screen	Explanation
	*_ *5_↵	Display the given line (line 5 in this example) for editing.
(*a*)	5: *THIS IS LINE FIVE 5: *_ [F1] *17 times* 5: *THIS IS LINE FIVE_	Striking **F1** will repeat each character, one at a time. The **F1** function key does the same thing as the right-cursor movement key (→) on the numeric keypad.
(*b*)	5: *THIS IS LINE FIVE 5: *_ [F2] [F] 5: *THIS IS LINE _	Striking **F2** then F will repeat all characters from the cursor location up to, but not including, the designated character (F in this example).
(*c*)	5: *THIS IS LINE FIVE 5: *_ [F3] 5: *THIS IS LINE FIVE_	Striking **F3** will repeat all characters from the cursor location to the end of the line.
	5: *THIS IS LINE FIVE 5: **bbbbbbbb* [F3] 5: * LINE FIVE_	Leading characters can be deleted and the cursor moved to the right with the space bar. In this example, the space bar was struck 8 times before striking **F3**, thus deleting the characters THIS IS*b* before repeating the characters LINE FIVE.
(*d*)	5: *THIS IS LINE FIVE 5: *_ [F4] [L] [F3] 5: : *LINE FIVE_	Striking **F4**, L, then **F3** will delete all characters from the cursor up to, but not including, the designated character (L in this example) and repeat the remaining characters beginning at the cursor location.
(*e*)	5: *THUS ARE FINE 5: * [F5] 5: *@ _ (*now try again*) 5: *THIS IS LINE FIVE_↵	Striking **F5** will display a @, delete the mistakenly typed line, and return the cursor to column 1 for a new start.

(*f*) The **F6** function key permits replacing or deleting one character (or string of characters) wherever that character (or string of characters) appears in a block of consecutive lines:

```
*L=↵
     1. THIS IS LINE ONE
     2. THIS IS LINE TWO
     3. THIS IS LINE THREE
     4. THIS IS LINE FOUR
     5. THIS IS LINE FIVE
```

In this example, the character N in the word LINE is to be replaced by the character * in lines 1 through 3, inclusive, and the character S is to be deleted in lines 4 and 5.

***1,3?RN** [F6] *

```
*1,3?RN^Z*=↵
     1: THIS IS LI*E ONE
 O.K.? Y
     1: THIS IS LI*E O*E
 O.K.? N
     2: THIS IS LI*E TWO
 O.K.? Y
     3: THIS IS LI*E THREE
 O.K.? Y
*L=↵
     1: THIS IS LI*E ONE
     2: THIS IS LI*E TWO
     3: THIS IS LI*E THREE
     4: THIS IS LINE FOUR
     5: THIS IS LINE FIVE
```

Key the inclusive line numbers 1 and 3, separated by a comma, a ?, R, and N (the character to be replaced). Strike the **F6** function key. Enter a * (the replacement character) and strike the ↵ key. (Note that striking the **F6** function key causes ^Z to be displayed on the screen.)

The question mark (?) provides for user control over the character replacement on a one-by-one basis.

Respond to the O.K.? prompt by keying Y if the replacement is to be made, N if the replacement is not desired.

***4,5RS** [F6]

```
*4,5RS^Z↵
     4: THI IS LINE FOUR
     4: THI I LINE FOUR
     5: THI IS LINE FIVE
     5: THI I LINE FIVE
*L=↵
     1: THIS IS LI*E ONE
     2: THIS IS LI*E TWO
     3: THIS IS LI*E THREE
     4: THI I LINE FOUR
     5: THI I LINE FIVE
*=
```

Note that in this instruction, no replacement character is indicated. The character S will not be replaced but deleted, and the remaining characters closed to the left.

Note also the absence of a ? in the instruction. No selective replacement is possible.

The final listing shows the text of lines 1 through 5 after both replacements have been executed.

D-10 To Insert or Delete Characters in a Given Line

(*a*) *=
*5=↵

5: *THIS IS LINE FIVE 5: * [F2] [L] [Ins]	To insert characters, strike **F2**, L, Ins, then key the characters to be inserted (NEW*b* in this example).
5: *THIS IS **NEW** = [F3]	Strike **F3** to complete the line.
5: *THIS IS NEW LINE FIVE=↵	Strike the ↵ key to enter the edited line.

(*b*)

5: *THIS IS NEW LINE FIVE 5: * [F2] [N] [Del] [F3] (*4 times*)	To delete characters NEW*b* strike **F2**, N, then Del 4 times—once for each character to be deleted, including the *blank* after NEW. Strike **F3** to complete the line.
5: *THIS IS LINE FIVE=↵	Strike the ↵ key to enter the edited line.

or

5: *THIS IS NEW LINE FIVE 5: * [F2] [N] [F4] [L] [F3]	Strike **F2**, N, **F4**, L, then **F3**.
5: *THIS IS LINE FIVE=↵	Strike the ↵ key to enter the edited line.

(*c*) An entire line can be moved to the right by inserting leading *blanks*. Hold down Ins and depress the space bar once for each column the line is to be moved. Release Ins and strike **F3** to repeat the line in the new position.

An entire line can be moved to the left by deleting leading *blanks*. Depress **Del** once for each column the line is to be moved. Strike **F3** to repeat the line in the new position.

D-11 The BAK File

When an existing file is recalled from diskette storage (App. D-3), edited, and reentered with the EDLIN line editor, the text of the old file is automatically copied and stored on the diskette under the same filename and assigned the extension BAK. The *backup* or

BAK file is created when the edited text is entered into diskette storage with the EDLIN command E (App. D-2). A directory listing will then include two files with the same filename: the edited file with the extension FOR, and the old file with the extension BAK. A BAK file cannot be recalled for editing; however, a BAK file can be renamed with a different extension and then recalled and edited.

Only one BAK file with a given filename can be stored at a time. If the newly edited file is edited a second time, the existing BAK file is erased and a new BAK file is created from the text of the file just recalled. BAK files should be deleted from the diskette when they are no longer needed.

APPENDIX **E**

COMPILING THE FORTRAN SOURCE PROGRAM

E-1 Introduction

FORTRAN is a compiler language; the source program written by the programmer must be translated (compiled) into a symbolic code or machine language that is understandable to the personal computer. An intermediate program called a *compiler* is required to make this translation. Several compilers are available. The compiler used for translating (compiling) the programs in this text, and briefly outlined in the following sections, is the Microsoft (MS) FORTRAN Compiler developed and marketed by the Microsoft Corporation of Bellevue, Washington. The MS-FORTRAN compiler is a superset of a subset of standard FORTRAN 77, specifically designed for compiling a FORTRAN source program on the personal computer. Several versions of this compiler are in use, with Version 3.31 (copyright 1985) being the latest at the time of this publication.

The MS-FORTRAN compiler consists of a set of diskettes and a reference manual and user's guide, providing detailed information about the files on the diskettes and how they can be applied. This appendix will describe how the files on the DOS master and the MS-FORTRAN master diskettes can be combined to create two "working" diskettes for use in writing, editing, compiling, and executing a FORTRAN source program. (For a more detailed discussion of the MS-FORTRAN compiler, refer to the reference manual and user's guide.) The instructions that follow assume the availability of a personal computer with two disk drives and 256 K of random-access memory operating from the Disk Operating System.

E-2 Preparing the Working Diskettes

Prepare two working diskettes as follows:

1 (*a*) With the DOS master diskette in drive A and a new diskette in drive B, format the new diskette using the /S and /V options.

A>**FORMAT B:/S/V**_ ↵	This will add the COMMAND.COM and the hidden files used to boot the system to the diskette in drive B.

At the prompt, label the volume on this diskette: PROGRAM A

(*b*) Copy the EDLIN.COM file from the DOS master diskette to the newly formatted PROGRAM A working diskette in drive B.

A>**COPY EDLIN.COM B:** ↵ The FORTRAN source program will be written and edited on the PROGRAM A diskette

(*c*) Remove the PROGRAM A diskette from drive B and label "PROGRAM A." Insert the second new diskette in drive B. Format this diskette using the /V option only.

A>**FORMAT B:/V** ↵ Neither the COMMAND.COM nor the EDLIN.COM files are needed on the second formatted diskette.

At the prompt, label the volume on this diskette: COMPILER B When formatting is complete, remove the COMPILER B working diskette from drive B and label "COMPILER B."

2 The next step is to copy the necessary files from the MS-FORTRAN master diskettes to the working diskettes. Obtain a directory of the files on the master diskettes and locate the following files:

```
FORTRAN.LIB     PAS2.EXE     MATH.LIB
FOR1.EXE        LINK.EXE
```

3 Using the COPY command:

(*a*) Copy the MATH.LIB and the LINK.EXE files from the FORTRAN master diskette to the PROGRAM A working diskette (App. C-11).

A>**COPY MATH.LIB B:** ↵
A>**COPY LINK.EXE B:** ↵

(*b*) Copy the FOR1.EXE, the PAS2.EXE, and the FORTRAN.LIB files from the MS-FORTRAN master diskette to the COMPILER B working diskette.

A>**COPY FOR1.EXE B:** ↵
A>**COPY PAS2.EXE B:** ↵
A>**COPY FORTRAN.LIB B:** ↵

(*c*) Display a directory listing of the two working diskettes. The working diskettes should now contain the following:

```
 PROGRAM A                          COMPILER B

COMMAND   COM                       FOR1      EXE
(including the hidden               PAS2      EXE
 files required to                  FORTRAN   LIB
 boot the system.)
EDLIN     COM
MATH      LIB
LINK      EXE
```

4 Write-protect the COMPILER B working diskette. *Do not* write-protect the PROGRAM A working diskette.

The working diskette labeled PROGRAM A goes in drive A. The working diskette labeled COMPILER B goes in drive B.

The FORTRAN source program is written and edited by using the EDLIN line editor and is entered on the PROGRAM A working diskette identified by an appropriate filename with the extension FOR. An *object program* (extension OBJ) and an *execute program* (extension EXE) with the same filename as the source program are created during compilation and stored on the PROGRAM A working diskette.

E-3 Compiling the FORTRAN Source Program

1 (*a*) Insert the PROGRAM A working diskette in drive A. (Remember, this diskette contains the COMMAND.COM files, the hidden files needed to boot the system, and the EDLIN.COM file.)

(*b*) Insert the COMPILER B working diskette in drive B.

(*c*) Boot (start up) the system. Enter DATE and TIME.

(*d*) Key in the FORTRAN source program by using the EDLIN line editor, and enter on the PROGRAM A diskette (App. D).

Assume the following example FORTRAN source program has been filed on the PROGRAM A working diskette identified by the filename and extension CIRCLE.FOR. (Note that the extension FOR is assigned to *all* FORTRAN source programs.)

```
      PROGRAM CIRCLE
      PI=3.141593
      R=7.5
      C=2.Ø*PI*R
      A=PI*R**2
      WRITE(*,1ØØ)R,C,A
 1ØØ  FORMAT(3F17.7)
      STOP
      END
```

2 Proceed as follows from the A> prompt:

```
A>B:FOR1 CIRCLE=↵ (Key in filename, only. No extension.)
The following messages will appear on the screen:
Microsoft FORTRAN77 V3.30 March 1985
(C) Copyright Microsoft Corp 1982, 1983, 1984, 1985

Object filename [CIRCLE.OBJ]: =↵
Source listing  [NUL.LST]: =↵          or    CIRCLE=↵
Object listing  [NUL.COD]: =↵
 Pass One     No Errors Detected          (see text below
              9 Source Lines               for explanation)
```

A>_

(*a*) Strike the ↵ key in response to each : prompt.
(*b*) If a source listing file is desired, key in the file name CIRCLE after [NUL.LST]: before striking the ↵ key. This file, identified CIRCLE.LST and stored on the PROGRAM A working diskette, can be displayed on the screen after compilation has been completed by using the TYPE command. A CIRCLE.LST file is not necessary, but it may be helpful in locating errors (App. E-6).
(*c*) If errors are detected after pass one, the source program must be recalled with the EDLIN line editor and the necessary corrections made.
After correcting the errors, begin again with the FOR1 step.

If no errors are detected:

3 Continue from the A> prompt:

A>**B:PAS2**_↵
The following messages will appear on the screen:

```
Code Area Size = #00DD (  221)
Cons Area Size = #001C (   28)
Data Area Size = #0028 (   40)

Pass Two   No Errors Detected.
```

A>_

(*a*) If errors are detected after pass two, the source program must be recalled with the EDLIN line editor and the necessary corrections made.
(*b*) After correcting the errors, begin again with the FOR1 step.

If no errors are detected:

4 Continue from the A> prompt:

A>**LINK CIRCLE,,,B:FORTRAN.LIB+A:MATH.LIB**_↵
The following messages will appear on the screen:

```
Microsoft 8086 Object Linker
Version 3.Ø2 (C) Copyright Microsoft Corp 1983, 1984, 1985
```

A>_

(Be patient . . . 90 to 95 seconds is required to complete the LINK step.) When the drive lights stop blinking, the A> prompt will return to the screen. Compilation is complete.

A directory listing of the files now stored on the PROGRAM A working diskette in drive A will include the following files:

COMMAND	COM	CIRCLE	FOR
EDLIN	COM	CIRCLE	OBJ
MATH	LIB	CIRCLE	EXE
LINK	EXE	CIRCLE	MAP

CIRCLE LST will also be included if a source listing was specified during pass one of compilation. The FORTRAN source program, CIRCLE.FOR, was entered by the programmer with the EDLIN line editor. The CIRCLE files with extensions OBJ, EXE, MAP, and LST were created and stored at the direction of the compiler program during compilation. The text of these files may be displayed using the TYPE command; however, only two, CIRCLE.FOR and CIRCLE.LST, will be displayed in readable form. The files with the OBJ, EXE, and MAP extensions will be displayed in symbolic code, and viewing them is usually of little value to the FORTRAN programmer.

E-4 Executing the FORTRAN Program

Results are obtained by *running* or *executing* the program. To execute the program:

1 Insert the PROGRAM A working diskette containing the CIRCLE.EXE file in drive A.
2 List the source program with the TYPE command:

```
A>TYPE CIRCLE.FOR_ ↵          (Listing the source program is not
                              necessary, but it is listed here
                              so the results can be compared
                              with the source program.)

      PROGRAM CIRCLE
      PI=3.141593
      R=7.5
      C=2.Ø*PI*R
      A=PI*R**2
      WRITE(*,1ØØ)R,C,A
  1ØØ FORMAT(3F17.7)
      STOP
      END
A>_
```

3 Following the A> prompt, key in the filename only (without extension), and strike the ↵ key.

```
A>CIRCLE_↵
          7.5ØØØØØØ        47.1238900        176.7146ØØØ
Stop - Program terminated.
A>_
```

After compilation has been completed, an execution file created and stored, and the desired results obtained, only the files with extensions FOR and EXE need be retained. All other files with the filename CIRCLE (CIRCLE.OBJ, CIRCLE.MAP, CIRCLE.LST, or, as the result of editing the source program, CIRCLE.BAK) may be deleted to make room for additional programs on the PROGRAM A working diskette (App. C-10). The FORTRAN source and execute files, CIRCLE.FOR and CIRCLE.EXE, should be copied to a storage diskette and deleted from the PROGRAM A working diskette. If this is not done, the PROGRAM A working diskette will soon become too full to accept any more files; eventually files must be transferred or a new PROGRAM A working diskette made.

E-5 Creating a Batch File for Controlling the Compiler

A batch file (App. C-20) can be created and stored on the PROGRAM A working diskette that will semiautomatically compile and execute the FORTRAN source program and delete the MAP and OBJ files from the PROGRAM A diskette.

With the EDLIN line editor, key in the following file and enter it on the PROGRAM A working diskette identified with the filename and extension COMPILE.BAT. (The extension BAT identifies a batch file.)

```
Path A:\;B:\;
FOR1 %1
PAS2
LINK %1,,,B:FORTRAN.LIB+A:MATH.LIB
ERASE %1.MAP
ERASE %1.OBJ
%1
```

Any suitable filename can be assigned to the batch file, i.e., COMP.BAT, C.BAT, etc.; however, the extension must be BAT.

To use the batch file, key in COMPILE followed by the filename of the source program, and strike the ↵ key. There will be three pauses in the automatic compilation during pass one. To continue compilation, strike the ↵ key after each : prompt (or, if a source listing is desired, key in the filename after [NUL.LST]: before striking the ↵ key).

To compile the CIRCLE.FOR source program used in the previous example, key in the command and filename, COMPILE CIRCLE, respectively, and strike the ↵ key. Note that only the filename, no extension, is keyed in.

```
A>COMPILE CIRCLE = ↵

(Three pauses will occur. Strike the ↵ key after each : )

Object filename  [CIRCLE.OBJ]: = ↵
Source listing   [NUL.LST]: = ↵          or    CIRCLE = ↵
Object listing   [nul.cod]: = ↵

(Automatic compilation and execution continues.)
```

When compilation is complete, execution will begin automatically.

If errors in the source program are detected, automatic compilation will be terminated after pass one, pass two, or during execution, depending on when the error was detected.

E-6 Errors

A first-run, error-free FORTRAN source program is highly desirable . . . and highly unlikely! Errors detected during compilation pass one and pass two are located by the source-program line number, and appropriate numbered *error messages* are displayed. The error-message numbers refer to the MS-FORTRAN error messages listed in the Microsoft FORTRAN User's Guide. Errors detected, during pass one and pass two are usually errors in FORTRAN syntax or procedure. Compilation is aborted at pass one or pass two when errors are detected, and the A> prompt is displayed. The FORTRAN source program must then be recalled with the EDLIN line editor, each error located and corrected, and the corrected file reentered on the diskette. When the corrected program is entered, the old error-infested program will be retained on the diskette (until erased) under the same filename but with the extension changed from FOR to BAK (App. D-11). The corrected program will have the extension FOR.

A source program still may not execute successfully even though no errors are detected during compilation pass one or pass two. These are known as *run-time errors*. Run-time errors abort execution and display error messages to assist in identifying the errors. These error messages may not be explicit and are sometimes difficult to interpret. Attempting to divide by zero, extract the square root of a negative number, or execute some other undefined operation are the usual causes of run-time errors.

Figures E-1 through E-11 list FORTRAN source programs containing errors with the resulting MS-FORTRAN error messages. The program in Fig. E-1 contains errors detected during pass one of compilation. The number of the line in which the error(s) occur is identified in each error message along with the probable cause of the error and a reference to the error number in the MS-FORTRAN User's Guide.

The first step in correcting errors is to recall the source program with the EDLIN line editor and display the line(s) containing the errors. However, when the editor is invoked, the display of error messages disappears from the screen. Unless a paper copy of the error messages has been made, they may be difficult to remember. A printout of the list file

FIGURE E-1 Compilation errors.

```
C234567890
      READ(3,100)A,B,C
      FORMAT(3F10.4)
      DISC=SQRT(B**2-4.*/A*C
      ROOT1=(-B+DISC)/(2.*A)
      ROOT2=(-B-DISC)/(2.*A)
     WRITE(7,200)ROOT1,ROOT2
      IF(LVAL)10,10,20
   20 STOP
      END

A>B:FOR1 APP-E-1

Microsoft FORTRAN77 V3.30 March 1985
(C) Copyright Microsoft Corp 1982, 1983, 1984, 1985

Object filename [APP-E-1.OBJ]:
Source listing  [NUL.LST]:
Object listing  [NUL.COD]:

***** Error 135,line 3 -- FORMAT label missing

***** Error 50,line 4 -- invalid symbol in expression

***** Error 26,line 4 -- ")" expected

***** Error 23,line 6 -- extra characters at end of statement
      Label  10      not defined.

***** Error 131,line 10 -- label not defined

***** Error 163,line 10 -- FORMAT not found
 Pass One       6 Errors Detected
               10 Source Lines
```

(Fig. E-2) will be helpful since the list file (APP-E-1B.LST) lists the source program with the error message(s) immediately following the line on which the error occurs.

The error in line 3 is obvious; the label on the FORMAT statement is missing. Two errors have been noted in line 4. The message *invalid symbol in expression* refers to the adjacent */ in the expression which computes and assigns a value to DISC; two arithmetic operators in succession are not permitted (Sec. 3-7*a*). The message *expected* indicates unbalanced parentheses: a closing (right) parenthesis is needed. Line 6 contains no errors. Then why the error message? Because the next line (line 7) begins with the first character, W, in column 6, the continuation field. The characters that follow are considered part of line 6 and are not recognizable as a valid statement. Messages such as *Label 1Ø not defined* indicate that somewhere in the program (in the arithmetic IF statement) a reference was made to a statement label (1Ø) that is not in the program. Finally, the line 1Ø message, *FORMAT not found*, is not in line 1Ø but is stated here because the END statement is the last statement in the program, and there is nowhere else to look for the FORMAT statement 1Ø referenced in the READ statement. The error is caused by the missing statement label in line 3. One other error, undetected by the compiler, is present in this program. No

FIGURE E-2 Compilation errors of Fig. E-1 as shown by the LST output.

```
                                                              Page    1
                                                              02-24-86
                                                              14:22:05
D Line# 1      7                      Microsoft FORTRAN77 V3.30 March 1985
      1 C234567890
      2         READ(3,100)A,B,C
      3         FORMAT(3F10.4)
***** Error 135 -- FORMAT label missing
      4         DISC=SQRT(B**2-4.*/A*C
***** Error 50 -- invalid symbol in expression
***** Error 26 -- ")" expected
      5         ROOT1=(-B+DISC)/(2.*A)
      6         ROOT2=(-B-DISC)/(2.*A)
      7        WRITE(7,200)ROOT1,ROOT2
***** Error 23 -- extra characters at end of statement
      8         IF(LVAL)10,10,20
      9      20 STOP
     10         END
     Label  10      not defined.
     Format 100     not defined.
***** Error 131 -- label not defined
***** Error 163 -- FORMAT not found

Name      Type          Offset P Class

A        REAL             16
B        REAL             20
C        REAL             24
DISC     REAL             28
LVAL     INTEGER*4        40
ROOT1    REAL             32
ROOT2    REAL             36
SQRT                              INTRINSIC


Name      Type             Size   Class

MAIN                              PROGRAM


 Pass One      6 Errors Detected
              10 Source Lines
```

value has been assigned to the variable name LVAL, the logical expression in the IF statement. A default value of zero has been assigned to LVAL, which may or may not be what the programmer intended.

Figure E-3 is the program of Fig. E-1 with the errors (presumably) corrected. No errors are detected during pass one and pass two; however, an error is detected during the LINK step. The intrinsic function, SQR, called in line 4 has not been located in the library files, and the obscure message, *Unresolved externals:* is printed. Fortunately, the message *SQR in files(s):* provides a clue to the trouble, and SQR can be changed to SQRT, the correct function name.

Figure E-4 (see p. 394) illustrates the third attempt to "get it right"! This time compilation is completed without error. However, execution is terminated with an error message indicating that the Unit 3 referenced in the READ statement does not exist. An OPEN statement is needed preceding the READ statement, identifying the data file from which the values to be assigned to the variable names in the read list can be read. Another OPEN statement is needed preceding the WRITE statement, identifying the Unit 6 referenced in

FIGURE E-3 LINK-step errors.

```
C234567890
   10 READ(3,100)A,B,C,LASTVALUE
  100 FORMAT(3F10.4,I5)
      DISC=SQR(B**2-4.*A*C)
      ROOT1=(-B+DISC)/(2.*A)
      ROOT2=(-B-DISC)/(2.*A)
      WRITE(6,200)ROOT1,ROOT2,
  200 FORMAT(1X,2F10.4)
      IF(LVAL)10,10,20
   20 STOP
      END

A>B:FOR1 APP-E-3

Microsoft FORTRAN77 V3.30 March 1985
(C) Copyright Microsoft Corp 1982, 1983, 1984, 1985

Object filename [APP-E-3.OBJ]:
Source listing  [NUL.LST]:
Object listing  [NUL.COD]:
 Pass One     No Errors Detected
              11 Source Lines

A>B:PAS2

 Code Area Size = #0189  (  393)
 Cons Area Size = #001C  (   28)
 Data Area Size = #0048  (   72)

 Pass Two     No Errors Detected.

A>LINK APP-E-3,,,B:FORTRAN.LIB+A:MATH.LIB

Microsoft 8086 Object Linker
Version 3.02 (C) Copyright Microsoft Corp 1983, 1984, 1985


Unresolved externals:


SQR in file(s):
 APP-E-3.OBJ(MAIN_)

There was 1 error detected
```

```
C234567890
   10 READ(3,100)A,B,C,LASTVALUE
  100 FORMAT(3F10.4,I5)
      DISC=SQRT(B**2-4.0*A*C)
      ROOT1=(-B+DISC)/(2.0*A)
      ROOT2=(-B-DISC)/(2.0*A)
      WRITE(6,200)ROOT1,ROOT2
  200 FORMAT(1X,2F10.4)
      IF(LVAL)10,10,20
   20 STOP
      END

A>B:FOR1 APP-E-4

Microsoft FORTRAN77 V3.30 March 1985
(C) Copyright Microsoft Corp 1982, 1983, 1984, 1985

Object filename [APP-E-4.OBJ]:
Source listing  [NUL.LST]:
Object listing  [NUL.COD]:
 Pass One     No Errors Detected
              11 Source Lines

A>B:PAS2

 Code Area Size = #0189  (  393)
 Cons Area Size = #001C  (   28)
 Data Area Size = #0048  (   72)

 Pass Two     No Errors Detected.

A>LINK APP-E-4,,,B:FORTRAN.LIB+A:MATH.LIB

Microsoft 8086 Object Linker
Version 3.02 (C) Copyright Microsoft Corp 1983, 1984, 1985


A>APP-E-4
File name missing or blank - Please enter name
```

FIGURE E-4 Another LINK-step error.

the WRITE statement as the printer or file to which the output is to be routed. Note two other errors in this program listing undetected by the compiler: the variable name LASTVALUE in the read list is an invalid variable name (more than six characters) which will be truncated to LASTVA; and two different variable names, LASTVALUE and LVAL, were used to represent the same quantity. The variable name LASTVALUE should be changed to LVAL. With all corrections made, and data file APP-E-4.DAT properly entered on the diskette, the source program is finally compiled and executed successfully as illustrated in Fig. E-5.

Figure E-6 (see p. 396) is a source-program listing which compiled without error but was terminated during the execution phase. The error message is general, indicating only that a problem exists in the output (PRN) file. A close examination of the source program reveals that the 100 FORMAT statement does not agree with the WRITE statement that references it. There are no edit descriptors in the FORMAT specification corresponding with the variable names A, B, C in the write list, nor should there be; the problem is with the WRITE statement. Since this output statement was written to print the character constants 'A B C' for column headings, no write list is needed; including a write list constitutes a run-time error.

The source-program listing of Fig. E-7 (see p. 397) repeats the listing of Fig. E-6 with the WRITE and 200 FORMAT statements added to print the values assigned to the variable names A, B, C. Again an error-free compilation but termination during execution! This time the error message signals a problem with the data (input) file. Look at the 10 READ statement and its associated 100 FORMAT statement. Note the real-variable names A, B in the read list. Compare with the integer edit descriptors (2I5) in the format specification. This mixed-mode combination will not work and results in an error every time. Why was this error not detected before and an error message printed with the listing

FIGURE E-5 A successful program.

```
C234567890
      OPEN(3,FILE='APP-E-5.DAT')
      OPEN(6,FILE='PRN')
   10 READ(3,100)A,B,C,LVAL
  100 FORMAT(3F10.4,I5)
      DISC=SQRT(B**2-4.0*A*C)
      ROOT1=(-B+DISC)/(2.0*A)
      ROOT2=(-B-DISC)/(2.0*A)
      WRITE(6,200)ROOT1,ROOT2
  200 FORMAT(1X,2F10.4)
      IF(LVAL)10,10,20
   20 WRITE(6,300)
  300 FORMAT(' ')
      STOP
      END
```

```
       1.0       2.0      -8.0    0
       1.0       2.0      -3.0    0
       1.0      -8.0     -15.0    1
```

```
A>B:FOR1 APP-E-5

Microsoft FORTRAN77 V3.30 March 1985
(C) Copyright Microsoft Corp 1982, 1983, 1984, 1985

Object filename [APP-E-5.OBJ]:
Source listing  [NUL.LST]:
Object listing  [NUL.COD]:
 Pass One     No Errors Detected
              15 Source Lines

A>B:PAS2

 Code Area Size = #01D9  (  473)
 Cons Area Size = #002A  (   42)
 Data Area Size = #004A  (   74)

 Pass Two     No Errors Detected.

A>LINK APP-E-5,,,B:FORTRAN.LIB+A:MATH.LIB

Microsoft 8086 Object Linker
Version 3.02 (C) Copyright Microsoft Corp 1983, 1984, 1985


A>APP-E-5

    2.0000   -4.0000
    1.0000   -3.0000
    9.5678   -1.5678

Stop - Program terminated.
```

```
C234567890
      OPEN(2,FILE='APP-E-6.DAT')
      OPEN(8,FILE='PRN')
      WRITE(8,100)A,B,C
  100 FORMAT(1X,'A    B    C')
   10 READ(2,200)A,B
  200 FORMAT(2I5)
      C=SQRT(A**2+B**2)
      GOTO 10
      STOP
      END
```

```
 2.00 3.00
 4.00 6.00
 6.40 8.30
 8.8011.40
10.9013.70
```

```
A>B:FOR1 APP-E-6

Microsoft FORTRAN77 V3.30 March 1985
(C) Copyright Microsoft Corp 1982, 1983, 1984, 1985

Object filename [APP-E-6.OBJ]:
Source listing  [NUL.LST]:
Object listing  [NUL.COD]:
 Pass One     No Errors Detected
              11 Source Lines

A>B:PAS2

 Code Area Size = #013D  (  317)
 Cons Area Size = #001E  (   30)
 Data Area Size = #0032  (   50)

 Pass Two     No Errors Detected.

A>LINK APP-E-6,,,B:FORTRAN.LIB+A:MATH.LIB

Microsoft 8086 Object Linker
Version 3.02 (C) Copyright Microsoft Corp 1983, 1984, 1985


A>APP-E-6

? Error: Data format error in file PRN
  Error Code 1244, Status  000E
PC = 000C: 0006; SS = 0FC3, FP = 0AED, SP = 1500
```

FIGURE E-6 **An execution error.**

in Fig. E-6? Remember that execution is sequential. Errors occurring during execution terminate execution at the point of occurrence; errors later in the program are not detected until an attempt is made to execute the statement in which the error occurs. So, correct the mixed mode and try again.

The results shown in Fig. E-8 (see p. 398) seem to have gone from bad to worse. There are column headings, but the output values do not appear in three neatly spaced columns. Rows of asterisks (****) have unaccountably appeared. The error message is about as helpful to the uninitiated as the asterisks! The trouble this time is in the output format. The specification in the 300 FORMAT statement, (3F4.2), provides for printing three real variables in a field of twelve output columns. Consider the values assigned to A, B, and C—the values to be printed. The three values to be printed each occupy an output field of five characters, including the decimal point. There must be fifteen columns of output, assuming only positive values and no *blank* between columns. And, a *blank* that must be provided in output column 1! These mistakes in Fig. E-8 are the result of poor planning. Note the truncation of leading digits when they are specified in output column 1. The asterisks are printed to indicate an insufficient field width to print the number of characters specified in the format specification. The number of asterisks printed corresponds to the actual field width specified (Sec. 6-8). Correct these errors and try again.

FIGURE E-7 Another execution error.

```
C234567890
      OPEN(2,FILE='APP-E-6.DAT')
      OPEN(8,FILE='PRN')
      WRITE(8,100)
  100 FORMAT(1X,'A    B    C')
   10 READ(2,200)A,B
  200 FORMAT(2I5)
      C=SQRT(A**2+B**2)
      WRITE(8,300)A,B,C
  300 FORMAT(3F4.2)
      GOTO 10
      STOP
      END
```

```
 2.00 3.00
 4.00 6.00
 6.40 8.30
 8.8011.40
10.9013.70
```

```
A>B:FOR1 APP-E-7

Microsoft FORTRAN77 V3.30 March 1985
(C) Copyright Microsoft Corp 1982, 1983, 1984, 1985

Object filename [APP-E-7.OBJ]:
Source listing  [NUL.LST]:
Object listing  [NUL.COD]:
 Pass One     No Errors Detected
              13 Source Lines

A>B:PAS2

 Code Area Size = #0157  (  343)
 Cons Area Size = #001E  (   30)
 Data Area Size = #003A  (   58)

 Pass Two     No Errors Detected.

A>LINK APP-E-7,,,B:FORTRAN.LIB+A:MATH.LIB

Microsoft 8086 Object Linker
Version 3.02 (C) Copyright Microsoft Corp 1983, 1984, 1985


A>APP-E-7

A   B   C
? Error: Data format error in file APP-E-6.DAT
  Error Code 1234, Status  000E
PC = 0070: 1528; SS = 0FC4, FP = 000C, SP = 14F8
```

```
C234567890
      OPEN(2,FILE='APP-E-6.DAT')
      OPEN(8,FILE='PRN')
      WRITE(8,100)
  100 FORMAT(1X,'A    B    C')
   10 READ(2,200)A,B
  200 FORMAT(2F5.1)
      C=SQRT(A**2+B**2)
      WRITE(8,300)A,B,C
  300 FORMAT(3F4.2)
      GOTO 10
      END
```

```
 2.00 3.00
 4.00 6.00
 6.40 8.30
 8.8011.40
10.9013.70
```

```
A>B:FOR1 APP-E-8

Microsoft FORTRAN77 V3.30 March 1985
(C) Copyright Microsoft Corp 1982, 1983, 1984, 1985

Object filename [APP-E-8.OBJ]:
Source listing  [NUL.LST]:
Object listing  [NUL.COD]:
 Pass One     No Errors Detected
              12 Source Lines

A>B:PAS2

 Code Area Size = #0145  (   325)
 Cons Area Size = #001E  (    30)
 Data Area Size = #003C  (    60)

 Pass Two     No Errors Detected.

A>LINK APP-E-8,,,B:FORTRAN.LIB+A:MATH.LIB

Microsoft 8086 Object Linker
Version 3.02 (C) Copyright Microsoft Corp 1983, 1984, 1985


A>APP-E-8

A   B   C
.003.003.61
.006.007.21
.408.30****
.80********
***********
? Error: Operation error in file APP-E-6.DAT
  Error Code 1298, Status  0003
PC = 0070: 1438; SS = 0F06, FP = 0006, SP = 1408
```

FIGURE E-8 A logic error.

Figure E-9 shows that it is possible to write, compile, and execute an error-free FORTRAN program. Figures E-10 (see p. 400) and E-11 (see p. 401) illustrate two more typical errors. Omission of the END statement in the program of Fig. E-10 is a compilation error detected during pass one. Attempting to perform an undefined operation in the program of Fig. E-11, taking the square root of a negative number, is a run-time error. The error messages for both of these errors are quite explicit.

These sample errors and error messages represent only a few of the many errors that can occur in the FORTRAN source program. In due time, and with experience, the programmer will discover most of them. Refer to Table E-1 (see p. 400) for a more comprehensive listing of typical errors.

FIGURE E-9 Another successful program.

```
C234567890
      OPEN(2,FILE='APP-E-6.DAT')
      OPEN(8,FILE='PRN')
      WRITE(8,100)
  100 FORMAT(3X,'A',5X,'B',5X,'C',/)
   10 READ(2,200,END=20)A,B
  200 FORMAT(2F5.2)
      C=SQRT(A**2+B**2)
      WRITE(8,300)A,B,C
  300 FORMAT(3(1X,F5.2))
      GOTO 10
   20 STOP
      END
```

```
 2.00 3.00
 4.00 6.00
 6.40 8.30
 8.8011.40
10.9013.70
```

```
A>B:FOR1 APP-E-9

Microsoft FORTRAN77 V3.30 March 1985
(C) Copyright Microsoft Corp 1982, 1983, 1984, 1985

Object filename [APP-E-9.OBJ]:
Source listing  [NUL.LST]:
Object listing  [NUL.COD]:
 Pass One       No Errors Detected
                13 Source Lines

A>B:PAS2

 Code Area Size = #0160  (  352)
 Cons Area Size = #001E  (   30)
 Data Area Size = #0048  (   72)

 Pass Two       No Errors Detected.

A>LINK APP-E-9,,,B:FORTRAN.LIB+A:MATH.LIB

Microsoft 8086 Object Linker
Version 3.02 (C) Copyright Microsoft Corp 1983, 1984, 1985


A>APP-E-9

   A     B     C

 2.00  3.00  3.61
 4.00  6.00  7.21
 6.40  8.30 10.48
 8.80 11.40 14.40
10.90 13.70 17.51
Stop - Program terminated.
```

```
C234567890
      OPEN(7,FILE='PRN')
      X=100.0
      Z=10.0
   10 X=X-Z
      Y=SQRT(X)
      WRITE(7,100)Y
      GOTO 10
  100 FORMAT(1X,F10.4)

A>B:FOR1 APP-E-10

Microsoft FORTRAN77 V3.30 March 1985
(C) Copyright Microsoft Corp 1982, 1983, 1984, 1985

Object filename [APP-E-10.OBJ]:
Source listing  [NUL.LST]:
Object listing  [NUL.COD]:

***** Error 91,line 9 -- missing END statement
 Pass One       1 Errors Detected
                9 Source Lines
```

FIGURE E-10 A different compilation error.

TABLE E-1 TYPICAL PROGRAMMING MISTAKES

Using mixed-mode expressions.
Using a variable name to which no value has been assigned.
Failing to consider and/or correctly apply the hierarchy of operations.
Adding or omitting a comma, period, or quotation character.
Using a statement label more than once.
Omitting a statement label.
Using unmatched parentheses.
Using an integer expression as the argument of a real function.
Using a real expression as the argument of an integer function.
Using degrees rather than radians as the argument of a trigonometric function.
Allowing insufficient field width in the WRITE/FORMAT edit descriptor to accommodate the number of characters to be displayed.
Using the wrong edit descriptor in a READ or WRITE FORMAT specification.
Inadvertently attempting to display a character in output position 1.
Using a real expression as the index, initial or limiting value, or increment of a DO statement.
Attempting to change the value of the index, initial or limiting value, or increment of a DO statement within the range of the loop.
Improperly nesting DO loops.
Failing to list declaration statements (i.e., DIMENSION or DOUBLE PRECISION) before the first executable statement.
Exceeding subscript limits defined by the DIMENSION statement.
Incorrectly relating the actual arguments in the calling statement with the dummy arguments in the defining statement.

E-7 Compiling the Main Program and Subprograms Separately

A long complex program is generally easier to understand, write, and debug if it is composed of a short main program that calls a series of subprograms (Chap. 10). Subprograms may be placed following the END statement of the main program, and compiled along with the main program under the filename of the main program as follows:

```
PROGRAM SPHERE
DIA=2.Ø
CALL SURFAR(DIA, AREA)
CALL VOLUME(DIA, VOL)
WRITE(*, *) DIA, AREA, VOL
STOP
END
SUBROUTINE SURFAR(D, A)
```

FIGURE E-11 A run-time error of logic.

```
C234567890
      OPEN(7,FILE='PRN')
      X=100.0
      Z=10.0
   10 X=X-Z
      Y=SQRT(X)
      WRITE(7,100)Y
  100 FORMAT(1X,F10.4)
      GOTO 10
      STOP
      END

A>B:FOR1 APP-E-11

Microsoft FORTRAN77 V3.30 March 1985
(C) Copyright Microsoft Corp 1982, 1983, 1984, 1985

Object filename [APP-E-11.OBJ]:
Source listing  [NUL.LST]:
Object listing  [NUL.COD]:
 Pass One     No Errors Detected
              11 Source Lines

A>B:PAS2

 Code Area Size = #00CD  (   205)
 Cons Area Size = #0017  (    23)
 Data Area Size = #002B  (    43)

 Pass Two     No Errors Detected.

A>LINK APP-E-11,,,B:FORTRAN.LIB+A:MATH.LIB

Microsoft 8086 Object Linker
Version 3.02 (C) Copyright Microsoft Corp 1983, 1984, 1985


A>APP-E-11

    9.4868
    8.9443
    8.3666
    7.7460
    7.0711
    6.3246
    5.4772
    4.4721
    3.1623
     .0000
? Error: SQRT of negative argument
  Error Code 2104
PC = 0A91: 000A; SS = 0F1A, FP = 0BB7, SP = 144E
```

```
A=3.141593*D**2
RETURN
END
SUBROUTINE VOLUME(D,VOL)
VOL=(3.141593*D**3)/6.Ø
RETURN
END
```

A subprogram may be written for general requirements, applicable to a variety of calling programs. It would be more efficient if, instead of recompiling the subprogram along with its calling program each time it was needed, the subprogram could be stored on the PROGRAM A working diskette ready to be called as needed by any other program. This would, in effect, permit the programmer to create and store a personal library of subprograms on the PROGRAM A working diskette.

In the example above, two subprograms, SUBROUTINE SURFAR and SUBROUTINE VOLUME, calculate and return to the main program values for the surface area and volume, respectively, of a sphere whose diameter is defined in the main program. Each of these subprograms can be entered with the EDLIN line editor as an independent FORTRAN source program filed under its subprogram name with the extension FOR, and an OBJ file created by executing the FOR1 (pass one) and PAS2 (pass two) steps of the compiler program.

Proceed as follows:

1 Using the EDLIN line editor, key in and enter each of the two subprograms filed under SURFAR.FOR and VOLUME.FOR, respectively.
2 Manually (do not use the batch file) compile each of these two subprograms through FOR1 (pass one) and PAS2 (pass two). This will enter the object programs SURFAR.OBJ and VOLUME.OBJ on the PROGRAM A working diskette. These two subprograms may now be linked with *any* main program desired.
3 Using the EDLIN line editor, key in and enter the main program, SPHERE.FOR, on the PROGRAM A working diskette.
4 Manually compile the main program through FOR1 (pass one) and PAS2 (pass two).
5 When PAS2 (pass two) has been completed and the A> prompt appears, link the main program with the two subprograms as follows:

   A>**LINK SPHERE+SURFAR+VOLUME,,,B:FORTRAN.LIB+A:MATH.LIB** ↵

   When compilation is complete (after about 90 seconds), the SPHERE.EXE program entered on the PROGRAM A working diskette will include both of the two subprograms, SURFAR and VOLUME, just as if they had been entered and compiled with the main program in the usual manner.
6 Execute the program by keying in the filename, SPHERE, following the A > prompt and striking the ↵ key.

   A>**SPHERE** ↵

Linking with a main program does not destroy the subprogram object file. Subprograms entered and compiled in this manner remain on the PROGRAM A working diskette ready to be linked with any main program that can make use of the values they were written to calculate.

The same result can be accomplished with the EDLIN line editor. With the main source program in EDLIN mode, use the T command (App. D-8) to merge the source file(s) of the subprogram(s) stored on the diskette with the main program in EDLIN. The main program and its subprogram(s) can then be compiled together by using the COMPILE batch file.

INDEX